Empirical Social
Research in and on
the Armed Forces

Sozialwissenschaftliche Studien des Zentrums für Militärgeschichte und Sozialwissenschaften der Bundeswehr

Herausgegeben vom
Zentrum für Militärgeschichte und Sozialwissenschaften
der Bundeswehr

Band 24

Markus Steinbrecher, Heiko Biehl,
Martin Elbe (Eds.)

——

Empirical Social Research in and on the Armed Forces

Comparative and National Perspectives

Berliner
Wissenschafts-Verlag

Studies in Social Science by the Center for Military History and Social Sciences of the Bundeswehr
Edited by the Center for Military History and Social Sciences of the Bundeswehr

Bibliografische Information der Deutschen Nationalbibliothek
Die Deutsche Nationalbibliothek verzeichnet diese Publikation in der Deutschen
Nationalbibliografie; detaillierte bibliografische Daten sind im Internet über
http://dnb.d-nb.de abrufbar.

Bibliographic information published by the German National Library
The German National Library lists this publication in the German National Bibliography;
detailed bibliographic information is available on the Internet at
http://dnb.d-nb.de

© 2022 BWV | BERLINER WISSENSCHAFTS-VERLAG GmbH,
Behaimstraße 25, 10585 Berlin,
E-Mail: bwv@bwv-verlag.de, Internet: http://www.bwv-verlag.de

Redaktion / *Editorial Office:* ZMSBw, Potsdam, Fachbereich Publikationen (0859-01)
Projektkoordination / *Project coordination:* Christian Adam, Annabel Franceschini
Lektorat / *Copyediting:* Nancy Pearson Mackie (Calgary)
Satz / *Typesetting:* Carola Klinke

Umschlagabbildung: Soldaten der NATO-Streitkräfte bei einer Veranstaltung in Heidelberg anlässlich
„60 Jahre NATO-Hauptquartier in Heidelberg", Oktober 2009. (picture alliance/dpa/Ronald Wittek)
Cover illustration: Soldiers of the NATO forces at an event in Heidelberg on the occasion of „60 years
of NATO headquarters in Heidelberg", October 2009. (picture alliance/dpa/Ronald Wittek)

Druck / *Print:* Memminger MedienCentrum, Memmingen
Gedruckt auf holzfreiem, chlor- und säurefreiem, alterungsbeständigem Papier.
Printed in Germany.

ISBN Print   978-3-8305-5144-7
ISBN E-Book   978-3-8305-4369-5

Contents

Foreword

It is one of the core missions of the Center for Military History and Social Sciences of the Bundeswehr (ZMSBw) to conduct and publish studies in military history and the social sciences on behalf of the German Federal Ministry of Defense. The main audience of these studies are the armed forces, the academic community, and the interested public. A central goal of our research is to provide information as a base for decision-making. Another core mission is to conduct basic research in both disciplines. Our military sociology research branch follows the latter by publishing this anthology on empirical social research in and on the armed forces. It provides an international comparison of the structures, methods, and results of empirical military sociology in different countries and analyses the impact of the national background on the respective research. The volume at hand offers an overview on current trends in international military sociology. The large number of renowned contributors from various countries points to the strong international links in military sociology that clearly go beyond joint participation in scientific conferences. This volume definitely is an important step towards a more standardized and comprehensive analysis of military sociology which reveals the strengths and weaknesses as well as the similarities and differences of the respective national military sociologies. The main purpose of the editors and contributors is to start and accelerate a debate on prerequisites, conditions, and consequences of research in military sociology by looking at research practices in a selected number of countries: France, Germany, Israel, Japan, Slovenia, Sweden, Switzerland, the United Kingdom, and the United States. They examine in which areas military sociology research is already widely independent of the national context, and where it pursues general questions with theories, methods, and instruments that leave the national context behind.

The international and comparative perspective of this volume is particularly important for me as commander of the ZMSBw with our institute's strong links to military history and military sociology research institutions across the world. The close cooperation with a large set of different partners on joint publication projects and scientific events is one of the strengths of our institute. Our connections across the world definitely help to gain deep and broad insights into the military as a prime topic of research. The book at hand is complemented by another volume in German ("Empirische Sozialforschung in den Streitkräften", edited by M. Elbe, H. Biehl, and M. Steinbrecher) that concentrates on the methodological problems, and selected areas of application of the discipline. It shows the breadth and depth of the discipline in a single country.

I would like to thank the editors of this book, Dr. Markus Steinbrecher, Dr. Heiko Biehl, and Prof. Dr. Martin Elbe for the realization of the project and the compilation of its content. In addition, I send my deepest gratitude to all contributors for their participation in the project and their support for the work of ZMSBw. Finally, I would like to thank our colleagues in the publications department at ZMSBw for realizing the book in cooperation with the Berliner Wissenschafts-Verlag. I wish this volume on empirical social research in the armed forces a large readership.

Dr. Sven Lange
Colonel (GS) and Commander of the
Center for Military History and
Social Sciences of the Bundeswehr

Research in Military Sociology. A Comparison of National Perspectives on Empirical Social Research on the Armed Forces

Markus Steinbrecher, Heiko Biehl, and Martin Elbe

1 Introduction

This edited volume is part of a larger publication project on empirical social research in and on the armed forces. The purpose of this and the other volume of the publication project (Elbe et al. 2021) is to start and accelerate a debate on prerequisites, conditions, and consequences of research in military sociology by looking at research practices in a selected number of countries. Our intention is to examine in which areas military sociology research in a selected number of countries (here and throughout the book in alphabetical order: France, Germany, Israel, Japan, Slovenia, Sweden, Switzerland, the United Kingdom, and the United States) is already widely independent of the national context, and where it pursues general questions with theories, methods, and instruments that leave the national context behind. In addition, we want to know where national constellations, characteristics and preferences still dominate military sociology. This book cannot be a panacea for how to overcome national imprinting, but it might show ways to deal more consciously with the impact national background has on military sociology. This introductory chapter presents some thoughts and arguments on the national versus the supranational character of military sociology in the second section picking up a discussion started by critical military sociologists. The third section provides some organizational remarks regarding the object and composition of the book. The fourth section goes beyond traditional introductory chapters in edited volumes: We do not only provide a broad overview but discuss and compare the content of the country chapters. After highlighting the similarities between the countries, we provide characterizations of the national styles in military sociologies and concentrate on the differences between them. The final section provides some thoughts on directions and topics of future research in our discipline.

2   Military Sociology as an Empirical Discipline

Military sociologists are used to justifying themselves to various addressees. First, there are the armed forces and the ministries of defense. Anyone who has ever conducted a research project in or for the armed forces is aware of the concerns and reservations about military sociology. Armed forces preserve a culture of military secrecy – or at least military restraint – and ministries are characterized by bureaucracy as well as reactive and passive public relations. While they may have an interest in empirical studies to obtain exclusive information, they often fear the publication of findings and cannot do much with sociological arguments or scientific debates in general. At the same time, military sociology has to justify itself to other social sciences. Sometimes there are explicit reservations about military sociology but the ignorance and indifference of other disciplines occurs more frequently. In their comprehensive history of ideas and literature, Hans Joas and Wolfgang Knöbl (2013) have demonstrated a neglect of war and military violence in the social sciences and social theory. Even if this diagnosis is considered too broad, the military is hardly the focus of the social sciences. There are studies that approach the armed forces from a political science, social psychology, or organization sociology perspective. However, the observation and analysis of armed forces and military violence is not common in leading journals and handbooks. Obviously, most social science approaches and theories assume that understanding the military is not essential for understanding contemporary societies.

In addition to this disregard for the armed forces, an internal criticism within the discipline has occurred in recent years. Some scholars contrast the established military sociology with a critical military sociology (e.g., Basham et al. 2015; Higate and Cameron 2006; Levy 2015). According to them, too many studies lack a sufficient distance between researchers and the armed forces. Too many studies focus on the solutions to practical military problems and challenges. Thus, these studies aim to increase military efficiency – and in the worst case – help to foster militarization. These kinds of studies would legitimize military force and power in the dominating political, social and normative context. According to the proponents of critical military sociology, a central reason for these shortcomings is the close interdependence of most researchers in military sociology with the military. Many researchers are members of the armed forces, whether as civilian employees or as active or reserve soldiers. In addition, the military often acts as a client and sponsor of studies. Last but not least, defense ministries control the access to the research field and often decide on the conduct of studies, the selection of methods, the design of research instruments such as questionnaires, and the release of results.

Critical military sociology aims to counter these deficits by taking into account the social and political preconditions of the armed forces, their power structures, and hidden assumptions. Critical military sociology demands a reflected view of the armed forces in their entirety. In doing so, the prevailing modes of operation, mechanisms, and structures are scrutinized. This means that researchers always take a critical look at their own theories and methods, that they recognize the limits and blind spots of their approach and point out and discuss the weaknesses of their investigations and findings. This has been the case in many ways in recent years. For example, the professional relationship between researchers and the armed forces has been inspected (Carreiras et al. 2016; Higate and Cameron 2006). The selection of quantitative and qualitative methods also has come under scrutiny (Carreiras and Castro 2013). Analyses that follow a West-centered perspective and "a heteronormative gender order" have been criticized. In many respects, tendencies of social militarization have come into view.[1]

Another aspect, equally constitutive for current armed forces and military sociological research, has been broadly ignored: The national imprinting and anchoring of the military and military sociology research is hardly critically examined. In major reference texts of critical military sociology (Basham et al. 2015; Levy 2015), for example, there is no corresponding reference on this issue. Although anyone who has ever attended a military sociology conference can grasp the national character of researchers, presentations, and projects with their hands, there has so far been no systematic survey to address this aspect.

This neglect is astounding for two reasons. Firstly, the armed forces themselves are a symbol and expression of the nation state. They like to present themselves as its guarantors who protect and defend nation state and national society against external enemies. Such a reading is entirely compatible with the militaristic school of statehood (Levy 2015; Shaw 1991) – albeit with critical intent. Charles Tilly (1992), Anthony Giddens (1985) and others have pointed to the connection between warfare, statehood, and citizenship. This close connection between nationhood and armed violence has to be problematized more intensely – especially under a critical approach – and current tendencies of trans-nationalization and globalization need to be questioned.

Secondly, there is already a debate in sociology about its methodological obsession with the nation state and national society. Many sociological studies think society in the nation-state framework and confirm and consolidate it. Ulrich Beck (2007), in particular, has voiced a well-founded criticism of methodological na-

---

1   See the website of the journal Critical Military Studies: <www.tandfonline.com/loi/rcms20> (last access 27 February 2020).

tionalism and called for its overcoming. For Beck, a large part of sociology has the weakness that it "subsumes society under the nation-state" (Beck 2007, 286). This is in the tradition of the classics, which like Durkheim, Weber and Parsons were also "the product of national struggles, the Franco-German War of 1870 and the First World War at the beginning of the 20th century" (Beck 2007, 286). Methodological nationalism

> equates society with nation-state societies, and sees states and their governments as the cornerstones of social sciences analysis. It assumes that humanity is naturally divided into a limited number of nations, which on the inside, organize themselves as nation-states, and on the outside, set boundaries to distinguish themselves from other nation-states. It goes even further: this outer delimination, as well as the competition between nation-states, presents the most fundamental category of political organization. (Beck 2007, 287)

Instead, Beck calls for a cosmopolitan methodology that does justice to the globalization of societies and makes it accessible for sociological analysis. In spite of the description of the problem and the appeals, Beck owes a robust proposal how such a methodology could look like. Although the core of his criticism is correct, in practice it is difficult to overcome the shortcomings of methodological nationalism pointed out by Beck. It is true that international comparison is of greater significance today than it was twenty or thirty years ago (see also the chapter by Kraft in this volume). But even in studies that make international comparisons, the nation-state represents the essential frame of reference – now in comparison and not as the only set of consideration. Thus, these studies also contribute to the stabilization of nation-state orientations and identities, regardless of their claim.

When applying these considerations to military sociology, their relevance becomes immediately apparent. First of all, the connection between armed forces and nation states is already an essential topic of military sociology (Giddens 1985; Shaw 1991). After all, it is the primary task of armed forces to protect and, if necessary, to defend the borders between nation states. However, this is not the only way in which the military is constitutive for nation states. It can also be a school of the nation, in which a national consciousness only develops among the (mostly male) citizens and replaces regional, corporative or class identities (Janowitz 1976). These mechanisms are part of the studies on civil-military relations in younger states and emerging nations. In his study on the armed forces in Europe, Anthony Forster (2006) points out the importance of the military for the Eastern European states and societies after the end of the Cold War. Secondly, there have been a considerable number of studies on military multi-nationality for about three decades. In most cases, they are considered as proof of the international character of military sociological research (see also the chapter by Soeters in this volume). At the same time, however, these studies should be questioned to the extent to which they replicate and confirm the nation-state paradigm. In any case, analyses of genuinely transnational military interdependence are rare. Rather, the question arises as to what these potential studies could look like at all. In addition, the question of the national character of military sociology arises: Are military sociology studies truly supranational? Is there more common ground across countries in the choice of topics, the way research is done, the relevant debates and discussions in military sociology? Or do national styles and characteristics dominate?

The ambition of military sociology cannot be to overcome the national character of research, but to reflect it sufficiently and, thus, to leave it at least a bit behind. National peculiarities must always be taken into account. The aim of military sociology, however, should always be supranational in its scope and reality. This means to strive for global theory and analysis of armed forces and society. Does the current military sociology already meet these ambitions? Or does military sociology – perhaps even more so than other fields of social sciences – stand in the tradition of methodological nationalism? The strong link between the nation-state and the military at least suggests such a connection.

3   Object and Composition of the Book

The present volume has set itself the task of investigating and testing these questions empirically. We will examine the areas where military sociology research is already widely independent of the national context, where it pursues general questions with theories, methods, and instruments that leave the national context behind. And we want to know where national characteristics and preferences still dominate. This book cannot be a panacea for how to overcome national imprinting, but it might show ways to deal more consciously with the national character of military sociology. To address these questions, the book is divided into two parts.

The *first part of the book* provides a rather general and broad picture on comparative research in general and its added value for research on military sociology. This is particularly relevant as comparative approaches and research projects can help to identify patterns and peculiarities of different national military sociologies. In her chapter, *Ina Kraft* explains and discusses the value of the comparative method in current research on the military, security, and war. She highlights the potential of comparative research on the armed forces in order to overcome the absence of theory as well as the West-centrist orientation in military sociology. *Joseph Soeters* focuses on a specific and widely researched topic of military sociology: multinational military cooperation. In his opinion, multinational military cooperation is and will be one of the most important topics of military sociology. He points to the serious challenges of multilateral military action, in particular with respect to decisions about the use of force and the optimization of the use of scarce resources (e.g., logistics). He regards research into multinational military cooperation as an important topic and urges researchers to focus on concrete events and behavior to give proper content to the analysis of more general developments related to the military.

The *second part of the book* presents case studies by experts who describe and analyze the state of the discipline in their respective countries. The rationale behind the country selection was to get a diverse set of countries in terms of geography, size as well as breadth and depth of the discipline. We have country chapters on France, Germany, Israel, Japan, Slovenia, Sweden, Switzerland, the United Kingdom, and the United States. This selection does not claim to be a representative sample. However, it offers a promising mix of countries. There are both larger and smaller countries, countries inside and outside NATO and EU as well as neutral countries. The sample includes countries whose armed forces are permanently involved in military conflicts, as well as Switzerland, a country that has not experienced war for around two hundred years. Some of the countries still have conscription, while others have all-volunteer forces. Three continents are represented, although the global South is missing. We asked our contributors to focus on the position of military sociology in the scientific arena in their country in general. Another issue was the status and visibility of military sociology in (mostly) civilian universities, in the professional associations and in the leading academic journals. The country chapters also focus on the institutional setup of military sociology: Do academics belonging to military institutes and academies provide the bulk of research on the armed forces? What influence does the Ministry of Defense (MoD) exercise on research projects? Is the ministry the/a gatekeeper to the field? Does the military sponsor and control most of the research in it? Our contributors should also describe how easy or hard it is to do research in and on the military. Important questions include: Who has a say in realizing these studies? Who provides the research funding – is it mostly the military itself or does it include civilian and academic organizations as well? The choice of research methods in empirical studies is another issue, including the following questions: Do quantitative or qualitative approaches dominate? What are methodological innovations? Military sociology has a core of relevant topics like civil-military relations, research on foreign deployments and missions, or gender issues. We asked our contributors to provide an overview on these and other relevant topics in their countries. Thereby, common trends and national particularities in military sociology become clear. The last point we asked about is the perception of military sociology findings in the public, covering the subsequent topics: Which impact do studies on the military have? Are they noticed at all? Does this only happen in the case of scandals or are military sociological studies a definite reference in public debates?

4   An Overview of Findings

Subsequently, we summarize, compare, and discuss our contributors' insights on the topics. After highlighting the similarities between the countries, we provide national characterizations and concentrate on the differences. The position of military sociology in the scientific arena in most of the countries seems to be rather marginal or fragile, in particular in Germany, Japan, and Switzerland. A majority of the chapters describe the discipline as an outsider in sociology and the social sciences in general. In Japan, it is one of the least developed areas of study in the social sciences. However, there seems to be an undeniable improvement in legitimacy and visibility of military sociology (France) or a recent growth and evolution as academic discipline (Germany) in some countries. In Israel, the United Kingdom, and the United States the position of the discipline is much stronger. Although even here researchers and institutions who work on military sociology seem to be scattered throughout the country and different academic disciplines. The position of military sociology also seems to be relatively stronger in Slovenia and Sweden, but in both countries most of the research is concentrated in one institution, mainly because of the small size of the country (Slovenia) or the dominant motive to profit from a decade-long peaceful development (Sweden). Accordingly, and already well known among military sociologists, there is enough room for improvement in all countries for the standing of the discipline.

4.1   Institutional Setup

The institutional setup of the discipline shows several similarities. First, all countries have at least one institution inside the armed forces that does research on military sociology issues. The specific institutional setup varies strongly. In some countries like Israel, Germany, or the United States, there are several research institutions which do research on behalf of the MoD or even on behalf of the different services. In other countries like Slovenia or France, there is a central research institution operated by the armed forces. However, the institutional setup also changes over time within each country, e.g., in France, Sweden, or Germany where different research institutions have merged or split apart. A second pattern is the strong international orientation of and cooperation within the discipline. All contributors describe the active and intense engagement of military sociologists and research institutions in international societies and associations of the discipline, especially in ERGOMAS (European Research Group on Military and Society), ISA RC 01 (International Sociological Association, Research Committee 01 Armed Forces and Conflict Resolution), and IUS (Inter-University Seminar on Armed Forces and Society). This cooperation includes active participation in the conferences of the respective associations, joint research as well as publication projects. Most of the countries also seem to have national professional associations with a focus on military sociology. However, cooperation across national institutions is limited (e.g., in Israel, Slovenia, Switzerland, and the United States). In most of the countries civilian academic institutions conduct military sociology research, too – although the number of researchers is rather limited. France has an institutional arrangement where researchers have double positions in civilian and armed forces institutions at the same time. However, looking at the general institutional setup of military sociology in civilian institutions, there is nothing like a department or a chair on military sociology in any of the countries. Accordingly, institutes that belong to the MoD or the military dominate the institutional landscape in all countries analyzed.

4.2   Publication Practices

The publication practices are rather similar in most of the countries and follow the general academic standards in the social sciences. Publications in military sociology include the whole range from research reports, academic journals, and monographs to edited volumes. Leading journals in the field are *Armed Forces & Society* and *Res Militaris*. However, military sociologists also publish their articles and papers in journals specialized in international relations, political science, sociology, psychology, or communication science. From time to time, French colleagues have been successful in editing special issues on military sociology in national political science or sociology journals, but this seems to be an exception in comparison to the other countries. The research institutions which belong to the realm of the MoD usually publish a large number of research reports that are available for the public at limited or no cost (e.g., in France, Germany, Slovenia, Sweden, or Switzerland). Some of these research institutes even have their own book series (e.g., in Germany) or academic journals (e.g., in France and Israel). In some countries military sociologists put an emphasis on publications in English to address an international audience (e.g., in Israel and Slovenia). In contrast French and German military sociologists publish in their native language to address larger francophone and German-speaking communities and publics. The overall picture shows that publication practices in military sociology are similar to the practices in other sub-disciplines of sociology or the social sciences in general.

4.3   Researchers and Research Funding

More national variations can be found with respect to the easiness and difficulties of research in and on the military. The two key issues here are the access to military personnel for research projects and the quick and unregulated publication of results. All country chapters indicate that the military and/or the MoD are gatekeepers for all kinds of research projects which focus on the armed forces. In some countries, it seems easier for military research institutions than for external civilian researchers to get access to the military field (e.g., in Germany and the United States), while some country chapters both speak of easy access and the lack of differences between internal and external researchers in terms of access restrictions (e.g., in France, Slovenia, and Sweden). Israel and Japan seem to be special cases on the access issue. On the one hand, the Japanese MoD is extremely hesitant to disclose information and to grant access which leads to a vicious circle. The hesitancy of the MoD has made the public more skeptical of the military and, thus, the MoD has become even more restrictive in supporting research projects. On the other hand, the Israeli MoD is usually incredibly open towards research on and within the armed forces even by outside researchers. In cases when the MoD does not grant access, it is easy for researchers to get at least access to former military members or reservists due to widespread conscription in Israel. The MoD, thus, can be bypassed by researchers who are interested in the Israeli Defense Force (IDF). Furthermore, in Germany, the UK, and Israel, the MoD can have an impact on project design, survey instruments, and (the publication of) research reports. The practices vary from country to country but very often the MoD is a gatekeeper for the conduct of projects and the publication of the results, confirming the concerns of critical military sociology (e.g., Basham et al. 2015; Higate and Cameron 2006; Levy 2015).

The MoD is also an important player with respect to research funding. The general rule of thumb is that research institutions which belong to the MoD are fully funded by the ministry or the national or ministerial budget, respectively. In some cases, researchers in a research institute run by the armed forces can also apply for external funds (e.g., in Germany, Israel, Slovenia, and Sweden). Researchers at the Swiss Military Academy (MILAC) are an exception from this rule. They are not allowed to acquire external funds. In some countries, the armed forces also provide funds for external researchers. France used this model very often until the creation of the IRSEM (Institute for Strategic Studies) in 2009. Until then, military sociology research in France was conducted to a large degree by external researchers who got their funding from the French MoD on a contract-per-project base. In Israel, Japan, and the United Kingdom, external researchers can apply for money from the military to do their research. However, this practice has been criticized by academics in all three countries.

4.4   Topics and Methods

Quantitative and qualitative approaches both are research methods applied by military sociologists in all countries. However, the preference for one school over another seems to depend on the topic of research. Projects on civil-military relations and public opinion usually use quantitative large-scale survey data, while qualitative approaches are more relevant for research projects which address military personnel or multinational military cooperation. In some cases, methodological triangulation or a mix of both approaches is used. This is particularly true for internal research projects, e.g., on topics like foreign deployments. France and Sweden, for example, reveal a strong national preference for qualitative methods in military sociology. This has also been reflected by a large amount of international methodological contributions published in the last decade (e.g., Carreiras and Castro 2013; Carreiras et al. 2016; Soeters et al. 2014).

A comparison of the main topics of research shows the multiple facets and the broadness of the discipline. We will focus here on some of the over-arching similarities, while the country chapters provide much more detailed information and show the differentiation and specialization of the discipline. Military sociologists in all subject countries do research on human resources. This includes the classical military sociology issues of recruitment and retention, professional motivation, career paths, and career development, as well as the social composition of the armed forces. Research on human resources has become even more important with the end of conscription (in France, the United Kingdom, and the United States) or its suspension (in Germany and Sweden) which urges the armed forces to attract enough volunteers to fill their ranks. Research on the military profession in general and on military identities are related topics of the discipline in almost all countries. This includes studies and publications on leadership, cohesion, values of military personnel, and their motivation, to mention just a few common examples. Gender and the integration of women in the armed forces has also become a popular topic of research in almost all countries included in our overview, reflecting the removal of access restrictions for women in recent decades. Some country chapters also indicate an increased emphasis of research on minorities (e.g., based on ethnicity, migration background, or sexual orientation) in the armed forces and questions of diversity.

International cooperation and military multi-nationality are topics widely studied by European military sociologists because almost all foreign deployments occur within the framework of international organizations (e.g., the EU or the UN), alliances (e.g., NATO), and mandates that usually require the close cooperation and interaction with forces from other countries (see also the chapter by Soeters in this volume). This topic is related to the widespread research on foreign deployments and their consequences for the armed forces in general and the military personnel in particular. Japan and Switzerland are the exceptions due to the very low number of missions abroad in which their armed forces take part. However, this topic is largely a domain of researchers who work for the MoD itself or research institutes within the realm of the national MoDs due to access restrictions and confidentiality requirements.

Another topic common to all countries in this book is civil-military relations. This includes large-scale public opinion surveys which provide information on a wide variety of topics in foreign, security, and defense policy. Civilian control of the armed forces is another well-established field in this category – although the country chapters provide the impression that this issue is more dominant in the US than in the other countries.

Our contributors also identified some research blind spots in their countries. The overall focus of Japanese military sociology seems to be quite narrow due to the small number of researchers and institutions devoted to the discipline and the strict access regulations by the Japanese Self-Defense Forces (JSDF). The German chapter indicates that there is not much research on the political dimension of civil-military relations, military violence in general, or the political attitudes and behavior of military personnel. In addition, against the background of the already existing research (e.g., Elbe and Richter 2012; Richter 2016, 2021) more research on the organizational logic of the armed forces is needed. The Israeli chapter emphasizes that there could be more studies on the use of military violence and the operational side of the IDF. This is quite surprising given the high level of operational experience in the IDF. It is not acceptable to transfer these deficits to all countries. However, it seems to be plausible that the reasons provided for Israel, including confidentiality requirements, access restrictions, and lack of interest in these topics by critical military sociologists, apply to other countries as well.

4.5   Impact of Research in Military Sociology

The last category of analysis was the perception of findings in military sociology in the respective public and national politics. In some countries like France, Germany, and Japan, military sociology findings do not have a strong impact in the public or on politics. The German MoD only uses research results of military sociology on occasion (see also Kümmel 2021 on this issue). This happens especially if results are suitable to create scandals or if they strengthen political demands and initiatives. In general, however, there is a lack of proper perception of military sociology and its findings in the scientific and public arena in Germany. In Japan, the dominant anti-militarism of the large majority of its citizens seems to create a taboo to speak of military topics and military experiences. Accordingly, there is a widespread ignorance towards research results of the discipline. One of the obstacles to the extensive use of the results by the French MoD is the extremely high turnover of (military) personnel. This might also explain, in part, why French decision-makers do not know how to use the results. In the United Kingdom, military sociology at least has a certain relevance. However, this statement seems primarily to apply for selected issues like veterans and experiences in and after deployments only which are widely perceived in the public and have an impact on the political debate and decision-making. Sweden can also be placed in the middle between ignorance and high levels of attention towards military sociology and its results. Contents and findings of military sociology are known in public, media, and politics but are not linked to the term *military sociology*. One example are the contributions on leadership theory and practice in the 1970s and 1980s.

The other four countries are examples for higher levels of public and political attention towards military sociology and its findings. For the United States, we have evidence that military sociology had a direct impact on some policies (e.g., the *Don't ask, don't tell*-policy regarding homosexuality in the armed forces). In Israel, military sociology results are not very prominently discussed and used by the media but have a strong impact in consultative processes by the MoD, the parliament, and the government. In addition, security and military issues matter a lot to large parts of the population. Most of Israel's citizens have military experience as conscripts and the IDF is constantly deployed and present in everyday life. Both aspects help to create strong links between the IDF and their society and make the public more attentive towards military sociology research and its findings. Public attention to military sociology findings is quite high in Switzerland. Results of empirical studies regularly make the frontpages and headlines in different media outlets. In addition, the monopoly position of the MILAC seems to increase the public acceptance and visibility of its findings. MILAC's results and publications also influence policies and political decisions. Slovenia seems to be an exception in terms of the impact of military sociology. It is not the high responsiveness towards military sociology findings in politics that makes Slovenian military sociology stand out. However, the strong impact of the discipline on concrete policies and political decision-making is remarkable. Military sociology seems to take on a cooperative relationship with the political sphere which becomes clear when looking at the central topics of research. Eventually, some Slovenian military sociologists have moved to the political arena and have even taken high-ranking public offices (e.g., as ambassadors, state secretaries, or ministers of defense).

4.6   Some National Characteristics of Research

So far, this summary has concentrated on common features and similarities between the different countries and has highlighted only occasionally their differences and specifics. Although we are concentrating on similarities and common trends, we must not lose sight of the national characteristics of research. Military sociology as an academic discipline seems to be highly dependent on the respective national context – which includes many aspects like historical developments and events, geography, security policy, military resources, political decisions, alliance membership, neutrality, voluntary force or conscription, or societal changes, to mention just a few. Scrutinizing the country portraits makes it clear that the way military sociology is conducted is foremost tied to three components: first, to the armed forces and their structure, mission, and orientation; second, to civil-military relations; and third, to the security policy of a country. The following short summaries characterize each countries specifics and illustrate how these three components have a strong impact on the respective institutional setup, the topics, and the impact of military sociology on the public and politics. Like the country chapters, these summaries are ordered alphabetically.

In *France*, two strands of military sociology coexist. A first strand is oriented towards international debates, themes, and standards. Accordingly, French military sociology is also strongly present at international conferences, in international publications, and associations. At the same time, however, there is an extensive domestic debate aimed at the French armed forces, politics, science and the French public. In addition, there is an attempt to bring francophone scientists worldwide together in their own associations and publications. Such an approach corresponds to French security policy, which for many decades has maintained a rather distanced relationship with NATO, attempted to shape European security policy decisively and pursued its own national component, manifested in the *force du frappe*. Military sociology in the motherland of conscription pays comparatively little attention to its end and the transition to a voluntary army. There are studies on recruitment and retention – as in all countries. However, a particular French imprint on this debate or on the relationship between citizenship and the military after the end of conscription is not prominent.

Military sociology in *Germany* is shaped by its security policy orientation and historical experiences. The reservations against the use of military force are the subject of various research efforts. In contrast to the former Japanese ally, the response of the young German democracy to the lessons of World War II is the deep integration of the armed forces into society. The intertwining of soldiers and civil society was intended to prevent militarization. This constellation offers diverse research questions. A remarkable part of the publications is devoted to the specific German concept of *Innere Führung*. Since reunification, new impulses for military sociology have become apparent. The foreign missions of the Bundeswehr have given rise to new research questions that are increasingly being taken up by civilian academics outside the Bundeswehr. It is true that a high proportion of publications is still addressed to a German-speaking audience. At the same time, an increasing number of attempts have been made to involve German military sociology in international associations, projects, and publications.

Israeli military sociology reflects the high value that politics and society in Israel have for the armed forces. Due to the permanent threat to Israel by its neighbors, the ongoing involvement of its forces in low-intensity conflicts, the extensive conscription of young men and women, and the political power of (former) generals, military sociology has an academic status that is unparalleled in any of the countries studied. Just as the role and tasks of the armed forces in Israeli democracy are subject to lively debate, there is a remarkable pluralism in Israeli military sociology. The spectrum ranges from internal surveys of the armed forces, which serve to optimize the military organization, to contributions that address traditional military sociological debates, to representatives of the critical military sociology that has its origins in Israel (and in the United Kingdom).

Japanese military sociology is described even by its representatives as very marginal. This corresponds to the low social standing of the military. After the Second World War, Japan tried to take precautions against a renewed militarization of society when rebuilding its armed forces. The key was the strict limitation of the military to defense tasks and the strict separation of civil society and military organization. This led to a low level of attention to and significance of the military in Japanese society. However, these conditions also brought with them the danger of isolation and, thus, a loss of control over the armed forces. Studies of military sociology would be able to provide insights into the isolated world of the military. However, neither the armed forces themselves nor politics, the general public and science have a great interest in this.

For almost thirty years, *Slovenian* military sociology has been in line with the aspirations of this young nation to become a state. The support provided during the Yugoslavian wars of disintegration and independence showed the strong instrumentalization of science for military purposes. After independence, the country strove for membership in NATO and the EU in the 1990s. The international orientation of military sociology in Slovenia became just as consistent. On the one hand, it served the problems, situations and interests of politics and the military. On the other hand, it consistently followed international scientific standards with regard to accounting, publication, and evaluation. A considerable part of the publications were published in English and in academic journals. Equally important was the participation in international professional associations and cooperation in research projects with international colleagues.

Swedish military sociology is characterized by the concept of total defense. During the Cold War, Sweden wanted to maintain its political independence from both the Western and Eastern blocs. At the same time, serious defense capabilities and military readiness were to be maintained. Early military sociological studies supported these objectives by recording the society's readiness for defense and showing ways of increasing it. The extensive conscription in Sweden explains the subsequent turn of research towards leadership problems in the military organization. This orientation had a dialectical effect. First, it emphasized the value of the individual in the military apparatus and strengthened the rights of the soldier in accordance with Sweden's democratic culture. At the same time, it legitimized the inclusion of wider social spheres in the defense effort, and, thus, did not necessarily contribute to the militarization of Swedish society, but at least to the legitimization of military force per se. This ambivalence was very consciously processed by sociology after the end of the Cold War. Since 2014, with the renewed perception of threat from Russia, Swedish military sociology has also been showing signs of a new political and military instrumentalization.

Military sociology in *Switzerland* can only be understood against the background of two particularities. Firstly, neutrality as a security policy guideline has kept the Swiss nation out of war for centuries. Switzerland is member of just a few international organizations, is outside of NATO and the EU and has only been a member of the United Nations since 2002. This strict neutrality goes hand in hand with a militia system that closely links (male) citizenship and military service. Although this symbiosis has been weakening for several decades, it continues to shape Switzerland's identity and is reflected in military sociology research. Thus, neutrality, the Swiss army and the militia system enjoy (almost) unbroken social support. With this approach, the questions of the internationalization of security policy and civil-military relations are posed in a very specific way that clearly differs from its European neighbors.

Military sociology in the *United Kingdom* is characterized by a lively pluralism. Admittedly, the preoccupation with the armed forces – as in all the other countries considered – is certainly expandable in sociology. Nevertheless, there are several strands of military sociology research in the UK taking place at universities, civilian institutes, and think tanks. What is striking in comparison to other countries is that internal military research plays a rather subordinate role. It does provide empirical studies, robust data, and reliable information. However, according to the UK chapter, it lags behind research conducted in civilian contexts. Researchers with a civilian background also dominate in international associations and publications. Critical military sociology, which has its origins here (and in Israel), is very much alive. Decisive impulses for reflection and new perspectives have come from the UK over the past decade and a half. Thus, on the one hand, British military sociology reflects the vitality and readiness for discussion of British society and democracy. On the other hand, the pluralism of British military sociology with its strong critical elements reflects the diversity and impact of British sociology and social sciences as a whole.

There are two characteristics that are reflected in military sociology in the *United States*. The USA is both the leading military power and the leading scientific power worldwide. Therefore, it sets many military as well as scientific standards. US military sociology dominates the academic field and sets topics that determine the debates in other countries: whether it is research on civil-military relations, the debates on the transition from conscription to a volunteer army, or the integration of women into the armed forces. The size of the country, and, thus, the large number of scientists, institutes, and universities, as well as the fact that English is the *lingua franca* of science, add to this. For many academics worldwide, US military practice and US academic literature serve as an impetus and starting point. The journal, *Armed Forces & Society*, and the IUS are important platforms for academic exchange in military sociology based in the US. Conversely, this can sometimes lead to a nationally limited perception of non-American developments and research efforts. In addition, the strong orientation of scholars from other countries towards the United States might lead to an inadequate transfer of theoretical and methodological approaches as well as research topics that do not match well with the respective national context and conditions.

5   Conclusion

What conclusions can be drawn from the country chapters and our observations for military sociological research? As indicated and presented above, there are international trends in military sociology, but also national developments and characteristics. In the future, it will be necessary to reflect more consciously on the national background of research and researchers. In order to do this, it is important to systematically investigate the influence of the national context on the selection of topics, the design of projects, the preferences for theories as well as on findings and debates. The present book needs to be expanded upon and supplemented in the future. The first step could be to describe and analyze military sociology in other countries. Regional expansion is decisive. Military sociology research in South America, in Africa and (apart from Japan) in Asia has been completely left out of the picture here. This has to be changed and the analyses presented need to be extended to countries of the Global South. In addition, the systematization of the analyses has to be increased. For the country portraits, we have provided our contributors with topics and questions as kind of guidelines. These have led to a certain degree of comparability between the country chapters. At the same time, the contributors have set their own priorities, depending on their preferences and the relevance of the criteria in the respective countries. In the next steps, the analyses should follow more narrowly defined guidelines. Perhaps even data about national military sociology need to be presented in order to increase the comparability and informative value of the country analyses.

At least as decisive as the empirical development is a comprehensive theoretical embedding of military sociology. In doing so, it is necessary to draw on the literature concerning national scientific styles and national scientific cultures, which we have only touched so far (e.g., Livingstone 2003). Equally necessary are social-theoretical contributions to the relationship between armed forces, nation states, and civil societies – especially in times of security policy globalization and military multi-nationality. Military sociology demands a conscious approach to the categories bound to the nation state. First proposals on how this could look like are available (e.g., King 2011), others should follow.

In this way, the present volume aims to advance the further discussion in three ways. First, it aims to present the current state of military sociology – based on a comparison of countries. Second, it aims to reflect the international orientation and national ties of military sociology. Third, the volume aims to continue the discussion initiated by critical military sociology and expand it to include the essential component of nationhood. We would be pleased if the volume contributes to the enrichment of military sociology on all three levels.

References

Basham, V., A. Belkin, and J. Gifkins. 2015. "What is Critical Military Studies?" *Critical Military Studies* 1(1): 1–2.

Beck, U. 2007. "The Cosmopolitan Condition. Why Methodological Nationalism Fails." *Theory, Culture & Society* 24(7–8): 286–290.

Carreiras, H., and C. Castro, eds. 2013. *Qualitative Methods in Military Studies. Research Experiences and Challenges*. Abingdon: Routledge.

Carreiras, H., C. Castro, and S. Frederic, eds. 2016. *Researching the Military*. Milton Park: Routledge.

Elbe, M., H. Biehl, and M. Steinbrecher, eds. 2021. *Empirische Sozialforschung in den Streitkräften. Positionen, Erfahrungen, Kontroversen*. Berlin: Berliner Wissenschafts-Verlag.

Elbe, M., and G. Richter. 2012. "Militär: Institution und Organisation." In *Militärsoziologie – Eine Einführung*. 2nd ed., edited by N. Leonhard and I.-J. Werkner, 244–263. Wiesbaden: VS Verlag für Sozialwissenschaften.

Forster, A. 2006. *Armed Forces* and *Society in Europe*. Basingstoke: Palgrave Macmillan.

Giddens, A. 1985. *The Nation-State and Violence*. Volume 2 of a Contemporary Critique of Historical Materialism. Berkley: University of California Press.

Higate, P., and A. Cameron. 2006. "Reflexivity and Researching the Military." *Armed Forces & Society* 32(2): 219–233.

Janowitz, M. 1976. "Military Institutions and Citizenship in Western Societies." *Armed Forces & Society* 2(2): 185–204.

Joas, H., and W. Knöbl. 2013. *War in Social Thought – Hobbes to the Present*. Princeton: Princeton University Press.

Kümmel, G. 2021. "Die Wissenschaft und die Politik: Zur politischen Nutzung militärsoziologischer Forschungsergebnisse." In *Empirische Sozialforschung in den Streitkräften. Positionen, Erfahrungen, Kontroversen*, edited by M. Elbe, H. Biehl, and M. Steinbrecher, 149–168. Berlin: Berliner Wissenschafts-Verlag.

King, A. 2011. *The Transformation of Europe's Armed Forces. From Rhine to Afghanistan*. Cambridge: Cambridge University Press.

Levy, Y. 2015. "Time for Critical Military Sociology." *Res Militaris* 5(2), 1–8.

Livingstone, D. 2003. *Putting Science in its Place. Geographies of Scientific Knowledge*. Chicago: The University of Chicago Press.

Richter, G. 2016. "Methoden und Daten zur Erforschung spezieller Organisationen: Bundeswehr." In *Handbuch Empirische Organisationsforschung*, edited by S. Liebig, W. Matiaske, and S. Rosenbohm, 657–674. Berlin: Springer.

Richter, G. 2021. "Ganz normale Organisationsforschung. Empirische Befragungen in der Bundeswehr." In *Empirische Sozialforschung in den Streitkräften. Positionen, Erfahrungen, Kontroversen*, edited by M. Elbe, H. Biehl, and M. Steinbrecher, 301–321. Berlin: Berliner Wissenschafts-Verlag.

Shaw, M. 1991. *Post-Military Society. Militarism, Demilitarization, and War at the End of the Twentieth Century*. Philadelphia: Temple University Press.

Soeters, J., P. Shields, and S. Rietjens, eds. 2014. *Routledge Handbook of Research Methods in Military Studies*. Milton Park: Routledge.

Tilly, C. 1992. *Coercion, Capital, and European States, AD 990-1992*. Cambridge: Basil Blackwell.

Part I:
Comparative Research in
and on the Armed Forces

International Comparative Military Sociology

Ina Kraft

> Most political and social science research,
> whether explicitly or implicitly, is
> comparative research. That is, most
> research is concerned with findings which
> are directly compared across countries
> or cases, or which can be tested against
> theories and inferences derived from such
> a comparison of countries and cases.
> *Peter Mair (2008, 177).*

1   Introduction

Comparisons are the engine of knowledge.[1] Whether we regard something as good or bad, as beneficial, or useless, any of our daily inferences have previously been put in relation to a frame of reference. As the quote by political scientist Peter Mair indicates, comparisons – implicit or explicit – also play a part in the academic context. The comparative method is a well-established path in social science research, and comparative politics, in addition to political theory and international relations, is one of the three sub-disciplines of political science.

Empirical social research on armed forces also often uses the comparative method to answer research questions. This paper provides an overview of the application of the comparative method in current research on the military, security, and war. First, the comparative method is introduced and its value in social science research is explained. Subsequently, selected international research studies on the military are organized according to the different ways of applying the comparative method; the challenges for practical research in comparative empirical military sociology are addressed as are the possibilities of meeting them. A summary weighs the possibility that comparative research on armed forces issues could overcome the absence of theory and the West-centrist orientation in military sociology. Finally, given its potential, this examination advocates an increased use of comparative case study research.

---

1   The author thanks Steffen Kraft, Martin Elbe, Heiko Biehl, Julius Heß and Markus Steinbrecher for comments on an earlier version of this chapter.

2   The Comparative Method

Unlike peace and conflict research, which often makes normative or critical claims, the majority of military sociologists make positivist claims. Scholars trace connections between phenomena and the factors conditioning them, trying to formulate and test hypotheses and to make assumptions about causal relations. They often are, however, limited by the research tools they can apply.

The strongest means to gather knowledge, the experiment, for example, is not applicable in many areas of social science research, especially not in military and conflict studies (Morton and Williams 2008; Teigen 2014). Partly for both ethical and practical research reasons, laboratory experiments are rarely conducted to answer questions concerning war and the armed forces. Quasi-experiments like field experiments, on the other hand, present researchers with the difficulty of controlling the conditions of social interactions. As a result, only a few scholars consider using experiments in their empirical research (Elbe and Steinbrecher 2020).

Quantitative analysis is another means of establishing relationships between independent factors and dependent phenomena (Franklin 2008). In the process, large data sets are analyzed to make statements regarding empirical phenomena and the factors potentially causing them. Important branches of military sociology as well as war and conflict studies make use of the statistical method to examine, for example, the attitudes of the population towards security policy (Biehl and Schoen 2015) or to establish connections between conflicts on the one hand and systemic and geopolitical factors, types of regimes or actors on the other (Gleditsch et al. 2014; Wallensteen 2017). Researchers using the quantitative method either collect the required data themselves or they commission respective surveys or databases. In addition, there are several openly accessible global data sets on the topics of war and armed forces for scholars to resort to. The Uppsala Conflict Data Program containing data on global wars and conflicts as well as the data sets of the Stockholm International Peace Research Institute on international military expenditures, arms sales, military companies, and peace operations are well-known examples.[2]

The statistical method, however, is not applicable when the number of cases is too small as is the case with many topics of armed forces research. A quantitative analysis of an armaments-related decision, of the development of an operational concept or of the culture of a military organization is hardly possible. Empirical social science research, therefore, often uses a third approach which complements experiment and statistical analysis: the case study. A case study shall be under-

---

2   For more information about these datasets see <http://ucdp.uu.se/downloads>, <www.sipri.org/databases> (last access: 18 May 2018).

stood as "the detailed examination of an aspect of a historical episode to develop or test historical explanations that may be generalisable to other events" (George and Bennett 2004, 5). This social scientist's definition differs from the historian's common understanding of case studies as the description of a singular event. Purely descriptive or narrative accounts of events, which represent a considerable share of publications on military subjects, may provide valuable information on specific events (Vennesson and Wiesner 2014, 96). However, they do not necessarily contribute to theory building because they do not meet the important criterion of the scientific case study, that is to generalize findings and thus apply them to other cases.

A social science case study differs from narrative approaches in its epistemological interest. The focus is not on the discovery of new information about a phenomenon but on the generation or validation of theoretical assumptions. In addition to the generation of empirical knowledge, case studies, just like experiments and quantitative methods, contribute to the further development of theories in military sociology and social sciences.

The methodical challenge of theory building, and testing lies in the small numbers. How can we draw theoretically relevant conclusions from only one case? At first glance, singular events like the 9/11 terrorist attacks, World War II, or the development of the US Armed Forces do not seem suitable for any theory building. Apparently, the formulation of generalizable statements from one single case is not possible. Or is it?

It is! The solution for the problem of small numbers lies in a comparative research design (Lijphart 1971; Muno 2009). As Detlef Jahn states: "(A comparative design) puts variables, and especially their relationship towards each other, in the focus and neglects the peculiarity of the cases" (Jahn 2011, 52, translation by the author). The orientation on variables instead of cases makes it possible to apply to research on topics with small case numbers the same positivist logics of inquiry that is known in quantitative research.

However, to study a singular case with the comparative method the researcher requires further cases. There are two possible ways to obtain them, either the internal differentiation of n=1, or external expansion. An internal differentiation is possible, for instance, if a case can be divided into temporal phases. For instance, Lynn Eden studied the assessment of the effect of firebombs and later of nuclear bombs in the United States Air Force. She demonstrated that despite the technological change from one type of bomb to the other, the calculation of the weapon effect remained the same and therefore, the predictions of damage became inaccurate (Eden 2004). The division of a case into temporal phases results in the creation of several cases which then can be compared to each other (longitudinal comparison). Another possible way to generate more cases from one single case is internal differentiation with a view to organizational sub-units (a functional comparison). Especially with regard to armed forces research, an internal differentiation of the single case *armed forces* into three separate cases – army, air force, navy – is feasible in order to make, for example, statements on factors leading to changes in military cultures.

In some instances, however, internal differentiation might not be possible if, for example, the effect of a certain event on a particular organization is analyzed. In this case, external expansion by the analysis of the studied phenomenon also in other military organizations might be feasible to develop and test theoretical statements (spatial/cross-sectional comparison).[3] Ina Wiesner, for example, examines the introduction of the concept of network-centric operations in the Bundeswehr and in the British armed forces (Wiesner 2013). The description of the individual development of the two cases is only a by-product of the work. The main objective is to answer the scientific question of why two similar military organizations like the British armed forces and the German Bundeswehr differ so profoundly in the adoption of the network-centric operations' concept. The British armed forces were quick to decide to introduce the concept and followed up its implementation promptly while it took the Bundeswehr years to develop its own version of network-centric operations. In addition, the German armed forces implemented the concept slowly and selectively (Wiesner 2013, 13). Based on this comparison, Wiesner developed an institutionalist explanatory model that can be generalized and thus be applied to other cases of concept adoption in the armed forces.

International comparative research is a way to engage in theory building in military sociology. Thus, the focus of comparative research is not on the narration of individual cases but – like with experiment and statistical method – on analyzing relations between variables (Jahn 2011, 44).

The prerequisite for a theory-driven analysis of variable relations is a systematic, i.e. structured, and focused approach (George and McKeown 1985). Structured means that researchers engage in theory-driven research using the same set of questions. Focused means the study of only (but also all) those aspects of the cases that are relevant to answering the research questions (George and McKeown 1985, 41).

In order to conduct comparative empirical research on the military, it is therefore not sufficient to simply present mere narratives about military organizations.

---

3   In addition to the inclusion of other countries as benchmarks, other external extensions are possible. Juanita M. Firestone studies the difference in the position of women and men in civilian professions and compares it with the distribution in military professions (Firestone 1992).

Instead, theory-derived variables need to be examined in the sub-cases (or phases) and put in relation to the respective outcomes of the case. Depending on the problem, the focus is either on the variables or on the outcomes.

The application of standardized procedures for the selection of cases is an important prerequisite for a structured and focused approach and thus for theory-building (Ebbinghaus 2009). Comparative empirical military sociology – as well as social sciences in general – often use a "most similar systems design". The researcher selects cases which – ideally – are similar in their independent variables but differ in the dependent variable, the outcome. The above-cited study by Wiesner follows this study design. It was ideally assumed that the cases of the Bundeswehr and the British armed forces were almost identical in size, equipment, and challenges faced in the Afghanistan operation. However, they differed in all dimensions of the outcome *introduction of network-enabled capabilities* (concept faithfulness, pace of introduction, faithfulness of implementation). The "most different systems design" with vastly different cases having the same outcome, is less often applied in social science research (George and Bennett 2004, Chapter 2). In both approaches, the researcher aims to identify those variables that are responsible for the observed outcomes.

Researchers using the quantitative method occasionally criticize the self-confidence displayed by those who use the qualitative method when deriving generalizations. They argue that with small case numbers and few variables one and the same data set is used in an unacceptable way to generate hypotheses and to verify them. Furthermore, they criticize the fact that the small number of cases only allows for a small number of variables to be tested since researchers have limited possibilities of controlling variables. From the perspective of qualitative research, the instrument of process tracing offers a solution for both issues; it establishes the causal relationship between variables and outcomes – in addition to the comparison of variables – by tracing the development within cases in a focused and structured way (Vennesson and Wiesner 2014).

3   Comparative Research on the Military

The case-study comparison is a research method. It is neither a theoretical proposition nor is it a substantial topic of armed forces research. Depending on the problem, any aspect of military sociology research can be examined by using the comparative approach. As a result, the range of studies on military topics that employ the comparative method is quite broad. Publications on country-specific aspects of national security and defense policies (Meijer and Wyss 2018) used this approach, as did publications on armed forces transformations (Terriff et al. 2010) and military operations (Farrell et al. 2013), studies on operations-related tactics (Ruffa 2014, 2018), on strategic cultures (Biehl et al. 2013c; Giegerich 2006), on the selection and training of officers (Caforio 2000a), on the position of reserve forces (James 2011), on military innovations (Posen 1984; Shamir 2011; Wiesner 2013) as well as on the relationship between society, politics and the military (Avant 1994; Moskos et al. 2000). There are, however, considerable differences in the respective strength of the comparison. Depending on the theoretical aspiration, there are different ways to employ the comparative method – from the mere presentation of similarly structured chapters on countries in edited volumes on the one hand, to the coherent research design with a strict comparative logic on the other.

The publication by Terry Terriff, Frans Osinga, and Theo Farrell on the introduction of three conceptual military innovations in the 2000s, for example, is an edited volume in which the individual country-specific chapters are each structured in a similar way to enable a comparison among the national cases (Terriff et al. 2010).

In contrast, the transnational public survey by Heiko Biehl et al. on the topic of strategic cultures in Europe (Biehl et al. 2011a) is an example for a centrally designed and conducted study with a strict structure and focus. For the purpose of the study, telephone interviews were conducted in Austria, the Czech Republic, Germany, France, Sweden, Spain, Turkey, and the United Kingdom with the objective of finding "similarities, differences and imminent changes in the strategic cultures of the selected European states which are reflected at population levels" (Biehl et al. 2011b, 16, translation by the author). The questions asked referred, for instance, to the interest in politics and security policy, media usage, the personal feeling of security and threat, the personal assessment of the national security situation, the attitude towards the role of NATO and EU in security policy, and the personal attitude towards the tasks of the state and the armed forces but also towards the interaction of state institutions of foreign, security and defense policy. The study is descriptive in character and does not have an explicit theoretical agenda – i.e., it is neither theory-generating nor theory-testing. However, the structured and focused collection of data allowed others at a later stage to make theoretical claims on the basis of the dataset (Biehl 2015; Endres 2018, 76 ff.; Mader 2017, 64 ff.).

The policy analysis by Ines-Jacqueline Werkner, who studied conscription systems in eight European states (Austria, Belgium, Denmark, Germany, France, the Netherlands, Spain, and Switzerland), is an example of a comparative and a theory-testing study (Werkner 2006). Werkner asked why some of the countries decided to abolish conscription while others decided to keep it even though they all faced similar security challenges (Werkner 2006, 32). Werkner employs an integrative multi-level approach to explain her puzzle, building especially on the significance of the political-military culture as an explanatory variable (Werkner 2006, 38–44, 273–283). Werkner not only applied the same set of questions to every case, but the set itself also embodies the operationalization of her theoretical assumptions. She studies the individual countries with regard to the constitutional provisions in national security, the relations between parliament, government, and armed forces as well as the norms and traditions in the field of security and defense. In her work, Werkner made extensive use of the theory potential of comparisons.

Although military sociology itself can be understood as a sub-discipline of sociology, it can be differentiated even further. There are expert discussions on different topics such as the armed forces and public opinion, military and gender, civil-military relations, the military profession, and veterans. *Comparative military sociology*, however, could not be included in this list. Rather, it runs across these topics. Comparative research is, thus, defined by its method and not by its content. This also means that the comparative method is not an end in itself. Like all social science methods, it is used according to its usefulness for approaching a specific research question.

4   Challenges and Chances of Comparative Military Sociology

In the social sciences, particular in Germany, the study of armed forces is a peripheral phenomenon (Bredow 2007, 47–53). This is often attributed to the problem of acquiring access to the research field. At a first glance, this problem has an intellectual, an ideological and an institutional dimension. First, the lack of military experience among sociologists might unwittingly trigger reservations about the topics of military and conflict and, thus, render the discovery of research puzzles difficult. Second, in liberal societies, science mostly has a progressive connotation whereas military and war are often perceived as "obscurantist and reactionary" (Edgerton 1990, 935). Therefore, researchers probably tend to avoid military topics. Third, institutional barriers should not be underestimated. Eyal Ben-Ari and Yagil Levy state that empirical researchers need to obtain access to the military organization. Yet, like most large-scale organizations the military is "bureaucratised, centralised, secretive [and] masculanised" (Ben-Ari and Levy 2014, 12) making it hard from the beginning to get access. And, to make matters more complicated, it is also entrusted with aspects of national security.

The institutional aspect is a major challenge for comparative research on the armed forces. It can be assumed that the difficulties of institutional access even increase if researchers who require access to the military organization have a foreign nationality. The reasons for this are manifold: beginning with language barriers, the lack of institutional knowledge about formal and informal access, to stricter decision-making rules regarding permits for non-nationals. Even after obtaining institutional access, there are often further challenges. Language barriers, for example, may result in a lack of understanding and a distortion of research findings as Chiara Ruffa and Joseph Soeters describe:

> Interviewing soldiers in their mother tongue is fundamental to enabling them to express themselves freely with all the nuances and complexities that come along with in-depth conversations. Relying on English as the general bridging language will often prove to be inadequate, because it will lead to biased selections of respondents/interviewees – to those who master that language – or to an insufficient quality of information exchange. (Ruffa and Soeters 2014, 223)

The lack of understanding does not only have an obvious linguistic dimension; it is also reflected in problems of interpretation if researchers, who did not serve in the military, lack the cultural access to the military organization. The potential deficiency to understanding symbols, signs, actions and the spoken word only further increases if the observed or interviewed person has another nationality. Depending on the researcher's cultural background, an observed behavior, for example, can be understood as servile or respectful, a certain symbol as including or excluding and a certain phrase as encouraging or deterring. These challenges influence the empirical collection of data in such a way that the three already identified obstacles to field access (intellectual, ideological, and institutional) need to be extended by a fourth challenge, the cultural dimension.

In case studies on military topics, a considerable share of the research resources is needed to obtain field access. Researchers must make even greater efforts if they want to access foreign armed forces with their foreign organizational codes and languages. In order to conduct telephone interviews in different countries for their survey, Heiko Biehl et al. had to hire a company that guaranteed the use of native speakers as interviewers to "ensure the acceptance and quality of the survey" (Biehl 2011, 110). This is a very cost-intensive approach. Unfortunately, research funds often are not available in the required amount. Research can also be very time-consuming. For her excellent contribution on how military culture affects international peacekeeping, Chiara Ruffa spent nine months embedded within the French and the Italian peacekeeping forces in Afghanistan and in Lebanon (Ruffa 2018). It took Ruffa about two months to gain access to the French military. In the French case, the process of acquiring access was decentralized and based on personal contacts to personnel deployed in the military theatre. The Italian army was more difficult to access and the whole process took about a year. It was, furthermore, much more centralized. At the same time, Ruffa had to put a lot of effort into identifying and contacting the relevant gatekeepers in the organization. Ruffa's permission was ultimately authorized by the office of the Joint Chief of Staff of the Italian Armed Forces – a top unit in the Italian military.[4]

Also, like the research budget, time is a scarce resource and not every researcher is able or willing to spend a year acquiring field access. In addition, not everyone can be away from home for a long period of time nor be embedded in a military unit deployed in a crisis theatre.

These kinds of challenges could force scholars to seek compromises with regards to how they ultimately approach their research subject. It is not uncommon in social science research – though not quite without problems in terms of research ethics – to repeatedly readjust the research design and, if necessary, the theoretical model and its operationalization to adjust to evolving difficulties of the empirical research phase (adjustment of research design). It can happen, for example, that in the course of a research process, one case is relinquished if it turns out that the administrative problems become overwhelming. Research publications usually do not raise this issue, and the altered research design is presented in a fitting relation to the theoretical question and the presentation of results.

Secondly, when selecting their cases, researchers will – either intentionally or unintentionally – consider those countries where access to the armed forces appears to be (rather) easy (selection bias). In practice, unfortunately, this often results in a West-centrist approach, which prevails in the present research on the military. This leads to an ever-increasing collection of secondary sources for these Western countries, which, in turn, further perpetuates the relative ease to gain access to this particular part of the field.

Thirdly, researchers might be forced to adjust the selection of empirical material as planned interviews might get cancelled, or a permission to enter a military facility might be withdrawn (adjustment of data collection). Researchers with limited personnel, time and budget are often forced to put up with these challenges of limited access.

What are the possibilities to limit the negative repercussions these challenges of international comparative empirical research on the military might have? When presenting one's research results, it is, firstly, to address these adjustments openly in view of the quality of the research. Thus, one solution to the problems of access is transparency in the presentation of research findings. Researchers need to be

---

4   E-mail communication with Chiara Ruffa on 11 November 2019. Ruffa has also reflected on her research method and the conduct of her case studies (Ruffa 2019).

open about any difference between their initial theoretical ambition and the actual obstacles in the collection of data. They also need to address the resulting potential limitations in the range of their own research findings.

Another possibility to cope with the problem of access is the smart operationalization of the research puzzle and the theoretical model. Which data are already available? How can unavailable data be obtained? Which data is mandatory to be collected by the researchers themselves? In some cases, researchers might be able to rely on published studies and secondary data. The problem is, of course, that data are only available in the way they were generated by other researchers before (possibly with different research questions). If collecting one's own data is required, researchers may decide in favor of a mixed approach using both secondary and primary data. In her above-mentioned study, Werkner (2006) resorted to secondary sources but also conducted expert interviews in the eight examined countries. Pluralism in sources and methods can be understood as a chance to conduct international research despite practical obstacles.

A third option is project-related research cooperation. By that, individual researchers or research teams cooperate with researchers from the countries that need to be included in a comparison. As a result, a number of access-related problems no longer apply. In a research cooperation, scholars collect empirical data based on a study design developed by the researcher in charge of the project. The focus and structure that are vital to a comparison are thus determined as a central guideline.[5] In the following, some examples of such research cooperations are provided.

In 2013, Biehl, Giegerich, and Jonas approached the issue of strategic cultures in Europe once again in a study, this time from the perspective of national foreign, security and defense policies (Biehl et al. 2013c). This particular study supplements research on the attitude of the national populations. The study examines the institutional conditions of national defense policies as well as their contents in all EU member states and Turkey with the help of national experts. The editors of the study prepared an analytic framework as a guideline for the authors (Biehl et al. 2013b, 13). It consists of four areas of interest: first, the national level of ambition in foreign and security policy, second, the scope of action for the executive in decision-making, third, the foreign policy orientation, and fourth, the readiness to use military force. These rather general topics are specified through further questions. Thanks to these specifications, all case studies end up having the same structure.

---

5   At this point, it is important to note that research cooperation can also give rise to a number of new problems. There is a potential problem of different academic and cultural influences among national experts from countries with their own research traditions (Peterson 2009). So far, this problem has not been mentioned in connection with comparative research on armed forces issues.

Despite the strict comparative logic, the development or testing of theories is not an explicit aim of this study. Instead, the project team's objective is to capture and map the strategic cultures in Europe in a "methodically controlled approach with the help of standardized dimensions and indicators".[6] Nevertheless, the editors are able to derive a theory-driven classification based on the empirical results. They categorize the 28 cases of national strategic cultures using a set of analytical dimensions (Biehl et al. 2013a, 394).

The study *The European Officer* is another example of research cooperation. The study focuses on the selection and training of officers in Europe (Bulgaria, Czech Republic, France, Germany, Greece, Italy, The Netherlands, Poland, Portugal, Sweden, Switzerland, United Kingdom) (Caforio 2000a). It had been organized by The Military Profession Working Group of the Research Group on Military and Society (ERGOMAS), an international association of scientists with an interest in the sociological research of the armed forces. Project manager Giuseppe Caforio provided the authors from the individual countries with an analytical framework according to which they structured their case studies (Caforio 2000b, 9). The framework consists of four parts: admission procedures to military academies, circumstances of training, further training, trends of change. Similar to the research cooperation on strategic cultures, the development and verification of theories were not the focus of analysis, however, this study nevertheless allows for some theory-based classifications of the countries according to their style of officer training (Caforio 2000b, 13–15).

A special form of research cooperation is collaboration. Different to a cooperative research setting with a central research team and decentralized contributors, in a collaborative setting, participating researchers hold the same degree of responsibility. Collaboration is often chosen when scholars jointly publish a comparative article in a professional journal. For instance, Özkan Duman and Dimitris Tsarouhas studied the impact of the European Union on the civil-military relations in Greece and Turkey and included their respective national perspectives in the paper (Duman and Tsarouhas 2006). Pascal Vennesson, Fabian Breuer, Chiara de Franco, and Ursula C. Schröder raised the question of whether there was a European way of waging war. To answer this question, they studied the role concepts and the organizational framework conditions of the military institutions in France, Germany, Italy, and the United Kingdom in a comparative way (Vennesson et al. 2008).

As with research cooperation, in research collaboration the inclusion of national experts facilitates the generation of empirical data. In contrast to cooperation, researchers participating in a collaboration are involved, from the beginning, in all

---

6   E-mail communication with Heiko Biehl on 8 March 2018, translation by the author.

stages of the research process – from the development of the study design to the execution of the study and the evaluation of the findings. Collaboration therefore is more close-knit than mere cooperation. It can be assumed, however, that with an increasing number of countries involved in a comparative design, the inclusion of all participating researchers in all phases of the research becomes more difficult. Therefore, research collaboration will be preferred in comparative studies with a smaller number of cases whereas research cooperation will be the method of choice in studies with a larger number of cases.

The scholars who participated in the above cited studies came together in different ways. For the study on strategic cultures in 28 European countries, project leaders were able to resort to existing personal networks in the field of the armed forces research. In addition, they identified national experts through publications.[7] The European Officer study resorted to the institutional network of the ERGOMAS Military Profession Working Group. As a result, only those countries probably were considered to be included in the study, for which an expert with the same nationality was a member of the group. The research collaboration including Pascal Vennesson was formed of researchers who were all working at the European University Institute in Florence, Italy, at the time.[8] Personal networks, the invitation to authors identified through their publications, contacting existing institutional arenas and familiarity through spatial proximity are the ways of initiating research cooperation.

As demonstrated, in an international comparative research project sometimes the challenges of access increase. Obvious institutional but also less apparent cultural obstacles render comparative empirical research on military topics abroad more difficult. Some of these obstacles simply need to be accepted. Some will result in the altering of the research design, perhaps even the research puzzle. Some might be approached by a smart selection of sources. And in some cases, international cooperation and collaboration will be the way to mitigate the problem of access.

5   Summary

Even though single-case studies still dominate research on the military, Ruffa and Soeters (2014) have found an increase in comparative case studies in recent years. By that, we can assume that the problem of access also increases. It was argued in this chapter, that research cooperation can provide a way forward.

---

7   E-mail communication with Heiko Biehl on 8 March 2018.
8   E-mail communication with Ursula Schröder on 14 March 2018.

It can be observed, however, that the potential of research cooperation is not fully utilized. Even with the possibility of research cooperation, the distinct West-centrist approach of military sociology prevails. The potential of cooperative research settings, that is to include non-Western militaries, could be used to broaden the scope of future research on military topics.

The use of the comparative approach could also increase the contribution of military sociology to theory building in the social sciences. Although most of the studies cited in this paper have a comparative study design, they do not claim to contribute to theory-building in military sociology, rather they are confined to generating descriptive knowledge and classifications. While collecting descriptive knowledge is a valid objective of social science research (Eckstein 1975, 96–99; Levy 2008, 4), international comparative empirical research on armed forces offers a chance to live up to the theoretical potential of military sociology even when the number of cases is small.

References

Avant, D.D. 1994. *Political Institutions and Military Change: Lessons from Peripheral Wars*. Ithaca: Cornell University Press.

Ben-Ari, E., and Y. Levy. 2014. "Getting Access to The Field: Insider/Outsider Perspectives." In *Routledge Handbook of Research Methods in Military Studies*, edited by J. Soeters, P. Shields, and S. Rietjens, 9–18. London: Routledge.

Biehl, H. 2011. "Die internationalen Bevölkerungsumfragen. Methodik, Datenbasis und Fragebogen." In *Strategische Kulturen in Europa. Die Bürger Europas und ihre Streitkräfte. Ergebnisse der Bevölkerungsbefragungen in acht europäischen Ländern 2010 des Sozialwissenschaftlichen Instituts der Bundeswehr*. Forschungsbericht 96, edited by H. Biehl, R. Fiebig, B. Giegerich, J. Jacobs, and A. Jonas, 109–112. Strausberg: Sozialwissenschaftliches Institut der Bundeswehr.

Biehl, H. 2015. "Support Our Troops!? Unterstützung und Ablehnung von Streitkräften im europäischen Vergleich." In *Sicherheitspolitik und Streitkräfte im Urteil der Bürger: Theorien, Methoden, Befunde*, edited by H. Biehl and H. Schoen, 237–262. Wiesbaden: Springer VS.

Biehl, H., R. Fiebig, B. Giegerich, J. Jacobs, and A. Jonas. 2011a. *Strategische Kulturen in Europa. Die Bürger Europas und ihre Streitkräfte. Ergebnisse der Bevölkerungsbefragungen in acht europäischen Ländern 2010 des Sozialwissenschaftlichen Instituts der Bundeswehr*. Forschungsbericht 96. Strausberg: Sozialwissenschaftliches Institut der Bundeswehr.

Biehl, H., B. Giegerich, and A. Jonas. 2011b. "Das Forschungsprojekt 'Strategische Kulturen in Europa' am Sozialwissenschaftlichen Institut der Bundeswehr." In *Strategische Kulturen in Europa. Die Bürger Europas und ihre Streitkräfte. Ergebnisse der Bevölkerungsbefragungen in acht europäischen Ländern 2010 des Sozialwissenschaftlichen Instituts der Bundeswehr.* Forschungsbericht 96, edited by H. Biehl, R. Fiebig, B. Giegerich, J. Jacobs, and A. Jonas, 9–16. Strausberg: Sozialwissenschaftliches Institut der Bundeswehr.

Biehl, H., B. Giegerich, and A. Jonas. 2013a. "Conclusion." In *Strategic Cultures in Europe. Security and Defence Policies Across the Continent*, edited by H. Biehl, B. Giegerich, and A. Jonas, 387–401. Wiesbaden: Springer VS.

Biehl, H., B. Giegerich, and A. Jonas. 2013b. "Introduction." In *Strategic Cultures in Europe. Security and Defence Policies Across the Continent*, edited by H. Biehl, B. Giegerich, and A. Jonas, 7–16. Wiesbaden: Springer VS.

Biehl, H., B. Giegerich, and A. Jonas, eds. 2013c. *Strategic Cultures in Europe. Security and Defence Policies Across the Continent.* Wiesbaden: Springer VS.

Biehl, H., and H. Schoen, eds. 2015. *Sicherheitspolitik und Streitkräfte im Urteil der Bürger; Theorien, Methoden, Befunde.* Wiesbaden: Springer VS.

Caforio, G., ed. 2000a. *The European Officer: A Comparative View on Selection and Education.* Pisa: Edizioni ETS.

Caforio, G. 2000b. "Introduction." In *The European Officer: A Comparative View on Selection and Education*, edited by G. Caforio, 7–18. Pisa: Edizioni ETS.

Duman, Ö., and D. Tsarouhas. 2006. "'Civilianization' in Greece versus 'Demilitarization' in Turkey: A Comparative Study of Civil-Military Relations and the Impact of the European Union." *Armed Forces & Society* 32(3): 405–423.

Ebbinghaus, B. 2009. "Mehr oder weniger? Quantitativer versus qualitativer Vergleich." In *Methoden der vergleichenden Politik- und Sozialwissenschaft: Neue Entwicklungen und Anwendungen*, edited by S. Pickel, G. Pickel, H.-J. Lauth, and D. Jahn, 197–212. Wiesbaden: Springer VS.

Eckstein, H. 1975. "Case Study and Theory in Political Science." In *Strategies of Inquiry*, edited by F.I. Greenstein and N.W. Polsby, 79–137. Reading: Addison-Wesley.

Eden, L. 2004. *Whole World on Fire. Organizations, Knowledge, and Nuclear Weapons Devastation.* New York: Cornell University Press.

Edgerton, D. 1990. "Science and War." In *Companion to the History of Modern Science*, edited by R.C. Olby, G.N. Cantor, J.R. Christie, and M.J.S. Hodge, 934–945. London: Routledge.

Endres, F. 2018. *Öffentliche Meinung und strategische Kulturen Außenpolitische Überzeugungen in Deutschland, Frankreich und Großbritannien.* Wiesbaden: Springer VS.

Farrell, T., F.P.B. Osinga, and J.A. Russell, eds. 2013. *Military Adaptation in Afghanistan.* Stanford: Stanford University Press.

Firestone Juanita, M. 1992. "Occupational Segregation: Comparing the Civilian and Military Work Force." *Armed Forces & Society* 18(3): 363−381.

Franklin, M. 2008. "Quantitative Analysis." In *Approaches and Methodologies in the Social Sciences: A Pluralist Perspective*, edited by D. Della Porta and M. Keating, 240−262. Cambridge: Cambridge University Press.

George, A.L., and A. Bennett. 2004. *Case Studies and Theory Development in the Social Sciences.* Cambridge: MIT Press.

George, A.L., and T. McKeown. 1985. "Case Studies and Theories of Organizational Decision Making." In *Advances in Information Processing In Organizations: A Research Annual*, edited by R.F. Coulam and R.A. Smith, 21−58. Greenwich: JAI Press.

Giegerich, B. 2006. *European Security and Strategic Culture: National Responses to the EU's Security and Defence Policy.* Baden-Baden: Nomos.

Gleditsch, K.S., N.W. Metternich, and A. Ruggeri. 2014. "Data and Progress in Peace and Conflict Research." *Journal of Peace Research* 51(2): 301−314.

Jahn, D. 2011. *Vergleichende Politikwissenschaft.* Wiesbaden: Springer VS.

James, G. 2011. "Reserve Forces − After the Cold War: An International Perspective." *Armed Forces & Society* 37(2): 209−215.

Levy, J.S. 2008. "Case Studies: Types, Designs, and Logics of Inference." *Conflict Management and Peace Science* 25(1): 1−18.

Lijphart, A. 1971. "Comparative Politics and the Comparative Method." *American Political Science Review* 65(3): 682−693.

Mader, M. 2017. *Öffentliche Meinung zu Auslandseinsätzen der Bundeswehr. Zwischen Antimilitarismus und transatlantischer Orientierung.* Wiesbaden: Springer VS.

Mair, P. 2008. "Concepts and concept formation." In *Approaches and Methodologies in the Social Sciences: A Pluralist Perspective*, edited by D. Della Porta and M. Keating, 177−197. Cambridge: Cambridge University Press.

Meijer, H., and M. Wyss, eds. 2018. *The Handbook of European Defence Policies and Armed Forces.* Oxford: Oxford University Press.

Morton, R.B., and K.C. Williams. 2008. "Experimentation in Political Science." In *The Oxford Handbook of Political Methodology*, edited by J.M. Box-Steffensmeier, H.E. Brady, and D. Collier, 339−356. Oxford: Oxford University Press.

Moskos, C.C., J.A. Williams and D.R. Segal, eds. 2000. *The Postmodern Military: Armed Forces After the Cold War*. Oxford: Oxford University Press.

Muno, W. 2009. "Fallstudien und die vergleichende Methode." In *Methoden der vergleichenden Politik- und Sozialwissenschaft: neue Entwicklungen und Anwendungen*, edited by S. Pickel, G. Pickel, H.-J. Lauth, and D. Jahn, 113–131. Wiesbaden: Springer VS.

Peterson, M. F. 2009. "Cross-Cultural Comparative Studies and Issues in International Research Collaboration." In *The SAGE Handbook of Organizational Research Methods*, edited by D.A. Buchanan and A. Bryman, 328–345. Los Angeles: SAGE.

Posen, B. 1984. *The Sources of Military Doctrine: France, Britain, and Germany Between the World Wars*. Ithaca: Cornell University Press.

Ruffa, C. 2014. "What Peacekeepers Think and Do: An Exploratory Study of French, Ghanaian, Italian, and South Korean Armies in the United Nations Interim Force in Lebanon." *Armed Forces & Society* 40(2): 199–225.

Ruffa, C. 2018. *Military Cultures in Peace and Stability Operations: Afghanistan and Lebanon*. Philadelphia: Penn Press.

Ruffa, C. 2019. "Designing and Conducting the Comparative Case Study Method." *In SAGE Research Methods Cases Part 2*. <https://doi.org/10.4135/9781526490827>.

Ruffa, C., and J. Soeters. 2014. "Cross-National Research in the Military. Comparing Operational Styles." In *Routledge Handbook of Research Methods in Military Studies*, edited by J. Soeters, J., P. Shields, and S. Rietjens, 216–227. London: Routledge.

Shamir, E. 2011. *Transforming Command: The Pursuit of Mission Command in the U.S., British, and Israeli Armies*. Stanford: Stanford University Press.

Teigen, J.M. 2014. "Experimental Methods in Military and Veteran Studies." In *Routledge Handbook of Research Methods in Military Studies*, edited by J. Soeters, P. Shields, and S. Rietjens, 228–237. London: Routledge.

Terriff, T., F.P.B. Osinga, and T. Farrell, eds. 2010. *A Transformation Gap? American Innovations and European Military Change*. Stanford: Stanford University Press.

Vennesson, P., F. Breuer, C. de Franco, and U.C. Schröder. 2008. "Is There a European Way of War? Role Conceptions, Organizational Frames, and the Utility of Force." *Armed Forces & Society* 35(4): 628–645.

Vennesson, P., and I. Wiesner. 2014. "Process Tracing in Case Studies." In *Routledge Handbook of Research Methods in Military Studies*, edited by J. Soeters, P. Shields, and S. Rietjens, 92–103. London: Routledge.

von Bredow, W. 2007. *Militär und Demokratie in Deutschland. Eine Einführung*. Wiesbaden: Springer VS.

Wallensteen, P. 2017. "Wars, Civil Wars and Armed Conflict: Patterns, Trends and Analytic Paradigms." In *States and peoples in conflict: transformations of conflict studies*, edited by M. Stohl, M.I. Lichbach, and P.N. Grabosky, 253–271. London: Routledge.

Werkner, I.-J. 2006. *Wehrpflicht oder Freiwilligenarmee? Wehrstrukturentscheidungen im europäischen Vergleich*. Frankfurt a.M.: Lang.

Wiesner, I. 2013. *Importing the American Way of War? Network-Centric Warfare in the UK and Germany*. Baden-Baden: Nomos.

Multinational Military Cooperation: An Overview of the Current State of Research

Joseph Soeters

1 Introduction

Historically, multinational cooperation is a relatively new phenomenon as it is connected to the rise of nation-states. The foundation of nations – for some states over four hundred years or longer ago, for other nations only about a century or less ago – was nearly almost accompanied by the formation of armed forces (e.g., Tilly 1992). More than anything, the military has been – and still is – a national phenomenon per se. It is an institution that relates to the core identity of the individual state, its population, its language(s), its economic interests, and its culture. What is more, the raison d'être of national militaries is to defend against other national forces. For these reasons, multinational military cooperation – i.e., cooperation between national armed forces – does not come naturally.

The crisis following the Boxer Rebellion in Beijing in the 1900s pushed various nations to join in a military operation. The participating nations ranged from the United States, the United Kingdom, France, Austria-Hungary and Germany to Russia and Japan. This operation was intended to relieve the foreign citizens in Beijing taken hostage during the rebellion. The operation was successful but did not evolve without friction between the participants. Tensions emerged not only during the march on Beijing but particularly after the goals had been achieved as fierce debates emerged about who had contributed most and who had in fact gained the victory (Preston 2002).

The liberation of Europe from the Nazis was a spectacular manifestation of effective multinational military cooperation. Yet, in the Italian campaign, there was rather intense inter-allied stress and disagreement, which improved after the Normandy invasion (Visser 2010, 347–348). American, British, Canadian, and later French and Polish troops joined in one mission but nonetheless followed separate routes to achieve the common goals. Because of their geographical separation, the Soviet troops' contributions to the victory have often even been considered as a military operation of its own.[1] Remarkably, while the mission gradually came to a successful ending, soldiers from the various cooperating nations did not turn out to like one another very much. Boasting their own efforts, American servicemen nicknamed French and British soldiers in a derogatory manner, and they generally voiced "anything from mild annoyance to extreme anger at French and British glorification of their own forces" (Glaser 1946, 436). Indeed, American soldiers were not the only ones to behave in such manner.

After the Second World War, the Cold War began, bringing with it, multinational military cooperation and alliance formation within both NATO and the Warsaw Pact. Without this cooperation, the Cold War would have been quite different. Today, multinational military cooperation has become even more a major and inevitable challenge for national armed forces (Haltiner and Klein 2004; King 2005). The globalization of security threats entails that military operations are conducted all over the globe but, more often, far away from than nearby the own national territories. Greater distances and more complex missions in culturally uncharted areas imply that relatively more financial, manpower and material resources are needed, which most national forces can hardly afford by themselves. Clearly, there are economic arguments related to international burden sharing and cost control that urge multinational military cooperation. Multinational military cooperation is even considered *smart defense* as a way to be more efficient and effective with the same level of resources (e.g., Giegerich 2012). But, even if armed forces are sizable and well-funded, they prefer their operations to be legitimized through multinational cooperation. Legitimation – political, societal, and institutional support – can best be achieved through the operational participation and support of other nations' militaries even if this participation is minor. The foundation of the French-German military cooperation in the last two decades provides a clear example of all these political, economic, and operational arguments coming together (Leonhard and Gareis 2008).

Hence, in today's world, multinational military cooperation is here to stay, and it is likely to become one of the main challenges facing militaries, particularly in Europe and the broader Western hemisphere (King 2010; Maniscalco 2018; Soeters and Manigart 2008). Such multinational cooperation is likely to come along with the internationalization of previously fully national militaries and their work forces

---

1   Very often, the Soviet or Russian hemisphere remains out of the equation, including unfortunately, in this chapter (e.g., Savic 2010). The same applies to the Chinese and many other militaries, for instance those in Africa (Very et al. 2013). For sure, there is no or hardly any cooperation with Russian and Chinese forces at the time but there may be opportunities to cooperate in the future; these options are out of the scope of this chapter, however. For a more global approach of multinational military affairs see Soeters 2021.

(Bagayoko-Penone 2006). All this is highly comparable to what has been occurring in the business world – such as the airlines, the automotive industry, or the telecom business – for over almost half a century. Multinational cooperation is not a specific military phenomenon these days.

Multinational military cooperation is practiced with allies, in partnerships such as NATO or the EU, or with other fellow militaries such as the ones from Australia, New Zealand, South Korea, and Japan. Moreover, the United Nations has identi-fied multinational military cooperation as an essential feature of its peace missions. Cooperation will sometimes also be required with host nationals or host nations in the areas of operation, such as the Afghan National Army, and even with im-promptu partners, including various African forces (Senegal, Nigeria, etc.). Even cooperation with actual enemies can be imagined. However, in this chapter, the focus is on cooperation between allies, near and far. Cooperation with enemies, accidental or not, deserves a different perspective that is beyond the context of this chapter.

This chapter first examines available comparative studies because military cul-tures, structures, and strategies – like languages for instance – differ between na-tional forces. In the study of multinational military cooperation, it is important to be aware of these differences. Then the focus will be on the actual encounter of military men and women from different nationalities working together in (recent) operations and three ways of organizing such encounters. Subsequently, it is im-portant to realize that everything is in movement, and so is military collaboration. Therefore, attention will be paid to time-sensitive developments. The chapter ends with a brief overview of methodological issues and implications of studying multi-national military cooperation.

2   Comparison

The first element that deserves attention in the study of inter-organizational coop-eration is the fact that there is no such thing as one way of organizing. In a similar manner, one can state that there is not one way of military organization nor is there one way of conducting military operations. As cognitive sociologists have taught us, people construe their own realities dependent on the context in which they live. To put it another way, people's values and cognitions are shaped – at least to a certain extent – by the structural and cultural environment they live in (e.g., Zerubavel 1997). Depending on where and how people live, where they are edu-cated, which languages they learned, which religious beliefs they acquired, and how they earn their living, people develop their own *social mindscapes*.

In international business practices, such cognitive and corresponding cultural and institutional variation has been acknowledged for a long time (e.g., Olie 1994). The Anglo-American managerial and business style and institutional environment are quite different from what one can observe in Northwestern Europe (Sorge et al. 2015, 112 ff.). In the Anglo-American context, the financial system imposes relatively short-term horizons on companies, whereas deregulation without strong employee representation is preferred and strong *between companies*-competition, rivalry and hostile take-overs are encouraged. In Northwestern Europe, these tendencies tend to be the opposite. In the Anglo-Saxon world, the interests of shareholders are considered most, whereas in their continental European counterparts the interests of customers and personnel count as well. As it is said, in the Anglo-Saxon world primarily, the interests of billionaires count, while in continental Western Europe the interests of billions or more customers are considered as well.

This translates to the military domain. It has long been recognized that nations display so-called *strategic cultures*, referring to shared beliefs, views, decisions and practices that are based on fundamentally distinct assumptions about security and defense (Biehl et al. 2013; Johnston 1995). Such strategic cultures are observed at the level of national societies and are quite stable, even though intra-national variation and changes over time may occur (Soeters 2018a). To use a well-known example: The United States' expenditures on defense and security are twice to three times as large as those of most continental European nations. This is an established difference despite changes in government and situational developments on both sides of the ocean. High military spending in the United States may seem surprising as this country is not likely to be attacked by its neighboring countries and possible adversaries are located at least an ocean away. Nonetheless, in the United States, the siren-call of Big Wars is never far away.[2]

Inside Europe, the United Kingdom and France spend systematically more money on the military than most continental nations do, including today's Germany. So-called small powers display their own strategic cultures, balancing between different views of how to act with military force (Angstrom and Honig 2012). In general, national differences in spending on security relate to larger *social things* such as strategic cultures (Lemert 2012), including ideas and views about when and how to use force in hostile confrontations. This is an important point to consider before engaging in the study of multinational military cooperation.[3]

---

2   Phrasing by Wilbur Scott in a personal communication.
3   In a comparable way, Beatrice de Graaf (2013) has demonstrated that in Europe there are considerable national differences in approaches to fight home-grown counterterrorism, with varying degrees of effectiveness. Such finding is important to know before one can start developing collaboration in combatting terrorism across borders within Europe.

Theoretically and inevitably simplifying, there are two approaches of viewing things militarily. In the literature on international relations, one discerns so-called *Hard Realpolitik* (the belief in the efficacy of violence, that conflicts have a ze-ro-sum nature and that conflicts occur frequently in human affairs) from Soft Realpolitik, to indicate the opposite way of viewing conflictual realities (Johnston 1995, 47).[4] There are comparable distinctions. Following in the footsteps of Morris Janowitz, Travis (2020) made a distinction between the so-called Absolutist and the Pragmatic approach. The Absolutist approach stresses the importance of (quick) victories, dominance over enemies, (major) combat and a warrior mind-set, whereas the Pragmatist approach emphasizes lasting success, adaptation to and from others, stability, peacekeeping, and reconstruction (Shields and Travis 2017; Travis 2020). In a different but intentionally comparable way, Soeters (2013) goes back to ancient Greek mythology and history, distinguishing between the fast and emotional Achilles versus the *polumetis* and *polumechanos* Odysseus. The former refers to the operational style in which emotion-based fierce combat as the natural means to solve problems prevails, whereas the latter refers to a pragmatist, com-munication-oriented and negotiating style of solving conflicts. Odysseus is also known for his tendency towards restraint and self-binding, benefitting from having fewer instead of more options to choose from (Elster 2000). Soeters connects this difference to case studies related to British and Dutch politics and military action in contemporary history, including the recent operations in Afghanistan.

This distinction can be applied more broadly. Despite differences, there are considerable commonalities in the strategic cultures of the United States and the United Kingdom as compared to continental European countries. Their partner-ship during the missions in Iraq and Afghanistan after 9/11 demonstrated their shared political-military perspective and that their strategic cultures belong to the same Anglo-Saxon military community. Both nations initiated the missions, were the first to enter those foreign nations, and were most active and persistent in combat-actions, which they deemed inevitable to solve the problems in the region. Because the attacks on 9/11 were considered to be an assault in the framework of NATO-article V, other NATO-partners were urged to participate in the missions as well. All continental European NATO member states deemed this obligation to

---

Going back further in history, in particular WWII, there are a number of publications in which the different operational styles of the various adversaries were studied (e.g., Ingesson 2016; Visser 2010). This chapter, however, focuses on studies dealing with more recent operations.

4   As an illustration of the belief that conflicts have a zero-sum character, a full colonel from the British army once at a reception stated that he had experienced all possible outcomes in his military career: a loss in Iraq, a draw in Afghanistan and a victory in Northern Ireland (!).

be legitimate, but they were nonetheless careful and hesitant about how to solve the problems at hand.

In the Netherlands, for instance, participation in the operations in the violent Southern Afghanistan provinces, starting in 2006, could only be *sold* to the general public by emphasizing the reconstruction and development aspect of the civil-military cooperation that would be initiated in the province of Uruzgan. And indeed, the *Dutch approach* turned out to be something different, compared to the war- and counter insurgency missions undertaken by British and American forces. The Dutch mission accentuated, more than others, co-optation of host-national power brokers as a means to de-escalate the hostilities (Kitzen 2012). But, when after some three years of presence in the region, the Dutch military itself gradually started to emphasize the combat-character of their actions, politicians in 2010 decided to put an end to the Dutch contribution. The more participation in combat was stressed by the military – most likely under the influence of the American and other English-speaking militaries involved – the more resistance towards the mission emerged in Dutch society and politics. The social-democratic party did not want to renew the mission, even if it were only for a year or only for a non-combat training mission (e.g., Massie 2016), particularly because of electoral calculations. Increasingly stressing the Dutch participation in combat-actions led to the termination of all Dutch contributions to the mission. While taking into account differences that are related to the political systems in both nations, Canada's pull-out in 2011 had a more or less comparable background (Massie 2016).

Italian scholar Ruffa (2014a, 2017) conducted a number of comparative studies in Lebanon and Afghanistan. In Lebanon, she carefully compared the operational performance of the French, Italian, South-Korean and Ghanaian contingents in the UNIFIL mission. It should be kept in mind that the area of operations in this mission, bordering Israel, is not large and that its mandate and goals are identical across all troops. Nonetheless, based on in-depth fieldwork, Ruffa discovered that the daily activities of the soldiers of the four contingents varied consistently and remarkably. While the Ghanaian and Italian units preferred to engage in humanitarian activities, the French and Korean contingents emphasized the importance of patrolling and force protection, on the road and in their camps. These different operational styles, for example, the definition of appropriate standards of behavior and actions were very much connected to the way the military of each contingent interpreted the context of the mission. In this interpretation, the echo of each force's memories of the past and institutional cultures could be clearly recognized (Ruffa 2014a). In another publication, Ruffa (2014b) compared societal beliefs about the use of force and casualty sensitivity in France, Italy, and Israel. Her comparison demonstrated that support for war and casualty sensitivity vary a lot across nations because they "are deeply nested in specific domestic institutional configurations and have deep historical origins" (Ruffa 2014b, 115).

In a follow-up study, Ruffa (2017) pursued the comparison between the French and Italian army culture as it influences operational styles, not only in Lebanon but also in the ISAF-mission in Afghanistan. She again demonstrated that, in similar operational contexts, there are different national perceptions as to what needs to be done in the operations. For the French soldiers, combat skills are as important in traditional operations as they are in peace building missions, whereas the Italians perceived humanitarian skills as the most important skills in both types of missions (Ruffa 2017, 407). In Afghanistan, the French soldiers behaved in a manner that was detached from the local population, even during their patrols. The Italians, however, relied on their relations with the population and interacted much more closely, also developing a number of larger humanitarian projects for the local population. In a similar vein, Ruffa and Vennesson (2017) studied how Italian and French NGO-military relations during their operations in Lebanon and Afghanistan were deeply influenced by institutional constellations in their respective civilian societies.

In a similar vein, Friesendorf compared the US army, the British army, and the German army in a number of recent operations, including the missions in Afghanistan (Friesendorf 2018, 1). He came to observations that were comparable to previous findings on the modes of operandi of these three national forces: US and British forces were keen on being warriors whereas German soldiers struggled to be robust peace enforcers in the Balkans and fight insurgents in Afghanistan.

To close this section on comparing strategic cultures and operational styles, the air campaign in Libya in 2011 provides a clear example of how individual nations and their politicians – advised by their military top brass(!) – can task their forces to approach conflictual situations in different ways, for example, with different goals, means, and actions. The United Kingdom and France, the European nations with the largest military budgets and with, traditionally, the largest belief in the superiority of military solutions, deployed most fighter aircraft and did most of the bombing. The aim was to prevent further hostilities against the insurgents inside the country. Some nations with participating air forces such as Canada, Norway and Denmark participated in the bombing as well but on a smaller scale, whereas other air forces – such as the Dutch – only flew reconnaissance and monitoring missions or delivered logistical support, predominantly at sea. The United States' military was first in launching attack missiles from navy vessels and provided the satellite communication links but, after the first stage, refrained from the actual bombing campaign as it already was engaged in other wars. Obama's administration was severely divided over the questions whether or not, and how to participate. Merkel's Germany abstained from all of this.[5]

Nothing of this decision-making is a coincidence; all of this relies on views and perceptions of threat, security and peace that are connected to national (strategic) military cultures, histories, institutional backgrounds, and power interests. Those views and perceptions, however, impact one another and are dynamic, at least to a certain degree, as we shall see by the end of this chapter. Certainly, different views on how operations need to be conducted play a large role in how to obtain effectiveness and success in multinational military operations.

3   Encounters

After having become aware of differences in national strategic cultures and military operational styles, it is time to focus on actual military cooperation in exercises, missions, and operations. These may be in a NATO, AU, EU or most frequently in an UN framework where a multinational composition is prerequisite. These concrete interactions may occur at various levels: in project teams in which individual military personnel from different nations work together, for instance on military research and development (R&D), but also in operational units and missions, small and large, and in international headquarters (HQs) or national HQs that are in the process of internationalizing their workforce. In UN missions these encounters are most significant, as the cultural variation among the troops-contributing nations generally is largest. In UN missions, the troops of so-called developing nations, such as India, Pakistan, and Nigeria, prevail, whereas some Western militaries participate in such missions too, but on a much smaller scale, and others do not.

These encounters are likely to produce tensions between differing mind-sets of national commitment and what may be referred to as feelings of transnational belonging (Ben-Ari and Elron 2001, 271). Based on close fieldwork in a UN mission, Ben-Ari and Elron discovered that the national identity and self-definition of soldiers in terms of their national background does not disappear or decrease in multinational military cooperation. The character of the multinational mission does not turn into a certain professional non-nationalism among the workforce, such as in the World Bank. The military which are deployed to a mission still very

---

5   This section is based on a comprehensive overview provided by bachelor student Stef
     Keulers, University of Tilburg. The information as to the military participation of various
     nations can be found on NATO-websites and websites of major international newspapers
     such as The Guardian.

much adhere to the orders that they receive from their national organization at home, and they stress their national identity, including their own language, ceaselessly. As such, those multi-national missions are also multi-cultural gatherings that resemble the Olympic Games, where national flags, uniforms, including hats(!), and ceremonial display are considered especially important to emphasize one's national belonging (e.g., Rafaeli and Pratt 1993).

This multi-nationalism also creates certain ways of viewing others dependent on the stereotypes that prevail not only in the mission but also in the domestic societies. Particularly the perceived differences between the troops deployed by so-called developed countries (e.g., NATO) and those of developing countries (i.e., the so-called Third World) are often an obstacle to obtain satisfactory rapprochement between the various troop contributors. The others are often seen as strangers, oftentimes connected with a certain aura of incompetence. Such negative stereotyping is not unique to multinational military environments as the fate of the military officers from East Germany after the integration with the West German Bundeswehr illustrates (Leonhard 2016). But even within a rather homogeneous community such as NATO there are perceptual differences that may lead to one group displaying subtle derogatory or patronizing behavior towards others despite the exhibition of politeness at the surface. Such subtle treatments may have an active impact, for instance, with respect to the question with whom one is inclined to share operational information (e.g., Goldenberg and Dean 2017).

Such different perceptions relate to different views of what military competency in fact is, in terms of technological orientation and military professionalism. The latter is oftentimes defined as being experienced and skillful in combat situations as well as being proficient in the dominating language, that is proficiency in English. The importance of these capabilities is simply taken for granted and creates power differentials between servicemen and servicewomen from different nations in multinational military encounters (e.g., Moskos 2001). Not being proficient in the English language prohibits active participation in strategic and tactical decision-making and may even lead to the sub-standard implementation of decisions, plans, and orders. By consequence, emotional conflicts among members of multinational groupings are likely to occur (von Glinow et al. 2004), but particularly in the military these are expected to be suppressed and, hence, are not likely to be perceived as problematic in the overall picture. It, however, may lead to differences in frontstage and backstage speech among the various national servicemen and servicewomen (Eliasoph and Lichterman 2003, 772).

However, gradually the broader awareness emerges that military competence needs to be more than just being technologically advanced and/or being combat-ready and speaking proper English. Military competence also needs to include skills that foster a positive encounter with host-nationals; being successful in such interaction is equally important, perhaps even more crucial for the general outcome of operations (Moskos 2007). These skills, for one, include knowing local languages, be they Arabic in the Middle East, Lingala in the Democratic Republic of Congo, or Russian at the borders between Russia and the Baltic states. This awareness may strengthen the position of other national militaries or personnel with specific backgrounds.

As can be seen from the previous discussion, in multinational military cooperation power balances play a dominating role. Dominating perceptions and views are very much related to who is in power, or, to phrase it differently, who has the largest economic, social, and reputational capital. Obviously, all these power- and culture-related dynamics are likely to be challenging with respect to the effectiveness of multinational missions. And yet, multinational military cooperation is inevitable today, as we saw before.

Speaking in general, there are three ways of dealing with the challenges that such cultural interaction provokes (Soeters 2018a, 2018b, 27–28; Soeters and Tresch 2010):

– *Assimilation* occurs when junior partners adapt to and often become akin to a majority or a senior partner on whom they are dependent or whom they deem superior; examples are smaller air forces (e.g., Belgium, Norway, or the Netherlands) that use the same aircraft as a senior partner, in particular the United States Air Force, and hence follow identical procedures with respect to training, exercise, maintenance and the use of language. Another example concerns Estonian and Danish infantry contingents that during the ISAF mission were attached to the considerably larger and higher standing British troops in the Afghan province of Helmand, which made them imitate and take part in the British war-like style of operating, quite deliberately ignoring the Civil-Military Cooperation (CIMIC) side of the mission (Osinga and Russell 2013, 302);

– *Separation* as a way of organizing is often applied in operations by
  • dividing the area of operations in smaller geographical boxes or areas that are assigned to different lead nations, such as during the ISAF mission the Southern Afghan province of Kandahar was assigned to the Canadian troops, Uruzgan to the Dutch military, Helmand to the British forces, and Zabul and others to the United States;
  • separating the operation in different periods of time, in which in one particular period of time a specific task, such as air patrolling across the Baltic States, is assigned to one national air force, and in the subsequent period to another,

- task-related separation, such as Operation Enduring Freedom being conducted by American and British troops and ISAF assigned to German and
  other continental European forces; or distributing different tasks, such as
  base protection, maintenance, and policing, each to specific national units.
- *Integration* is the most complicated way of obtaining cooperation among militaries of different nations, as it relies on the idea that all partners are equal
  counterparts and can have a comparable contribution. However difficult, this
  is most likely to occur in multinational HQs (e.g., Richter 2018), where the
  participation of nations is more based on individual personnel than on whole
  large-sized units. At the operational level, a system of crisscrossing through
  which cooperating militaries are assigned alternating minority and majority
  positions in units that belong together, seems promising in this regard, as the
  examples of French-German cooperation (Abel 2008) and the integration of
  Dutch tank units into a German armored brigade illustrates.

These strategies have different implications. The *assimilation* strategy is easiest in
multinational military cooperation as cultural differences between national forces
are levelled out. In particular, this way of cooperating is more likely to occur successfully in technology-driven actions such as the air campaign over Libya that
boasted to have incurred no fatalities during the execution of the mission. In flying
sorties language and other culture-related problems are virtually absent because of
the assimilating power of science and technology. The problem, however, is that
the advantage of having and probing multiple views on a certain problem is likely
to disappear. The risks of organizational *myopia*, leading for instance to a disregard
of possible consequences of actions, are likely to increase; the broader spectrum
tends to get lost. Assimilation is a much less successful cooperation strategy when
the goals of a mission are ambiguous. Again, the air campaign over Libya, but now
seen from another angle, provides an example.

The *separation* strategy – also known as federalization or *working apart together* –
creates a sense of territoriality and ownership that has both positive and negative
consequences. On the positive side, a feeling of territoriality and ownership en-
hances the ambition to take responsibility for the space or task assigned. Besides,
it offers the troops a feeling of being connected to home (same language, same
food, etc.). On the negative side, however, this may culminate in the risk of losing
oversight of what is happening outside one's *own* territory and of being too much
directed internally (e.g., Brown et al. 2005). The benefits, thus, are curvilinear,
which has been demonstrated in many military operations that took place in the
last few decades, for instance in Afghanistan. To a certain degree this strategy has
many advantages, but in excess it is likely to create organizational myopia within a
particular area of operations.

Challenges of the *integration* strategy emerge specifically in the composition and performance of multinational groups. The distribution of nationalities over the various group members plays a role here. A distribution of 50 percent-50 percent in a two-party-cooperation must be treated with most care, a 10 percent to 90 percent-distribution is likely to lead to the easy assimilation-solutions that we saw before, whereas a solution in which 10 countries provide 10 percent- or 20 countries provide 5 percent, such as in a multinational HQs, is probably best to achieve integration at a high-quality level (e.g., Soeters and Manigart 2008). Next, the type of task that needs to be conducted has an impact. Creative tasks are most, and coordinative tasks are least, conducive to achieving adequate performance in multinational groups (Hambrick et al. 1998).

4   Developments

As nothing ever stands still, multinational military cooperation is in full development. Ten years from now, the then current state of affairs will definitely look different from the situation now. The general tendency in the near future will undoubtedly turn towards more and more intensive multinational cooperation. In terms of striving for a so-called *smart defense* via multinational cooperation (getting more value out of your money), supra-national institutions such as NATO have a number of policies available. NATO may urge its member states to align their national investment decisions with the priorities that NATO has set, and/or increase cooperation by pooling and sharing scarce resources, and/or specialize in certain activities leaving other specialties to other national armed forces. The latter option – for instance, as a nation, specializing in ground forces, leaving air force activities to other nations – obviously is politically and militarily most difficult to accept. It is clearly at odds with the idea of the sovereignty of nations and it requires nations to rely on others and trust these other nations will do a proper job when needed (Giegerich 2012). Up until now, this is a bridge too far for most nations.

However, the second option, in particular, proves promising as there are already a number of successful examples, such as the European Air Transport Command (EATC), in which military air transport capacity of Germany, France, Italy, Spain, the Netherlands, Belgium and Luxembourg are used in combination to increase efficiencies of scale and scope. Also, the Strategic Airlift Capabilities (SAC) making use of jointly purchased C-17 aircraft – based in Hungary – is an excellent example of how things will work out in the near future. In addition, jointly operated educational and training facilities all over the Western hemisphere are examples of where multinational military cooperation is going.

Such pooling and sharing are possible because of dynamics that organizational sociologists identified as *isomorphism* (Dimaggio and Powell 1983). *Isomorphism* refers to the tendency among organizations in the same organizational field or domain – e.g., health care, automotive industry – to become more similar to one another. This development emerges under the influence of competitive pressure or governmental and legal *coercion*, or because organizations tend to *mimic* one another – particularly the most prestigious ones –, or because of *normative* pressures stemming from professionalization. There are various patterns in these dynamics (e.g., Sahlin and Wedlin 2008), but for the moment it suffices to accept that these *isomorphing* dynamics do exist and can be seen in the military. Using NATO again as example, coercion can clearly be observed in NATO's strategic formulation of common policies and priorities (for instance the notorious 2 percent-expenditure norm) and its constant issuing and applying of doctrines and standard operating and certifying procedures, particularly in training, maintenance, and operational capabilities. Mimetic and normative *isomorphing* pressures can be seen in joint training and exercises, the application of systems of quality management, mentoring, and monitoring activities as well as in an increasing multinational exchange of personnel (e.g., Bagayoko-Penone 2006; King 2010).

This works particularly well if cooperative activities have a relatively neutral character; not much political risk or possible factual harm occur in military air transport or general training, referring to the examples just mentioned. This is different when it comes to decision-making about real military operations. As explained before, there is a continuum that connects two extremes of approaching conflicts and hostile tensions. At the one end, this refers to accentuating threat perceptions and tensions and responding predominantly with the threat and use of military force (absolutism). At the other end, conflicts are approached with negotiation, non-military force and only as a very *ultimum remedium* by military force (pragmatism).

The different strategic cultures render *isomorphism* among national militaries not a fully preordained development. As Kümmel correctly stated (2013, 198), threat perceptions and expenditures for the military still diverge quite substantially among the various NATO member states, aligning with the two ends of the continuum. Today's Germany – like Japan – stresses the pragmatist approach as do various smaller continental nations in Western Europe. This in comparison with the Anglo-Saxon nations – the United States and the United Kingdom in particular – who stress security threats and subsequent military options ceaselessly. Therefore, if one can identify tendencies towards *isomorphism* these will predominantly pertain to logistics, as well as technical and training activities. Intentions towards war fighting are much more varied, even among the fairly homogeneous community of

NATO member states. The participation in the air campaign over Libya in 2011 discussed before constitutes a prime example in this vein.

Yet, also with respect to the latter, conducting military operations, a certain *isomorphism* or adaptation seems to have emerged recently. There are at least two reasons for this development to occur. First, the current United States administration is strong on viewing things militarily (= absolutist approach), admonishing NATO member states for not complying with the 2 percent-expenditure norm, even quasi-coercively threatening them with financial, trade-related sanctions because of the *unpaid bills*. Second, the operations in Afghanistan – under the impact of British and American actions – turned out to be quite combat-oriented and affected many other troops-contributing militaries, in a number of cases helping them overcome reluctance to operate robustly (Osinga and Russell 2013, 308). Counter Insurgency (COIN) and even mechanized warfare had come to dominate over CIMIC (Osinga and Russell 2013). Mild-mannered forces such as the ones from the Netherlands, Norway, Denmark, Germany, and Canada swiftly or gradually adopted a war-prone discourse and ambition, that lasts until now, even after some of these nations withdrew their troops from Afghanistan (Soeters 2018a).

The first reason leading to *isomorphism* with respect to conducting operations has a coercive setting, the second a mimetic and normative background; in both reasons power and power-related reputation play a role. The question is, in which direction this development will continue to go. That is a matter of speculating about the future of course, but theoretically one can argue the following.

Isomorphism is closely connected to the diffusion – if one wishes: the travelling, proliferation, and final adoption – of ideas, views, ambitions, policies, and practices (Braun and Gilardi 2006). Theoretically there are at least three ways, through which ideas, views, policies, and practices can be diffused and adopted (Sahlin and Wedlin 2008, 227–230):

– via the *broadcasting mode* – a central model inspiring (or leaving no alternative to) others;
– via the *chain mode of imitation* – an idea, policy or practice being repeated but in different links without the origin of the development becoming known;
– via the *mediation by others, so-called carriers* – diffusion of ideas, policies and practices via international organizations, media, and researchers/expert committees.

With some imagination, one could combine those three modes with the three ways of organizing cultural interaction that we saw before. The *broadcasting* mode then fits with the *assimilation* approach, the *chain* mode with *federalization* or *separation* (assuming that the chain not only has different links but also different branches), and *mediation by others* with the *integration* approach. Using this combination of concepts, one could contend that the current wave of operational *isomorphism* – next to the ongoing movement towards convergence in the field of logistics, maintenance, and training – is predominantly based on *broadcasting/assimilation* and the *chain mode/separation*. Obviously, the American centrality and way of *broadcasting* tends to aim at and in fact lead to assimilation. The current practice of organizing operations in separate *national* areas of operations connects to the *chain mode*, in which the same message is copied in every branch of the chain but in different manners. However, *integration* in which all voices are brought together in a harmonious choir is most difficult to achieve and does not seem fashionable these days. However, mediation by others, such as international NGO's, experts and researchers, journalists and particularly politicians may – at some point in time – have an impact on how multinational military cooperation will develop. This would be beneficial to civil-military relations in general.

The first two modes of policy diffusion originate from within the militaries themselves or governments who are strongly affiliated with the military. The other mode is more of an external affair, giving leeway to the proliferation of – more civilian – views that stress de-escalation, negotiation, inside-up indigenous development, and reconstruction (Kitzen 2012; Mintzberg 2006). Even though the current wave towards operational *isomorphism* is characterized by an increasing orientation towards the solutions that war offers, things may become to look differently in the foreseeable future. Taking into account that inside nations' views as to the use of force and its consequences are quite heterogeneous (Ruffa 2014b, 115) and considering the possibilities of social and governmental power changes over time, *isomorphism* in multinational military cooperation may switch to a more pragmatist view in the foreseeable future.

For sure, such developments are not likely to come without serious challenges and tensions. These developments will be accompanied by the need for *hybrid organizing*. That is coming to terms with different group identities, varying organizational forms and diverse societal rationales that will come along with the cooperation between the various national armed forces. The legitimacy of such cooperation will be tested, there will be strive between competing identification targets and guidelines to action and possibly there will be mission drift. However, there will also be opportunities for innovation and creativity, and in general a broader base for legitimacy and resources (Battilana et al. 2017).

5   Research Methods and Implications

As said previously, multinational military cooperation is here to stay, and it is likely to become increasingly more important in the near future. As has been stated too, this will not come without serious challenges, more so with respect to decisions about the use of force than regarding the optimization of the use of scarce resources that have a more neutral impact (e.g., logistics). For these reasons, research into multinational military cooperation remains a prerequisite. It is imperative that such research focuses on concrete events and behavior to give proper content to the analysis of more general developments, such as *isomorphism*.

One may be able to observe how multinational military cooperation develops towards a natural instead of an exceptional state of affairs through the study of organizational practices, new practice creation, and the organizations' selective and hybrid ways of dealing with institutional complexity (Lounsbury and Crumley 2007; Nicolini 2012; Schildt and Perkmann 2017). Specific topics of study may include information sharing, the exchange of personnel, discussions on operational decisions, the actual conduct of military operations, and the organization of collaborative efforts in exercises and missions. Most of all, the comparative assessment of the effectiveness of different operational actions – the degree of their goal attainment – must be central in the study of multinational military cooperation in the near future.

As to methodological specificities of such research projects, it is important to keep in mind that the selection of cases should be done carefully and that blended methods are most preferred. One is not likely to achieve the best results if one limits oneself to either quantitative or qualitative methods. Ethnographic, participatory observation can be combined with statistical survey research and possibly big data analysis – based for instance on visuals on soldiers' mobile phones (De Rond 2012) or digitalized operations' reports that so far were only stored in archives. Next, mastering the languages that soldiers under study use is prerequisite. Relying on English as the bridging language will often prove to be insufficient. The researcher should, therefore, be as proficient in as many relevant languages as possible. Preferably, this includes languages of the host-nationals. If this is not or only limitedly doable, it makes sense to collect data with a team of researchers that have different national and language backgrounds. This will also help the researcher(s) to prevent acting and thinking ethnocentrically, which is probably the biggest trap in doing research into multinational military cooperation (Ruffa and Soeters 2013).

In this vein, it makes sense to pay attention to the four blind spots that have been identified in general research on inter-organizational relationships (Lumineau and Oliveira 2018). These are: a single party focus, the assumption of a single valence in relationships (either cooperative or conflictual), a single level of analysis and a single conception of time (only clock time). All these blind spots can be recognized in the study of multinational military cooperation, and they should all be dealt with in future research. At the same time, being aware of these blind spots will help commanding practitioners to improve their operations in the context of multinational military cooperation. To illustrate the blind spots in research on multinational military cooperation, a few examples suffice.

Coinciding with the assimilation tendencies discussed before, researchers and practitioners often tend to forget the smaller nations' experiences in the cooperation which demonstrates the single party focus on many missions and research projects. Also, the fact that researchers most of the time only have access to their own national troops, may strengthen this single party focus on research. This needs not always be the case, though. In a study of Swedish-Irish military cooperation in the UN mission in Liberia initiated by the Swedish Ministry of Defence (MOD), Hedlund and colleagues (2008) deliberately included interviews with Irish soldiers to come to grips with their views of the Swedes and the effectiveness of the cooperation, hence avoiding the single party focus. The results turned out to be challenging because cultural friction in the cooperation was observed. However, their interviews focused on privates and other personnel at the work floor level, neglecting the relatively harmonious working relations in the staff and the operations room between officers and NCOs of both nations. This is an example of a blind spot related to multiple levels of analysis.

That the valence between cooperating parties can be cooperative and problematic at the same time does not seem easy to understand, but in the study of social and organizational phenomena dialectic tensions are not unknown at all (e.g., De Rond and Bouchikhi 2004). In the field of multinational military cooperation, one can often observe that the support of more sizable, better funded and more reputed partners is much appreciated, whereas at the same time irritation and friction may occur because of the others' overwhelming dominance. The omnipresence and pressure of the United States and other coalition forces in teaching others how to *conduct war* may be a case in point. One only needs to think of the formation and the training of the Afghan National Army by coalition troops that are accompanied by numerous inside attacks by individual members of Afghan security forces on soldiers from coalition troops (e.g., Long 2013). Also, the perception of time between both parties is likely to differ. For coalition forces, the basic idea is that their presence will be temporary, but Afghan security forces are there to stay. Thus, future research – and again practice – needs to include the multiple time orientations of the multiple partners in the cooperation.

Taking these blind spots into account (Lumineau and Oliveira 2018), a next overview several years from now will demonstrate flourishing practices of multinational military cooperation accompanied by more elaborated and more refined research.

References

Abel, H. 2008. "Criss-crossing – Ein alternatives Modell der Gruppenzusammensetzung." In *Vereint Marschieren – Marcher Uni. Die deutsch-französische Streitkräftekooperation als Paradigma europäischer Streitkräfte?*, edited by N. Leonhard and S. Gareis, 183–222. Wiesbaden: VS Verlag für Sozialwissenschaften.

Angstrom, J., and J.W. Honig. 2012. "Regaining Strategy: Small Powers, Strategic Culture, and Escalation in Afghanistan." *Journal of Strategic Studies* 35(5): 663–687.

Bagayoko-Penone, N. 2006. "L'Européanisation des Militaires Français. Socialisation Institutionelle et Culture Stratégique." *Revue Française de Science Politique* 56(1): 49–77.

Batilana, J., M. Besharov, and B. Mitzinneck. 2017. "On Hybrids and Hybrid Organizing: A Review and Roadmap for Future Research." In *The SAGE Handbook of Organizational Institutionalism*, edited by R. Greenwood, C. Oliver, T.B. Lawrence, and R.E. Meyer, 128–162. Thousand Oaks: Sage.

Ben-Ari, E., and E. Elron. 2001. "Blue Helmets and White Armor: Multi-Nationalism and Multi-Culturalism Among UN Peacekeeping Forces." *City & Society* 13(2): 271–302.

Biehl, H., B. Giegerich, and A. Jonas, eds. 2013. *Strategic Cultures in Europe. Security and Defence Policies Across the Continent*. Wiesbaden: Springer VS.

Braun, D., and F. Gilardi. 2006. "Taking 'Galton's Problem' seriously. Towards a Theory of Policy Diffusion." *Journal of Theoretical Politics* 18(3): 298–322.

Brown, G., T.B. Lawrence, and S.L. Robinson. 2005. "Territoriality in Organizations." *Academy of Management Review* 30(3): 577–594.

De Graaf, B. 2013. *Evaluating Counterterrorism Performance. A Comparative Study*. London/New York: Routledge.

De Rond, M. 2012. "Soldier, Surgeon, Photographer, Fly: Fieldwork Beyond the Comfort Zone." *Strategic Organization* 10(3): 256–262.

De Rond, M., and H. Bouchikhi. 2004. "On the Dialectics of Strategic Alliances." *Organization Science* 15(1): 56–69.

Dimaggio, P., and W.W. Powell. 1983. "The Iron Cage Revisited: Institutional Isomorphism and Collective Rationality in Organizational Fields." *American Sociological Review* 48(April): 147–160.

Eliasoph, N., and P. Lichterman. 2003. "Culture in Interaction." *American Journal of Sociology* 108(4): 735–794.

Elster, J. 2000. *Ulysses Unbound. Studies in Rationality, Precommitment, and Constraints*. Cambridge: Cambridge University Press.

Friesendorf, C. 2018. *How Western Soldiers Fight. Organizational Routines in Multinational Missions*. Cambridge: Cambridge University Press.

Giegerich, B. 2012. "NATO's Smart Defence: Who's buying?" Survival 54(3): 69–77.

Glaser, D. 1946. "The Sentiments of American Soldiers Abroad Toward Europeans." *American Journal of Sociology* 51(5): 433–438.

Goldenberg I., and W. Dean. 2017. "Enablers and Barriers to Information Sharing in Military and Security Operations: Lessons Learned." In *Information Sharing in Military Operations*, edited by I. Goldenberg, J. Soeters, and W. Dean, 251–267. Cham: Springer.

Haltiner, K.W., and P. Klein, eds. 2004. *Multinationalität als Herausforderung für die Streitkräfte*. Baden-Baden: Nomos.

Hambrick, D.C., S. Canney Davison, S.A. Snell, and C.C. Snow. 1998. "When Groups Consist of Multiple Nationalities: Towards a New Understanding of the Implications." *Organization Studies* 19(2): 181–205.

Hedlund, E., L. Weibull, and J. Soeters. 2008. "Swedish-Irish Collaboration in Liberia." In *Military Cooperation in Multinational Peace Operations. Managing Cultural Diversity and Crisis Response*, edited by J. Soeters and P. Manigart, 153–165. London & New York: Routledge.

Ingesson, T. 2016. "The Political and Strategic Impact of Tactical-Level Subcultures, 1939–1995." Doctoral Dissertation, University of Lund.

Johnston, A.I. 1995. "Thinking about Strategic Culture." *International Security* 19(4): 32–64.

King, A. 2005. "Towards a Transnational Europe: The Case of the Armed Forces." *European Journal of Social Theory* 8(3): 321–340.

King, A. 2010. *The Transformation of Europe's Armed Forces. From the Rhine to Afghanistan*. Cambridge: Cambridge University Press.

Kitzen, M. 2012. "Close Encounters of the Tribal Kind: The Implementation of Co-Optation as a Tool for De-Escalation of Conflict." *Journal of Strategic Studies* 35(5): 713–734.

Kümmel, G. 2013. "Isomorphism Within NATO? Soldiers and Armed Forces Before and After 9/11." In *How 9/11 Changed Our Ways of* War, edited by J. Burk, 183–208. Stanford: Stanford University Press.

Lemert, C. 2012. *Social Things. An Introduction to the Sociological Life.* 5th edition. Lanham et al.: Rowman & Littlefield.

Leonhard, N. 2016. *Integration und Gedächtnis: NVA-Offiziere im Vereinigten Deutschland.* Köln: Herbert von Halem.

Leonhard, N., and S.B. Gareis, eds. 2008. *Vereint Marschieren – Marcher Uni. Die Deutsch-Französische Streitkräftekooperation als Paradigma europäischer Streitkräfte?* Wiesbaden: VS Verlag für Sozialwissenschaften.

Long, A. 2013. "'Green on Blue': Insider Attacks in Afghanistan." *Survival* 55(3): 167–182.

Lounsbury, M., and E.T. Crumley. 2007. "New Practice Creation: An Institutional Perspective on Innovation." *Organization Studies* 28(7): 993–1012.

Lumineau, F., and N. Oiveira. 2018. "A Pluralistic Perspective Towards Major Blind Spots in Research on Interorganizational Relationships." *Academy of Management Annals* 12(1): 1–25.

Maniscalco, M.L. 2018. "Military Cooperation in Multinational Missions." In *Handbook of the Sociology of the Military*, edited by G. Caforio, 535–551 Cham: Springer.

Massie, J. 2016. "Why Democratic Allies Defect Prematurely: Canadian and Dutch Unilateral Pullouts from the War in Afghanistan." *Democracy and Security* 12(2): 85–113.

Mintzberg, H. 2006. "Developing Leaders? Developing Countries?" *Development in Practice* 16(1): 4–14.

Moskos, C. 2001. "Multinational Military Cooperation: Enhancing American Military Effectiveness." Unpublished memo. Chicago: Northwestern University.

Moskos, C. 2007. "American Military Interaction with Locals in Operation Iraqi Freedom (OEF)." Unpublished memo. Chicago: Northwestern University.

Nagl, J. 2002. *Learning to Eat Soup with a Knife: Counterinsurgency Lessons from Malaya and Vietnam.* Chicago: Chicago University Press.

Nicolini, D. 2012. *Practice Theory, Work, & Organization.* Oxford: Oxford University Press.

Olie, R. 1994. "Shades of Culture and Institutions in International Mergers." *Organization Studies* 15(3): 381–405.

Osinga, F., and J.A. Russell. 2013. "Conclusion: Military Adaptation and the War in Afghanistan." In *Military Adaptation in Afghanistan*, edited by T. Farrell, F. Osinga and J.A. Russell, 288–326. Stanford: Stanford University Press.

Preston, D. 2002. *The Boxer Rebellion: China's War on Foreigners.* London: Robinson.

Rafaeli, A., and M.G. Pratt. 1993. "Tailored Meanings: On the Meaning and Impact of Organizational Dress." *Academy of Management Review* 18(1): 32–55.

Richter, G. 2018. "Antecedents and Consequences of Leadership Styles: Findings from Empirical Research in Multinational Headquarters." *Armed Forces & Society* 44(1): 72–91.

Ruffa, C. 2014a. "What Peacekeepers Think and Do: An Exploratory Study of French, Ghanaian, Italian, and South Korean Armies in the United Nations Interim Force in Lebanon." *Armed Forces & Society* 40(2): 199–225.

Ruffa, C. 2014b. "Societal Beliefs about the Use of Force in Israel, Italy and France." *The Tocqueville Review* 35(2): 101–117.

Ruffa, C. 2017. "Military Cultures and Force Employment in Peace Operations." *Security Studies* 26(3): 391–422.

Ruffa, C., and J. Soeters. 2014. "Cross-national Research in the Military: Comparing Operational Styles." In *Routledge Handbook of Research Methods in Military Studies*, edited by J. Soeters, P. Shields and S. Rietjens, 216–227. London & New York: Routledge.

Ruffa, C., and P. Venesson. 2014. "Fighting or Helping? A Historical-Institutionalist Explanation of NGO-Military Relations." *Security Studies* 23(3): 582–621.

Savic, I. 2010. "The Russian Soldier Today." *Journal of International Affairs* 63(2): 219–229.

Sahlin, K., and L. Wedlin. 2008. "Circulating Ideas: Imitation, Translation and Editing." In *The Sage Handbook of Organizational Institutionalism*, edited by R. Greenwood, C. Oliver, R. Suddaby and K. Sahlin-Andersson, 218–242. Thousand Oaks: Sage.

Schildt, H., and M. Perkmann. 2017. "Organizational Settlements: Theorizing How Organizations Respond to Institutional Complexity." *Journal of Management Inquiry* 26(2): 139–145.

Shields, P., and D.S. Travis. 2017. "Achieving Organizational Flexibility Through Ambidexterity." *Parameters* 47(2): 65–76.

Soeters, J. 2013. "Odysseus Prevails Over Achilles: A Warrior Model Suited to Post-9/11 Conflicts." In *How 9/11 Changed Our Ways of War*, edited by J. Burk, 89–115. Stanford: Stanford University Press.

Soeters, J. 2018a. "Organizational Cultures in the Military." In *Handbook of the Sociology of the Military*, edited by G. Caforio, 251–272. Cham: Springer.

Soeters, J. 2018b. *Sociology and Military Studies. Classical and Current Foundations.* London & New York: Routledge.

Soeters, J. 2021. "Militaries' Organizational Cultures in a Globalizing World". *Oxford Research Encyclopedia of Politics.* Oxford University Press. <https://doi.org/10.1093/acrefore/9780190228637.013.1937>.

Soeters, J., and P. Manigart, eds. 2008. *Military Cooperation in Multinational Peace Operations. Managing Cultural Diversity and Crisis Response.* London & New York: Routledge.

Soeters, J. and T. Szvircsev Tresch. 2010. "Towards Cultural Integration in Multinational Peace Operations." *Defence Studies* 10(1/2): 272–287.

Sorge, A., N. Noorderhaven and C. Koen. 2015. *Comparative International Management.* London & New York: Routledge.

Tilly, C. 1992. *Coercion, Capital and European States AD 990–1990.* Cambridge: Blackwell.

Travis, D.S. 2020. "Decoding Morris Janowitz: Limited War and Pragmatic Doctrine." *Armed Forces & Society* 46(1): 68–91.

Visser, M. 2010. "Configurations of Human Resource Practices and Battlefield Performance: A Comparison of Two Armies." *Human Resource Management Review* 20(4): 340–349.

von Glinow, M.A., D.L. Shapiro, D.L. and J.M. Brett. 2004. "Can We Talk, And Should We? Managing Emotional Conflict in Multicultural Teams." *Academy of Management* Review 29(4): 578–592.

Vrey, F., A. Esterhuyse and T. Mandrup, eds. 2013. *On Military Culture: Theory, Practice and African Armed Forces.* Claremont, CT: University of Connecticut Press.

Zerubavel, E. 1997. *Social Mindscapes. An invitation to Cognitive Sociology.* Cambridge, MA & London: Harvard University Press.

Part II:
National Perspectives

Military Sociology in France: Development and Limits since the 1990s

Barbara Jankowski

1   Introduction

Until recently, the country that witnessed the institutionalization of sociology as an autonomous discipline more than hundred years ago had maintained a distant relationship with the armed forces as a research object. It is only since the mid-1990s that French military sociology has known an unprecedented, although far from being linear, development. A combination of changes in the academic field and foremost in the institutional setting has made it more visible both within the Ministry of Defense and in the academic field.

Of course, military sociology has a history that goes back well before the 1990s (Bardiès 2008; Les Champs de Mars 2001, 2002). This decade is taken as a starting point for this review because the previous period has already been the subject of detailed analysis (Gresle 2003; Jankowski and Vennesson 2005; Martin 1999). Moreover, in 1995, a crucial institutional change took place. The *Centre d'Etudes en Sciences Sociales de la Défense* (C2SD)[1] was established and has ever since developed military sociology far beyond the circle in which it was confined until then. This rise in military sociology over the past 25 years was also driven by President Chirac's decision to end conscription in February 1996. Thus, as in the United States, military sociology has benefited from the major issues raised by this important reform.

Before 1996, studies on the military mostly focused on military history or on human resources such as recruitment, motivation, and career paths of the military personnel.[2] Since the 1990s, thanks to the C2SD, military sociology in France has widely expanded and diversified. The research has rapidly covered a wide range of themes. In 2009, with the endowment of the *Institut de Recherche Stratégique de l'Ecole Militaire* (IRSEM),[3] amalgamating the C2SD and three other institutes of

---

1   The Center for Social Sciences Research in Defense.
2   These include studies conducted by the *Centre de Sociologie de la défense nationale* (CSDN) by Hubert Jean-Pierre Thomas and his staff (Gadbois 1996; Jankowski and Vennesson 2005, 270).
3   Institute for Strategic Studies.

research, the situation changed once more. The emphasis was on strategic studies, of which military sociology was only one component, not very visible from outside given the name of the institute. In addition, a shift has occurred from commissioned research, with a budget to fund between twelve and fifteen empirical studies a year, to internal research conducted by a team of permanent researchers.

Today, French military sociology is an interdisciplinary endeavor connecting a whole range of disciplines such as political science, social psychology, anthropology, and philosophy. In France, as in many other countries, military sociology has neither a single definition nor well-defined contours. As an interdisciplinary field, it covers studies on the military in its broadest sense, including the military institution, its organization, its personnel, its relations to the state and to civil society. The issues of military sociology are constantly evolving, according to current events such as army reforms or new types of military interventions, as well as to changes in academic approaches and debates. The growing interest in the Europeanization of defense policies on which a large amount of research has been done (Bagayoko-Penone 2006; Faure 2016; Hoeffler 2008, 2011; Irondelle 2008, 2009; Irondelle and Vennesson 2002; Nivet 2006, 2012; Sheppard 2010) is a good example for the development of the discipline.

This article provides an overview of recent developments in military sociology in France, with an emphasis on the institutional framework. My core argument is that the institutional setting is decisive for the advancement and achievements of French military sociology. The second section outlines the position of military sociology in relation to other academic disciplines. The third section is devoted to institutional changes and the establishment of IRSEM. The fourth section presents the publication practices of French military sociology and the fifth section its main research topics. The conclusion summarizes the findings and identifies future opportunities and risks for the discipline in France.

2   Military Sociology in the French Academic Arena: A Legitimate but Fragile and Challenged Position

Two contrasting trends are at work concerning the position of military sociology in the academic field in France. The first one is positive, an undeniable gain in legitimacy. The second one is less promising in the medium term: the newly fragile position of military sociology in the academic field, because of a rising competition with security studies in the last decade. Security studies have seen a boom and made military sociology less visible and less attractive than in the past.

2.1   An Increased Legitimacy

Today doing research on the armed forces in France is considered fully legitimate. This has not always been the case. In the 1970s, parts of sociology, strongly influenced by Marxism, considered state institutions as instruments of class domination and oppression. Furthermore, the Algerian war and the May 1968 events left an enduring footprint in France. For these reasons researchers working on the military institution were seen as suspicious until the 1990s and, in most cases, military sociology was an outcast in academia.

The changes that occurred very slowly concerning the status of military sociology within academia can be observed in small but significant details. The examples for the various fields of sociology (health, culture, media, education) now include military sociology, which would not have been the case at the end of the 1990s.

The legitimacy and the visibility of military sociology today are undoubtedly much higher than they were 25 years ago. Only historians and a few social or political scientists were working on the military at that time, such as Bernard Boëne (1990, 1991, 1998), Raoul Girardet (1964, 1998), François Gresle (1996, 1997) or Michel Louis Martin (1981, 1991). The first generation of young PhDs that defended their theses in military sociology in the late 1990s and early 2000s did not find positions in a university and a lot of them left the academic field. Almost no researcher in military sociology actually taught military sociology, except those hired by military schools, such as Claude Weber[4] or Christophe Pajon[5]. Those who entered the academic market a little later were more fortunate and now form the core of the senior lecturers and professors of sociology and political science who teach one or some of the many aspects of military sociology and continue the research in this field. Today there are around thirty of them. From this point of view, the long-term effects of the efforts made over the past 25 years are therefore positive.

2.2   Unstable Contours and Competition with Other Subfields

Despite the presence of academics teaching military sociology, the subfield has not broken out of the margins at the university nor at the CNRS (French National

---

4   Claude Weber is a senior lecturer at the University of Rennes 2, teaching at the *Ecoles Militaires de St-Cyr Coëtquidan.*
5   Christophe Pajon is deputy head of the Research Department of the *Centre de Recherche de l'Ecole de l'Air.*

Centre for Scientific Research).[6] Its development has stagnated mainly because other connected sub-disciplines and fields of research have taken over. For the last ten years military sociology has competed with other subfields, such as security and defense studies, in a field dominated by political science and, within it, by studies on international relations. Military sociology could have been counted among these disciplines and their curricula, but this is far from being the case. Defense and security studies do not generally include the study of the military. Furthermore, the titles given to the courses very rarely refer to military sociology even if their content covers the field. Consequently, what military sociology suffers from mostly is a lack of visibility and autonomy *vis-à-vis* other sub-disciplines and related fields, such as strategic studies, defense and security studies, or studies on war and peace.

The book entitled *Military Sociology,* published by Caplow and Vennesson (2000), included three relevant chapters, one on armies, another on war and a third one on peace. Thus, twenty years ago, military sociology had a broad and inclusive definition. Even today, in some libraries, one finds the books on strategy in the military sociology section. It should not be unusual or surprising for a research center on security and strategy to have a section dedicated to military sociology. Yet, today in France when one thinks about strategic research, one associates it more spontaneously with security studies, international relations, and threats on global security. The study of the military *per se* has been relegated to the background.

This assessment is strengthened and illustrated by the composition of the recruitment and evaluation commissions for the CNRS and the universities in which military sociology could be found (at CNU: in sections 04 (Political Science) and 19 (Sociology); at CNRS: in section 40 (Politics, Power, Organization) and 36 (Sociology and Law)). There are only around 5 percent of the professors, senior lecturers or researchers who can be directly or indirectly related to military sociology even in a very loose sense, even if they have only either participated just once in their career in research on military sociology or they have supervised a PhD thesis in military sociology.

Military sociology is not alone. Other fields which are not yet fully legitimized within their discipline are facing the same challenges. The problem is, however, worse for military sociology since it is an interdisciplinary field and as such, lacking recognition from each of the involved disciplines. Therefore, military sociology in France does not have the visibility it has in the United States or in the UK. Yet it

---

6   In France, scholars in social sciences mostly belong to two entities: The University and the CNRS (French National Centre for Scientific Research). One can add the *Grandes Ecoles*, a French specificity, such as Sciences Po, and the EHESS (*Ecole des Hautes Etudes en Sciences Sociales* – School of Advanced Studies in Social Sciences), institutions that host PhD students.

has made tremendous progress in 25 years and its medium-term future is secured due to a new generation of academics in different kinds of positions. The endeavor must be pursued and especially reiterated regarding young doctoral students because there is no more succession among the new waves of PhD students which became evident in recent recruitment efforts at IRSEM.

2.3 Belonging to a Network: The Importance of the Professional Associations

Researchers in military sociology are extremely dispersed: on the one hand, they belong to different disciplines (sociology, political science, etc.) and teach diverse curricula within those disciplines, with each university having its particularities. On the other hand, they are geographically scattered throughout the country. In addition, military sociology is not usually their only field of research. In parallel, young PhD students, funded by doctoral fellowships from the Ministry of Defense in the 1990s and early 2000s, have become professional scholars, allowing military sociology to be more present within universities and no longer confined to a few scattered courses in military schools as was the case before. This diversity in professional profiles reflects the French academic landscape in military sociology, excluding the other places where military sociology is practiced like in military schools, a few think tanks and especially at IRSEM.

Due to this heterogeneity, the socialization of researchers takes place within academic networks dedicated to military sociology. Those networks are small compared to other countries where military sociologists can exchange and debate their issues at various venues, not just conferences. If this phenomenon is true for researchers in general, it is more crucial when it comes to military sociology as the networks are the only opportunities to debate because military sociology researchers, being few in number, are very isolated in their institutions. There are three relevant networks in France which are linked to international networks: the *Association Française de Sociologie* (AFS, French Association of Sociology) linked to the International Sociological Association (ISA), the *Association Internationale des Sociologues de Langue Française* (AISLF, International Association of French-speaking Sociologists), and the *Association pour les Etudes sur la Guerre et la Stratégie* (AEGES, Association for War and Strategic Studies).

The AFS brings together more than a thousand sociologists, a third of them doctoral students, grouped in about forty thematic networks. Within it, the thematic network, *Sociology of the Military: Security, Armed Forces & Society*, initiated by François Gresle in 2002, a pioneer in French military sociology, analyzes the actors and the challenges in the defense and security sector. This network, now led by Sébastien Jakubowski, organizes panels at each biennial congress some of which are published.In addition to its permanent members, this network occasionally attracts researchers from other fields of sociological research such as youth, conflict, profession, or gender relations, applying their approaches to military issues.

The AISLF organizes an international symposium every four years, the last one was held in Montreal in 2016. Within it, the working group GT05 *Armed Forces and Society* led by Claude Weber brings together French-speaking military sociologists. This network has an international character since it ties together academics from French-speaking countries such as Switzerland, Canada, and Belgium, Lebanon, many African countries, and Maghreb countries as Tunisia or Morocco.

The AEGES is a trans-disciplinary platform that develops war studies in the French academic world. The more than three hundred affiliated researchers have initiated a dozen working groups and there is one on military sociology called *Military Institution: Action, Cultures, Society*, whose members are mostly the same as those of the AFS working group related to military sociology. In a network in which international relations and history dominate, the purpose of the working group is to demonstrate that military sociology has full legitimacy within war studies and strategic studies. It also aims to show that war studies can gain a great deal from military sociology approaches on the transformations of military institutions, the patterns of civil-military relations, military training, or gender in the armed forces.

I will not go into the details of the affiliation of French researchers with international networks such as the International Studies Association (ISA), the Inter-University Seminar on Armed Forces and Society (IUS) of which Bernard Boëne was an active member, or the European Group for Military and Social Research (ERGOMAS) in which French researchers try to be present and active. These international networks connect relatively isolated French researchers to more visible and important groups, thus reinforcing the feeling of belonging to a global community of researchers.

3   The Institutional Setup of Military Sociology in France and its Funding

The main development of military sociology in France is the increasing participation of the Ministry of Defense in funding research over the last thirty years. However, this main trend must be described in a nuanced way. Although the financial support for research in the social sciences within the Ministry of Defense has dramatically increased in the past ten years, the effort has mainly benefited strategic research, making current military sociology much less visible, compared to its undeniable progress between 1995 and 2009.

3.1   1995–2009 – The C2SD. A Structure Dedicated to Military Sociology

Compared to other French public institutions, the interest of the Ministry of Defense in the social sciences became apparent early on. In a chapter in an edited volume on research within the French administration (Jankowski and Vennesson, 2005), the authors describe the various research organizations developed since the 1960s with the aim of financing and promoting studies in the social sciences within the French administration. Each one studies the specific field of the respective ministry. The chapter on the armed forces analyzed the experience with the C2SD. The C2SD was created within the Ministry of Defense to commission research on military sociology and existed for fifteen years. In 2009, it was merged with other research organizations of the MoD to form the IRSEM. Three directors have led the C2SD: Gérard Hoffmann, its founder, Pascal Vennesson, from 1999 to 2003, and Frédéric Charillon, from 2003 to 2009.

During this period, the C2SD published 120 research reports, produced by more than 90 academics, consultants or think tank researchers. These studies have covered four dimensions of military sociology: recruitment, training, retention, and careers; the relations between armed forces and civil society; the adaptation of the military to the evolution of the missions; and the analysis of defense policy as public policy. The C2SD primarily commissioned research. Accordingly, its own research team was small in numbers, as the studies were done by outside researchers. Each year, a research program was launched that considered both the needs of the military and the proposals made by the C2SD. After a call for proposals, selected teams carried out primarily empirical studies within a time frame ranging from 6 to 15 months, depending on the scope of the field survey.

The large number of researchers who have worked with the C2SD can be explained by the fact that most contractors were not military sociologists. They were, for example, labor sociologists applying their approaches to analyze the upheavals due to professionalization, youth sociologists who helped the armed forces to identify young people who are interested in military careers, specialists in political sociology, in sociology of immigration, public policy analysis, devoting themselves to military sociology on a temporary basis. During this fifteen-year period, the Ministry of Defense's financial support for the research done by the C2SD has increased from almost nothing in 1995 to 50,000 euros per year at the end of the 2000s.

3.2   Since 2009 – The IRSEM. The Rise of Strategic Studies and the Deceleration of Military Sociology

The IRSEM[7] established in 2009, merged four institutes[8] with complementary specializations: military sociology, history, strategic thinking, and defense armament. This was completely changing the way social science research was carried out within the Ministry of Defense. The staff of each of the centers were usually not researchers. It took a few years to achieve the current balance between research and research support, which was initially more important in terms of personnel because of the orientation of the centers before their integration into the IRSEM. The C2SD, which was essentially dedicated to financing projects carried out by external teams and therefore had a limited number of researchers, was transformed into the IRSEM with a team of about thirty scholars who produce in-house research. In addition, the financial support for PhD and post-doctoral fellowships has also considerably increased.

This change had several implications for military sociology. The C2SD had allowed military sociology to expand because it only did research in this discipline. At IRSEM a much greater importance has been given to research in the social sciences within the Ministry of Defense, a very positive development. However, the merge also had the effect of making military sociology less visible within the new entity dedicated to strategic research. Just at the same time, military sociology was losing the interest and attention it generated in the late 1990s and early 2000s. This is particularly evident with respect to the attractiveness of security studies and international relations for students choosing a master's degree course. Due to a lack of applicants, the IRSEM has not funded a single student in military sociology for the past six years.

Despite the institutional changes, military sociology is still as fragmented as it was twenty-five years ago when the C2SD was created. It is split between the following poles: the IRSEM with its Defense and Society Department, about fifteen university or CNRS research units in which researchers work either partially or entirely on topics related to military sociology, military schools where social scientists teach military sociology and, finally, small centers within each service, which

---

7   The IRSEM is a research institute attached to the Ministry of Defense's General Directorate for International Relations and Strategy (DGRIS). IRSEM is made up of a team of 40 civilian and military personnel working on defense and security issues.

8   The C2SD on military sociology, the CEHD (Centre *D'études D'histoire de la Défense*) on military history, the CEREMS (*Centre D'études et de Recherches de L'enseignement Militaire Supérieur*) on strategic studies and the CHEAr (*Centre des Hautes Études de L'Armement*) on armament and procurement.

study issues concerning their personnel. Accordingly, the IRSEM is not a unique institution involved in military sociology in France and it works as often as possible with the scholars, PhD students, research units, or think tanks. It should also be mentioned that nothing has ever prevented a researcher from working on military issues without having any link with the Ministry of Defense, and there are some recent examples in different universities such as Christel Coton (2017).

The research team of the IRSEM is divided into five departments: Regions of the global North which covers Europe, the United States, Russia, the post-Soviet area, China, Japan and the Korean peninsula; Regions of the global South with a focus on Africa, the Middle East, the Gulf, the Indian Subcontinent, South East Asia and the Pacific; Armament and defense economics, which focuses on economic issues concerning defense and questions of strategy arising from technological development; Defense and Society, which looks at the relationship between the state and the armed forces, at public opinion on defense matters, and at the sociology of violence; and finally strategic thought, which focuses on the conduct of armed conflict at strategic, operational, and tactical levels.

Within the IRSEM, the Defense and Society department is dedicated to military sociology. There are three permanent researchers. Anne Muxel is the chief of the department and studies youth values, engagement, radicalization (2017, 2018a, 2018b). Her research highlighted that, contrary to common belief, young people are not depoliticized. They express their interest in politics and in collective matters differently. They are no longer involved in traditional long-term ways of engagement, such as political party or trade union activism but are more attracted to associative or humanitarian commitments that produce concrete results. Camille Boutron works on different aspects of women's engagement in wars and armed conflicts (2015, 2017, 2018, 2019). She started a research program on women involved in jihadist organizations, French military females in combat operations, and FARC (Revolutionary Armed Forces of Colombia) women combatants as they reintegrate into civil society which should allow her to produce an innovative analysis of the female combat experience at the beginning of the 21st century. Barbara Jankowski studies civil-military relations (2001, 2003, 2018a, 2018b, 2019) as well as public opinion and war (2011, 2013, 2017a, 2017b).[9]

Both the C2SD and the IRSEM have been subordinated to three different directorates or military units inside the Ministry of Defense throughout their history. It is important to point out that the institutional setting does not influence the

---

9   Since this chapter was written, Barbara Jankowski has retired. Florian Opillard, a geographer, who works on the adaptation of the army to climate change and on the role of the armed forces in the management of the Covid 19 pandemic crisis, and a lieutenant of the Air Force, Camille Trotoux, have joined the team.

definition of missions, but it impacts the research subjects that are valued, the resources allocated and the type of recognition inside the MOD. Each of these institutional connections had their advantages and disadvantages and there is no universal lesson to be drawn, apart from this one: the existence of a unit of military sociology within a center dedicated to strategic research whose aim is to shed light on the international context and provide essential information about security actors is not self-evident and cannot be taken for granted. It is not unthinkable that, if the IRSEM had been created *ex-nihilo* ten years ago, military sociology would not have found a place.

The role of strategic research has been confirmed by the Ministry of Defense recently. An agreement between the Ministry of Higher Education and the Ministry of Defense in 2018 affirmed the Ministry's financial support to research units at universities and to young PhD students.[10] An article by the current director of the IRSEM, Jean-Baptiste Jeangène Vilmer, retraces all the actions undertaken since the creation of the C2SD in 1995 to help young researchers by providing them with research grants, facilitating their access to the field and allowing them to publish their research, first in military sociology, then more broadly in war studies (Jeangène Vilmer 2018). In return, the continuity of military sociology is now rather ensured within universities, more thanks to the lecturers and professors who will promote it, than through the institutional support inside the Ministry, which is quite fragile.

3.3   Military Personnel in Military Sociology: Officers as Sociologists

This section does not attempt to sum up the long history of the links between officers and social sciences (see Jankowski and Vennesson 2005; Les Champs de Mars 2001, 2002; Martin 1999). However, it should be underlined that, in the late 1970s and in the 1980s, the armed forces encouraged their officers to undertake higher studies in sociology. Each year an officer of the Army was part of the group of around twenty students taking the course of the DEA (*Diplôme d'Etudes Approfondies*, now a master's degree) in sociology of organizations at the *Institut d'Etudes Politiques de Paris* (now Sciences Po), set up by Michel Crozier. This has led to the existence of a group of officers who were sensitive towards the social sciences and who have carried out empirical research, not only for their master's thesis

---

10   Cf. *Pacte Enseignement Supérieur*, <www.defense.gouv.fr/dgris/recherche-et-prospective/pacte-enseignement-superieur/pacte-enseignement-superieur> (last access: 3 February 2020).

but also, for some of them, for their PhD thesis. Since the late 1990s, the process has been interrupted and not been renewed in any other form. Each year there are officers from the National War College who study a master's degree at a university at the same time, but the curriculums they generally choose rarely include military sociology. We must look at research in history for substantial contributions of officers to the production of academic knowledge related to military sociology. However, institutionally in the Ministry of Defense, historical research has always been separated from military sociology, except for a short period just after the IRSEM was created.

The Defense and Society department of IRSEM is supposed to welcome a senior officer among its researchers, but research is not highly valued in a professional career as an officer and there are only atypical officers who know that they sacrifice part of their career if they accept a research position at the Institute. In addition, there are still very few senior military officials with a PhD in any discipline, although this is gradually changing. However, between 2015 and 2018 the Defense and Society department has benefited from the active presence of an Army lieutenant colonel who has published on women in the armed forces, military resilience, or the military and new technologies (Planiol 2016, 2017a, 2017b)

Some officers write articles in military journals, publish books mostly outside university presses and focus on history or strategy. There is a persistent concern about the risk of voicing one's opinion publicly, even if the articles that have been problematic in the past were released in the press, not in books. I would like to highlight the edited volume by a future Chief of Defense Staff (Lecointre 2017) and the many works of Colonel Michel Goya, a historian and former researcher at the IRSEM, who published some extremely relevant works during his career and, since his retirement, some of them on military sociology (Goya 2010, 2015).

Finally, I would like to mention André Thiéblemont, former colonel of the army, whose contributions on the ethnographic approach to combat, and wartime field work are numerous and cannot be fully cited here. He has contributed widely to the analysis of military cultures and his book *Cultures et Logiques Militaires* (Thiéblemont 1999) is a reference to this day.

4 Publishing in Military Sociology: Quality, but Rarity and Dispersion

Publications in military sociology are divided into three types of products: open access editions on the Internet, articles, or special thematic issues in academic journals, edited volumes, or monographs. I will focus on publications in French only because this literature is not as visible in international discussions as publications in English.[11]

4.1 An Active Editorial Policy within the Ministry of Defense on Military Sociology

For the IRSEM and, previously, the C2SD, publishing and wide access to the results of the studies have always been a priority. Before the internet era, studies were published in printed paper series and sent to mailing lists or, on request, to civilian and military authorities, to libraries, journalists, and researchers. Since its foundation, IRSEM's website has published online and free of charge all the institute's productions in two types of paper series: *Notes de Recherche* (Research Paper): a short format between 5 and 15 pages dealing with a specific topic; *Etudes* (Studies): extensive research work of at least forty pages. Since 2009, the IRSEM has published 70 issues in its *Etudes* collection. Of these, 27 percent belong to military sociology. Aside from that, of 75 Research papers, only 10 percent are related to military sociology. In the previous paper series, which can be found on ARES[12] (*Paris Papers, Laboratoires de l'IRSEM, Cahiers de l'IRSEM*), the proportion of military sociology was around 15 to 20 percent of the total publications.

Thus, in terms of publication within the IRSEM, military sociology is not to be outdone. As a percentage of the volume of publications available online, the share of military sociology represents at least one fifth and is equivalent to what the field represents in the institute overall, being one of the five research fields.

4.2 The Limited Number of Specialized Journals on Military Sociology

There are three military sociology journals published in French: *Les Champs de Mars, Res Militaris*, and *Inflexions. Civils et Militaires: Pouvoir Dire*. Since its foundation in 1995, one of the objectives of the C2SD was to launch an academic journal and it founded *Les Champs de Mars* in 1996, publishing two issues per year. The journal has changed its publisher three times during its existence and has recently turned from a social sciences journal on defense issues and military sociology into the peer-reviewed journal of war studies in French. The journal is now called: *Les Champs de Mars, Revue D'études sur la Guerre et la Paix* and is published by Les

---

11   One can mention among many others, e.g., Irondelle et al. 2011; Jankowski 2017c; Martin 1981; Vennesson 2013, 2015.
12   ARES, *Portail Documentaire de la Recherche Stratégique* (Documentary Portal for Strategic Research): <www.irsem.fr/search.html>.

Presses de Sciences Po, one of the leading academic editors in France. The entire collection of volumes is available on CAIRN.info.[13]

A special remark should be made regarding the online journal launched by Bernard Boëne in 2010, *Res Militaris. European Journal of Military Studies*. It is an academic journal devoted entirely to military sociology, published both in French and English. It includes a relevant section dedicated to the analysis of the fundamental texts of the discipline called *Classics of the Military Field in the Social Sciences*. *Res Militaris* also edits works produced by ERGOMAS. The journal *Inflexions. Civils et Militaires: Pouvoir Dire* is not strictly speaking an academic journal but it has an interesting position because of its combined focus on theory and practice for each of its thematic issues. Its aim is to take part in the intellectual debate around military topics which it has been doing for 38 issues. Finally, I would like to mention the *Revue Défense Nationale*, which is not an academic journal. However, it is the oldest journal of all, publishing mainly on strategic issues, but occasionally devoting space to military sociology. All French military sociologists regularly write in this journal.

4.3 Examples for Special issues on Military Sociology of Major General Journals

Academic journals in sociology and political science publish special issues on military affairs from time to time. The first initiative of this kind came from the *Revue Française de Sociologie*, with a special issue on the military during the Algerian war in 1961 entitled: *Guerre, Armée, Société,* with fourteen articles covering war, peace and relations between armed forces and society (Revue Française de Sociologie 1961). Since then, only thirty articles related to military sociology have been published in this journal, one every two years. However, most of them have been published before the early 1990s. It is worth to mention the special issue edited by François Gresle in 2003, entitled *Military Profession*, with first analyses on the shift to an all-volunteer armed force in France (Gresle 2003) or the article by Jean Joana on civil-military relations (Joana 2007).

Another academic journal in the field, the *Revue Française de Science Politique,* published an issue on military sociology oriented on defense policies and edited by Pascal Vennesson (2004). In this journal, two articles are significant: an article by Jean Joana in 2002 on the legal status and life conditions of the military (Joana 2002) and the latest article on the relationship between sociology and the military published by Laure Bardiès in 2017. The French journal of political science published only one special issue and 7 papers on military sociology in twenty years.

---

13   <www.cairn.info/revue-les-champs-de-mars.htm>.

L'Année Sociologique, a French semi-annual journal in sociology, founded in 1896 by Émile Durkheim, published a special issue entitled: "Values, profession and action: evolutions and permanencies of the military institution" edited by Eric Letonturier in 2011 (2011a, 2011b) with seven major contributions (L'année Sociologique 2011). The thematic journal *Pouvoirs*, a French review of constitutional and political studies, published an issue on the army in 1986 and then another one in 2008 entitled *The French Armies* (Pouvoirs 1986, 2008).

Cultures & Conflits, the journal of international relations focusing on conflicts, created by Didier Bigo in 1990, regularly publishes issues on security and defense matters. Of particular note are the issues devoted to armed forces and domestic security and to military and missions abroad (Bigo and Guittet 2004; Olsson and Vermeren 2007) as well as numerous articles in issues devoted to related topics, like Daho (2015) on the socialization of professional groups in foreign policy and how civil-military activities in former Yugoslavia have been institutionalized in France. Aside from these French journals I would like to highlight the Belgian journal The *Revue Internationale de Politique Comparée* that publishes a lot in military sociology in French.[14]

The problem encountered by researchers trying to publish is not as much the lack of academic journals in French than the fact that, first, military issues are not considered sufficiently promising and valuable enough. This observation unfortunately repeats itself over the decades. Second, building a solid academic profile requires now to imperatively publish in English and the younger generation of researchers publishes sometimes more in English than in French. One good example are the works of the late Bastien Irondelle who analyzed the reforms of the armed forces as well as the process of Europeanization of security policies (Irondelle 2008a, 2008b, 2009; Irondelle and Vennesson 2002). In addition, the obstacle of low interest in defense issues of French readers, considerably limits the interest of publishing on military sociology, compared to the attractiveness aroused by history, international security, and the studies on geographical areas.

4.4   Examples for French-Language Books on Military Sociology

For many years, Theodor Caplow's and Pascal Vennesson's *Sociologie militaire* (Caplow and Vennesson 2000) was the only book on military sociology in French. Since then, the landscape has significantly expanded. First, in the 2000s some collective books following conferences and edited by senior academics allowed the

---

14   See for example the special issue edited by Jean Joana in 2008 on civil-military relations (Joana 2008).

young doctoral and post-doctoral students to publish the results of their empirical research such as in Vennesson (2000a), Gresle (2005) or Porteret (2007). These three books present approximately twenty chapters dealing with the impact of the professionalization of the armed forces, their Europeanization and internationalization that largely modified the patterns of military actions in the early 2000s.

Other researchers have published books which provided major steps forward for the discipline in terms of content, findings, and methodological approaches, e.g., Claude Weber (2012) and his cohort study on the socialization of young army officers who join the Saint-Cyr Coëtquidan Military School, or Christel Coton (2017) and her work on the army officer corps.

The collection *l'Homme et la guerre* (Man and War), edited by Jean Baechler, analyzes the multiple aspects of war such as war and law or war and religion in edited volumes for more than a decade. Contributions to these volumes mostly follow a historical approach, but the series includes many papers or even entire volumes related to military sociology like *L'Arrière*, on public opinion and war (Baechler and Ramel 2017) or the one on War and Politics (Baechler and Holeindre 2014).

In the past decade, book series have been initiated by renowned publishers devoted to war and strategy, mostly on history, but from time to time including books on military sociology, such as Tallandier (*Guerres et Militaires*), *Economica*, that includes 12 series dedicated to military history and strategy, and one related to military sociology (*Guerres et Opinions Publiques*). Another example is Armand Colin which recently published Bénédicte Chéron's book on armed forces and French society (Chéron 2018) or a manual on intelligence in France presenting the main features of this field of study (Chopin and Oudet 2019). Perrin, a famous publisher in history, published *La ruse et la force* (Holeindre 2017), a book on strategy by Jean-Vincent Holeindre. The Presses Universitaires de France (PUF) published Louis Gautier's book on French defense policy since the Cold War (Gautier 2009). Finally, Les Presses de Sciences Po have published three fundamental works on political sociology of the military: Jean Joana (2013), Bastien Irondelle (2011) and William Genieys (2008) and the chapter on defense policy in the book on public policies in France (Irondelle 2008a). It becomes evident from this description that there is a relatively large number of publishers and as a result, publications are quite scattered. Two very recent and major works gather most of the French researchers working in the field. The first is a collective volume edited by Jakubowski and Cardona Gil (2020) on the transformation of the armed forces and their adaptation to changes in their environment. The second one (Jankowski, Muxel and Thura 2021) is entitled *La Sociologie Militaire. Héritages et nouvelles perspectives* and offers a broad overview of the latest research in France and internationally. The twenty chapters examine the social functions of the armed forces, military occupations, civil-military relations, terrorism and the redefinition of the missions, and finally, how military sociology can contribute helping the armed forces.

5   Research on the Military: Mostly Empirical Methods and a Large Scope of Topics

Knowing that military sociology "touches upon a variety of topics and borrows from many theoretical frames" (Ouellet et al. 2005, 5), what makes French research on military sociology original? While research topics are the same as in many other countries, some are more developed or studied with a specific approach: defense policy analyses use the tools of public action or public policy analysis, for example, in particular with regard to the Europeanization processes. The relationship between armed forces and society is a recurring concern, especially since the end of conscription. However, studies focus less on the relationship between decision-makers and the military leadership, under the prism of civilian control over the military, but focus on the distance between military and society in its various components (youth, elites, elected officials).

The most prominent characteristics of French military sociology are, first, based on empirical and qualitative methods and second, as far as theoretical approaches are concerned, references to American military sociology have remained the rule. For an overview of the specificities of French approaches to military sociology, it is useful to refer to Sébastien Jakubowski's chapter (Jakubowski 2013).

5.1   Mainly Empirical Research with Qualitative Methods

French research in military sociology has been and is based on qualitative empirical methods, e.g., social interactions using in-depth interviews with actors, field observations, including also missions abroad, focus groups, or oral history. Some researchers have become reservists to be sent on a mission with the military and thus gain insight from participating observation (Prévot-Forni 2006). *Women in the Armed Forces*, the first PhD-thesis on women in the military by Katia Sorin was based on more than 250 interviews (Sorin 2003). There are many more similar examples. If we take into account all the theses and studies carried out over the past 25 years, around 5000 interviews were carried out with military personnel of all ranks and branches, mainly from the French but also from other European or North American armed forces.

The use of qualitative methodology has been analyzed over time in highly relevant articles (Deschaux-Beaume 2011; Deschaux-Dutard 2015). The author of these studies focuses on and questions the practice of qualitative interviews in the military field and the status of those interviews which provide the only access to military actors and thus are the only chance for generating data. Another important contribution from a methodological perspective is Samy Cohen's book, *The Art of Interviewing Leaders*, including military ones, making it an essential reference in this field (Cohen 1999). A special issue of the journal *Les Champs de Mars* (Lafaye et al. 2015) is devoted to the predominant use of qualitative methodology in French military sociology, with a preface of Frédéric Charillon (Charillon 2015b), and articles from many post-docs (Martin and Pajon 2015; Paya y Pastor et al. 2015; Settoul 2015b).

5.2   A Large Scope of Topics

What are the main topics of French military sociology? To answer that question would require a separate chapter as the themes addressed by military sociology in France are numerous and have been studied for decades. France is, thus, characterized by the fact that, on the one hand, few researchers invest in military sociology and are willing to devote themselves to it throughout their careers. However, on the other hand, almost all fields generally referred to as part of military sociology have been investigated.

In the 1990s, the C2SD concentrated on five topics of research in military sociology: the adaptation of the military to the evolution of its missions, human resources challenges, relations between the military institution and civil society, defense policies, and the military in the system of international cooperation. In 2001, the themes were reorganized into four: the soldier in Europe, with a comparative approach, the adaptation of the military to the evolution of their missions, armed forces and society, and defense policies.

In 2003, Vincent Porteret published an overview of the state of the art of military sociology developed by the C2SD since 1995 (Porteret 2003) detailing more precisely three topics: women and the military institution, the military profession facing new operational contexts, and new expectations in the relationship between the armed forces and society.

As described above, the foundation of the IRSEM led to a much broader approach in terms of research topics: The IRSEM did no longer focus on *military sociology* but on *social sciences in defense*, encompassing issues on the military personnel (profiles, values, behavior, working conditions, combat experience), the study of their interactions with decision-makers, politicians, senior civil servants, or media, and their interactions with society at large (support of public opinion). "In fact, it even includes issues where the word 'defense' does not appear: the values of young people (potential recruits), the impact of digital technology and social networks on individual and collective behavior, the state of public and intellectual debate (on cultural insecurity, resilience)" (Charillon 2015a, 7).

Currently the areas studied in military sociology inside the IRSEM are the following: changes at work for military personnel, relations between the military leaders and the civilian decision-makers, public opinion and war, gender within the military, the different forms of youth engagement, the renewal of conscription, and the rise of radicalism and violence.

There is undoubtfully a convergence between what is studied in France and in other European countries. The consequences of the professionalization of the armed forces gave an impulse to military sociology in France from the suspension of conscription in 1996 for at least a decade, with a book as a starting point (Boëne and Martin 1998) and an assessment in 2004 (C2SD 2004).

The end of mandatory military service has resulted in numerous studies on the motivations of young people to join the army and on their return to civilian life with an assessment after four years and a half dozen of studies made in 1999 and further on (Besse and Coton 2019; Hatto et al. 2011; Léger 2004).More recent studies focus on the attractiveness of the careers of senior military officers or on the work-life balance for the military.

Other important topics are the role of women in the military, quantitatively few in number but regularly undertaken (Planiol 2017; Porteret 2003; Sorin 2003; Weber 2015), or the integration of minorities in the armed forces, an issue much less developed, except by two researchers (Settoul 2015a, 2015b, 2016, 2017; Wihtol de Wenden and Bertossi 2005).

Since the professionalization and the increase of the missions abroad went hand in hand, the studies also focused on the changes they induced in the military profession, first in peacekeeping operations and then in war operations, such as in Afghanistan. A third of the studies of the C2SD and of the IRSEM deals with this theme, based on in-depth interviews with military personnel during deployments or after coming back from a mission (Lafaye 2016; Prévot 2006, 2008; Teboul 2017; Thiéblemont 2000, 2002, 2011, 2013, 2015; Thura 2014).

The relations between armed forces and society are a second broad area of French military sociology. In France, the focus has been more on the links between the armed forces and the nation (*le lien armée-nation*, the *army-nation link*) than on other aspects. It refers to the role played by military service from its origin in 1798 until its abolition, in defending national sovereignty and building citizenship. Researchers must constantly distance themselves from this normative approach, far from the objective measurement of what these relations are and especially how one can analyze their evolution since the professionalization (Jankowski 2003, 2008; Vennesson 2000c).

Themes like the perception of the armed forces of public opinion attitudes towards war and casualties have been studied during the 2000s by both external researchers (Irondelle and Foucault 2008; La Balme 2002; Thiebaut 2015), and within the IRSEM (Jankowski 2011, 2013, 2017a, 2017b, 2018a, 2018b). This theme also includes research on the military and the media (Chéron 2012, 2019). Civil-military relations in terms of civilian supremacy over the military in decision-making processes have been an important topic in military sociology for many decades (Cohen 1980, 1984, 1985, 1986, 1995; Daho 2015, 2016; Gautier 1999, 2009; Genieys 2008; Irondelle 2008a, 2011; Jankowski 2019; Joana 2007, 2008, 2013).

Still, the use of research results remains problematic. Decision-makers do not know how to use research. In addition, researchers do not intend political use of their findings and have not learned how to operationalize their results. The military leadership's lack of time and interest in research is real and difficult to dispel. Civilian and military leaders only read short notes, which researchers cannot write alone, because they usually do not obey the logic of action and decision. Another obstacle for the political use of research results is the extremely high turnover of the personnel in the military compared to other public institutions, the main reason being that the military top hierarchy changes frequently due to age limits in each grade. The officers and the generals do not stay in their position more than three years, and often only two. So just as a relationship of trust is established between researchers and military officials, the relationship must be rebuilt again with new leaders.

The question of the usefulness of research for decision-making support, which arises repeatedly, was analyzed a long time ago by Pascal Vennesson (2000b, 2002) who demonstrated all the underlying presuppositions and showed how the social sciences make a useful contribution to the work and decisions of the Ministry of Defense: by establishing knowledge, contributing to the pluralism of social representations and arguments, and promoting a debate based on empirical surveys and by situating the transformations of the armed forces in their social and political context. In the field of public policy and decision-making, military sociology contributes mainly by helping to identify the problems. There is no fool proof recipe for this accumulated knowledge to be used by decision-makers.

6   Conclusion

If one defines military sociology as similar to other subfield studies, such as the sociology of education, family, youth, or religion, as taking the general concepts and methods of social sciences and applying them to the military institution and to the military personnel, the least that can be observed is that its place is more marginal than that of other subfields, taking into account the highly significant role played by the state and its sovereign institution.

The major obstacle faced by military sociology in France today is still the insufficient number of researchers and the fact that they are very dispersed among institutions. Reading this overview, however, it would seem that a lot of research has been accumulated in 25 years and it is impossible to deny that there is a solid base today. French military sociology is alive and well and has been re-invigorated. However, the small size of the field and the regular institutional changes have caused many discontinuities, for example, with respect to career patterns, and more importantly, the topics which are in the focus of research.

Since 2009, military sociology in France has been integrated into strategic research while not necessarily recognized in the same way as area studies. Since the IRSEM mainly carries out strategic studies, what is military sociology doing there? Strategic research focuses on everything that affects the interests, values and sovereignty of a country. It must first enlighten the international landscape by trying to discern what may limit the freedom of action of the country's strategy. One may wonder how military sociology is strategic or how it can help strategic studies. With regard to the relationship between the armed forces and society, the analyses should help to identify the trends at work in French society likely to have repercussions on the military institution or the relationship between the military and society. Their usefulness depends on the choice of the issues on which to focus.

Some topics are evident blind spots in French military sociology, such as, for example, the values and concerns of the youth and their understanding of security or military sacrifice. The recurring questions among the military officers about the nature of the links between the military and the society prove to what extent the social environment has a strategic dimension. The changes that affect our society have consequences for the military and knowing them is crucial to prepare for the future.

References

Baechler, J., and B. Boëne, eds. 2018. *Les Armées*. Paris: Hermann.

Baechler, J., and J.-V. Holeindre, eds. 2014. *Guerre et Politique*. Paris: Hermann.

Baechler, J., and F. Ramel, eds. 2017. *L'arrière*. Paris: Hermann.

Bagayoko-Penone, N. 2006. "L'Européanisation des Militaires Français. Socialisation Institutionelle et Culture Stratégique." *Revue Française de Science Politique* 56(1): 49–77.

Bardiès, L. 2008. "Deux Siècles de Sociologie Militaire en France (1815–1991). Sociologie d'une Sociologie." Doctoral dissertation, Université Toulouse 1.

Bardiès, L. 2017. "La Sociologie Française et la Chose Militaire. Une Tradition Antipolitique." *Revue Française de Science Politique* 67(5): 879–898.

Barrera, B. 2015. *Opération Serval. Notes de Guerre – Mali 2013*. Paris: Seuil.

Besse, L., and C. Coton. 2019. "Armée-Jeunesse: Vocations, Engagement et Deuxième Chance." *Agora. Débats/Jeunesses* 82(2) 7–142.

Bezes P., M. Chauviere, J. Chevallier, N. de Montricher, and F. Oqueteau, eds. 2005. *L'Etat à L'épreuve des Sciences Sociales. La Fonction Recherche dans les Administrations sous la Ve République*. Paris: La Découverte.

Bigo, D., and E.-P. Guittet. 2004. "Militaires et Sécurité Intérieure." *Cultures & Conflits* 56(4): 5–182.

Boëne, B. 2014. *Les Sciences Sociales, La Guerre et L'armée. Objets, Approches, Perspectives*. Paris: Presses de l'université Paris-Sorbonne.

Boëne, B., and D. Auverlot. 1990. *La Spécificité Militaire: Actes du Colloque de Coëtquidan*. Paris: Armand Colin.

Boëne, B., and C. Dandeker. 1998. *Les Armées en Europe*. Paris: La Découverte.

Boëne, B., and M.L. Martin, eds. 1991. *Conscription et Armée de Métier*. Paris: Fondation des Etudes de Défense Nationale.

Boutron, C. 2015. "Women at War, War on Women: Reconciliation and Patriarchy in Peru." In *Female Combatants in Conflict and Peace. Challenging Gender in Violence and Post-Conflict Reintegration*, edited by S. Shekhawat, 149–166. London: Palgrave Macmillan.

Boutron, C. 2017. "Colombie: la Longue Marche Vers la Paix?" *IdeAs. Idées d'Amériques* 9. <https://doi.org/10.4000/ideas.1838>

Boutron, C. 2018. "Engendering Peacebuilding: The International Gender Nomenclature of Peace Politics and Women's Participation in the Colombian Peace Process." *Journal of Peacebuilding & Development* 13(2): 116–121.

Boutron, C. 2019. *Femmes en Armes – Itinéraires de Combattantes au Pérou (1980–2010)*. Rennes: Presses Universitaires de Rennes.

Caplow, T., and P. Vennesson. 2000. *Sociologie Militaire*. Paris: Armand Colin.

C2SD – Centre d'Études en Sciences Sociales de la Défense. 2004. "Catalogue des publications du C2SD: 1996–2001. Mis à jour en 2004". *Les Documents du C2SD*. <www.irsem.fr/data/files/irsem/documents/document/file/1585/c2sd_publications_catalogue2003.pdf> (last access: 3 February 2020).

Centre de Sociologie de la Défense Nationale. 1993. *Centre de Sociologie de la Défense Nationale, 1969–1994*. Paris: CSDN.

Charillon, F. 2015a. "L'IRSEM et le Chantier Stratégique. Entretien." *Stratégique* 110 (3): 175–181.

Charillon, F. 2015b. "Préface." *Les Champs de Mars* 27(2): 7–8.

Charillon, F., T. Balzacq, and F. Ramel, F. 2018. "La Diplomatie de Défense." In *Manuel de Diplomatie*, edited by T. Balzacq, 307–319. Paris: Presses de Sciences Po.

Chéron, B. 2012. "L'image des Militaires Français à la Télévision. 2001–2011." *Etude de l'IRSEM 21*. Paris: Irsem.

Chéron, B. 2018. *Le Soldat Méconnu. Les Français et Leurs Armées: Un État des Lieux*. Malakoff: Armand Colin.

Chéron, B. 2019. "L'expérience Militaire dans les Médias (2008–2018). Une Diversification des Formes de Récits." *Etude de l'IRSEM* 66. Paris: Irsem.

Chopin, O., ed. 2011. "Etudier le Renseignement, État de l'Art et Perspectives De Recherche." *Etude de l'IRSEM 9*. Paris: Irsem.

Chopin, O., and B. Oudet. 2019. *Renseignement et Sécurité*. 2nd edition. Malakoff: Armand Colin.

Clément, M., and C. Pajon. 2015. "La Sociologie Militaire par les Personnels de la Défense: Une Sociologie D'insiders?" *Les Champs de Mars* 27(2): 23–30.

Cohen, S. 1980. *Les Conseillers du Président. De Charles de Gaulle à Valéry Giscard d'Estaing*. Paris: PUF.

Cohen, S. 1984. *La Défaite des Généraux*. Paris: Fayard.

Cohen, S. 1985. *La Politique Extérieure de Valéry Giscard d'Estaing*. Paris: Presses de Sciences Po.

Cohen, S. 1986. *La Monarchie Nucléaire*. Paris: Hachette.

Cohen, S. 1995. *La Bombe Atomique: La Stratégie de L'épouvante*. Paris: Gallimard.

Cohen, S. 1999. *L'art d'Interviewer les Dirigeants*. Paris: PUF.

Coton, C. 2017. *Officiers. Des Classes en Lutte Sous l'Uniforme*. Marseille: Agone.

Daho, G. 2015. "La Socialisation Entre Groupes Professionnels de la Politique Étrangère: Le Cas de l'Institutionnalisation des Activités Civilo-Militaires Françaises en Ex-Yougoslavie." *Cultures & Conflits* 98(2): 101–131.

Daho, G. 2016. *La Transformation des Armées. Enquête sur les Relations Civilo-Militaires en France*. Paris: Editions de la Maison des sciences de l'homme.

Deschaux-Beaume, D. 2011. "Enquêter en Milieu Militaire. Stratégie Qualitative et Conduite D'entretiens dans le Domaine de la Défense." *Res Militaris* 1(2): 1–16.

Deschaux-Dutard, D. 2015. "Stratégie Qualitative et Défense: L'entretien Comme Interaction Sociale en Milieu Militaire." *Les Champs de Mars* 27(2): 42–47.

Durieux, B., J.-B. Jeangène Vilmer, and F. Ramel, eds. 2017. *Dictionnaire de la Guerre et de la Paix*. Paris: PUF.

Faure, S. 2016. *La Défense Européenne. L'émergence d'une Culture Stratégique Commune*. Montréal: Athéna éditions.

Gadbois, S. 1996. "Recrutement, Mobilité et Reconversion des Militaires. Un État des Recherches Menées au Centre de Sociologie de la Défense Nationale (1969–1994)." *Les Documents du C2SD 1*. Paris: Centre d'Études en Sciences Sociales de la Défense.

Gautier, L. 1999. *Mitterrand et son Armée: 1990–1995*. Paris: Grasset.

Gautier, L. 2009. *La Défense de la France après la Guerre Froide: Politique Militaire et forces armées depuis 1991*. Paris. PUF.

Genieys, W. 2008. *L'élite des Politiques de L'Etat*. Paris: Les Presses de Sciences Po.

Girardet, R. 1964. *La Crise Militaire Française: 1945–1962: Aspects Sociologiques et Idéologiques*. Paris: Armand Colin.

Girardet, R. 1998. *La Société Militaire de 1815 à nos Jours*. Paris: Perrin.

Goya, M. 2010. *Res Militaris: de L'emploi des Forces Armées au XXIème siècle*. Paris: Economica.

Goya, M. 2015. *Sous le Feu. La Mort comme Hypothèse de Travail*. Paris: Tallandier.

Gresle, F. 1996. "Le Citoyen-Soldat Garant du Pacte Républicain: à propos des Origines et de la Persistance d'une Idée Reçue." *L'Année Sociologique* 46(1): 105–125.

Gresle, F. 1997. *Le Service National*. Paris: PUF.

Gresle, F. 2003. "Présentation." *Revue Française de Sociologie* 44(4): 637–645.

Hoeffler, C. 2008. "Les Réformes des Systèmes D'acquisition D'armement en France et en Allemagne: Un Retour Paradoxal des Militaires?" *Revue Internationale de Politique Comparée* 15(1): 133–150.

Hoeffler, C. 2011. "Les Politiques D'armement en Europe: L'adieu aux Armes de l'État Nation? Une Comparaison entre l'Allemagne, la France, le Royaume-Uni et l'Union Européenne de 1976 à 2010." Doctoral dissertation, Institut d'Etudes Politiques de Paris.

Hoeffler, C., and S. Faure. 2015. "L'européanisation sans l'Union Européenne: Penser le Changement des Politiques Militaires." *Politique Européenne* 48(2): 8–27.

Holeindre, J.-V. 2017. *La Ruse et La Force – Une Autre Histoire de la Stratégie*. Paris: Perrin.

Irondelle, B. 2008a. "Les Politiques de Défense." In *Politiques Publiques 1, La France dans la Gouvernance Européenne*, edited by O. Borraz and V. Guiraudon, 93–112. Paris: Presses de Sciences Po.

Irondelle, B. 2008b. "Quelle Européanisation de la Sécurité au sein de l'Union Européenne?" *Les Champs de Mars* 19(1): 39–51.

Irondelle, B. 2009. "De la PESC à la PESD." In *Politiques Européennes*, edited by R. Dehousse, 303–330. Paris: Presses de Sciences Po.

Irondelle, B. 2011. *La Réforme des Armées en France: Sociologie de la Décision*. Paris: Presses de Sciences Po.

Irondelle, B., and M. Foucault. 2008. "Opinion Publique et Transformation de la Sécurité en Europe: Une Perspective Comparée." *Les Documents du C2SD*. Paris: Centre d'Études en Sciences Sociales de la Défense.

Irondelle B., M. Foucault, and F. Mérand, eds. 2011. *European Security since the Fall of the Berlin Wall*. Toronto: Toronto University Press.

Irondelle, B., and P. Vennesson, eds. 2002. "L'Europe de la Défense: Institution-nalisation, Européanisation." *Politique Européenne* 8(4): 5–129.

Jakubowski, S. 2007. *La Professionnalisation de l'Armée Française: Conséquences sur l'Autorité*. Paris: L'Harmattan.

Jakubowski, S. 2013. "Etat des Lieux et Enjeux d'Avenir de la Sociologie de la 'Société' Militaire." In *Les Études Stratégiques au XXIe Siècle*, edited by E. Ouellet, P. Pahlavi and M. Chennoufi, 201–237. Montréal, Athéna.

Jakubowski, S. and Cardona Gil, E.(eds). 2020. *Les Logiques de Transformation des Armées*. Villeneuve d'Ascq: Les Presses Universitaires du Septentrion.

Jankowski, B. 2003. "Valeurs des Français, Valeurs des Officiers." *Les Champs de Mars* 14(2): 59–70.

Jankowski, B. 2008. "Les Relations Armées-Société en France." *Pouvoirs* 125(2): 93–107.

Jankowski, B. 2011. "French Public Support for Military Operations: The Challenge of the War in Afghanistan." In *Security and the Military between Reality and Perception*, edited by M. Malešič and G. Kümmel, 43–54. Baden Baden: Nomos.

Jankowski, B. 2013a. "Opinion Publique et Armées à l'Épreuve de la Guerre en Afghanistan." *Etude de l'IRSEM* 34. Paris: Irsem.

Jankowski, B. 2013b. "War Narratives in a World of Information Age." *IRSEM Paper 8*. Paris: Irsem.

Jankowski, B. 2017a. "L'érosion du Soutien de l'Opinion Publique à l'Intervention Militaire en Afghanistan: l'Impact des Récits." In *L'arrière*, edited by J. Baechler and F. Ramel, 191–211. Paris: Hermann.

Jankowski, B. 2017b. "L'opinion des Français sur leur Armée." In *Guerre, Armée et Communication*, edited by E. Letonturier, 81–98. Paris: Les essentiels d'Hermès, CNRS Editions.

Jankowski, B. 2017c. "Information Sharing Among Military Operational Staff: The French Officers' Experience." In *Information Sharing in Military Operations*, edited by I. Goldenberg, J. Soeters, and W.H. Heads, 67–80. Cham: Springer.

Jankowski, B. 2018a. "Armed Forces and Society in France: A Positive Relationship." In *France and Poland Facing the Evolution of the Security Environment*, edited by B. Jankowski and A. Zima, 95–106. *Etude de l'IRSEM* 59. Paris: Irsem.

Jankowski, B. 2018b. "Le Rôle des Armées dans la Fonction Intégration de l'Etat." *Etude de l'IRSEM* 63. Paris: Irsem.

Jankowski, B. 2020. "L'influence des Militaires dans les Processus Décisionnels: Quelles Ressources ?" In *Les Logiques de Transformation des Armées*, edited by S. Jakubowski and E. Cardona-Gil, 57–86. Villeneuve d'Ascq: Les Presses Universitaires du Septentrion.

Jankowski, B., and P. Vennesson. 2005. "Les Sciences Sociales au Ministère de la Défense. Inventer, Négocier et Promouvoir un Rôle." In *L'Etat à l'Épreuve des Sciences Sociales. La Fonction Recherche dans les Administrations sous la Ve République*, edited by P. Bezes, P., M. Chauviere, J. Chevallier, N. de Montricher, and F. Oqueteau, 267–294. Paris: La Découverte.

Jankowski, B., A. Muxel, and M. Thura, eds. 2021. *La Sociologie Militaire. Héritages et nouvelles perspectives*. Oxford: Peter Lang.

Jeangène Vilmer, J.-B. 2018. "La Relève Stratégique: une Première Histoire du Soutien aux Jeunes Chercheurs sur les Questions de Défense et de Sécurité." *Les Champs de Mars* 30(1): 9–43.

Joana, J. 2002. "La 'Condition Militaire:' Inventions et Réinventions d'une Catégorie d'Action Publique." *Revue Française de Science Politique* 52(4): 449–467.

Joana, J. 2007. "La Démocratie Face à ses Militaires. Où en est l'Analyse des Relations Civils-Militaires?" *Revue Française de Sociologie* 48(1): 133–159.

Joana, J. 2008. "La Démocratie Face aux Relations Civils-Militaires." *Revue Internationale de Politique Comparée* 5(1): 7–150.

Joana, J. 2013. Les armées contemporaines. Paris: Presses de Sciences Po.

L'Année Sociologique. 2011. "Valeurs, Métier et Action. Evolutions et Permanences de L'institution Militaire." *L'Année sociologique* 61(2): 267–451.

La Balme, N. 2002. Partir en Guerre. *Décideurs et Politiques face à l'Opinion Publique*. Paris: Autrement.

Lafaye, C. 2016. *L'armée Française en Afghanistan (2001–2012). Le Génie au Combat*. Paris: CNRS éditions/DMPA.

Lafaye, C., A. Paya y Pastor, and M. Thura, eds. 2015. "La Pratique des Sciences Sociales en milieu Militaire: une Opération Spéciale? Dossier." *Les Champs de Mars* 27(2): 7–81.

Lecointre, F., ed. 2017. *Le Soldat: XXe-XXIe siècle*. Paris: Gallimard.

Léger, J.-F. 2003/4. "Pourquoi les Jeunes s'Engagent-ils Aujourd'hui dans les Armées?" *Revue Française de Sociologie* 44(4): 713–734.

Léger, J.-F. 2004. *Les Jeunes et l'Armée*. Paris: L'Harmattan.

Letonturier, E. 2011a. "Présentation." *L'Année Sociologique* 61(2): 267–271.

Letonturier, E. 2011b. "Reconnaissance, Institution et Identités Militaires." *L'Année Sociologique* 61(2): 323–350.

Le Roux, H., and A. Sabbagh. 2018. *Paroles de Soldats*. Paris: Tallandier.

Les Champs de Mars. 2001. "Les Précurseurs Français de la Sociologie Militaire. Dossier (première partie)." *Les Champs de Mars* 10(2): 7–101.

Les Champs de Mars. 2002. "Les Précurseurs Français de la Sociologie Militaire. Dossier (deuxième partie)." *Les Champs de Mars* 12(2): 7–83.

Makki, S. 2004. *Militarisation de l'Humanitaire, Privatisation du Militaire*. Paris: CIRPES-EHESS.

Martin, C., and C. Pajon, (2015). La sociologie militaire par les personnels de la défense: une sociologie d'insiders? *Les Champs de Mars* 27(2): 23–30.

Martin, M.L. 1981. *Warriors to Managers: The French Military Establishment Since 1945*. Chapel Hill: University of North Carolina Press.

Martin, M.L. 1999. "Prometteur ou Marginal? Le Champ de la Sociologie Militaire en France." *Les Champs de Mars* 1(6): 5–36.

Michelin, J. 2017. *Jonquille*. Paris: Gallimard.

Muxel, A., ed. 2017. *Croire et Faire Croire. Usages Politiques de la Croyance*. Paris: Presses de Sciences Po.

Muxel, A. 2018a. *Politiquement Jeune*. Paris: L'Aube.

Muxel, A., and O. Galland, eds. 2018b. *La Tentation Radicale. Enquête auprès des Lycéens*. Paris: PUF.

Nivet, B. 2006. "Complexe Européen de la Puissance: Une Analyse Critique du Concept d' Europe puissance." Doctoral dissertation, Université de Lille 2.

Nivet, B. 2012. "L'Europe de la Sécurité et de la Défense par-delà l'Européanisation: Un Champ Politique entre Normalisation et Renationalisations." *Les Champs de Mars* 24: 63–68.

Olsson, C., and P. Vermeren. 2007. "Militaires et Engagements Extérieurs: À la Conquête des Cœurs et des Esprits." *Cultures & Conflits* 67(3): 7–174.

Ouellet, E., P. Pahlavi, and M. Chennoufi, eds. 2005. *Les Études Stratégiques au XXIe siècle*. Montréal: Athéna.

Pajon, C. 2001. *Forces Armées et Société dans l'Allemagne Contemporaine*. Paris: L'Harmattan.

Pajon, C. 2005. "Le Sociologue Enrégimenté: Méthodes et Techniques d'Enquête en Milieu Militaire." In *Sociologie du Milieu Militaire. Les Conséquences de la Professionnalisation sur les Armées et l'Identité Militaire,* edited by F. Gresle, 45–56. Paris: L'Harmattan.

Paya y Pastor, A., C. Lafaye, and M. Thura. 2015. "Introduction", *Les Champs de Mars* 27(2): 9–22.

Planiol, A. 2016. "L'intégration des Femmes dans les Armées Américaines." *Etude de l'IRSEM* 43. Paris: Irsem.

Planiol, A. 2017a. "Les Blogs de Défense en France." *Etude de l'IRSEM* 47. Paris: Irsem.

Planiol, A., ed. 2017b. "Femmes Militaires, et Maintenant?" *Actes du Colloque, Mercredi 8 mars 2017*. Paris: École Militaire, Les Cahiers de la RDN/IRSEM.

Politique Européenne. 2015. "Les Politiques Militaires en Europe." *Héritage de Bastien Irondelle* 48(2): 8–200.

Porteret, V. 2003. "A la Recherche du Nouveau Visage des Armées et des Militaires Français: les Études Sociologiques du Centre d'Études en Sciences Sociales de la Défense." *Revue Française de Sociologie* 44(4): 799–822.

Porteret, V. 2005. *Etat-nation et Professionnalisation des Armées: Les Députés Français face au Déclin de l'Armée de Masse de 1962 à Nos Jours*. Paris: L'Harmattan.

Porteret, V., ed. 2007. *La Défense: Acteurs, Légitimité, Missions: Perspectives Sociologiques*. Paris: L'Harmattan.

Pouvoirs. 1986. "Les Armées." *Pouvoirs* 38: 3–125.

Pouvoirs. 2008. "L'armée Française." *Pouvoirs* 125(2): 5–120.

Prévot, E. 2008. *Corps et Armes. L'influence des 'Nouvelles Missions' sur le Sens du Métier Militaire*. Paris: L'Harmattan.

Prévot-Forni, E. 2006. "L'influence des *Nouvelles Missions* sur le Sens du Métier Militaire: La Fonction Identitaire des Représentations Professionnelles dans une Armée en Cours de Professionnalisation." Doctoral dissertation, Université de Paris 1.

Revue Française de Sociologie. 1961. "Guerre, Armée, Société." *Revue Française de Sociologie* 2(2).

Settoul, E. 2015a. "Classes Populaires et Engagement Militaire: Des Affinités Électives aux Stratégies d'Intégration Professionnelle." *Lien Social et Politiques* (74): 95–112.

Settoul, E. 2015b. "Analyser l'Immigration Postcoloniale en Milieu Militaire: Retour sur les Enseignements d'une Enquête ethnographique." *Les Champs de Mars* 27(2): 31–41.

Settoul, E. 2016. "Les Jeunes Issus de l'Immigration sont-ils moins Patriotes que les Autres?" In *Migrants, Migrations. 50 Questions pour Vous faire Votre Opinion*, edited by H. Thiollet, 76–78. Malakoff: Armand Colin.

Settoul, E. 2017. "Un Regard sur les Descendants de l'Immigration dans les Institutions Sécuritaires Françaises." *Migrations & Sociétés* 169(3): 13–24.

Sheppard, E. 2010. "L'européanisation des Politiques de Défense? Les Cas de la France et du Royaume-Uni 1995–2002." Doctoral dissertation, Paris, Institut d'Études Politiques.

Sorin, K. 2003. *Femmes en Armes, une Place Introuvable. Le Cas de la Féminisation des Armées Françaises.* Paris: L'Harmattan.

Teboul, J. 2017. *Corps Combattant: la Production du Soldat.* Paris: Editions de la Maison des Sciences de l'homme.

Thiebaut, C. 2015. "Opinions, Information et Réception: la Réactivité du Public Français aux Représentations Médiatiques de l'Europe de la Défense (1991–2008)." Doctoral dissertation, Université de Paris 1.

Thiéblemont, A. 1999. *Cultures et Logiques Militaires.* Paris: PUF.

Thiéblemont, A. 2000. "Contribution à une Socio-Ethnologie du Combat: La Vie Quotidienne d'Unités de Combat de l'Armée Française dans les Conflits Contemporains, Bosnie 1993–1995." *Les Champs de Mars* 7(1): 41–52.

Thiéblemont, A. 2002. "Unités de Combat en Bosnie (1992–95): La Tactique Déstructurée, la Débrouille, le Ludique." *Les Champs de Mars* 12(2): 85–122.

Thiéblemont, A. 2011. "Il n'est pas plutôt revenu qu'il lui faut repartir." *Inflexions* 18(3): 129–140.

Thiéblemont, A. 2013. Retours de Guerre et Parole en Berne. *Inflexions* 23(2): 135–142.

Thiéblemont, A. 2015. "Les Rapports du Combattant Français à l'Ennemi. Le Lointain et le Proche." *Inflexions* 28(1): 37–47.

Thura, M. 2014. "En Avant! Sociologie de l'Action Militaire et de l'Anticipation du Combat: Un Régiment d'Infanterie en route pour l'Afghanistan." Doctoral dissertation, Paris, Ecole des Hautes Etudes en Sciences Sociales.

Thura, M. 2015. "Armer le Lecteur. Relire la Sociologie Militaire à l'aune de ses Conditions de Production en France." *Dynamiques Internationales* 11, <http://dynamiques-internationales.com/wp-content/uploads/2016/02/Thura-DI-11.pdf> (last access: 3 February 2020).

Vennesson, P., ed. 2000a. *Politiques de Défense: Institutions, Innovations, Européanisation*. Paris: L'Harmattan.

Vennesson, P. 2000b. "Les sciences sociales. Quels apports pour la défense?" *Les Champs de Mars* 1(7): 7–18.

Vennesson, P. 2000c. "La Nouvelle Armée: La société Militaire Française en Tendances, 1962–2000." *Les Documents du C2SD*. Paris: Centre d'Études en Sciences Sociales de la Défense.

Vennesson, P. 2002. "Sciences Sociales et Défense: de 'l'Aide à la Decision' aux Contributions à l'Action Publique." *Les Champs de Mars* 11(1): 341–348.

Vennesson, P., ed. 2004. "Idées, Politiques de Défense et Stratégie. Dossier." *La Revue Française de Science Politique* 54(5): 749–858.

Vennesson, P. 2013. "Globalization and Al Qaeda's challenge to American." In *How 9/11 Changed our Ways of War*, edited by J. Burk, 232–260. Stanford: Stanford University Press.

Vennesson, P. 2015. "Cohesion and Misconduct: The French Army and the Mahé Affair." In *Frontline. Combat and Cohesion in the Twenty-First Century*, edited by A. King, 234–249. Oxford: Oxford University Press.

Weber, C. 2012. *A Genou les Hommes, Debout les Officiers: La Socialisation des Saints-Cyriens*. Rennes: Presses Universitaires de Rennes.

Weber, C., ed. 2015. *Les Femmes Militaires*. Rennes: Presses Universitaires de Rennes.

Wihtol de Wenden, C., and C. Bertossi. 2005. "Les Militaires Français Issus de l'Immigration." *Les Documents du C2SD* 78. Paris: Centre d'Études en Sciences Sociales de la Défense.

On the Rise? State and Challenges of Military Sociology in Germany

Heiko Biehl, Martin Elbe, and Markus Steinbrecher

1   Introduction

The Bundeswehr has been the army of the Federal Republic of Germany for more than six decades. As a close ally in the EU and NATO, it has been and still is engaged in numerous international missions from the Balkans to Afghanistan and Mali and enjoys a good reputation among the German public. Thus, the Bundeswehr could be regarded as a typical army of Western democracies. But its foundation and history were highly controversial. The rearmament of West Germany in the 1950s was met with considerable political and social resistance. Less than ten years after the end of World War II, broad sections of the German public protested vehemently against the re-introduction of armed forces. In order to overcome public resistance and gain the trust of the German population and its Western allies, the Bundeswehr was committed to close ties with civil society from the outset. The concept of *Leadership Development and Civic Education (Innere Führung)* – together with con-scription – was supposed to ensure that the Bundeswehr was adaptive to social developments and did not separate itself from society as a *state within a state* as was the case with the German armed forces in the first half of the 20th century. From the very beginning the Bundeswehr has been associated with a specific idea of civil-military relations. The concept of *Innere Führung* which is an overarching principle that affects all aspects of military service advocates a close relationship between armed forces and society. This guiding idea is a trademark of the Bundeswehr up to this day and close to the concept of civil-military relations presented by Morris Janowitz (1960) subsequently. *Innere Führung* has been the normative, political, and legal ideal of how the new West German armed forces should integrate into the young democracy and was accompanied by the founding of two civil Universities of the Bundeswehr (not to be mistaken as military academies) and a Bundeswehr Institute of Social Sciences in the early 1970s.

This ideal has defined a yardstick to provide sufficient grounds for military sociology research. However, as in many other Western countries, even this con-stellation did not lead to an unbroken success story. On the contrary, to this day, military sociology in Germany shares some deficits and weaknesses that are common in Western countries. Its position at universities is still rather marginal and it plays an outsider role within the institutionalized social sciences. Most of the empirical research is done on behalf of the armed forces and the Ministry of Defense (MoD). The Bundeswehr is often the subject of research and the gatekeeper, sponsor, and client for research at once. At the same time, German military sociology has some specifics. Due to the continuing relevance and presence of World War II in German public and academia, it is lagging behind military history in many regards. Furthermore, the concept of *Innere Führung* and the ubiquitous presence of theologians and lawyers within the armed forces have a normative imprint on internal and public discussions. Accordingly, a portrait of German military sociology promises both insights into the functioning of the sub-discipline in general and into the national specifics.

The following section analyzes the institutional setting of military sociology in Germany. Our focus is on the research institutes of the Bundeswehr which provide the bulk of empirical studies. We describe the conditions of their research and discuss the relations to civilian universities and neighbor disciplines. Furthermore, we analyze the practices of military sociology: How are studies on the armed forces carried out? Who influences them? Where and how are the results published? The third section outlines the main issues of military sociology in Germany. We mention relevant studies and findings and identify new topics and trends. The last section summarizes the relevant insights, provides an outlook on possible developments, and tries to characterize military sociology in Germany.

2   The Institutional Setting of Military Sociology in Germany

West German military sociology started in the 1960s. The works by the *Evangelische Studiengemeinschaft* (Picht 1965/66) as well as the studies under the guidance of René König (1980, 206 f.) at the University of Cologne have been references for military sociology research to this day. Since the 1970s institutes founded and funded by the Bundeswehr took over most of the research in military sociology. Two causes contributed to this development: On the one hand, civilian universities turned successively away from the armed forces as an object of investigation. On the other hand, the armed forces effectively tried to incorporate social research (Heinemann 2016). The establishment of the Bundeswehr Institute of Social Sciences (SOWI in German) was the immediate result of these efforts. The SOWI conducted military sociology mostly in the sense of empirical social research (for an overview see Dörfler-Dierken and Kümmel 2016b). Founded in 1974, the SOWI dominated military sociology in Germany for decades. First located in Munich and transferred to Strausberg (east of Berlin) after unification it was a research institute on behalf of the Bundeswehr. Approximately 20 scientists from various disciplines worked on joint projects. The SOWI brought together sociologists, political scientists, psychologists, theologians, anthropologists, historians, and even some natural scientists in an interdisciplinary endeavor. On behalf of the MoD, the SOWI carried out numerous surveys within the armed forces as well as among the civilian population.[1] The research ranged from questions of military socialization and training to studies on the cooperation of soldiers from different nations to surveys on the attitudes of the population, in particular of young people, to security policy (Dörfler-Dierken and Kümmel 2016a). Among its most prolific social scientists were Detlef Bald, Ekkehard Lippert, Paul Klein, Jürgen Kuhlmann, Günther Wachtler, and Ralf Zoll.

Charles Moskos drew a euphoric balance on the occasion of the 25th anniversary of the SOWI when declaring that the SOWI has been a "leader in research" (Moskos 1999; translation by the authors). In contrast, the evaluation by the *Wissenschaftsrat* (German Council of Science and Humanities) was more balanced – and certainly more accurate. The agency, responsible for scientific audits in Germany, certified in its report the SOWI's "predominantly good research performance" (Wissenschaftsrat 2009, 11; translation by the authors). The council criticized the appointment of management positions with non-academics from the political realm and the MoD's excessive influence on research projects. The dominant orientation towards the short-term demand of the MoD resulted in an insufficient theoretical base of the projects according to the evaluation report.

In 2013, the SOWI merged with the Military History Research Office (MGFA in German). The resulting Center for Military History and Social Sciences of the Bundeswehr (ZMSBw in German)[2] comprises about 60 academics, of whom about two thirds are historians and roughly one third social scientists. The ZMSBw stands in the tradition of the SOWI but with a different focus. Studies still follow the needs of the MoD, for example when analyzing how to improve retention (Richter 2016) or reporting on public opinion on security and defense policy (Steinbrecher et al. 2019). However, sociological debates and theoretical interests guide the research to a larger degree than was previously the case. The rising number of PhD theses (Hess 2020; Kramer 2017; Rothbart, forthcoming; Wanner 2019) is a concrete result of this development. First interdisciplinary projects are underway which analyze historical sources and use social science theories and methods (Loch 2021).

---

1   More than 120 research papers from 1975 on can be downloaded on the website of the succeeding institution <www.zmsbw.de> or via the ZMSBw's publication server and online repository: <https://opus4.kobv.de/opus4-zmsbw>.
2   <www.zmsbw.de> (last access: 17 December 2019).

The ZMSBw releases a whole range of publications from research reports and articles to anthologies and monographs. Its social scientists participate in the relevant international forums of military sociology like ISA (International Sociological Association), ERGOMAS (European Research Group on Military and Society), and IUS (Inter-University Seminar on Armed Forces and Society). Several of its members have held positions in these organizations. Gerhard Kümmel was secretary general and president of ISA's RC 01 (Research Committee on Armed Forces and Conflict Resolution). Ralf Zoll, Heinz-Ulrich Kohr, and Mathias Schönborn were among the founders of ERGOMAS in 1986. Currently, Markus Steinbrecher is coordinator of its working group on public opinion, mass media and the military. The ZMSBw also organizes its own national and international conferences on military sociology. Furthermore, its members participate in different international working groups within the NATO framework. A special feature are the many research projects carried out by the ZMSBw (and the former SOWI) with colleagues from different nations. When investigating military cooperation there have been numerous multinational projects on common structures (vom Hagen et al. 2006), international missions (Leonhard and Gareis 2008) and common security and defense policies (Biehl et al. 2013) (see section 3).

Outside the ZMSBw, other military institutions employ military sociologists. For example, the Bundeswehr Command and Staff College *(Führungsakademie der Bundeswehr)* in Hamburg, which is responsible for training staff officers. Social scientists at the Bundeswehr Centre for Public Affairs *(Zentrum Informationsarbeit Bundeswehr)* in Strausberg investigate public perceptions of the Bundeswehr from a public relations and information perspective. Some research can be found at the Leadership Development and Civic Education Centre *(Zentrum Innere Führung)* in Koblenz and at the George C. Marshall European Center for Security Studies in Garmisch-Partenkirchen, an institution jointly operated by the German and American armed forces. Military sociology, in contrast, is hardly present at the two Bundeswehr universities in Hamburg and Munich – reflecting the low degree of institutional establishment of the discipline at German universities in general.

Looking at the academic community in Germany as a whole, a comprehensive, continuous, and substantial presence of military sociology is still missing. Internationally, with RC 01 military sociology is a prominent part of the ISA, but there is no equivalent representation at the national level. The German Sociological Association (DGS in German) currently consists of 36 sections (plus additional committees and associations) none of which explicitly deals with military sociology issues. The same applies to the German Association for Political Science (DVPW in German). However, there are collaborations between military sociologists and other social scientists when researching the military as a case study for general sociological concepts. For example, Martin Elbe and Gregor Richter (2019) have compared retention in the military to other employers together with other colleagues. Nina Leonhard and Oliver Dimbath (2021) have used military tradition and memorials as case studies for collective memory. In addition, a group of researchers from the ZMSBw and civilian universities has analyzed public views on the balance between freedom and security (Steinbrecher et al. 2018). Although these efforts may be meritorious, there remains a lack of institutionalization of military sociology at German universities. There are only a few courses on military sociology at German universities and still no chair or even a department with a designation for military sociology (Potsdam University has a chair for military history which is unique in Germany). The only continuous academic circle on military sociology is the *Arbeitskreis Militär und Sozialwissenschaften* (AMS – Working Group on Military and Social Sciences).[3] Established in the early 1970s, it has held annual conferences bringing together academics, soldiers, journalists, bureaucrats, and politicians. The AMS has published over 50 books which tackle a range of topics from security policy and civil-military relations to research on recruitment and retention.

Although there is enough evidence to diagnose a marginalization of military sociology at universities and in established academia, there is also a glimmer of hope. In recent years, an increasing number of newcomers has entered the field and has provided fresh perspectives. The study of Rabea Haß (2016), for example, explicitly follows a critical perspective on the recruitment motivation of young soldiers. Sarah Kayß' (2018) comparison of young officers' collective memory in the British and German army and their different understanding of military tradition is another example. Some handbooks and textbooks provide an overview on military sociology from a German perspective: Volker Heins' and Jens Warburg's book (2004) provides a critical introduction to military sociology including international and German research. A large-scale handbook on military and social sciences by Sven B. Gareis and Paul Klein (2006) is available in a second edition. The same applies to the standard German textbook on military sociology (Leonhard and Werkner 2015). The latest summary on military sociology in German has been published by the ZMSBw (Dörfler-Dierken and Kümmel 2016b). Recent efforts to combine sociological and historical perspectives have received broad resonance in the academic field and in the broader public. Neitzel and Welzer (2011) as well as Römer (2012) have analyzed wiretap protocols of Wehrmacht soldiers in allied captivity and tried to explain their actions in the war. Kühl (2014) also has, based on (military) sociology theory and historical records, studied the murderous escalation in World War II. These new approaches have further expanded the methodological

---

3   <https://mil-soz.de> (last access: 11 December 2019).

approaches in German military sociology. While quantitative methods dominate in some fields like public opinion, qualitative methods dominate in other areas like research on military identities. More often than usual in general sociology, quantitative and qualitative approaches complement each other and go hand in hand in military sociology (see Biehl and Tomforde 2021). Studies on military missions often rely on a method mix combining questionnaires, group discussions, documents analysis, interviews, and participating observation (see section 3). When looking at the background of the researchers, a rule of thumb applies: Whereas the Bundeswehr institutes often carry out quantitative surveys, external researchers prefer qualitative methods. This division of labor has to do with the fact that access to the field is easier for internal military researchers. They are more likely to get authorization to carry out quantitative surveys (see below) – not least because the MoD hopes to be able to exercise greater influence on the use and communication of the data and results obtained.

Moreover, in recent years, the interest in theorizing on the armed forces and military violence has increased. Hans Joas and Wolfgang Knöbl (2008) were the first to trace the relevance of war in the sociological history of ideas. Their verdict is that sociology after World War II turned its gaze away from the armed forces and drew a far too peaceful picture of modern societies. This deficit provoked several attempts to grasp military violence in social theory (Kruse 2015; Spreen 2008). Remarkably, several authors (Kohl 2009; Kuchler 2013) rely on the systems theory by Niklas Luhmann, although (or because?) Luhmann himself has never systematically investigated war and the military.

The renewed interest in the armed forces is more than a coincidence with the changed tasks of the Bundeswehr after the end of the Cold War. The missions abroad, beginning immediately after German unification, led to a redefinition of civil-military relations. Sociology is becoming more and more aware of this, albeit with a clear division of labor. The ZMSBw provides the bulk of empirical research, external researchers prefer theoretical perspectives. These separate focuses are the result of the conditions of military sociology, especially of the multiple roles the armed forces have in the research process.

The Bundeswehr often is subject, gatekeeper and sponsor of research simultaneously and, in addition, politically responsible for the results. There are codified regulations when doing research in the armed forces (Bundesministerium der Verteidigung 2008). All empirical projects require approval by the German MoD – this holds true for internal and external researchers. Ministerial regulations define how and when research can be done. Some of these conditions, such as anonymity and voluntary participation in surveys, are self-evident. Other regulations provide room for political interpretation. This provides a tool by which studies that promise politically dangerous results, like possible right-wing extremist attitudes among soldiers, may be prohibited. Most projects sponsored by the MoD are problem-oriented and aim at practical insights and impact, often based on surveys among soldiers. These studies provide exclusive results. As a consequence, the MoD has a strong impact on research projects: it reviews concepts and designs, approves questionnaires, and evaluates the results before publication. The supervision is even closer when the Bundeswehr provides research funding. This is regularly the case for Bundeswehr institutes but also the case for some studies by external researchers.[4] Although this constellation is not optimal for independent academic research, military sociology in Germany has taken a remarkable development in recent years as the following overview on relevant research topics and issues illustrates.

3 Topics and Issues of Military Sociology in Germany

The previous section has made clear that military sociology in Germany institutionally resembles the situation in most other Western countries. On the one hand, a similar conclusion holds true with regard to the main topics of German military sociology. The research on military and social issues, military missions and public opinion largely follows international trends. On the other hand, German military sociology can be seen as a pioneer with regard to studies on military multi-nationality. The following sections offer a concentrated overview of the most important empirical studies on some core topics.

3.1 Recruitment and Retention, Female Soldiers and Military Identities

The Bundeswehr institutes have carried out most of the internal surveys on the armed forces.[5] Since the suspension of compulsory military service in 2011, recruitment and retention have become increasingly important in internal surveys. The armed forces are interested in how to recruit and retain soldiers. Before the suspen-

---

4   See e.g., <www.ispk.uni-kiel.de/de/projekte> and <www.ipw.rwth-aachen.de/wp/lehr-und-forschungsgebiet-internationale-beziehungen-und-politische-oekonomie> (last access: 20 December 2019).

5   Unfortunately, Bundeswehr psychologists have conducted various surveys among soldiers without publishing the results. Consequently, these empirically rich studies have no influence on public perceptions and academic discussions about the Bundeswehr. See the website of the Bundeswehr psychology research unit for further information: <www.bundeswehr.de/de/organisation/streitkraeftebasis/organisation/streitkraefteamt> (last access: 6 January 2020).

sion of the draft, there were concerns among the wider public that the Bundeswehr as an all-voluntary force would mainly attract people from underprivileged classes. Public intellectuals (Wolffsohn 2011) as well as the Protestant military bishop (Rink 2018) expressed this concern without corresponding empirical evidence, causing a public debate. The available empirical studies do not support these fears but point to the importance of identification with the military organization. Although incentives such as good pay, family-army-adjustment and other benefits have some relevance, the decisive factor is the match of individual values and preferences with those of the Bundeswehr as an employer (Richter 2016). Studies on short-serving soldiers have shown that the armed forces have deficits in clarifying the meaning of military service (Haß 2016; Kramer 2014). This mismatch may lead to frustration, disappointment, and the desire to leave the armed forces. There have been several studies on the civil careers of former soldiers (especially former officers). Broad public interest was drawn recently to a ZMSBw study on dual careers, with the participation of 1,028 former officers and 1,054 civil employers (Elbe 2019a). An up-to-date overview on research and concepts in military human resource management in Germany has been published by Martin Elbe and Gregor Richter (2019).

Like the contributions on personnel management, research on the integration of women has attracted considerable academic and public attention (Kümmel 2016). Since 2001, women have access to all services and positions in the Bundeswehr. As in other Western armies, the integration of women is not proceeding without setbacks. Sometimes, female soldiers encounter male comrades with reservations for which empirical research has identified two sources. On the one hand, conservative ideas of military professionalism and of a gendered division of labor favor a masculine image of the military and of the identity of soldiers. On the other hand, some male soldiers see women as competitors in the workplace and as a threat to their careers. The hope that a successful integration of women is just a question of time has not come true. Studies reveal that reservations about women do not diminish automatically over time (Kümmel 2016).

Another relevant field of research is that of military identities. Ulrich vom Hagen (2012) has presented theoretically ambitious work on the military profession. Drawing on Max Weber and Pierre Bourdieu, he develops a model of officers' habitus and traces it along empirical data. Philipp Münch (2016) relies on the work of vom Hagen and investigates its relevance in the mission in Afghanistan. He shows that internal criteria and orientations are more relevant for military decisions and soldiers' behavior than the impact on the Afghan society. Leonhard (2017, 2007) developed a typology of military identities based on a qualitative study of 55 in-depth interviews with young officers and non-commissioned officers. The typology was constructed along four independent dimensions, reflecting the attitudes of the interviewees towards (1) one's own military function; (2) one's own military status; (3) military values; and (4) the (German) armed forces' mission. This typology has been cited and used frequently. Jens Warburg (2008) has also dealt with the contradictions of the military profession. He illustrates that the current requirements of deployments abroad contribute simultaneously to the re-professionalization and de-professionalization of the military. As a result, soldiers' identity is overburdened and overstretched. Both works have identified the paradoxes that arise from the functional expansion of military action during missions abroad.

3.2   Out of Area – Research on and in Deployments Abroad

After German unification, the Bundeswehr has taken part in multiple missions abroad. From the end of the 1990s, military sociology in Germany has picked up this topic. Although a latecomer by international standards, twenty years of research have produced a wealth of studies. There have been research projects on all of the Bundeswehr's major operational areas: Bosnia-Hercegovina (Keller et al. 2004; Leonhard et al. 2008; Seiffert 2005), Kosovo (Biehl et al. 2001; Keller 2005), Afghanistan (Keller and Tomforde 2005a; Seiffert et al. 2012; Seiffert and Heß 2020) and Congo (Keller et al. 2008). Only the navy deployments are still missing, representing a serious gap given the specifics of maritime missions. Some of the studies cover the entire mission and accompany the soldiers before, during, and after the deployments. This research demands a lot from the researchers. They have to make contact with the units in the pre-training phase and take part in the training phases. The researchers accompany the soldiers for several weeks in the field and expose themselves to the same dangers. Methodologically, the studies mix quantitative and qualitative instruments. The quantitative questionnaires rely on comprehensive samples and get response rates of one third to almost half (the surveys are voluntary and anonymous), often leading to the sampling of several thousand soldiers. Various qualitative instruments such as participating observation, interviews, group discussions, and document analysis enrich the empirical picture.

Thematically, the tackled issues are extremely broad. One of the core topics is motivation and morale. The studies show that the motivation of Bundeswehr soldiers for and during deployment is consistently high (Pietsch 2012). A decisive factor is identification with the deployment, an insight that confirms the concept of latent ideology developed by Moskos (1970) in his Vietnam studies. Conversely, the main burden of the mission is the separation from the family, both for the soldiers and for those at home.

A further issue that runs through the studies are possible changes in the soldier's identity. Since the beginning of the missions abroad, the public and academic debate has been concerned that the experiences of conflict, war, and violence will shift the soldiers' professional identity away from the ideal of the socially anchored citizen in uniform – as manifested in *Innere Führung* – towards warrior mindsets detached from civilian life. The studies do not confirm these fears but paint a rather differentiated picture. The study on Afghanistan, for example, showed that deployments are not only associated with burdens. A remarkable proportion of mission veterans report that they have made strengthening experiences during missions. Nevertheless, a generational conflict is emerging within the armed forces (Seiffert and Heß 2020). Different levels of experience in deployments abroad between the military leadership on the one hand and the younger generation on the other hand may contribute to a change in organizational culture with long-term effects.

There are some valuable studies on military missions outside the Bundeswehr research institutions. For example, the studies presented by a project team of Freie Universität Berlin led by Michael Daxner and Christoph Zürcher made a significant contribution (Bonacker et al. 2010). They combine empirical insights with theoretical, normative, and questions of international law. In this way, they overcome the internal perspective that dominates most of the studies conducted by Bundeswehr institutions.

3.3   Fighting Together or Fighting Each Other? – Studies on Military Multi-Nationality

Just like the Bundeswehr as an organization has been a driver of military integration, military sociology in Germany has been a pioneer in research on multi-nationality. The commissioning of the first multinational military units in the late 1980s triggered a whole wave of research on this topic (Thießen 2016). The research focused on the integrated units: the Franco-German Brigade, the German-Dutch Corps and the Corps North-East, in which Germany, Denmark and Poland participate. The focus of interest has been on the interactions between soldiers of different nationalities and the conditions that facilitate and complicate cooperation (vom Hagen et al. 2006). The study designs have reflected the military cooperation: Most projects were carried out by a team of researchers from different countries. As a result, a whole range of publications is available, especially anthologies and journal articles (for an overview see Thießen 2016). A central finding of the research has been that the success of military cooperation is not solely due to the (military) cultural imprint of the soldiers. Structures and processes of the military organization also influence the formation of an identification with the multinational units.

Subsequent studies have supplemented and broadened these perspectives. A team of researchers from each of the four countries has investigated the cooperation of German, French, Italian and Spanish soldiers in Bosnia-Hercegovina (Leonhard et al. 2008). The deployment of the German-Dutch Corps in Afghanistan has also been the subject of a project (Keller and Tomforde 2006). A study by German and Dutch researchers has focused on the organizational culture at NATO headquarters SHAPE (Supreme Headquarters Allied Powers Europe) in Mons (Goldenberg et al. 2018). While all these studies focused on the micro-level of military subjects and interactions, the project, *Strategic Cultures in Europe,* has tried to consider the social and political macro-level. Comparative population surveys covering security policy preferences of eight European nations and a volume with country case studies covering all members of the European Union have complemented each other (Biehl et al 2011; Biehl et al. 2013). The analyses have led to the identification of three types of strategic cultures in Europe, with most states (e.g., Germany, Austria, or the United Kingdom) showing similarities and some (e.g., France) certain differences between the elite and population levels. Thus, extensive studies on military cooperation at the micro level of soldierly interaction and the macro level of security and defense policy are available. What is lacking are studies focusing on the cooperation between military organizations. A comparison of military cultures and their influence on military multi-nationality is a central research desideratum.

3.4   What do the Citizens Think?
Research on German Public Opinion

A main interest of German military sociology is public opinion on security policy and the armed forces. Even during the Cold War, the German MoD conducted regular surveys on security policy. The study called *Wehrpolitische Lage* (defense policy conditions, translation by the authors) primarily served to inform political decision-makers about public attitudes on defense policy. Especially in times of massive political mobilization – as during the debate in the early 1980s on nuclear arms modernization and the peace movement following the NATO Double-Track Decision – the surveys were a reliable instrument for tracking the opinions of citizens independently of demonstrations and protests or media coverage. In addition, external social scientists have used this survey data. In particular, Hans Rattinger and his team drew a dense picture of attitudes on security policy in Germany during the 1980s and early 1990s. They analyzed specific topics such as the public's perception of security and threats (Holst 1993) and methodologically relevant questions on the individual and aggregate (Isernia et al. 2002) stability of security policy attitudes. Following the rational public theorem of Page and Shapiro (1988, 1992), the results showed, in contrast to widespread presumptions in the political arena, in the armed forces, and in the literature, that public opinion on security and defense issues has been rather stable – at least as stable as with regard to other policies.

Since the mid-1990s, the SOWI and later the ZMSBw have conducted their annual population survey. Previously, the SOWI already conducted separate surveys on specific topics and selected population groups – mostly young people (Kohr 1988). Whereas these studies were sporadic and did not aim to generate time series, the current survey offers a representative and comprehensive overview of the security policy attitudes of German society based on a rather stable set of questions and instruments (Steinbrecher et al. 2019). The study covers perceptions of security and threats, attitudes towards the Bundeswehr and its tasks, preferences regarding defense spending, missions abroad and the interaction between citizens and soldiers. In addition, attitudes towards other nations, international cooperation, NATO, and the EU as well as general security postures are part of the survey. In a first step, the data serve to inform the German MoD. In a second step, the ZMSBw reports the main findings to the broader public. Finally, different academic publications use these data. Articles shed light on the attitude of Germans towards foreign deployments (Steinbrecher and Wanner 2020), to alliance defense (Biehl et al. 2017) or to knowledge of defense policy (Steinbrecher and Biehl 2020). The public availability of the data ensures their broad use – also by researchers from civilian universities. As a result, several dissertations (Endres 2018; Mader 2017; Pötzschke 2016; Rothbart, forthcoming; Wanner 2019) are based on the ZMSBw public opinion data.

It is not possible to summarize the richness of the findings and studies concisely. However, three results are worth mentioning because they run counter to widespread perceptions. Firstly, citizens' attitudes towards security policy are by no means arbitrary, coincidental, unsystematic and, as a result, easily manipulable. On the contrary, Germans have certain attitudes, such as preferences for multilateral cooperation and non-military solutions, which enjoy remarkable stability over time and influence other attitudes (Mader 2017; Steinbrecher et al. 2019). Secondly, this consistency in public opinion is due, among other things, to the fact that citizens' knowledge of defense issues is broader than often assumed. In fact, it corresponds to the average of their knowledge of other policies (Steinbrecher and Biehl 2020). Thirdly, the social standing of the Bundeswehr is better than many soldiers, political elites, and the public itself believe. It is true that a lot of Germans reject the use of military force. However, the armed forces and the soldiers themselves enjoy a high reputation. They have societal trust, and far more citizens support it than oppose it (Steinbrecher et al. 2019, 82–109).

3.5   Blind Spots in German Military Sociology

The topics and studies described so far highlight the strengths of military sociology in Germany. However, the picture is not complete without discussing the existing weaknesses. The blind spots of military sociology in Germany are relevant beyond doubt. To mention just a few examples, there are many studies on the social dimension of civil-military relations which are mostly based on public opinion surveys. However, there are hardly any studies on the political dimension of civil-military relations. Although Aurel Croissant and David Kühn have published on this issue their case studies mostly tackle Asian or American countries (for an exception see Croissant and Kühn 2011, 76−97). This gap is problematic because it is a central question from a historical perspective. From the German Empire to the Weimar Republic, the Third Reich and the Federal Republic of Germany, the question of how to integrate armed forces into the political system was a central component of constitutional controversies and political disputes. The large number of historical studies on these questions contrasts with the small number of military sociology studies (see Franke 2012). German military sociology thus lacks an element of the international debate on civil-military relations, which Samuel Huntington (1957) and Morris Janowitz (1960) have dominated to this day with their contrasting concepts.

Another gap in German military sociology is the analysis of military violence. Although this is the core purpose of armed forces, surprisingly few studies have devoted themselves to this topic. One can rightly accuse German military sociology (like that in other countries) of focusing too much on soft issues rather than on the hard issue of military force. An empirical analysis of public opinion towards military violence in Germany can be found in Kümmel, Klein, and Kozielski (2002). Studies on missions abroad also address this phenomenon (see above and Münch 2016). Aside from these examples, there are theoretical analyses by Leonhard and Franke (2015) and Elbe (2019b). Considering the boom in the sociology of violence in the last decade, which is only slowly approaching military violence, there are opportunities for cooperation that have remained largely untapped so far.

A third blind spot is the lack of current studies on the political attitudes of soldiers (for the US see Dempsey 2010, 45−151). As mentioned in the introduction the concept of *Innere Führung* aims to bind soldiers politically to the democratic system. It is therefore important to counteract anti-democratic convictions – from the left and from the right – within the armed forces. As in other countries, there are repeated prejudices in the public that a certain proportion of soldiers adhere to right-wing ideas. The extent to which this allegation is true cannot be determined on the basis of empirical data yet, as hardly any studies are available. The last relevant study dealt with the attitudes of young officers studying at the Bundeswehr universities (Bulmahn et al. 2010). It concluded that about 15 percent of them attach to positions of the New Right, which is remarkably less than among all civilian youngsters. In view of German history, the democratic reliability of the armed forces and the recent political polarization in Germany with the rise of the right-wing party, *Alternative für Deutschland* (Alternative for Germany – AfD), it is extremely interesting to know how popular this party is in the armed forces and how widespread right-wing positions are among soldiers. So far, there have been only speculations by outsiders but no reliable study. Given the political, social, and normative implications of the issue, it is difficult to capture the political attitudes of soldiers through simple surveys.

Another gap is related to the preference of German military sociology for micro-sociological approaches and qualitative and quantitative interviews among soldiers. More studies on the organizational logic of the armed forces are needed. During the Cold War, René König (1968) and Hans Geser (1983) provided important preliminary work, but current military sociology has rarely expanded on them (see as exception Kühl 2014). Theoretical analyses from an institutional perspective are provided by Apelt (2010) and Elbe and Richter (2012). Richter (2021) focuses on the organizational perspective of empirical research in the military. But still, in general, there is a shortcoming of analyses on military structures and processes that could complement the perspective of military actors. After all, a comprehensive understanding of the armed forces should more intensely look at the interplay between military structures, processes, and subjects.

4   Conclusion: The Way Ahead for German Military Sociology

German military sociology is an academic discipline that is evolving. For more than 20 years there has been a growing interest in military sociology research albeit – and this must be emphasized again – at a still limited level in the academic field. The overview of the state and development of military sociology has identified both strengths and weaknesses. Among the strengths of German military sociology are its rich empirical studies, its strong international ties, and its pioneering role in research projects on military multi-nationality. Obvious weaknesses are the dependence of research on the armed forces and its low resonance at civilian universities. At least three connected obstacles stand in the way of the further development, appreciation, and establishment of military sociology. First, military sociological research too often lacks the ability to connect to general sociological questions. Second, the Bundeswehr continues to exert a strong influence on empirical research. Third, there is a lack of a proper perception of military sociological research in academia and the public. The question therefore becomes: What steps does military sociology have to take in order to establish itself further as an academic discipline in the making. It must be clear, however, that its establishment does not depend solely on military sociology and its research. External factors in politics, society, science, and the military also influence the development of the field. German military sociology can take at least the following three steps to evolve.

First, cooperation with other fields of sociology should be strengthened. Studies should be undertaken which examine the armed forces from different angles as a case study for an overarching sociological question. Thus, the comparison of the armed forces with other organizations such as the police and fire departments, but also with companies, administrations, parties, or associations from an organizational-sociological perspective is most promising (see Elbe 2018; Kern et al. 2020). The integration of female soldiers could serve as an example of a gendered labor market. The relationship between military and politics is comparable to the relations between other functional elites from business, media, churches, academia, etc. Through these connections, military sociology as a sub-discipline could leave its echo chamber and its approaches, concepts and insights could have an impact on sociology in general.

Second, existing innovative approaches should be developed further. In particular, interdisciplinary studies promise exclusive insights and academic and public resonance. The aforementioned works by Neitzel and Welzer (2011) as well as by Kühl (2014) show that it is possible to profitably combine historical archive material with social science concepts. On the one hand, theoretical approaches gain in empirical density and resilience. On the other hand, it may be possible to better assess the broad and rich historical findings and discuss their generalizability. In particular, the ZMSBw brings together history and the social sciences and thus could play a pioneering role in this endeavor.

Third, closer links between existing empirical findings and theoretical discussions are necessary. So far, there seems to be a division of labor. The researchers who work for the Bundeswehr compile a wealth of empirical material and paint a robust picture of the inner workings of the armed forces and their relations with civil society. Sociologists outside the military, on the contrary, try to connect armed forces and war with social theory. Too often, however, there is a lack of mutual references and exchanges. This calls for studies that succeed both in arguing theoretically, in taking the empirical findings seriously, and testing the validity of the theoretical premises.

If the outlined measures were successful, the result could be a military sociology that would gain visibility, resonance, and impact not only as an academic discipline. The gain in academic reputation would also be an asset to use in intra-military conflicts and to secure the independence within the social sciences. Equally important would be a broader public perception. So far, the public often learns about the findings of military sociology when they are suitable for scandalization (Kümmel 2021). This is indeed a legitimate view on research in military sociology. All too often, however, the broader public ignores the interpretations and arguments offered by military sociology even if they could make a fruitful contribution to the public perception and to the control of the Bundeswehr. It is not only *Innere Führung* which demands such a control. For armed forces in a democracy, this close integration should be a matter of course.

References

Apelt, M., ed. 2010. *Forschungsthema: Militär. Militärische Organisationen im Spannungsfeld von Krieg, Gesellschaft und soldatischen Subjekten*. Wiesbaden: VS Verlag für Sozialwissenschaften.

Aulenbacher, B., M. Burawoy, K. Dörre, and J. Sittel, eds. 2017. *Öffentliche Soziologie. Wissenschaft im Dialog mit der Gesellschaft*. Frankfurt: Campus.

Bacevich, A. 2013. *Breach of Trust. How Americans Failed Their Soldiers and Their Country*. New York: Metropolitan Books.

Barlösius, E. 2008. *Zwischen Wissenschaft und Staat? Die Verortung der Ressortforschung*. Berlin: Wissenschaftszentrum Berlin für Sozialforschung.

Basham, V., A. Belkin, and J. Gifkins. 2015. "What is Critical Military Studies?" *Critical Military Studies* 1(1): 1−2.

Biehl, H. 2012. "Einsatzmotivation und Kampfmoral." In *Militärsoziologie – eine Einführung, 2nd updated and revised edition*, edited by N. Leonhard and I.-J. Werkner, 447−474. Wiesbaden: Springer VS.

Biehl, H., R. Fiebig, B. Giegerich, J. Jacobs, and A. Jonas. 2011. *Strategische Kulturen in Europa. Die Bürger Europas und ihre Streitkräfte*. Strausberg: Sozialwissenschaftliches Institut der Bundeswehr.

Biehl, H., B. Giegerich, and A. Jonas, eds. 2013. Strategic Cultures in Europe. Security and Defence Policies Across the Continent. Wiesbaden: Springer VS.

Biehl, H., and H. Schoen, eds. 2015. *Sicherheitspolitik und Streitkräfte im Urteil der Bürger. Theorien, Methoden, Befunde*. Wiesbaden: Springer VS.

Biehl, H., and M. Tomforde. 2021. "Quantitative und qualitative Methoden in der militärsoziologischen Forschung. Grundzüge, Gemeinsamkeiten, Unterschiede, Verknüpfungen." In *Empirische Sozialforschung in den Streitkräften. Positionen, Erfahrungen, Kontroversen*, edited by M. Elbe, H. Biehl, and M. Steinbrecher, 171–196. Berlin: Berliner Wissenschafts-Verlag. .

Biehl, H., U. vom Hagen, and R. Mackewitsch. 2001. "Motivating Soldiers. A Challenge for Officer Education." In *The Challenging Continuity of Change and the Military. Female Soldiers – Conflict Resolution – South America*, edited by G. Kümmel, 399–410. Proceedings of the Interim Conference 2000 of ISA RC 01. Strausberg: Sozialwissenschaftliches Institut der Bundeswehr.

Bonacker, T., M. Daxner, J. Free, and C. Zürcher, eds. 2010. *Interventionskultur. Zur Soziologie von Interventionsgesellschaften*. Wiesbaden: VS Verlag für Sozialwissenschaften.

Bulmahn, T., R. Fiebig, V. Wieninger, S. Greif, M.H. Flach, and M.A. Priewisch. 2010. *Ergebnisse der Studentenbefragung an den Universitäten der Bundeswehr Hamburg und München* 2007. Strausberg: Sozialwissenschaftliches Institut der Bundeswehr.

Bundesministerium der Verteidigung. 2008. "Zentrale Dienstvorschrift A-2600/1. Innere Führung. Selbstverständnis und Führungskultur." Berlin.

Bundesministerium der Verteidigung. 2014. "Zentrale Dienstvorschrift A-2713/2. Wissenschaftliche Arbeit des Zentrums für Militärgeschichte und Sozialwissenschaften der Bundeswehr." Berlin.

Bundesministerium der Verteidigung. 2015. "Ressortforschungsplan des Bundesministeriums der Verteidigung für 2016ff." Berlin.

Burawoy, M. 2005. "For Public Sociology." American *Sociological Review* 70(1): 4–28.

Burawoy, M. 2015. *Public Sociology. Öffentliche Soziologie gegen Marktfundamentalismus und globale Ungleichheit*. Translated by B. Aulenbacher and K. Dörre. Weinheim: Beltz Juventa.

Callaghan, J., and F. Kernic, eds. 2003. *Armed Forces and International Security. Global Trends and Issues*. Münster: Lit.

Carreiras, H., and C. Castro, eds. 2012. *Qualitative Methods in Military Studies. Research Experiences and Challenges*. Abingdon: Routledge.

Collmer, S., and G. Kümmel. 2007. "The Civil-Military Gap Among German Future Elites." In *Cultural Differences between the Military and Parent Society in Democratic Countries*, edited by G. Caforio, 255–259. Amsterdam: Elsevier.

Croissant, A., and D. Kühn. 2011. *Militär und zivile Politik*. München: Oldenbourg.

Dempsey, J. 2010. *Our Army. Soldiers, Politics, and American Civil-Military Relations*. Princeton: Princeton University Press.

Dörfler-Dierken, A., and G. Kümmel. 2016a. "Die Militärsoziologie, das Militär und die Zukunft." In *Am Puls der Bundeswehr. Militärsoziologie in Deutschland zwischen Wissenschaft, Politik, Bundeswehr und Gesellschaft*, edited by A. Dörfler-Dierken and G. Kümmel, 345–354. Wiesbaden: Springer VS.

Dörfler-Dierken, A., and G. Kümmel, eds. 2016b. *Am Puls der Bundeswehr. Militärsoziologie in Deutschland zwischen Wissenschaft, Politik, Bundeswehr und Gesellschaft*. Wiesbaden: Springer VS.

Elbe, M. 2018. "Failure in Public Institutions: Characteristics of Organizational Culture in the Military." In *Strategies in Failure Management. Scientific Insights, Case Studies and Tools*, edited by S. Kunert, 231–239. New York: Springer.

Elbe, M., ed. 2019a. *Duale Karriere als Institution. Perspektiven ziviler Karrieren ehemaliger Offiziere*. Berlin: Berliner Wissenschaftsverlag.

Elbe, M. 2019b. "Gewalt und Ethik als Bezugsgrößen militärischen Handelns – eine militärsoziologische Betrachtung." In *Soziologie für den öffentlichen Dienst (II): Konflikt und Gewalt in öffentlichen Organisationen*, edited by J. Groß, 26–40. Hamburg: Maximilian.

Elbe, M., and G. Richter, eds. 2019. *Personalmanagement in der Bundeswehr. Strategien, Zielgruppen, Kompetenzen*. Berlin: Berliner Wissenschafts-Verlag.

Elbe, M., and G. Richter. 2012. "Militär: Institution und Organisation." In *Militärsoziologie – Eine Einführung*. 2. ed., edited by N. Leonhard and I.-J. Werkner, 244–263. Wiesbaden: VS Verlag für Sozialwissenschaften.

Endres, F. 2018. "Öffentliche Meinung und strategische Kulturen. Außenpolitische Überzeugungen in Deutschland, Frankreich und Großbritannien." Doctoral dissertation, University of Mannheim. Wiesbaden: Springer VS.

Endres, F., H. Schoen, and H. Rattinger. 2015. "Außen- und Sicherheitspolitik aus Sicht der Bürger. Theoretische Perspektiven und ein Überblick über den Forschungsstand." In Sicherheitspolitik und Streitkräfte im Urteil der Bürger. Theorien, Methoden, Befunde, edited by H. Biehl and H. Schoen, 39–65. Wiesbaden: Springer VS.

Feaver, P.D., and R.H. Kohn, eds. 2001. *Soldiers and Civilians. The Civil-Military Gap and American National Security*. Cambridge, MA: MIT Press.

Franke, J. 2012. *Wie integriert ist die Bundeswehr? Eine Untersuchung zur Integrationssituation der Bundeswehr als Verteidigungs- und Einsatzarmee*. Baden-Baden: Nomos.

Gareis, S.B., and P. Klein, eds. 2006. *Handbuch Militär und Sozialwissenschaft*. 2nd updated and extended edition. Wiesbaden: VS Verlag für Sozialwissenschaften.

Geser, H. 1983. "Organisationsprobleme des Militärs." In Militär, Krieg, Gesellschaft. Texte zur Militärsoziologie, edited by Günther Wachtler, 139–164. Frankfurt a.M.: Campus.

Giegerich, B. 2006. *European Security and Strategic Culture. National Responses to the EU's Security and Defence Policy*. Baden-Baden: Nomos.

Goldenberg, I., H. Biehl, G. Richter, and J. Soeters. 2018. "Military-Civilian Organisational Culture within NATO SHAPE." In *STO Technical Report TR-HFM-226: Civilian and Military Personnel Integration and Collaboration in Defence Organizations*. 1–19. Brüssel: NATO.

Hartmann, U., C. von Rosen, and C. Walther, eds. 2012. *Jahrbuch Innere Führung 2012. Der Soldatenberuf im Spagat zwischen gesellschaftlicher Integration und sui generis-Ansprüchen. Gedanken zur Weiterentwicklung der Inneren Führung*. Berlin: Miles.

Haß, R. 2016. *Der Freiwillige Wehrdienst in der Bundeswehr. Ein Beitrag zur kritischen Militärsoziologie*. Wiesbaden: Springer VS.

Heinemann, W. 2016. "Das SOWI im Lichte der Akten." In *Am Puls der Bundeswehr. Militärsoziologie in Deutschland zwischen Wissenschaft, Politik, Bundeswehr und Gesellschaft*, edited by A. Dörfler-Dierken and G. Kümmel, 35–50. Wiesbaden: Springer VS.

Heins, V., and J. Warburg. 2004. *Kampf der Zivilisten. Militär und Gesellschaft im Wandel*. Bielefeld: transcript.

Hess, J. 2020. *Leviathan Staggering. A Quantitative Analysis of the State's Coercive Capacity and Intrastate Violence*. Berlin: Berliner Wissenschafts-Verlag.

Höfig, C. 2017. "'Man Shall Not Live by Bread Alone': Occupational Needs of Military Personnel and their Significance for the Attractiveness of the German Armed Forces as an Employer." *Res Militaris* Ergomas Issue 4: 1–15.

Hoffmann, H.-V. 1993. *Demoskopisches Meinungsbild in Deutschland zur Sicherheits- und Verteidigungspolitik 1992*. Waldbröl: AIK.

Holst, C. 1993. "Sicherheitsorientierung und status quo – Einstellungen zur Bundeswehr in der Bevölkerung in Ost- und Westdeutschland 1992 bis 1993. DFG-project 'Struktur und Determinanten außen- und sicherheitspolitischer Einstellungen in der Bundesrepublik Deutschland'." *Research Report 6*. Bamberg: Universität Bamberg.

Holsti, O. 1992. "Public Opinion and Foreign Policy: Challenges to the Almond-Lippmann Consensus." *International Studies Quarterly* 36(4): 439–466.

Huntington, S.P. 1957. *The Soldier and the State: The Theory and Politics of Civil-Military Relations*. Cambridge, MA: Belknap Press.

Hurwitz, J., and M. Peffley. 1987. "How Are Foreign Policy Attitudes Structured? A Hierarchical Model." *American Political Science Review* 81(4): 1099–1120.

Hurwitz, J., M. Peffley, and M. Seligson. 1993. "Foreign Policy Belief Systems in Comparative Perspective: The United States and Costa Rica." *International Studies Quarterly* 37(3): 245–270.

Isernia, P., Z. Juhász and H. Rattinger. 2002. "Foreign Policy and the Rational Public in Comparative Perspective." *Journal of Conflict Resolution* 46(2): 201–224.

Janowitz, M. 1960. *The Professional Soldier. A Social and Political Portrait.* New York: The Free Press.

Joas, H., and W. Knöbl. 2008. *Kriegsverdrängung. Ein Problem in der Geschichte der Sozialtheorie.* Frankfurt a.M.: Suhrkamp.

Junk, J., and C. Daase. 2013. "Germany." In *Strategic Cultures in Europe. Security and Defence Policies Across the Continent*, edited by H. Biehl, B. Giegerich, and A. Jonas, 139–152. Wiesbaden: Springer VS.

Kayß, S. 2018. *Identity, Motivation and Memory. The Role of History in the British and German Forces.* Abingdon: Routledge.

Keller, J. 2005. *Stimmungslage im 8. Einsatzkontingent KFOR nach dem Einsatz – Ergebnisbericht. Gutachten.* Strausberg: Sozialwissenschaftliches Institut der Bundeswehr.

Keller, J., J. Hennig, and I. Menke. 2008. *EUFOR RD CONGO. SOWI-Gutachten 2/2008.* Strausberg: Sozialwissenschaftliches Institut der Bundeswehr.

Keller, J., and M. Tomforde. 2006. *Multinationalität im Einsatz – 3. Einsatzkontingent ISAF. Gutachten.* Strausberg: Sozialwissenschaftliches Institut der Bundeswehr.

Keller, J., M. Tomforde, H. Biehl, C. Reinholz, and P. Kozielski. 2004. *Einsatzmotivation im 7. und 8. Einsatzkontingent SFOR – Ergebnisbericht. Gutachten.* Strausberg: Sozialwissenschaftliches Institut der Bundeswehr.

Kern, E.-M., G. Richter, J. Müller, and F.-H. Voß, eds. 2020. *Einsatzorganisationen: Erfolgreiches Handeln in Hochrisikosituationen.* Wiesbaden: Springer Gabler.

Kernic, F. 2001. *Sozialwissenschaften und Militär. Eine kritische Analyse.* Wiesbaden: Deutscher Universitäts-Verlag.

Klein, P. 2002. "Das Sozialwissenschaftliche Institut der Bundeswehr in der Politikberatung." In *Wissenschaft, Politik und Politikberatung. Erkundungen zu einem schwierigen Verhältnis*, edited by G. Kümmel, 31–49. Frankfurt a.M.: Peter Lang.

König, R. 1968. "Einige Bemerkungen zu den speziellen Problemen der Begründung einer Militärsoziologie." In *Beiträge zur Militärsoziologie. Kölner Zeitschrift für Soziologie und Sozialpsychologie. Special Issue 12*, edited by R. König, 7–12. Köln: Westdeutscher Verlag.

König, R. 1980. *Leben im Widerspruch. Versuch einer intellektuellen Biographie.* München: Carl Hanser.

Kohl, T. 2009. "Zum Militär der Politik." *Soziale Systeme. Zeitschrift für soziologische Theorie* 15(1): 160–188.

Kohn, R. 1997 "How Democracies Control the Military." *Journal of Democracy* 8(4): 140–153.

Kohr, H.-U. 1989. "Public Opinion Surveys on Security Policy and the Armed Forces: Policy Polling or Scientific Research?" *SOWI-Working Paper 25.* München: Sozialwissenschaftliches Institut der Bundeswehr.

Kramer, R. 2014. "Sozialwissenschaftliche Begleitstudie zur Evaluation des Freiwilligen Wehrdienstes. Ergebnisse der Zweitbefragung der Freiwilligen Wehrdienst Leistenden mit Diensteintritt im Zeitraum von Juli 2011 bis April 2012." *Forschungsbericht 108.* Potsdam: Zentrum für Militärgeschichte und Sozialwissenschaften der Bundeswehr.

Kramer, R. 2017. *Vergleichende Werbung für die Positionierung neuer Marken. Untersuchung der Werbewirkung mittels Strukturgleichungsanalyse.* Wiesbaden: Springer Gabler.

Kruse, V. 2015. *Kriegsgesellschaftliche Moderne. Zur strukturbildenden Dynamik großer Kriege.* Konstanz: UVK.

Kuchler, B. 2013. *Kriege. Eine Gesellschaftstheorie gewaltsamer Konflikte.* Frankfurt a.M.: Campus.

Kühl, S. 2014. *Ganz normale Organisationen. Zur Soziologie des Holocaust.* Frankfurt a.M.: Suhrkamp.

Kümmel, G. 2016. "Halb zog man sie, halb sank sie hin ... Die Bundeswehr und ihre Öffnung für Frauen." In *Am Puls der Bundeswehr. Militärsoziologie in Deutschland zwischen Wissenschaft, Politik, Bundeswehr und Gesellschaft*, edited by A. Dörfler-Dierken and G. Kümmel, 277–301. Wiesbaden: Springer VS.

Kümmel, G. 2021. "Die Wissenschaft und die Politik: Zur politischen Nutzung militärsoziologischer Forschungsergebnisse." In *Empirische Sozialforschung in den Streitkräften. Positionen, Erfahrungen, Kontroversen*, edited by M. Elbe, H. Biehl, and M. Steinbrecher, 149–168. Berlin: Berliner Wissenschafts-Verlag.

Kümmel, G., P. Klein, and P. Kozielski. 2002. *Die gewalttätige Gesellschaft. Erscheinungsformen und Ursachen von Gewalt – Handlungsmöglichkeiten für die Bundeswehr.* Strausberg: Sozialwissenschaftliches Institut der Bundeswehr.

Kümmel, G., and A.D. Prüfert, eds. 2000. *Military Sociology. The Richness of a Discipline.* Baden-Baden: Nomos.

Langer, P., and G. Kümmel, eds. 2015. *"Wir sind Bundeswehr" – Wie viel Vielfalt benötigen/vertragen die Streitkräfte?* Berlin: Miles.

Leonhard, N. 2007. *Berufliche Identität von Soldaten. Eine qualitative Untersuchung von jungen männlichen Soldaten der Bundeswehr aus den neuen und alten Bundesländern. SOWI-Gutachten 3/2007.* Strausberg: Sozialwissenschaftliches Institut der Bundeswehr.

Leonhard, N. 2017. "Towards a New German Military Identity? Change and Continuity of Military Representations of Self and Other(s) in Germany." *Critical Military Studies*. Online First: <https://doi.org/10.1080/23337486.2 017.1385586>.

Leonhard, N., G. Aubry, M. Casas Santero, and B. Jankowski, eds. 2008. *Military Co-operation in Multinational Missions: The Case of EUFOR in Bosnia and Herzegovina*. Strausberg: Sozialwissenschaftliches Institut der Bundeswehr.

Leonhard, N., and O. Dimbath, eds. 2021. *Gewaltgedächtnisse. Analysen zur Präsenz vergangener Gewalt*. Wiesbaden: Springer.

Leonhard, N., and J. Franke, eds. 2015. *Militär und Gewalt: Sozialwissenschaftliche und ethische Perspektiven*. Berlin: Duncker & Humblot.

Leonhard, N., and S.B. Gareis, eds. 2008. *Vereint marschieren – Marcher uni. Die deutsch-französische Streitkräftekooperation als Paradigma europäischer Streitkräfte?* Wiesbaden: VS Verlag für Sozialwissenschaften.

Leonhard, N., and I.-J. Werkner, eds. 2012. *Militärsoziologie – Eine Einführung*. 2nd updated and revised edition. Wiesbaden: VS Verlag für Sozialwissenschaften.

Lippert, E. 1995. "Verzögerte Aufklärung. Zur jämmerlichen Lage der deutschen Militärsoziologie." *Mittelweg 36*(4): 18–31.

Lippert, E., and G. Wachtler. 1982. "Militärsoziologie – eine Soziologie 'nur für den Dienstgebrauch'?" In *Soziologie und Praxis. Erfahrungen, Konflikte, Perspektiven*, edited by U. Beck, 335–355. Göttingen: Otto Schwartz & Co.

Loch, T. 2021. "Sozialforschung und Geschichtsschreibung: Betrachtungen eines Grenzgängers." In *Empirische Sozialforschung in den Streitkräften. Positionen, Erfahrungen, Kontroversen*, edited by M. Elbe, H. Biehl, and M. Steinbrecher, 437–459. Berlin: Berliner Wissenschafts-Verlag.

Mader, M. 2015. "Grundhaltungen zur Außen- und Sicherheitspolitik in Deutschland." In *Sicherheitspolitik und Streitkräfte im Urteil der Bürger. Theorien, Methoden, Befunde*, edited by H. Biehl and H. Schoen, 69–96. Wiesbaden: Springer VS.

Mader, M. 2017. *Öffentliche Meinung zu Auslandseinsätzen der Bundeswehr. Zwischen Antimilitarismus und transatlantischer Orientierung*. Wiesbaden: Springer VS.

Mader, M., and R. Fiebig. 2015. "Determinanten der Bevölkerungseinstellungen zum Afghanistaneinsatz. Prädispositionen, Erfolgswahrnehmungen und die moderierende Wirkung individueller Mediennutzung." In *Sicherheitspolitik und Streitkräfte im Urteil der Bürger. Theorien, Methoden, Befunde*, edited by H. Biehl and H. Schoen, 97–121. Wiesbaden: Springer VS.

Manigart, P. 2005. "Risks and Recruitment in Postmodern Armed Forces: The Case of Belgium." *Armed Forces & Society* 31(4): 559–582.

Mannitz, S., ed. 2012. *Democratic Civil-Military Relations. Soldiering in 21st Century Europe.* Abingdon: Routledge.

Moskos, C. 1970. *The American Enlisted Man.* New York: Russell Sage.

Moskos, C. 1977. "From Institution to Occupation: Trends in Military Organization." *Armed Forces & Society* 4(1): 41–50.

Moskos, C. 1999. "SOWI – 25 Jahre an der Spitze der militärsoziologischen Forschung." In *25 Jahre Sozialwissenschaftliches Institut der Bundeswehr. Eine zukunftsorientierte Standortbestimmung,* edited by SOWI, 33–36. Strausberg: Sozialwissenschaftliches Institut der Bundeswehr.

Moskos, C., J.A. Williams, and D. Segal, eds. 2000. *The Postmodern Military. Armed Forces after the Cold War.* Oxford: Oxford University Press.

Müller, H.-P. 2017. "Die Grenzen der Soziologie." In *Öffentliche Soziologie. Wissenschaft im Dialog mit der Gesellschaft,* edited by B. Aulenbacher, M. Burawoy, K. Dörre, and J. Sittel, 113–118. Frankfurt a.M.: Campus.

Münch, P. 2016. *Die Bundeswehr in Afghanistan. Militärische Handlungslogik in internationalen Interventionen.* Freiburg: Rombach.

Münkler, H. 2002. *Die neuen Kriege.* Reinbek: Rowohlt.

Nachtwei, W. 2016. "Sicherheitspolitische Entscheidungsprozesse und Ergebnisse militärsoziologischer Forschungen." In *Am Puls der Bundeswehr. Militärsoziologie in Deutschland zwischen Wissenschaft, Politik, Bundeswehr und Gesellschaft,* edited by A. Dörfler-Dierken and G. Kümmel, 151–165. Wiesbaden: Springer VS.

Naumann, K. 2012. "Zwischen Auftragsforschung und Gesellschaftsdiagnostik. Zum gegenwärtigen Stand der Militärsoziologie. WestEnd." *Neue Zeitschrift für Sozialforschung* 9(1/2): 126–138.

Neitzel, S., and H. Welzer. 2011. *Soldaten. Protokolle vom Kämpfen, Töten und Sterben.* Frankfurt a.M.: Fischer.

Page, B., and R. Shapiro. 1992. *The Rational Public: Fifty Years of Trends in Americans' Policy Preferences.* Chicago: University of Chicago Press.

Peffley, M., and J. Hurwitz. 1993. "Models of Attitude Constraint in Foreign Affairs." *Political Behavior* 15(1): 61–90.

Picht, G., ed. 1965/66. *Studien zur politischen und gesellschaftlichen Situation der Bundeswehr. Drei Bände.* Witten & Berlin: Eckart.

Pietsch, C. 2012. "Zur Motivation deutscher Soldatinnen und Soldaten für den Afghanistaneinsatz." In *Der Einsatz der Bundeswehr in Afghanistan. Sozial- und politikwissenschaftliche Perspektiven,* edited by A. Seiffert, P. Langer, and C. Pietsch, 101–121. Wiesbaden: Springer VS.

Pötzschke, J., H. Rattinger, and H. Schoen. 2012. "Persönlichkeit, Wertorientie-rungen und Einstellungen zu Außen- und Sicherheitspolitik in den Vereinigten Staaten." *Politische Psychologie* 2(2): 4–29.

Rahbek-Clemmensen, J., E.M. Archer, J. Barr, A. Belkin, M. Guerrero, C. Hall, and K.E.O. Swain. 2012. "Conceptualizing the Civil–Military Gap: A Research Note." *Armed Forces & Society* 38(4): 669–678.

Rattinger, H. 1990. "Bestimmungsfaktoren des Wahlverhaltens bei der amerikan-ischen Präsidentschaftswahl 1988 unter besonderer Berücksichtigung politis-cher Sachfragen." *Politische Vierteljahresschrift* 31(1): 54–78.

Rattinger, H., J. Behnke, and C. Holst. 1995. *Außenpolitik und öffentliche Meinung in der Bundesrepublik: Ein Datenhandbuch zu Umfragen seit 1954.* Frank-furt a.M.: Peter Lang.

Rattinger, H., H. Schoen, F. Endres, S. Jungkunz, M. Mader, and J. Pötzschke. 2016. *Old Friends in Troubled Waters. Policy Principles, Elites, and U.S.-German Relations at the Citizen Level After the Cold War.* Baden-Baden: Nomos.

Richter, G. 2016. "Wie attraktiv ist die Bundeswehr als Arbeitgeber? Ergebnisse der Personalbefragung 2016". *Forschungsbericht 113.* Potsdam: Zentrum für Militärgeschichte und Sozialwissenschaften der Bundeswehr.

Richter, G. 2021. "Ganz normale Organisationsforschung. Empirische Befragungen in der Bundeswehr." In *Empirische Sozialforschung in den Streitkräften. Positionen, Erfahrungen, Kontroversen,* edited by M. Elbe, H. Biehl, and M. Steinbrecher, 301–321. Berlin: Berliner Wissenschafts-Verlag.

Rink, S. 2018. "Neue Söldner?" *Tagesspiegel,* February 14, 2018. <https://causa.tagesspiegel.de/kolumnen/causa-autoren-1/neue-soeldner.html> (last access: 17 December 2019).

Risse-Kappen, T. 1991. "Public Opinion, Domestic Structure, and Foreign Policy in Liberal Democracies." *World Politics* 43(4): 479–512.

Römer, F. 2012. *Kameraden. Die Wehrmacht von innen.* München: Piper.

Roghmann, K., and R. Ziegler. 1977. "Militärsoziologie." In *Organisation Militär,* edited by R. Mayntz, K. Roghmann, and R. Ziegler, 142–227. Stuttgart: Ferdinand Enke.

Rothbart, C. Forthcoming. "Messfehler in interviewer-administrierten Befragun-gen zu politischen Einstellungen. Eine systematische Untersuchung zum Ein-fluss des Erhebungsinstruments, des Befragten, des Interviewers und der Inter-viewsituation auf die Qualität der Daten." Doctoral dissertation, Universität Potsdam.

Rowley, E., F. Weitz, and I.-J. Werkner. 2012. "Militärsoziologische Forschung in den USA und in Deutschland. Eine Literaturanalyse über fünf Jahrzehnte." In *Militärsoziologie – Eine Einführung*. 2nd updated and revised edition, edited by N. Leonhard and I.-J. Werkner, 495–519. Wiesbaden: VS Verlag für Sozialwissenschaften.

Schoen, H. 2004. "Winning by Priming? Campaign Strategies, Changing Determinants of Voting Intention, and the Outcome of the 2002 German Federal Election." *German Politics and Society* 22(3): 65–82.

Schoen, H. 2008. "Identity, Instrumental Self-Interest and Institutional Evaluations. Explaining Public Opinion on Common European Policies in Foreign Affairs and Defence." *European Union Politics* 9(1): 5–29.

Seiffert, A., and J. Heß. 2020. *Leben nach Afghanistan: Die Soldaten und Veteranen der Generation Einsatz der Bundeswehr. Ergebnisse der sozialwissenschaftlichen Langzeitbegleitung des 22. Kontingents ISAF*. Potsdam: Zentrum für Militärgeschichte und Sozialwissenschaften der Bundeswehr.

Seiffert, A., P. Langer and C. Pietsch, eds. 2012. *Der Einsatz der Bundeswehr in Afghanistan. Sozial- und politikwissenschaftliche Perspektiven*. Wiesbaden: Springer VS.

Shapiro, R., and B. Page. 1988. "Foreign Policy and the Rational Public." *Journal of Conflict Resolution* 32(2): 211–247.

Shils, E.A., and M. Janowitz. 1948. "Cohesion and Disintegration in the Wehrmacht in World War II." *Public Opinion Quarterly* 12(2): 280–315.

Spreen, D. 2008. *Krieg und Gesellschaft. Die Konstitutionsfunktion des Krieges für moderne Gesellschaften*. Berlin: Duncker & Humblot.

Steinbrecher, M., and H. Biehl. 2020. "Military Know-Nothings or (At Least) Military Know-Somethings? Knowledge of Defense Policy in Germany and Its Determinants." *Armed Forces & Society* 46(2): 302–322. Online First: <https://doi.org/10.1177/0095327X18811384>.

Steinbrecher, M., and H. Biehl. 2019. "Nur 'Freundliches Desinteresse'? Ausmaß und Determinanten Verteidigungspolitischen Wissens in Deutschland." In *Politisches Wissen. Relevanz, Messung und Befunde*, edited by B. Westle and M. Tausendpfund, 145–175. Wiesbaden: Springer VS.

Steinbrecher, M., H. Biehl, E. Bytzek, and U. Rosar, eds. 2018. *Freiheit oder Sicherheit? Ein Spannungsverhältnis aus Sicht der Bürgerinnen und Bürger*. Wiesbaden: Springer VS.

Steinbrecher, M., T. Graf, and H. Biehl. 2019. "Sicherheits- und verteidigungspolitisches Meinungsbild in der Bundesrepublik Deutschland. Ergebnisse der Bevölkerungsbefragung 2019." *Forschungsbericht 122*. Potsdam: Zentrum für Militärgeschichte und Sozialwissenschaften der Bundeswehr.

Steinbrecher, M., and M. Wanner. 2020. "Alles eine Frage des Erfolgs? Einstellungen zum internationalen Engagement Deutschlands und zum Einsatz in Afghanistan." In *Einsatz ohne Krieg? Die Bundeswehr nach 1990 zwischen politischem Auftrag und militärischer Wirklichkeit*, edited by M. Rink and J. Maurer, 255–275. Göttingen: Vandenhoeck & Ruprecht.

Stouffer, S., E. Suchman, L. Devinney, S. Star, and R. Williams. 1949/50. *The American Soldier. Studies in Social Psychology in World War II*. Four Volumes. Princeton, NJ: Princeton University Press.

Thießen, J. 2016. "True love? Neue Herausforderungen für die Militärsoziologie nach der Wende." In *Am Puls der Bundeswehr. Militärsoziologie in Deutschland zwischen Wissenschaft, Politik, Bundeswehr und Gesellschaf*, edited by A. Dörfler-Dierken and G. Kümmel, 57–66. Wiesbaden: Springer VS.

Tresch, T., and C. Leuprecht, eds. 2010. *Europe without Soldiers? Recruitment and Retention across the Armed Forces of Europe*. Kingston: McGill-Queen's University Press.

Viehrig, H. 2010. *Militärische Auslandseinsätze. Die Entscheidungen europäischer Staaten zwischen 2000 und 2006*. Wiesbaden: VS Verlag für Sozialwissenschaften.

von Bredow, W. 2008. *Militär und Demokratie in Deutschland. Eine Einführung*. Wiesbaden: VS Verlag für Sozialwissenschaften.

vom Hagen, U. 2012. *Homo militaris. Perspektiven einer kritischen Militärsoziologie*. Bielefeld: transcript.

vom Hagen, U., R. Moelker, and J. Soeters, eds. 2006. *Cultural Interoperability. Ten Years of Research into Co-operation in the First German-Netherlands Corps*. Strausberg: Sozialwissenschaftliches Institut der Bundeswehr.

Wachtler, G., ed. 1983. *Militär, Krieg, Gesellschaft. Texte zur Militärsoziologie*. Frankfurt a.M.: Campus.

Wanner, M. 2019. *Das Ansehen der Bundeswehr. Persönliche Einstellung versus Meinungsklimawahrnehmung*. Baden-Baden: Nomos.

Warburg, J. 2008. *Das Militär und seine Subjekte. Zur Soziologie des Krieges*. Bielefeld: transcript.

Werkner, I.-J. 2003. *Allgemeine Trends und Entwicklungslinien in den europäischen Wehrsystemen*. Strausberg: Sozialwissenschaftliches Institut der Bundeswehr.

West, B., and S. Matthewman. 2016. "Towards a Strong Program in the Sociology of War, the Military and Civil Society." *Journal of Sociology* 52(3): 482–499.

Wiesendahl, E. 2016. "Vom Nutzen und Nachteil sozialwissenschaftlicher Forschung für die Bundeswehr." In *Am Puls der Bundeswehr. Militärsoziologie in Deutschland zwischen Wissenschaft, Politik, Bundeswehr und Gesellschaft*, edited by A. Dörfler-Dierken and G. Kümmel, 85–103. Wiesbaden: Springer VS.

Wissenschaftsrat. 2009. *Stellungnahme zum Sozialwissenschaftlichen Institut der Bundeswehr (SWInstBw), Strausberg.* Bonn: Wissenschaftsrat.

Wolffsohn, M. 2011. "Die Unterschicht übernimmt die Landesverteidigung." *Die Welt*, January 11, 2011.

Zoll, R. 2016. "Von wissenschaftlicher Politikberatung zur militärischen Dienststelle. Eine Kurzgeschichte des Sozialwissenschaftlichen Instituts der Bundeswehr (SOWI)." In *Am Puls der Bundeswehr. Militärsoziologie in Deutschland zwischen Wissenschaft, Politik, Bundeswehr und Gesellschaft*, edited by A. Dörfler-Dierken and G. Kümmel, 21–33. Wiesbaden: Springer VS.

Military Sociology in Israel

Eyal Ben-Ari

1   Introduction[1]

The field of military sociology – and its allied disciplines of social psychology and parts of political science – in Israel is alive and well. Key scholars continue to supervise students and publish substantial studies about the Israeli Defense Forces (IDF). This review will argue the field is marked by a continued expansion of topics for research, embeddedness of Israeli scholars in the global academic system, expanded theoretical pluralization and an emerging consensus about critical sociological perspectives being of higher academic status than others. While I use *military sociologist* as a convenient shorthand for the scholars I refer to, be cautioned that the term may miss the self-labelling of many scholars who see themselves as critical of the IDF, who view the military as an arena for exploring other theoretical issues (such as gender, power, or inequality) or who study multiple areas and topics. To be clear, I use the term simply to denote sociologists (and allied scholars) who investigate the armed forces.

In this chapter, I chart out the main developments only during the past decade and a half. My analysis is based on being a rather active participant in the community, previous reviews (Barak and Sheffer 2010; Cohen 2008; Rosman 2018b; Sasson-Levy 2011b) and many discussions with fellow scholars. Accordingly, consider three provisos related to its limits. First, my emphasis is on recent, ongoing work and not on historical developments. Second, the citations I offer are not sustained overviews but exemplifications of trends and topics. And third, the issues that military sociology deals with in Israel are closely related both to the changed forms of armed conflict and the military occupation that the IDF is involved in (Ben-Eliezer 2012; Sher et al. 2014) as well as to the substantial transformations that Israeli society has been undergoing since the late 1980s (Cohen 2008; Levy 2008). These include increasingly contested politics and the advent of neo-liberal ideologies governing many parts of society, a thriving economy with greater social

1   Acknowledgements: Thanks are due to Uzi Ben-Shalom, Nir Gazit, Yagil Levy, Edna Lomsky-Feder, Elisheva Rosman and to the editors of this volume for very good comments and discussions leading to this chapter.

inequality, a move towards more nationalist sentiments among the general voting public along with a continued *normalization* of the military occupation and the mediatization and judicialization of society leading to the IDF being ever more closely scrutinized. Thus, a sustained analysis of the impact of these trends on the study of the military is beyond the confines of this essay.

This chapter is structured along the following lines. I begin by tracing out the main institutions and funding through which research takes place and then will explain its impact. I then look at the main theoretical frameworks and topics that characterize military sociology in Israel. This section will be followed by an explanation of the main gaps in current studies and how Israeli academics are influenced by global trends in publication. I end with a conclusion about the reasons for the richness of the field in Israel.

2   Military Sociology: Institutions, Funding, and Impact

2.1   Academic institutions

Scholarly work in military sociology is carried out and presented in various contexts. Scholars who do relevant research belong to many of Israel's civilian universities and colleges. There is no program devoted solely to the field and research and teaching is carried out by individual scholars according to their interests and decisions. These institutions are populated by scholars who carried out their doctoral studies in the 1980s (many of them in or approaching retirement) and by younger researchers who have completed their PhDs since that period. Almost all of these scholars have either studied abroad or spent significant periods in academic institutions outside Israel. I shall return to the studies carried out by these scholars in later sections. Here I add a number of other institutional frameworks that are of importance.

2.2   Internal IDF Research

Within the IDF it is primarily members of the Behavioral Sciences Center (known as MAMDA by its Hebrew acronym) and its offshoots that carry out research in military sociology either by themselves or along with external academics through a special research branch. In existence since 1980 when established by Reuven Gal, the Center also oversees research carried out by other units such as the Gender Advisor to the Chief of Staff, the Air Force, the Home Front Command, or the Intelligence Corps. All these units carry out repeated studies (of public opinion for instance) and one-time projects either dictated by senior commanders or un-dertaken by members' own initiative. The topics that have or are studied include leadership and cohesion, motivation and civil-military relations or organizational culture. During the past two decades two journals (now defunct) were published within the units affiliated with MAMDA: *Mirrors of Leadership* published by the School for Leadership Development and *Military Psychology* which was, despite its name, actually dominated by sociological studies. Another journal called *Between the Arenas* has been published by MAMDA for many years but is only for an audi-ence within the IDF.

While initially dominated by a social psychological orientation, over the years MAMDA has moved towards various forms of sociology, partly a result of dealing with the place of the IDF in Israeli society and systemic organizational problems the military faced (Ben-Ishai 2017; Lehrer and Amram-Katz 2011; Sher and Ben-Eliyahu 2011). This move was reinforced by the addition of organizational psy-chology to the analytical toolbox of the Center, and by a blurred borderline with organizational sociology (Ben-Shalom and Fox 2009). MAMDA is now marked by two major orientations: a critical functional perspective, that is, one not derived from questions about inequality or changing power relations but rather employed to improve operational effectiveness and efficiency; and cultural approaches de-voted to deciphering key logics or codes of action out of an understanding that assumptions shape behavior. While many studies carried out within MAMDA have critical potential (for example, to gender relations or social inequality), they have been results of research intended and framed as contributing to the smoother running of the IDF.

Almost all researchers within the IDF are serving military officers (there are less than a handful of civilians employed directly by the force). As such they are subject to the same conditions and discipline as other regular officers. However, to an ex-tent since they are considered experts – for example, military engineers or lawyers – they are granted a separate status based primarily on their educational achieve-ments. More important, this expertise awards them a degree of independence both to pursue research and to voice their findings in internal military forums.

2.3   Professional Associations

The Association for Civil-Military Studies in Israel brings together most of the sociologists of the military in conferences held every two years and in occasional additional seminars. It too was established in the mid-2000s by Reuven Gal, long a member in the field, and has successfully gathered scholars from military sociology and other disciplines (for example geographers, economists, clinical psychologists and even occasionally philosophers). No less important, it is a forum where military research officers present some of their own work and interact with civilian scholars. However, sadly, the meetings of the Association are boycotted by some of the self-labelled critical sociologists who see it as a bastion of conservative thought and a forum too open and subservient to the IDF. Ironically, however, many students supervised by these very scholars regularly appear in the conferences and have even won some of its prizes. In addition, it is important to note the activities of the section of military and security of the Israel Sociological Association. It organizes panels at the Association's annual conferences, occasional workshops that yield publications and tours of conflict areas. This section is also an important forum for bringing together military and civilian scholars.

2.4   Cooperation across Institutions

A positive development is a host of cooperative projects linking scholars from different institutions. These include studies by Oren Barak and Gabi Sheffer on the military and militarization in Israel, Orna Sasson-Levy and Edna Lomsky-Feder on gender, Edna Lomsky-Feder as well as myself on militarism in Israel and the management of diversity, or Gabriel (Gabi) Ben-Dor and Ami Pedahzur on reserves. In addition, some academics have been key actors in working with others on various issues such as Kobi Michael and others on civil-military relations, Ami Oren and others on geography and the military, Uzi Ben-Shalom and others on social psychology, or Udi Lebel and others on commemoration. In addition, Sasson-Levy, Lomsky-Feder, Stuart Cohen and myself have published jointly with many former students.

2.5   International Contacts

Finally, turning outward, it is important to note that Israeli scholars regularly appear in great numbers in relevant international forums: the US based Inter-University Seminar on Armed Forces and Society (IUS), the European Research Group on Military and Society (ERGOMAS) and the global Research Committee 01 (RC 01) on Armed Forces and Conflict Resolution of the International Sociological Association (ISA). And indeed, my impression is that, per-capita, Israel is one of the countries with the highest participation ratios in international forums. In fact, several Israelis have been highly active members in committees related to these forums and Yagil Levy is past president of ERGOMAS and initiated its ties with Springer Publishers. These forums and committees have provided important arenas for cross-fertilization of ideas and the forging of interpersonal research links across national boundaries. In this respect, a major impetus for change has been the expansion of European centers and associations and the close alliance of Israelis with them. As I argue elsewhere (Ben-Ari 2016), the most theoretically innovative ideas in military sociology have been generated in Europe (and in other countries) and not the US where military sociology is in the doldrums.

2.6   Doing Research in and on the Military

A turning point in doing research within the military took place in the mid-2000s after the Second Lebanon War. While MAMDA encourages research and the IDF Chief Censor's Office covers only operational matters, the main problem is with the IDF Spokesperson's office since it also has the power to vet all academic publications based on official funding or research allowed within the armed forces. Vetting does not refer only to pre-checking research so that the office can react to media enquiries but much more importantly to control publication practices. Due to the IDF's perceived failure in the Second Lebanon War and the fact that the missions the armed forces execute are politically contested (for example, policing the Occupied Territories or targeted assassinations), any research deemed damaging to the image of the army is regarded problematic by the Spokesperson's office.

This situation has been exacerbated by the fact that so many issues in Israel are politically contested. In effect, this situation means that IDF control over publication (rather than research per se) is wielded directly by this office. Moreover, this is essentially an organizational control over (some) topics rather than political control in the sense of party politicians influencing subjects of study. The control of the IDF Spokesperson's office arises primarily out of considerations related to maintaining a good public image of the IDF and especially to how military themes are reported about in the media.

However, since Israel is an open society and since there are numerous people who have served in the military due to conscription, reserve duty or as regulars (primarily retired officers) and due to the country's relatively small geographical size, much work can be done outside the confines of the IDF. Accordingly, scholars have frequently interviewed or sent out questionnaires to people with past military experience as part of their research (e.g., Ben-Ari et al. 2010; Sasson-Levy and Lomsky-Feder 2018). To the best of my knowledge, there has not been any limitation placed on publication of these kinds of findings. In addition, a very significant amount of data about the IDF in traditional and new media (including news sites and a host of blogs, forums, and discussion groups) has been used in recent studies (Golan and Ben-Ari 2017; Israeli and Rosman-Stollman 2015; Kuntzman and Stein 2014).

2.7   Funding

Funding for research includes both internal and external sources. Thus, in the past MAMDA has been a key funder of research that it saw as relevant. Research enabled by this funding has primarily involved coalitions of internal and external researchers (Ben-Ari et al. 2010; Lomsky-Feder and Ben-Ari 2012; Sasson-Levy and Amram-Katz 2007). With the downsizing of the IDF for the past decade or so, however, the amount of sociological research funded and enabled by the IDF has greatly diminished. Among some critical scholars there is at best an ambivalent attitude towards receiving official funding for research or even a complete rejection of such funds lest the researchers be seen as somehow collaborating or subservient to the needs and interests of the military. These scholars, as well as some scholars cooperating with the IDF have been funded by either national funding agencies or by their universities' research bodies.

2.8   Public Perceptions of the Findings of Military Sociology

With the exception of Yagil Levy, who regularly appears in Haaretz which is Israel's prime left-leaning daily newspaper, military sociology is not very prominent in public media forums. There is some activity of scholars in the new media and various blogs and discussion forums, but these are mostly limited in their breadth and often involve preaching to the converted. In addition, members of the Institute for National Strategic Studies, a policy-oriented body located in Tel Aviv, report about social issues related to the military in press releases and very occasionally the heads of MAMDA and the IDF Mental Health Unit are involved in media reports. For a time as the *gender wars* waged over the service of women in new military occupations and over the joint service of religious men and women, Orna Sasson-Levy was subject to rather vicious attacks in some media outlets, but this controversy has died down. A particular Israeli problem is that with so many people having military experience very often scholarly opinions are met with anecdotal evidence in public non-academic venues.

At the same time, much activity takes place in committees or internal reviews in which some researchers participate. While not open to the public they nevertheless are a form of participation in various consultative processes. Finally, Yagil Levy of the Open University and, to a certain extent, myself (sometimes together) regularly organize(s) working groups, conferences and workshops that are open to the public and which are occasionally reported by the media. The Institute for National Strategic Studies also occasionally organizes working groups or meetings related to military sociology although these are often closed to the academic public or are merely public relations events. In general, this institute is analytically and conceptually quite conservative and the academic level of most (but not all) of its members leaves much to be desired.

3   Theories, Topics and Themes

Even a cursory inspection of the field reveals an impressive array of themes and topics that have been and are being studied. What follows is a very rough typology of clusters of themes that seem, to me, to be closely related. To begin, many of the issues now studied are a continuation of research interests sometimes harking back decades but often using more contemporary theoretical frames. These include the study of military elites (Barak and Tzur 2012), decision-making (Peri 2006), civil-military relations (Gal 2014b; Lebel and Lewin 2015) or public opinion (Tiargan and Eran Jona 2015). To these important macro and meso levels, studies of motivation (Ben-Shalom and Benbenisty 2016), leadership (Padan 2017) and families (Eran Jona 2009) can be added. The major emerging fields include the following.

3.1   Militarism and Militarization

The critical study of militarization includes investigations into inequality, material militarism or militarism in general (Levy 2007, 2008, 2012b; Livio 2018; Weiss 2014) and has been closely allied with analyses of the cultural processes undergirding militarism to include projects on the social legitimation of the enlargement of the IDF (Safrai 2018), how conscientious objection highlights militarism (Weiss 2014), Gazit and Levy's (2016) anthology that looks at education and the military, Levy and Sasson-Levy's (2008) examination of military socialization as a form of class reproduction, or the militarization of the country's geography (Oren and Michael 2013; Tzfadia et al. 2010). Intertwined with this work are studies of cultural discourses centered on the IDF including investigations of psychological discourses (Lomsky-Feder and Ben-Ari 2010), discourses about suicide of soldiers (Rothem 2018b) those centered on refusers and conscientious objectors (Livio 2014, 2015; Perez 2014, 2018; Weiss 2014, 2016, 2018) or of protest and dissent (Katriel and Shavit 2013; Sasson-Levy et al. 2011) as well as studies of the culture and politics of trauma within which troops are a central actor (Friedman Peleg 2017; Friedman-Peleg and Bilu 2011; Friedman-Peleg and Goodman 2010).

3.2   Gender

By far, the most numerous studies (reflecting global preoccupations) are on gender. These have been spearheaded by Orna Sasson-Levy alone (2006) or (later) by
Edna Lomsky-Feder to cover a very impressive array of issues. The wider move
in gender studies has been an analysis of inequality regimes and intersectionality
but also to women as agents of change (Sasson-Levy 2011a, 2011b). Prime examples of relevant studies include citizenship (Lomsky-Feder and Sasson-Levy 2015),
multiple models of women's service (Amram-Katz 2018); the intersection of ethnicity and gender among female secretaries (Lomsky-Feder et al. 2018), the links
between ethnicity and gender among male combat soldiers (Grosswirth-Kachtan
2016, 2017, 2018; Kachtan 2012), gender at the individual soldier and unit levels (Sasson-Levy and Lomsky-Feder 2018), gender integration in officer training
(Sasson-Levy and Amram-Katz 2007), the experience of junior female officers in
wielding power (Karazi-Presler 2018; Karazi-Presler et al. 2018), visual imagery
reinforcing gender images (Brownfield-Stein 2010; 2018), or organizational forms
reproducing masculinities (Wasserman et al. 2018). Included in this last regard are
also investigations of the image of warrior and alternative ideals of masculinities
(Hakak 2016; Kachtan and Wasserman 2015; Sasson-Levy 2008) or sexual orientation (Kaplan and Rosenman 2012). A focus on gender and the military can also
be found in studies of the management of diversity (Lomsky-Feder and Ben-Ari
2007, 2012).

3.3   Religionization

Another major area of study – and one fiercely contested both among the wider
public and among academics – is the religionization or theocratization of the military (Cohen 2008; Drory 2008, 2015; Gal and Libel 2012; Hakak 2016; Libel and
Gal 2015; Rosman 2014, 2015, 2018). These studies have charted out the effects
of the growing power of Jewish religious groups outside and within the IDF, the
role of chaplains and the Chief Military Rabbinate (Cohen et al. 2016; Kampinsky
2015) and the contradictions between religiosity and feminism as they impact lo-
cal-unit dynamics (Levy 2010b, 2014, 2015b).

3.4   A Market Army

Led singlehandedly by Yagil Levy, the study of the spread of neo-liberal ideas into
Israel and its effect on the country's armed forces has emerged as a new cluster of
projects. These studies go beyond previous ones about the privatization of the IDF

or the introduction of management methods into it (Seidman 2010) by introducing the theoretical concept of market army (Levy 2010a; Levy et al. 2020). Among the issues dealt with are the IDF's policy towards the recruitment and retention of technological versus combat soldiers (Harness 2020), changes in officers' career model within neoliberal concepts coloring IDF practices (Safrai 2020), or the recruitment of ultra-Orthodox men to the army as a mechanism generated primarily by market forces and economic incentives (Malchi 2020).

3.5   Death, Mourning and Commemoration

A large corpus of studies involves the study of mourning, commemoration and bereavement including the power of bereaved parents as a political force (Hermoni and Lebel 2012; Kaplan 2012, 2013; Lebel 2007, 2013a; Lebel and Rochlin 2009; Lomsky-Feder 2009) or the dynamics of social representation leading to casualty aversion (Lebel 2010b). A no less important set of issues involves what Levy (2012b) calls a society's death hierarchy or how the calculation of casualties ranges along an axis of socially constructed values.

3.6   Media, Representations, and Discourses

Work on the media has developed in two directions. The first involves internal changes within the military centered on how the old and new media have become part of the arsenal of the IDF and are managed by a hugely expanded IDF Spokesperson's Office (Golan and Ben-Ari 2017; Lebel 2010a; Peri 2017; Shavit 2017). The second centers on images and depictions of the IDF and soldiers in the media. These studies include work on rear-echelon troops in film (Barak and Inbar 2018), combat soldiers in the media (Israeli and Rosman-Stollman 2015; Rosman and Israeli 2015) or how militarism is reproduced via new media (Kuntsman and Stein 2015).

3.7   The New Wars and the Old Military Occupation

Studies of conflicts the IDF is involved in have also developed in several directions. The main preoccupation of the IDF (in terms of time and personnel if not resources) is the military occupation of Palestine (Azulai and Ophir 2008; Berda 2012, 2017; Gazit 2009; Gordon 2008; Ram 2017; Weizman 2017). The thrust of these works is the continued expansion and transformation of military rule over the Palestinian population and the mechanisms by which occupation is maintained and adapted. A small number of studies has also examined how the military occupation is saturated with violence (or its potential) (Grossman et al. 2015; Manekin 2013, 2017) and how sporadic episodes of high-intensity fighting are experienced by ground-level units (Ben-Ari et al. 2010; Gazit and Ben-Ari 2017) and the violence wielded by Jewish settlers with IDF consent (Gazit 2015). Nevertheless, to follow Ben-Eliezer (2017), relatively few studies have traced out the implications of the occupation for wider Israeli society. A theme that touches upon another aspect of the IDF's actions is that of the dynamics of borders within which military units are centrally involved (Ben-Eliezer and Feinstein 2009; Ben-Zeev and Gazit 2018).

3.8   Resilience

Closely related to the high-intensity conflicts that the IDF has been involved in and a very *hot* public topic is research on resilience. These studies include a focus on the individual psychological level and the communal, regional, and even national levels (Ajdukovic et al. 2015; Canetti et al. 2013; Elran and Padan 2018; Gal 2014a; Kimhi and Eshel 2009; Kimhi et al. 2017; Lewin 2012). As the IDF's Home Front Command has been charged with aiding municipalities during times of emergency, its research unit (affiliated with MAMDA) carries out relevant research. However, it is not publicly accessible.

3.9   Intra-Organizational Issues

Studies on the internal organizational dynamics of the army include projects on the reserves based on both quantitative and qualitative methods (Ben-Dor and Pedahzur 2006; Ben-Dor et al. 2008; Lomsky-Feder 2008; Sion and Ben-Ari 2005, 2009). In addition, research on the professionalization of the IDF, long a staple of military sociology around the world, has recently been initiated by a handful of scholars (Ben-Shalom 2014; Libel 2014; Libel and Gal 2010).

3.10   Other Forces and External Scholars

Finally, while still a distinct minority, there are a few Israeli scholars who have or are working on the armed forces of other countries: Michael and Ben-Ari on peacekeeping forces (Michael et al. 2009; Michael and Ben-Ari 2011), or on special operations forces (Glicken et al. 2017; Shamir and Ben-Ari 2017), Sion on the Dutch military (2006, 2008a, b), Barak on the Lebanese army (2009) or myself on the Japanese forces (Ben-Ari 2011a). Others have undertaken comparative work (Rosman 2016, Rosman-Stollman 2016) or edited comparative volumes (Grassiani and Ben-Ari 2011; Yden and Ben-Ari 2016). However, like much of Israeli social science in general, most scholars are inward looking and usually carry out research about Israel only. In this respect, Barak's (2011) proposal to compare the IDF to other Middle East militaries (rather than to the industrial democracies) is fascinating. Finally, while not the focus of this chapter, it should be mentioned that a small number of scholars based outside of Israel also carry out relevant sociological research: Sergio Catignani (2004a, 2004b) or Rebecca Stein (Kuntzman and Stein 2015).

4   Theories, (Publication) Practices and Gaps

4.1   A Continued Expansion of Theoretical Orientations

Diversification of the subject matter has been accompanied by a continued expansion of theoretical orientations. While a consensus around the centrality of critical sociology has not emerged, it is certainly the type of theoretical orientation that is the dominant one in most academic institutions and one accorded with the highest status. At the same time, there is still a highly active group of non-critical sociologists concentrated mainly at Bar-Ilan and Ariel Universities. This situation is related to global academic developments and to generational dynamics in Israeli academia. Because Israeli academics are embedded in global structures it is not surprising that, as critical approaches have taken front and center in the social sciences, these have influenced Israeli scholars. In addition, to mark their uniqueness, the second generation of scholars has often developed their work out of opposition to the older structural functionalists.

International contacts mean that to a great degree Israeli academics often depend on scholars from other academic centers to set their military sociological agendas. Only rarely has Israeli data been used by Israelis to develop major theories related to the military and war or to offer alternative theoretical models to those dominant in other global centers. This state of affairs is slowly changing with Israeli scholars generating new theoretical developments. For example, take Levy's work on the market army (Levy 2010a, 2012a), the death hierarchy (Levy 2012b), or theocratization of armed forces (2014, 2015b), gender and citizenship (Lomksy-Feder and Sasson-Levy 2017), my own work with colleagues on ground units in the new wars (Ben-Ari et al. 2010) or urban combat (Ben-Ari 2012), new approaches to civilian control of the military (Barak and Sheffer 2013; Levy 2012b, 2017; Levy and Michael 2011; Michael 2010), or the relations between conscience and military service (Weiss 2014).

A related and rather new direction has been reflective work on research and publication (Ben-Ari 2011b; Gazit and Maoz-Shai 2010), theory building (Ben-Ari 2014) access to the field (Ben-Ari and Levy 2014), or a plea for critical approaches (Levy 2015a). Attesting to the centrality of Israeli scholars in the global community is the fact that some have been asked to write overviews not only of Israel but of other more general issues such as gender and the military (Sasson-Levy 2011a, 2017), sense-making in combat (Ben-Shalom et al. 2012), leadership (Lebel and Ben-Shalom 2018), or military death (Ben-Ari 2005).

4.2   Publication Practices

The dynamics that have created these patterns are related to publication practices. The major language of publication about military affairs in Israel – as in most Israeli academia – is English although the proportion of Hebrew publications has grown during the past two decades. This is the result of Israel's continued embeddedness in the US-dominated global academia with its patterns of 'publish or perish', ongoing attempts to keep up with major theoretical developments outside the country and the dependence of Israeli scholars on promotion via recommendation letters from scholars abroad. As in most academic realms there is a strong incentive to publish in English in peer reviewed journals, for single authorship, and in outlets in the centers of world scholarship. Moreover, by now it has become a prerequisite for advancement in many Israeli institutions to be trained or to spend time outside the country and many military sociologists fit this pattern. In this respect, though, it has become slightly more acceptable to publish serious academic work in one of the following Hebrew-language journals: Theory and Criticism, The Public Sphere, Israeli Sociology and Megamot.

4.3   A Gap

Much of current military sociology, to follow Soeters (2018) lacks a focus on the core, the expertise of the armed forces: the deployment of violence. To be sure, militaries carry out multiple missions, but it is surprising how few studies of the actual workings of the IDF exist. With only some exceptions (Ben-Ari et al. 2010; Ben-Shalom and Tsur 2018; Cohen and Ben-Ari 2014; Gazit and Ben-Ari 2017; Grassiani 2013, 2015; Grassiani and Verweij 2014; Menekin 2013, 2017; Padan 2017) there has been very little sustained work on the operational side of the IDF, a fact that starkly differs from the kind of work published following the wars of 1967, 1973, and 1982. Thus, we know relatively little about the actual military experiences of individuals and how these experiences are related to such classic issues of military sociology as leadership or small-group dynamics. One could argue that this results from the fact that, since the early 1980s, the IDF has not been directly involved in any major war. However, it has been involved in major high-intensity episodes in Gaza and Lebanon, has continued to occupy (at times violently) the Palestinian Territories, maintains a blockade of Gaza, and constantly uses armed patrols around its borders. All of these create the potential for extended research or even short-term investigations.

There seems to be a number of interrelated reasons for this gap. First, the contested political nature of the theaters where the IDF is deployed. Accordingly, while MAMDA may have carried out relevant internal studies, as an organization, the IDF does not have an interest in inviting external scholars to devote their – and more generally, public – attention to its actions in these arenas. Second, the large-scale entry of organizational consultants (regular officers and occasionally external civilians hired for the job) into the behavioral sciences departments of the IDF has led to a situation in which there is less chance for academic scholars to find potential coalition partners inside the IDF for joint research. Third, a major part of research about the IDF since the 1980s has been carried out by critical sociologists who, it seems, tend to be interested foremost in the effects of the military on society and less in the internal aspects of the military itself. Generally, therefore, while there is a growth of interest in, and publications about the IDF, this interest focuses on issues other than those involving the actual use of units.

5   Towards a Conclusion

Israel, like many other countries, figures in a global division of labor where theory is developed in the centers and the *others* provide the data or the application of theories. As I have shown, however, Israel is less a periphery than a semi-center of military sociology with global recognition of the quality of work undertaken within the country. Indeed, the conspicuousness of Israeli scholars in international forums (often heartily arguing with each other), the fact that some Israeli scholars have been asked to write general reviews of sub-fields or attempts at independent theoretical development all attest to its global standing.

The uniqueness of Israel, though, lies in being the only democracy that is mobilized for continuous war. It is for this reason that military sociology in this country seems to constantly move between criticism and support, between accepting key images (e.g., of the IDF being a *People's Army*) and challenging these very images. This movement or tension is heightened by the political polarization marking the country and the dominance of the left-leaning scholars in academia making it difficult for the voices of other scholars to be truly heard. The influence of global trends, in turn, has been significant in legitimizing subjects of study such as the demographic composition of the IDF, its effects on gender relations, or the reproduction of inequality. However, these have often been thwarted by the unwillingness of the IDF to cooperate or allow research that may be seen as threatening to its public image.

All in all, the continued richness of military sociology in Israel is the result of both the continued necessity of the IDF in the face of continued threats as well as the fact that the country is an open and vibrant democracy. Indeed, as this review has shown military sociology is deeply intertwined not only with security issues but with central social issues such as gender relations, social inequality, or the militarization of society implying that part of the wealth of issues it deals with are the product of public debates in the country. Moreover, the fact that Israel is marked both by a continued system of conscription and the presence of so many former generals in all walks of life and across most of the political spectrum means that the security concerns and issues centered on military service continue to be important for very wide parts of the country's population.

References

Ajdukovic, D., S. Kimhi, and M. Lahad, eds. 2015. *Resiliency: Enhancing Coping with Crisis and Terrorism*. Amsterdam: IOS Press.

Amram-Katz, S. 2018. "Between the Coffee and the Rifle: Models of Women's Service in the IDF." In *Gender at the Base: Women, Men and Military Service in Israel*, edited by O. Sasson-Levy and E. Lomsky-Feder, 52–75. Jerusalem: Van Leer and Hakibutz Hameuchad (Hebrew).

Azulai, A., and A. Ophir. 2008. *This is not One Regime*. Tel Aviv: Resling. (Hebrew).

Bar, N., and E. Ben-Ari. 2005. "Israeli Snipers in the Al-Aqsa Intifada: Killing, Humanity and Lived Experience." *Third World Quarterly* 26(1): 133–152.

Barak, O. 2009. *The Lebanese Army*. Albany: State University of New York Press.

Barak, O. 2011. "Studying Middle Eastern Militaries: Where Do We Go from Here?" *International Journal of Middle East Studies* 43(3): 406–407.

Barak, O., and D. Inbar. 2018. "'Revenge of the Jobniks': A Critical Analysis of Daily Resistance of Soldiers to the Military in Contemporary Israeli Cinema." *Public Sphere* 14: 123–144. (Hebrew).

Barak, O., and G. Sheffer. 2010. *Militarism and Israeli Society*. Bloomington: Indiana University Press.

Barak, O., and G. Sheffer. 2013. *Israel's Security Networks*. New York: Cambridge University Press.

Barak, O., and E. Tzur. 2012. "Continuity and Change in the Social Background of Israel's Military Elite." *Middle East Journal* 66(2): 211–230.

Ben-Ari, E. 2005. "A 'Good' Military Death: Cultural Scripts, Organizational Experts and Contemporary Armed Forces." *Armed Forces & Society* 31(4): 651–664.

Ben-Ari, E. 2011a. "Public Events and Japanese Self-Defense Forces: Aesthetics, Ritual Density and the Normalization of Military Violence." In *Violence Expressed*, edited by M. Six-Hohenbalken and N. Weiss, 55–70. Farnham: Ashgate.

Ben-Ari, E. 2011b. "Anthropological Research, and State Violence: Some Observations of an Israeli Anthropologist." In *Dangerous Liaisons*, edited by L.A. McNamara and R.A. Rubinstein, 167–184. Santa Fe: SAR Press.

Ben-Ari, E. 2014. "Theory building in research on the military." In *Routledge Handbook of Methods in Military Research*, edited by J. Soeters, P. Shields, and S. Rietjens, 301–311. London: Routledge.

Ben-Ari, E. 2015. "From a Sociology of Units to a Sociology of Combat Formations: Militaries in Urban Combat." In *Frontline: Combat and Cohesion in the Twenty-First Century*, edited by A. King, 73–92. Oxford: Oxford University Press.

Ben-Ari, E. 2016. "What is Worthy of Study about the Military? The Sociology of Militaries-in-use in Current Conflicts." In *Researching the Military*, edited by H. Carreiras, C. Castro and S. Frederic, 26–45. London: Routledge.

Ben-Ari, E., Z. Lehrer, U. Ben-Shalom and A. Vainer. 2010. *Rethinking Contemporary Warfare: A Sociological View of the Al-Aqsa Intifada*. Albany: State University of New York Press.

Ben-Ari E., and Y. Levy. 2014. "Getting Access to the Field: Insider/Outsider Perspectives." In *Routledge Handbook of Methods in Military Research*, edited by J. Soeters, P. Shields and S. Rietjens, 9–18. London: Routledge.

Ben-Dor, G., and A. Pedahzur. 2006. "Under the Threat of Terrorism: A Reassessment of the Factors Influencing the Motivation to Serve in the Israeli Reserves." *Israel Affairs* 12(3): 430–438.

Ben-Dor, G., A. Pedahzur, D. Canetti-Nisim, E. Zaidise, A. Perliger, and S. Bermanis. 2008. "I vs. We: Collective and Individual Factors of Reserve Service Motivation during War and Peace." *Armed Forces & Society* 34(4): 565–592.

Ben-Eliezer, U. 2012. *Israel's New Wars*. Tel Aviv: Tel Aviv University Press. (Hebrew)

Ben-Eliezer, U. 2017. "The Sociology of No-War in Israel." *Megamont* 31(2): 115–142. (Hebrew).

Ben-Eliezer, U., and Y. Feinstein. 2009. "Politics of borders and the borders of politics: sovereignty and autonomy around Israel's human rights abuses in the Separation Barrier project." *Mobilization* 14(3): 357–374.

Ben-Ishai, O. 2017. "From *Decision* to *Resolution*: Change in the Doctrinal Language of Israel's Security Discourse as a New Legitimization for Military Action, since 2010." Doctoral Dissertation, Ben-Gurion University.

Ben-Shalom, U. 2014. "Trends in Training for the Military Profession in Israel – The Case Study of the Tactical Command College." *Political and Military Sociology* 42: 51–73.

Ben-Shalom, U., and I. Benbenisty. 2016. "Coping Styles and Combat Motivation During Operations – An IDF Case Study." *Armed Forces & Society* 42(4): 1–20.

Ben-Shalom, U., and S. Fox. 2009. "Military psychologists in the IDF: A perspective of continuity and change." *Armed Forces & Society* 36: 103–119.

Ben-Shalom, U., Y. Klar, and I. Benbenisty. 2012. "Characteristics of sense making during combat." In *Handbook of Military Psychology*, edited by J.A. Lawrence and M. Mathews, 218–230. London: Oxford University Press.

Ben-Shalom, U., S. Engel and E. Lewin. 2018. "Collective Action in Operational Mixed-Gender Units on Israel's Borders." *Res Militaris* Ergomas Issue 6: 1–17.

Ben-Shalom, U., and Y. Tsur. 2018. "Scripts of Service Culture and Joint Operations of Air and Ground Forces: An IDF Case Study." *Israel Affairs* 24(1): 84–98.

Ben-Zeev, E., and N. Gazit. 2018. "Juggling Logics on the Egyptian-Israeli Borderland: Soldiers between Securitization and Arbitrary Humanitarianism." *Journal of Contemporary Ethnography* 47(2): 255–277.

Berda, Y. 2012. *The Bureaucracy of the Occupation: The Permit Regime in the West Bank*. Tel Aviv: Hakibutz Hameuhad Publishers. (Hebrew).

Berda, Y. 2017. *Managing Dangerous Populations: The Permit Regime in the West Bank*. Stanford, CA: Stanford University Press.

Brownfield-Stein, C. 2010. "Visual representations of IDF women soldiers and 'civil-militarism' in Israel." In *Militarism and Israeli Society*, edited by G. Sheffer and O. Barak, 304–328. Bloomington, IN: Indiana University Press.

Brownfield-Stein, C. 2014. *Fantasy of a State: Photographs of Female Soldiers and the Eroticization of Civil-Militarism in Israel*. Tel Aviv: Resling. (Hebrew).

Brownfield-Stein, C. 2018. "The Chief of Staff Officiated in a Female Soldier's Wedding: Photographs and the Recruitment of Women." In *Gender at the Base: Women, Men and Military Service in Israel*, edited by O. Sasson-Levy and E. Lomsky-Feder, 87–99. Jerusalem: Van Leer and Hakibutz Hameuchad. (Hebrew).

Canetti, D., I. Waismel-Manor, N. Cohen, and C. Rapaport. 2013. "What Does National Resilience Mean in a Democracy? Evidence from the United States and Israel." *Armed Forces & Society* 40(3): 504–520.

Catignani, S. 2004a. "Israel Defence Forces Organizational Changes in an Era of Budgetary Cutbacks." *RUSI Journal* 149(5): 72–76.

Catignani, S. 2004b. "Trapped fools: Thirty Years of Israeli Policy in the Territories." *Millennium* 33(2): 423–425.

Cohen, A., and E. Ben-Ari. 2014. "Legal-advisors in the Armed Forces: Military Lawyers in the Israeli Defence Forces as Mediators, Interpreters and Arbitrators of Meaning During Operations." *Journal of Political and Military Sociology* 42: 125–148.

Cohen, S. 2008. *Israel and its Army: From Cohesion to Confusion.* Routledge: London.

Cohen, S. 2013. *Divine Service? Judaism and Israel's Armed Forces.* Ashgate: London.

Cohen, S., A. Kampinsky, and E. Rosman-Stollman. 2016. "Swimming Against the Tide: The Changing Functions and Status of Chaplains in the Israel Defense Force." *Religion, State and Society* 44(1): 65–74.

Drory, Z. 2009. "The Nahal Haredi: The God-Fearing Battalion of the IDF." *Journal of Political and Military Sociology* 37(2): 153–169.

Drory, Z. 2015. "The 'Religionizing' of the Israel Defence Force: Its Impact on Military Culture and Professionalism." *Res Militaris* 5(1): 1–21.

Elran, M., and C. Padan. 2018. "The Civilian Home Front: In Search of Societal Resilience?" In *Handbook of Israeli Security* edited by S.A. Cohen and A. Kleinman, 117–136. Routledge: London.

Eran Jona, M. 2011. "Married to the Military: Military-Family Relations in the Israel Defense Forces." *Armed Forces & Society* 37(1): 19–41.

Friedman-Peleg, K. 2017. *PTSD and the Politics of Trauma in Israel.* Toronto: The University of Toronto Press.

Friedman-Peleg, K., and Y. Bilu. 2011. "From PTSD to National Trauma: The Case of the Israeli Center for Victims of Terror and War." *Transcultural Psychiatry* 48(4): 416–436.

Friedman-Peleg, K., and Y. Goodman. 2010. "From Post-Trauma Intervention to Immunizing the Social Body: Pragmatics and Politics of a Resilience Program in Israel's Periphery." *Culture, Medicine and Psychiatry* 34(3): 421–442.

Gal, R. 2014a. "Social Resilience in Times of Protracted Crises: An Israeli Case Study." *Armed Forces & Society* 40(3): 452–475.

Gal, R. 2014b. "Civil-Military Relations in Israel: Who Influences Whom?" In *Civil-Military Relations in Israel,* edited by E. Rosman-Stolman and A. Kampinsky, 23–42. London: Lexington Books.

Gal, R., and T. Libel, eds. 2012. *Between the Kippa and Beret: Religion, Politics and Military in Israel.* Ben-Shemen: Modan. (Hebrew).

Gavriely-Nuri, D. 2006. "Israel's Cultural Code of Captivity and the Personal Stories of Yom-Kippur War ex-POWs." *Armed Forces & Society* 33(1): 94–105.

Gavriely-Nuri, D. 2012. "Cultural Codes and Military Ethics: The Case of Israeli POWs." *Journal of Multicultural Discourses* 7(3): 213–226.

Gazit, N. 2009. "Social Agency, Spatial Practices and Power: The Micro-Foundations of Fragmented Sovereignty in the Occupied Territories." *International Journal of Politics, Culture and Society* 22(1): 83–103

Gazit, N. 2015. "State-Sponsored Vigilantism: Jewish Settlers Violence in Occupied Palestinian Territories." *Sociology* 49(3): 438–454.

Gazit, N., and E. Ben-Ari. 2017. "Doing Violence is Hard: The Micro-Social Foundations of Military Violence in Non-Combat Situations." *Conflict and Society* 3(1): 189–207.

Gazit N., and Y. Levy, eds. 2016. *An Army Educates a Nation: The Role of the Military in the Israeli School System.* Ra'anana: The Open University of Israel. (Hebrew).

Gazit, N., and Y. Maoz-Shai. 2010. "Studying-up and Studying-across: Researching Governmental Violence Organizations at Home." *Qualitative Sociology* 33(3): 275–295.

Glicken Turnley, J., K. Michael, and E. Ben-Ari, eds. 2017. *Special Operations Forces in the 21st Century: Perspectives from the Social Sciences.* London: Routledge.

Golan, O., and E. Ben-Ari. 2017. "Armed Forces, Cyberspace and Global Images: The Official Website of the Israeli Defense Forces." *Armed Forces & Society* 44(2): 280–300.

Gordon, N. 2008. *Israel's Occupation.* Berkeley: University of California Press.

Grassiani, E. 2013. *Soldiering Under Occupation: Processes of Numbing among Israeli Soldiers in the Al-Aqsa Intifada.* New York: Berghahn Books.

Grassiani, E. 2015. "Moral Othering at the Checkpoint: The Case of Israeli Soldiers and Palestinian Civilians." *Critique of Anthropology* 35(4): 373–388.

Grassiani, E. 2018. "Between Security and Military Identities: The Case of Israeli Security Experts." *Security Dialogue* 49(1–2): 83–95.

Grassiani, E., and E. Ben-Ari, eds. 2011. "State/Violence." *Special Issue of Etnofoor* 23(2): 1–114.

Grassiani, E., and D. Verweij. 2014. "The Disciplinary Gaze of the Camera's Eye: Soldiers' Conscience and Moral Responsibility." *Journal of Military and Strategic Studies* 15(3): 5–22.

Grossman, G., D. Manekin, and D. Miodownik. 2015. "The Political Legacies of Combat: Attitudes Towards War and Peace Among Israeli Ex-Combatants." *International Organization* 69(4): 981–1009.

Grosswirth Kachtan, D. 2016. "Deconstructing the Military's Hegemonic Masculinity: An Intersectional Observation of the Combat Soldier." *Res Militaris* Ergomas Issue 2: 1–14.

Grosswirth Kachtan, D. 2017. "Acting Ethnic – Performance of Ethnicity and the Process of Ethnicization." *Ethnicities* 17(5): 707–726.

Grosswirth Kachtan, D. 2018. "In a Red Dress and a Brown Beret: Gender, Ethnicity and the Military." In *Gender at the Base: Women, Men and Military Service in Israel*, edited by O. Sasson-Levy and E. Lomsky-Feder, 122–146. Tel-Aviv: Hakibbutz Hameuchad.

Hakak, Y. 2016. *Haredi Masculinities between the Yeshiva, the Army, Work and Politics the Sage, the Warrior and the Entrepreneur*. Amsterdam: Brill.

Harness, A. 2020. "The Institution, The Occupation and the Market: Analyzing Military and Market-Society Relations from an Institutional Logics Perspective." In *The Army and the Market Society in Israel*, edited by Y. Levy, N. Gazit, R. Moshe, and A. Harness, 56–88. Ra'anana: The Open University of Israel Press. (Hebrew).

Hermoni, G., and U. Lebel. 2012. "Politicizing Memory: An Ethnographical Study of a Remembrance Ceremony." *Cultural Studies* 26(4): 469–491.

Israeli, Z., and E. Rosman-Stollman. 2015. "Men and Boys: Representations of Israeli Combat Soldiers in the Media." *Israel Studies Review* 30(1): 66–85.

Kachtan, D. 2012. "The Construction of Ethnic Identity in the Military – From the Bottom Up." *Israel Studies Journal* 17(3): 150–175.

Kachtan, D., and V. Wasserman. 2015. "Undressing Masculinity: The Body as a Site of Ethno-Gendered Resistance." *Organization* 22(3): 390–417.

Kampinsky, A. 2015. *By Order of the Rabbinate*. Jerusalem: Carmel. (Hebrew).

Kaplan, D. 2012. "Commemorating a Suspended Death: Missing Soldiers and National Solidarity in Israel." *American Ethnologist* 35(3): 413–427.

Kaplan, D. 2013. "National Mood Stations: The 'Commemorative Mode' of Israeli Radio Broadcasting during Memorial Days and Times of Emergency." *Megamot* 49(2): 232–256. (Hebrew).

Kaplan, D., and A. Rosenmann. 2012. "Unit Social Cohesion in the Israeli Military as a Case Study of 'Don't Ask Don't Tell'." *Political Psychology* 33(4): 419–436.

Karazi-Presler, T. 2018. "Between Empowerment and Shame: The Experience of Power among Junior Female Officers." In *Gender at the Base: Women, Men and Military Service in Israel*, edited by O. Sasson-Levy and E. Lomsky-Feder, 102–117. Jerusalem: Van Leer and Hakibutz Hameuchad. (Hebrew).

Karazi-Presler, T., O. Sasson-Levy, and E. Lomsky-Feder. 2018. "Gender, Emotions Management, and Power in Organizations: The Case of Israeli Women Junior Military Officers." *Sex Roles* 78(7–8): 573–586.

Katriel, T., and N. Shavit. 2013. "Speaking Out: Testimonial Rhetoric in Israeli Soldiers' Dissent." *Versus* 116: 81–105.

Kimhi, S., and Y. Eshel. 2009. "Individual and Public Resilience and Coping with Long Term Outcomes of War." *Journal of Applied Biobehavioral Research* 14: 70–89.

Kimhi, S., Y. Eshel, D. Leykin, and M. Lahad. 2017. "Individual, Community and National Resilience in the Peace-Time and in face of Terror: A Longitudinal Study." *Journal of Loss and Trauma* 22(8): 698–713.

Kuntsman, A., and R.L. Stein. 2015. *Digital Militarism Israel's Occupation in the Social Media Age.* Stanford: Stanford University Press.

Lebel, U. 2007. "Civil Society vs. Military Sovereignty: Cultural, Political and Operational Aspects." *Armed Forces & Society* 34(1): 67–89.

Lebel, U., ed. 2010a. *Communicating Security: Civil-Military Relations in Israel.* London: Routledge.

Lebel, U. 2010b: "'Casualty Panic': Military Recruitment Models, Civil-military Gap and their Implications for the Legitimacy of Military Loss." *Democracy and Security* 6(2): 183–206.

Lebel, U. 2013a. *Politics of Memory – The Israeli Underground's Struggle for Inclusion in the National Pantheon and Military Commemoralization.* London & New York: Routledge.

Lebel, U. 2013b. "Postmodern or Conservative? Competing Security Communities over Military Doctrine – Israeli National-Religious Soldiers as Counter [Strategic] Culture Agents." *Political and Military Sociology* (40): 23–57.

Lebel, U., and U. Ben-Shalom. 2018. "Military Leadership in Heroic and Post-Heroic Conditions." In *Handbook of the Sociology of the Military*, edited by G. Caforio, 126–143. Rotterdam: Springer.

Lebel, U. and L. Lewin, eds. 2015. *The 1973 Yom Kippur War and the Reshaping of Israeli Civil-Military Relations.* Lanham, MD: Lexington.

Lebel, U., and Y. Rochlin. 2009. "From 'Fighting Family' to 'Belligerent Families': Family-Military-Nation Interrelationships and the Forming of Israeli Public Behavior among Families of Fallen Soldiers and Families of MIAs and POWs." *Social Movements Studies* 8(4): 359–374.

Lehrer, Z., and S. Amram-Katz. 2011. "The Sociology of Military Knowledge in the IDF: From 'Forging' to 'Deciphering'." *Israel Studies Review* 26(2): 54–72.

Levy, G., and O. Sasson-Levy. 2008. "Militarized Socialization, Military Service and Class Reproduction: The Experiences of Israeli Soldiers." *Sociological Perspectives* 51(2): 349–374.

Levy, Y. 2008. *From People's Army to the Army of the Peripheries.* Jerusalem: Carmel. (Hebrew).

Levy, Y. 2010a. "The Essence of the 'Market Army'." *Public Administration Review* 70(3): 378–389.

Levy, Y. 2010b. "The Clash between Feminism and Religion in the Israeli Military: A Multilayered Analysis." *Social Politics* 17(2): 185–209.

Levy, Y. 2012a. "A Revised Model of Civilian Control of the Military: The Interaction between the Republican Exchange and the Control Exchange." *Armed Forces & Society* 38(4): 529–556.

Levy, Y. 2012b. *Israel's Death Hierarchy: Casualty Aversion in a Militarized Democracy.* New York: New York University Press.

Levy, Y. 2014. "The Theocratization of the Israeli Military." *Armed Forces and Society* 4(2): 269–294.

Levy, Y. 2015a. "Time for Critical Military Sociology." *Res Militaris* 5(2): 1–8.

Levy, Y. 2015b. *The Divine Commander: The Theocratization of the Israeli Military.* Tel Aviv: Am Oved. (Hebrew).

Levy, Y. 2017. "Control from Within: How Soldiers Control the Military." *European Journal of International Relations* 23(1): 192–216.

Levy, Y. 2018. "Conceptualizing the Spectrum of the Bereavement Discourse." *Armed Forces and Society* 44(1): 3–24.

Levy, Y., and K. Michael. 2011. "Conceptualizing Extra-Institutional Control of the Military: Israel as a Case Study." *Res Militaris* 1(2): 1–22.

Levy Y., G. Nir, M. Rinat, and A. Harness. 2020. *The Army and the Market Society in Israel.* Ra'anana: The Open University of Israel Press. (Hebrew).

Lewin, E. 2012. *National Resilience during War: Refining the Decision-Making Model.* Lanham, MD: Lexington.

Libel, T. 2014. "From the People's Army to the Jewish People's Army: The IDF's Force Structure Between Professionalization and Militarization." *Defense & Security Analysis* 29(4): 280–292.

Libel T., and R. Gal. 2010. "Teaching Citizens to be Professional Soldiers: IDF Responses and Their Implications." In *The Decline of Citizen Armies*, edited by S.A. Cohen, 215–233. London: Routledge.

Libel, T., and R. Gal. 2015. "Between Military–Society and Religion–Military Relations: Different Aspects of the Growing Religiosity in the Israeli Defense Forces." *Defense & Security Analysis* 31(3): 213–227.

Livio, O. 2012. "Avoidance of Military Service in Israel: Exploring the Role of Discourse." *Israel Studies Review* 27(1): 78–97.

Livio, O. 2015. "The Path of Least Resistance: Constructions of Space in the Discourse of Israeli Military Refuseniks." *Discourse, Context & Media* 10: 1–9.

Livio, O. 2018. "Producing Soldier Boy: Sperm Donor Discourse and Militarism in Israeli Media Culture." *Critical Studies in Media Communication* 35(3): 259–272.

Lomsky-Feder, E. 2009. "The Canonical Generation: Trapped between Personal and National Memories." *Sociology* 43(6): 1047–1065.

Lomsky-Feder, E., and E. Ben-Ari. 2007. "Diversity in the Israeli Defense Forces." In *Cultural Diversity in the Armed Forces*, edited by J. Soeters and J. van der Meulen, 125–140. London & New York: Routledge.

Lomsky-Feder, E., and E. Ben-Ari. 2010. "The Discourse of 'Psychology' and the 'Normalization' of War in Contemporary Israel." In *Militarism and Israeli Society*, edited by G. Sheffer and O. Barak, 280–330. Bloomington: Indiana University Press.

Lomsky-Feder, E., and E. Ben-Ari. 2012. "Managing Diversity in Context: Unit Level Dynamics in the Israel Defense Forces." *Armed Forces & Society* 39(2): 193–212.

Lomsky-Feder, E., G. Nir, and E. Ben-Ari. 2008. "Reserve Soldiers as Transmigrants: Moving Between the Civilian and Military Worlds." *Armed Forces & Society* 34(4): 593–614.

Lomsky-Feder, E., and O. Sasson-Levy. 2015. "Serving the Army as Secretaries: Intersectionality, Social Contracts and Subjective Experience of Citizenship." *British Journal of Sociology* 66(1): 173–192.

Lomsky-Feder, E., and O. Sasson-Levy. 2017. *Women Soldiers and Citizenship in Israel: Gendered Encounters with the State*. Oxfordshire: Routledge.

Lomsky-Feder, E., O. Sasson-Levy, and N. Dotan-Man. 2018. "'Social Respect' versus 'A Right to Self-fulfillment': Ethno-Class Interpretations of the Role of Female Secretaries." In *Gender at the Base: Women, Men and Military Service in Israel*, edited by O. Sasson-Levy and E. Lomsky-Feder, 36–54. Jerusalem: Van Leer and Hakibutz Hameuchad. (Hebrew).

Malchi, A. 2020. "The Market Army and the Ultra-Orthodox Paradox." In *The Army and the Market Society in Israel*, edited by Y. Levy, G. Nir., M. Rinat and A. Harness, 78–97. Raanana: The Open University of Israel Press. (Hebrew).

Manekin, D. 2013. "The Limits of Socialization and the Underproduction of Military Violence." *Journal of Peace Research* 54(5): 606–619.

Manekin, D. 2017. "Violence Against Civilians in the Second Intifada: The Moderating Effect of Armed Structure on Opportunistic Violence." *Comparative Political Studies* 46(10): 1273–1300.

Michael, K. 2010. "Military Knowledge and Weak Civilian Control in the Reality of Low Intensity Conflict – The Israeli Case." In *Militarism and Israeli Society*, edited by G. Sheffer and O. Barak, 42–66. Bloomington: Indiana University Press.

Michael, K., and E. Ben-Ari. 2011. "Contemporary Peace Support Operations: The Primacy of the Military and Internal Contradictions." *Armed Forces & Society* 37(4): 657–679.

Michael, K., D. Kellen, and E. Ben-Ari. 2009. *The Transformations in the World of War and Peace Support Operations*. New Haven: Praeger.

Oren, A., and K. Michael. 2013. "Civil Control with Regard to the Territorial Dimension of Security in Israel." *Floersheimer Studies* 1/84. Jerusalem: The Hebrew University of Jerusalem.

Padan, C. 2017. "Constructing 'Crisis Events' in Military Contexts – an Israeli Perspective." In *Leadership in Extreme Situations*, edited by M. Holenweger, M.K. Jager, and F. Kernic, 217–247. Cham: Springer.

Perez, M. 2014. "It Wasn't Ideology but Saving My Soul: Emotional Individualism and Avoidance of Military Service in Israel." *Theory and Criticism* 43: 131–153. (Hebrew).

Perez, M. 2018. "Avoidance of Military Service: A Lingering Resistance to Hegemonic Masculinity." In *Gender at the Base: Women, Men and Military Service in Israel*, edited by O. Sasson-Levy and E. Lomsky-Feder, 146–153. Jerusalem: Van Leer and Hakibutz Hameuchad. (Hebrew).

Peri, Y. 2006. *Generals in the Cabinet Room: How the Military Shapes Israeli Policy*. Washington, DC: United States Institute of Peace Press.

Peri, Y. 2017. *Media Directed Wars: The Paradox of Power and the Strategic Dilemma of the IDF*. Tel Aviv: Institute of National Security. (Hebrew).

Ram, U. 2017. "Sociology in the Time of Netanyahu: Critical Patterns in Israeli Sociology at the Beginning of the 21st Century." *Megamot* 31(2): 13–68.

Rosman, E. 2014. *For God and Country? Religious Student-Soldiers in the Israel Defense Forces*. Austin: University of Texas Press.

Rosman, E. 2015. "Religious Accommodation as a Civil-Military Looking Glass: The Case of the Indian and Israeli Armed Forces." *Journal of Church and State* 58(3): 440–461.

Rosman, E. 2016. "Towards a Classification of Managing Religious Diversity in the Ranks: The Case of the Turkish and Israeli Armed Forces." *Armed Forces & Society* 42(4): 675–696.

Rosman E. 2018a. "(Not) Becoming the Norm: Military Service by Religious Israeli Women as a Process of Social Legitimation." *Israel Studies Review* 33(1): 42–60.

Rosman, E. 2018b. "The Study of Civil-Military Relations in Israel: From Where and to Where?" Presented at the Bi-Annual Conference of the Israel Association of Civil-Military Relations.

Rosman, E., and Z. Israeli. 2015. "From Rambo to Sitting Ducks and Back Again – The Media Image of the Israeli Soldier." *Israel Affairs* 21(1): 112–130.

Rosman-Stollman, E. 2016. "Religious Accommodation as a Civil-Military Looking Glass: The Case of the Indian and Israeli Armed Forces." *Journal of Church and State* 58(3): 440–461.

Rosman-Stollman, E., and Z. Israeli. 2015. "'Our Forces' Become Alexei, Yuval and Liran: The Transition of the Israeli Soldier's Media Image from the Collective to an Individual." *Res Militaris* 5(2): 1–18.

Rothem, N. 2018a. "Suicide, Heroism and the Gender Between Them." In *Gender and Military*, edited by O. Sasson-Levy and E. Lomsky-Feder, 145–159. Jerusalem: The Van Leer Jerusalem Institute. (in Hebrew).

Rothem, N. 2018b. *Suicide and Our Shared Fate: Soldiers' Suicide in Psychology, Law and Modern Hebrew Literature*. Tel Aviv: Tel Aviv University Press. (Hebrew).

Safrai, M. Z. 2018. "Legitimizing Military Growth and Conscription: The Yom Kippur Mechanism." *Armed Forces & Society* 45(3): 491–510.

Safrai, M. Z. 2020. "When Neoliberalism Meets the 'People's Army': The Changes in the IDF Career Force Model." In *The Army and the Market Society in Israel*, edited by Y. Levy, G. Nir, M. Rinat, and A. Harness, 69–86. Raanana: The Open University of Israel Press. (Hebrew).

Sasson-Levy, O. 2006. *Identities in Uniform: Masculinities and Femininities in the Israeli Military*. Jerusalem: Magnes Press. (Hebrew).

Sasson-Levy, O. 2008. "Individual Bodies, Collective State Interests: The Case of Israeli Combat Soldiers." *Men and Masculinities* 10(3): 296–321.

Sasson-Levy, O. 2011a. "The Military in a Globalized Environment: Perpetuating an 'Extremely Gendered' Organization." In *Handbook of Gender, Work and Organization*, edited by E. Jeanes, D. Knights and P. Yancey Martin, 391–411. New York: Wiley-Blackwell.

Sasson-Levy, O. 2011b. "Research on Gender and the Military in Israel: From a Gendered Organization to Inequality Regimes." *Israel Studies Review* 26(2): 73–98.

Sasson-Levy, O. 2017. "Ethnicity and Gender in Militaries: An Intersectional Analysis." In *The Palgrave International Handbook of Gender and the Military*, edited by R. Woodward and C. Duncanson, 125–143. London: Palgrave Macmillan.

Sasson-Levy, O., and S. Amram-Katz. 2007. "Gender Integration in Israeli Officer Training: Degendering and Regendering the Military." *Signs* 33(1): 105–135.

Sasson-Levy, O., and E. Lomsky-Feder, eds. 2018. *Gender at the Base: Women, Men and Military Service in Israel.* Jerusalem: Van Leer and Hakibutz Hameuchad. (Hebrew).

Sasson-Levy, O., Y. Levy, and E. Lomsky-Feder. 2011. "Women Breaking the Silence: Military Service, Gender and Antiwar Protest." *Gender & Society* 25(6): 740–763.

Seidman, G. 2010. "From Nationalization to Privatization: The Case of the IDF." *Armed Forces & Society* 36(4): 716–749.

Shamir, E., and E. Ben-Ari. 2016. "The Rise of Special Operations Forces: Generalized Specialization, Boundary Spanning and Military Autonomy." *Journal of Strategic Studies* 41(3): 1–37.

Shavit, M. 2017. *Media Strategy and Military Operations in the 21st Century: Mediatizing the Israel Defence Forces.* London: Routledge.

Sher, Y., and H. Ben-Eliyahu. 2011. "Looking Out from the Tent: Internal Social Research at the IDF." *Israel Studies Review* 26(2): 99–108.

Sher, Y., A. Vainer and E. Ben-Ari. 2014. "The IDF Moving Towards a Professional Force: Hybrid Wars, Multiple Logics-of-Action and an Incremental Military." In *Civil-Military Relations in Israel*, edited by E. Rosman-Stillman and A. Kampinsky, 69–81. Lanham: Lexington Books.

Sion, L. 2006. "'Too Sweet and Innocent for War'? Dutch Peacekeepers and the Use of Violence." *Armed Forces & Society* 32(4): 454–474.

Sion, L. 2008a. "Dutch Peacekeepers and Host Environments in the Balkans: An Ethnographic Perspective." *International Peacekeeping* 15(2): 201–213.

Sion, L. 2008b. "Peacekeeping and the Gender Regime: Dutch Female Peacekeepers in Bosnia and Kosovo." *Journal of Contemporary Ethnography* 37(5): 561–585.

Sion, L., and E. Ben-Ari. (2005): "'Hungry, Weary and Horny': Joking and Jesting Among Israel's Combat Reserves." *Israel Affairs* 11(4): 656–672.

Sion, L., and E. Ben-Ari. 2009. "Imagined Masculinity: Body, Sexuality and Family among Israeli Military Reserves." *Symbolic Interaction* 32(1): 21–43.

Soeters, J. 2018. *Sociology and Military Studies.* London: Routledge.

Tiargan-Orr R., and M. Eran Jona. 2015. "The Israeli Public's Perception of the IDF: Stability and Change." *Armed Forces & Society* 42(2): 324–343.

Tzfadia, E., Y. Levy, and A. Oren. 2010. "Symbolic Meanings and the Feasibility of Policy Images: Relocating Military Bases to the Periphery in Israel." *Policy Studies Journal* 38(4): 723–744.

Wasserman, V., I. Dayan, and E. Ben-Ari. 2018. "Upgraded Masculinity: A Gendered Analysis of The Debriefing in the Israeli Air Force." *Gender and Society* 32(2): 228–251.

Weiss, E. 2014. *Conscientious Objectors in Israel: Sacrifice, Citizenship, Trials of Fealty.* Philadelphia: University of Pennsylvania Press.

Weiss, E. 2016. "Incentivized Obedience: How a Gentler Israeli Military Prevents Organized Resistance." *American Anthropologist* 118(1): 93–103.

Weiss, E. 2018. "Gendered Pathologization of Pacifism in the IDF." In *Gender at the Base: Women, Men and Military Service in Israel,* edited by O. Sasson-Levy and E. Lomsky-Feder, 123–137. Jerusalem: Van Leer and Hakibutz Hameuchad. (Hebrew).

Weizman, E. 2017. *Hollow Land: The Architecture of Israel's Occupation.* London: Verso.

Yden, K., and E. Ben-Ari, eds. 2016. "Special Issue: After Afghanistan." *Res Militaris* Ergomas Issue 3.

Military Sociology in Japan

Atsushi Yasutomi and Saya Kiba

1 Introduction: The State of Military Sociology in the Scientific Arena in Japan

Military sociology is not a popular field of study in Japan. A mere handful of military sociologists and scholars in related fields have contributed to research on the subject. Courses on military sociology are only offered to Japan Self-Defense Force (JSDF) cadets and graduate students enrolled in the National Defense Academy of Japan, where they are practically run by one professor. Hence, military sociology remains one of the least developed areas of study in the social sciences in Japan.

This lack of development is rooted in three interrelated problems. First, there are ongoing legal disputes over whether the JSDF – as well as its combat-related activities at home and abroad – are prohibited by the Constitution of Japan. This paradox sees no easy solution as a static portion of the Japanese population is strongly allergic to state force, espousing an anti-militarism that is grounded in the fear that any attempts to alter the constitution could allow Japan to engage in war.

Secondly, scholars in military sociology and related subjects have been accused of being disloyal to the spirit of Japan's peaceful constitution and of supporting violent conflicts and wars in the world. A lack of understanding and misinterpretation of current studies and methods– often based on public anti-war biases– makes it difficult for scholars to obtain research funds. This is particularly true at Japan's national research institutions (see section 3).

Thirdly, it is difficult for military sociologists to access primary information from the JSDF and the Ministry of Defense (MoD). The JSDF remains extremely hesitant to disclose information to researchers for fear that disclosure could provoke public criticism from journalists, scholars, and anti-military groups. The JSDF fears that heavy criticism could easily ruin their public image. At the same time, the JSDF's hesitancy to disclose military records and reports has made the public even more skeptical about the JSDF's mission and constitutional justification. This situation makes it difficult for military sociologists to gain access to primary sources. As a result, the public is less informed about and less interested in understanding the nature of the problems facing the JSDF. This vicious circle has constrained the development of military sociology and related studies in Japan.

While these challenging and unfavorable academic circumstances persist, the drastically changing security environment around Japan has prompted new attention to military sociology and related subjects over the past few years. The Japanese have been increasingly concerned by China's rapid expansion of military activities in the East China Sea, particularly since Japan nationalized the disputed Senkaku Islands in 2012. China's naval vessels have repeatedly intruded upon Japan's territorial waters, and Chinese military aircrafts have conducted operations near the Senkaku Islands, leading the Japan Air Self Defense Force's combat aircrafts to intercept. The Japanese government reports that interceptions of Chinese planes comprise 63 percent of 725 total intercepts during a one-year period ending March 2020 (Ministry of Defense 2021). The Defense Ministry also reported that two Chinese vessels, a submerged submarine, and a frigate, entered the contiguous zone off the Senkaku Islands in January 2018 (Lies 2018). The Japanese government believes China's military activities represent an attempt to unilaterally change the status quo by use of force, thus, posing a security threat to Japan (Ministry of Defense 2018: 47).

Under these circumstances, the urgent need for pragmatic and drastic legal reforms in response to Japan's security demands have given the public more opportunities to discuss the risks, conditions, and wellbeing of the soldiers serving in the homeland as well as those who are deployed abroad. Meanwhile, the JSDF, facing a serious shortage of new recruits, has been compelled to offer increasingly attractive and fulfilling working conditions, even while public discourse surrounding its existence has grown highly contentious.

Against this background, this chapter will provide an overview of military sociology in Japan. Since readers who are not familiar with Japan and Japanese politics cannot understand the status and discussions around the JSDF without some additional knowledge of Japanese history and the Japanese constitution, section 2 will provide the necessary information and will also cover recent debates about changes in the constitutional settings and related public perceptions. Section 3 will highlight topics and main results of military sociology research in Japan while section 4 will deal with the issue of research funding in Japan. Section 5 concentrates on some central obstacles to military sociology and section 6 provides a short summary of the previous sections.

2 Characteristics of the Relations between the JSDF and Society

The relationship between the JSDF and Japanese society is notable for its contradictions. On the one hand, a majority of the public trusts, respects, and appreciates the JSDF's disaster relief tasks within Japan as well as abroad. On the other hand, a majority of citizens also fears that any constitutional amendments or related legal reforms on defense could increase the risk that a newly re-militarized Japan would be dragged into war.

2.1 Debates over a Constitutional Amendment Legitimizing the JSDF

The Constitution of Japan was drafted in 1946 and promulgated in the following year. The peace clause in Article 9 stipulates that "Aspiring sincerely to an international peace based on justice and order, the Japanese people forever renounce war as a sovereign right of the nation and the threat or use of force as means of settling international disputes. In order to accomplish the aim of the preceding paragraph, land, sea, and air forces, as well as other war potential, will never be maintained. The right of belligerency of the state will not be recognized".[1] Despite this clause, the JSDF came into being in 1954, transforming from the *Keisatsu Yobitai*, the National Police Reserve established by the US in the wake of the Korean War. The JSDF is now the 20th strongest military in the world, staffed by approximately 220,000 men and women (roughly the size of the German *Bundeswehr*).

It is no exaggeration to say that the relationship between the JSDF and society in Japan has been shaped by the decades-long debate over the JSDF's constitutional legitimacy. The pacifist constitution, which renounces war and denies any form of military, appears to some to contradict the very nature of today's JSDF. For most opponents of the JSDF's legitimacy, any form of its combat or combat-related activities leads to a violation of the constitution.[2]

---

1   The English translation of the Constitution of Japan is available at <https://japan.kantei. go.jp/constitution_and_government_of_japan/constitution_e.html> (last access: 1 July 2018).

2   *The Asahi Shimbun* (newspaper) conducted online interviews of 122 scholars of law in June 2015, asking whether relaxing the regulations regarding the JSDF's use of force as stipulated in the 2015 Security Legislation (see the subsequent section) is a violation of the constitution or not. The survey shows that 119 respondents said that the legislation does violate or seems to violate the constitution. The same survey also shows that 77 scholars believe the presence of the JSDF does violate or seems to violate the constitution (The Asahi Shimbun, 30 June 2015).

The seriousness of recent constitutional debates in Japan points to the fact that the public still questions the legality of the JSDF as a military entity. Clause 1, Article 9 of the constitution renounces war and the threat or use of force as a means of settling international disputes, while the aforementioned Clause 2(a) stipulates that land, sea, and air forces will never be maintained, and (b) renounces the right of state belligerency. Debate over these details is focused on two issues: Whether the very existence of the JSDF violates Clause 2, and whether any military activities not aimed at homeland self-defense against foreign attack violate Clauses 1 and 2(b).

According to a survey conducted in March 2017 by the Nihon Hoso Kyokai (*NHK*), the Japanese public news channel, 62 percent of the respondents believe the JSDF is constitutionally legitimate, whereas 33 percent answered either *illegitimate* or *not sure* (NHK 2018). This study suggests nearly one-third of the population in Japan is not yet confident with the legal justification for their national defense institution, nor that their peaceful constitution and the JSDF can coexist.

The public's uncertainty about the JSDF's legality has been further deepened by former Prime Minister Abe's proposal to keep the two clauses as they are in Article 9 and to supplement a new Clause 3 stipulating that the JSDF is a legitimate military organization named the *Armed Forces of Japan*.[3]

Abe argued his case at the National Diet in November 2017, saying, "the Japanese government must no longer tell the JSDF personnel that their service and social roles are indeed unconstitutional while requiring them to swear in their personal sacrifices to their services."[4] Further, on 3 May 2018 (the national holiday celebrating enactment of the Constitution), Abe sent a video message to the 20th constitutional forum in Tokyo held amongst his Liberal Democratic Party members and supporters of his constitutional agenda. In his message, which was relayed to more than 150 similar conservative meetings concurrently held outside Tokyo, Abe argued that the JSDF must be declared a legal entity in a revised constitution; in this way, he said, the constitutional debate must end.[5]

---

3   The Asahi Shimbun, 4 May 2017.
4   His statement in the National Diet was in response to a question raised by the Democratic Party on 21 November 2017: "It is extremely irresponsible to tell SDF personnel, 'You may be unconstitutional, but risk your lives if anything should happen.' It is our generation's responsibility to eliminate room for such discussions." *The Mainichi Japan*, 22 November 2017. <https://mainichi.jp/english/articles/20171122/p2a/00m/0na/009000c> (last access: 1 July 2018).
5   "PM Abe's video message: 'Putting the constitutional debate to an end'", *The Sankei Shimbun*, 3 May 2018; and Osaki and Kikuchi (2018).

The public is split over Abe's proposed amendment to the constitution. According to an opinion poll published by *The Yomiuri Shimbun* on 30 April 2018, 51 percent of the respondents support the amendment whereas 46 percent do not.[6] This represents an increase from polls conducted in 2016 by *The Mainichi Shimbun*. More than half of their respondents opposed any constitutional amendments whereas only 30 percent supported such changes.[7] Most recently, in major newspaper opinion polls focused on Abe's idea of adding Clause 3, 41 percent *support*, 50 percent *do not support*, highlighting just how contentious and muddy public opinion is on this issue.[8]

2.2   Public Opinion on the JSDF's Activities

Public opinion of the JSDF's services can be characterized in four ways. Firstly, the vast majority of the Japanese population favors the *presence* of the JSDF itself. According to an official public opinion poll conducted in 2015, 92 percent of the respondents supported the JSDF (Cabinet Office of Japan 2015). Public opinion polls conducted by the Cabinet Office of Japan show that 81 percent of the respondents in 1997 held the JSDF in positive regard, categorizing their general services as *good* (31 percent) or *relatively good* (50 percent); these numbers had increased to 90 percent by 2018 (*good* (37 percent) and *relatively good* (53 percent)) (Cabinet Office of Japan 2018) (see Table 1).

Table 1:   General evaluation of the JSDF in 1997 and 2018

Response	1997	2018
Good	31 %	37 %
Relatively good	50 %	53 %
Relatively bad	11 %	5 %
Bad	1 %	1 %
Don't know	8 %	n/a

Source: Cabinet Office of Japan 1997 and 2018.
Note: Question wording: What is your general evaluation of the JSDF?

---

6   The Yomiuri Shimbun, 30 April 2018.
7   The Mainichi Shimbun, 17 April 2016.
8   The Asahi Shimbun, 3 May 2020.

Secondly, such high approval for the JSDF appears to be limited to its non-combat services related to disaster and humanitarian relief in Japan and abroad. 79 percent of the respondents to the 2018 poll believe disaster relief to be the JSDF's primary function, an increase from 67 percent in the 1997 poll (see Table 2; Cabinet Office of Japan 2018). The 2018 poll also shows that 87 percent highly approve of the JSDF's current overseas activities, including United Nations peacekeeping operations (UNPKO) (legally limited to engineering activities at the time of the poll) and disaster relief outside Japan (see Table 3). It notes that 89 percent of the respondents believe that the JSDF should continue with such activities in the future (see Table 4; Cabinet Office of Japan 2018).[9]

The Yomiuri Shimbun's 2003 poll indicates similar support levels for emergency disaster relief (78 percent), UNPKO (engineering activities) (42 percent), and non-UNPKO humanitarian assistance such as that conducted in Iraq (engineering support) (39 percent) (Midford 2011, 40).

Table 2:   Primary mission of the JSDF

Response	1997	2018
National security	57 %	61 %
Domestic security and order	26 %	50 %
Disaster relief	67 %	79 %
International cooperation	25 %	35 %
Respond to ballistic missile attacks	n/a	40 %

Source: Cabinet Office of Japan 1997 and 2018.
Note: Question wording: "What do you think is the JSDF's primary mission? Choose as many as you wish from the list below".
n/a: not available.

---

9   It is critical to note that the Japanese government treats UN peacekeeping operations and disaster relief activities abroad in the same category under "international peace cooperation activities". This mingling of the two separate activities into one "international activity" has confused the public and blurred the understanding of various roles and responsibilities *within* units of the JSDF (Yasutomi and Kiba 2015).

Table 3:   Evaluation of the JSDF's overseas activities

Response	2018
Very positive	37 %
Relatively positive	51 %
Relatively negative	6 %
Very negative	1 %

Source: Cabinet Office of Japan 2018.
Note: Question wording: "How do you evaluate the JSDF's overseas activities?"

Table 4:   Expectations about future JSDF overseas activities

Response	2018
Commit to the activities more actively	21 %
Continue with the current activities	67 %
Reduce the activities	5 %
Discontinue all activities	2 %

Source: Cabinet Office of Japan 2018
Note: Question wording: Question: "International Peace Cooperation Activities refer to the JSDF's overseas activities including participation in UNPKO and disaster relief & humanitarian assistance abroad. What do you think the JSDF should do in the future?"

Thirdly, the public is not fully opposed to the use of force if it is strictly limited to national territorial defense. In his book, *Rethinking Japanese Public Opinion and Security*, Paul Midford, a leading scholar of Japanese public opinion, argues that the public views the use of military power as appropriate and acceptable only when Japan faces foreign invasion (Midford 2011, 32). He claims that, according to a poll conducted by Washington State University and its collaborating institutes, more than 78 percent of the respondents believe that it is legitimate for Japan to go to war when Japan is attacked (Midford 2011, 32). His claim was supported by a Cabinet Office poll in 2018. More than 60 percent of the respondents said they would support the JSDF's fight to resist foreign invasion (Cabinet Office of Japan 2018).[10]

---

10   For the question *How would you respond … if Japan faces foreign invasion?*, the supportive answers were: *Enlist Myself in the JSDF and fight together with other JSDF soldiers* (6 percent); *Support the JSDF in some way* (do not join the JSDF but support its defensive activities) (55 percent).

Finally, a larger part of the public is skeptical about the use of the military in foreign countries. According to Midford's analysis, the Japanese tend to view the use of military power as ineffective and inappropriate for preventing human rights abuses, genocide, and terrorism in other countries (Midford 2011, 32–38).[11] As Japan's role in UNPKO is concerned, respondents believe that non-military, non-combat humanitarian contributions are more appropriate (Midford 2011, 39).

3   Studies in Military Sociology and the Related Fields conducted in Japan

3.1   Research on Military Sociology in Japan

The study of military sociology is limited in Japan. Research in the field primarily focuses on challenges facing soldiers and their families, support for military families, and issues regarding soldier identity and morale.

Hitoshi Kawano (2015) takes up the topic of military family support in Japan in his article, "The JSDF and Family Support: Building Community Capacity in Japan". Based on his comparative studies of the models of community capacity in the US and British armed forces, he concludes that Japan should follow the US/UK model of supplementing formal support infrastructure with informal support for families. Saya Kiba also analyses the family support system for JSDF soldiers, particularly from the perspective of disaster relief. In her article, "Parliamentary debate on Family Support Programs for the Japan Ground Self-Defense Force (JGSDF)", she explains that Japanese lawmakers have paid greater attention to the need to develop family support systems since the Great East Japan Earthquake of 2011, but many of the requests and demands from JSDF soldiers and their families have yet to be met (Kiba 2019).

In her article, "Ambiguous Positioning of Military Wives: Exclusion and Reliance Techniques in Japan," Atsuko Fukuura (2017) summarizes her interviews

---

11   Midford analyzed polls conducted by the *Asahi Shimbun*, the *Yomiuri Shimbun*, and Washington State University/SAGE measuring Japanese public opinion about the US invasions in Afghanistan in 2001 and Iraq in 2003. He examined public attitudes toward the use of the military in another country for reasons including promoting human rights and democracy, preventing genocide, and combating terrorism. The polls, Midford notes, indicate that Japanese people believe using the military for these purposes is ineffective and illegitimate. Only 9 percent of respondents answered that promoting human rights abroad was a "legitimate" use of the military, compared to "somewhat legitimate" (33 percent), "not very legitimate" (33 percent), and "not legitimate" (20 percent).

with wives of JSDF members, analyzing the way their husbands' service-related mental health issues have impacted their relationships. The issue of mental health in relation to both the military and society is also studied in detail by Hitoshi Kawano (2013a). His article, "Studies in Clinical Sociology on the JSDF's Overseas Activities", compares the US, UK, and Japanese systems for mental health treatment for soldiers and their families serving abroad. He argues that, while some US and UK examples should be learnt and followed, more extended measures are necessary to accommodate the specific circumstances of JSDF requirements.

Takako Hikotani (2007), in her article, "Does a Civil-military Gap Exist in Japan?", presents the quantitative results of her interviews with JSDF soldiers and civilians, exposing gaps in both their values and perceptions of national defense. Yuko Whitestone (2007) analyses changes in professional identities amongst the soldiers participating in UNPKO in 2002. Hitoshi Kawano (2001, 2004) conducted a similar analysis, evaluating the changing morale of JSDF soldiers enlisted in past UNPKO missions. He finds that their participation in UNPKO is more likely to be motivated by family-related reasons than career-related grounds.

Noriko Sudo (2013) examines more than 30 films produced in cooperation with the JSDF and analyses how their scenes, scenarios, and stage effects carefully reflect the political situation at the time of their production. She also points out that the JSDF was an active and cooperative partner in the production of such films (e.g., providing specific information on uniforms, terminology, etc.) in the hope that the films would attract more recruits in the future.

Another set of studies in military sociology in Japan is comprised by Japanese-language works that introduce and explain the latest trends in military sociology in the West. These efforts are particularly important in that they can familiarize the Japanese audience with the fundamental theoretical frameworks and current critical issues in the area of military sociology, which is still foreign to many students in Japan.

Hitoshi Kawano (2007), in his article, "Studies of 'the Military and Society' of Today", describes the core arguments of and discussions amongst Western military sociologists and scholars. He covers topics ranging from the Huntington-Janowitz arguments (Huntington 1957, 1996; Janowitz 1964) to traits and issues in postmodern militaries (Moskos 2000), explaining how scholars in Japan should extend these theories and models to various cases in the JSDF. Kawano (2013b) captures sociologists' attention with the title and topic of his article, "How should we think about 'New War'?", introducing the concept of a *hybrid military* that poses major changes to the roles of civilians within the military, recruitment patterns, roles of female soldiers, support for military families, and LGBT[12] soldiers.

Fumika Sato's (2013) work sheds crucial light on the developments of sociological discussions of gender perspectives in the Japanese language. In her book chapter, "Sociology of War and the Military from the Gender Perspective", she introduces leading scholars in the field such as Helena Carreiras (2006) and explores how gender identities and ideologies have affected the performance of militaries in the West. She highlights Marina Nuciari's (2018) work, which includes important questions for future research on issues related to women in the military, such as the recruitment and retention of female soldiers. Atsushi Yasutomi (2018) introduces studies from the West in his book chapter entitled "Revolution in Information Technology and the Changes in Military Culture." He explains how modern information technology (such as Social Networking Service) has changed the behavior of soldiers on the battlefield and how technology has affected performance in their missions abroad.

3.2   War Sociology as opposed to Military Sociology

It should be noted that most of the sociological studies done in Japan which are related to the military have focused on war experiences and memories, the role of media in society, and peace education. They have typically spotlighted the civilians who were victims of World War II (WWII), shining light on the memories of surviving soldiers, the fate of pupils drafted to serve the Japanese Imperial Army/Navy, the treatment of Koreans during the Japanese occupation, and more recently, Okinawans' resistance to the presence of US bases and soldiers in the Islands.

In 2015 and 2016, the Japan Sociological Society hosted panels specifically on war and the military. The panels discussed many of the aforementioned issues, including the relationship between society and the US bases in Japan (particularly in Okinawa), the memories of WWII, and the wartime draft system. These topics seem to be favorites in the field, including issues – all related to peace studies – that Japanese sociologists typically want to discuss. The resulting volume, *War Sociology: A Conception – The Institutions, the Experiences, and the Media*, edited by Yoshiaki Fukuma et al. (2013) compiles the content of the Society's conference panels. Fukuma and his colleagues seek to distance themselves from other military sociologists by focusing on the current state of *warfare*, broadly construed. They argue that the military and the field of military sociology require new, more comprehensive methods of addressing *War Sociology*. They place particular stress on Japanese

---

12   Lesbian, Gay, Bisexual, and Transgender.

experiences in WWII, seeking to identify the relationship between Japanese society and war while adopting aspects and methods of academic disciplines developed in the West and elsewhere. Similar works in this line of studies can be found in *War Sociology* (Yoshii and Seki 2016).

3.3   Military Anthropology

Scholars with an anthropological background have paid particular attention to the JSDF soldiers and their families. *Military Anthropology*, edited by Masakazu Tanaka (2015), is a collection of innovative works on anthropological studies related to the JSDF, which may be the only published book in this field in Japan. It contains a series of chapters on topics including female JSDF personnel, family support for soldiers, military death and remembrance, and war museums.

In her book on female soldiers and recruitment, *Military Organization and Gender: Women in the JSDF*, Fumika Sato (2004) carefully documents working conditions inside the JSDF from the female perspective, cases of sexual harassment, and life for female cadets in the National Defense Academy. Sato warns that work is needed to improve the status and guarantee the equal rights of women in the JSDF while describing the simultaneous and urgent need for more female recruits.

Atsuko Fukuura (2012) contributed another perspective in her 2012 article, "Getting Involved: Relocation, Overseas deployment and Spouse Clubs for Japan Self Defense Officers." Fukuura sheds light on the wives of JSDF soldiers, presenting ethnographic details about a number of spouses of soldiers serving abroad, with a focus on the JSDF's informal dimensions of assistance (in addition to the institutional support provided) to military families.

Anthropological studies of JSDF soldiers from non-Japanese scholars have provided fresh, eye-opening analyses of the public's relationship to the JSDF. Sabine Frühstück and Eyal Ben-Ari (2002), in their article "'Now We Show It All!' – Normalization and the Management of Violence in Japan's Armed Forces," argue that institutional change requires shifts in two key areas: public support for the JSDF and, in turn, the JSDF's attitude toward the public. They also observed that the roles and expected functions of the JSDF changed in the aftermath of the Cold War. Shifting expectations compelled the JSDF to euphemize its inevitable transformation to a more realistic organization of violence, using the word *normalization* with the Japanese public while avoiding words such as *re-militarization*. Furthermore, Frühstück (2007)'s book *Uneasy Warriors: Gender, Memory, and Popular Culture in the Japanese Army* described how Japanese soldiers feel uneasy about appearing as *ordinary* and *real* warriors in the eyes of the Japanese public. Soldiers fear that they will receive criticism for representing a threatening, unconstitutional being in Japanese society. She explains that the Japanese public in general still holds firm reservations against the JSDF's war training and exercises, which they have deemed contradictory to the war-renouncing constitution. Such confining circumstances, she concludes, prevent Japanese soldiers from achieving maturity as warriors.

3.4   Critical Studies on the JSDF

A number of sociological policy studies have examined the JSDF, with notable examples emerging from the fields of international security and of governance. Katsuhiro Musashi (2009), in his book, *Civilian Control in Post-Cold War Japan*, surveys the involvement of Japanese military officials in law-making processes related to defense and security issues since the end of the Cold War. He notes the increasing degree of influence that military officials had in a series of law-making processes and warns that civilian control needs to be strengthened in the Japanese parliament.

Other scholars have focused on the study of civil-military cooperation. Based on arguments that collaborations between the JSDF and other state and non-state agencies have met little success during past overseas activities of the JSDF (for example, peacekeeping operations and humanitarian assistance/disaster relief operations), scholars like Yuji Uesugi and his colleagues (2016) suggest a comprehensive approach to civil-military cooperation among Japanese institutions. Labelling it the *All-Japan Approach*, Uesugi and others argue that the state and non-state agencies in Japan involved in peace support operations (PSO) abroad – the JSDF, Ministry of Defense, Ministry of Foreign Affairs, and non-governmental organizations (NGO) – should be coordinated so as to maintain a more coherent Japanese assistance policy while avoiding overlaps and misunderstandings.

A comparatively vast number of policy studies have been done about the role of the JSDF in large-scale natural disaster emergencies. Research on this topic became especially popular after the Great East Japan Earthquake, which prompted the deployment of more than 107,000 soldiers for relief efforts (Yoshizaki 2011). For example, Yutaka Katayama's edited book, *Managing International Cooperation for Disaster Relief*, contains a number of policy studies on the lessons learnt from the cooperation and coordination amongst the JSDF and other state and non-state actors involved in relief efforts following the earthquake (Katayama 2017).

Critical research on the JSDF's foreign deployment is much more abundant than on the topics mentioned above. Since it first dispatched its UNPKO unit to Cambodia in 1992, Japan has sent the JSDF and civilian experts to 13 UN missions through 2017.[13] Japan has also deployed the JSDF to several non-UN missions. After the 2001 terrorist attacks in the US, Japan passed a law allowing the deployment of two military vessels – such as the supply ship *Tokiwa* and the destroyer *Kirisame* – to the Indian Ocean to refuel US, British and other vessels operating in the theatre. Japan also deployed to Iraq from 2003 to 2009 under a special law valid for a set period of time, allowing for humanitarian and engineering activities in the Samawa region (Ministry of Defense 2009, 2010). A number of studies in this area discuss the effects of the JSDF's foreign deployments on international relations and the impact of Japanese contributions to international peace and stability in post-conflict areas (e.g., Honda 2018; Imanishi 2014). Others criticize the legal paradox wherein the JSDF must respond to day-to-day combat-related realities in the UNPKO and other peace mission theatres whilst such activities are restricted under domestic laws and Article 9 of the Constitution. They suggest amendments to relevant laws and drastic transformation of the JSDF into a force that is more compatible with other militaries and capable of meeting the needs of international peace efforts. By the same token, other studies seek realistic – if temporary at best – compromises whereby the JSDF could find itself within the restrictions of current laws without precipitating constitutional change (e.g., Kiba and Yasutomi 2013).

3.5   Non-academic Works, Reports, Exposés, and Essays on the JSDF

It is noteworthy that an increasing number of non-academic reports and exposés have explored negative factors surrounding the JSDF's foreign deployments. These works commonly describe the dangers and sacrifices expected of JSDF soldiers, as well as the public's increasing anxieties and distrust toward the JSDF and Japanese government in general.

The popularity of non-academic works expressing public confusion and concerns about the future of the JSDF saw remarkable growth following nationwide disputes over the Diet's passing of the 2015 Security Legislation bill. The legislation is a package of eleven laws aimed at preparing Japan for the changing security landscape in Asia by relaxing regulations on the use of force. The bill's passing allowed the Japanese government to reinterpret the right of collective self-defense – previously understood to have been banned by the Constitution[14] – though the

---

13   Cabinet Office, Secretariat of the International Peace Cooperation Headquarters (2019)

14   On 14 October 1972, the government explained to the Diet that use of force for exercising the right of collective self-defense (for the purpose of inhibiting armed attack against other countries) shall not be permitted under the Constitution. See: "Relationship between the Right of Collective Self-Defense and the Constitution", submitted by the Government

right itself is endowed under the UN Charter.[15] As a result, the Security Legislation expanded conditions under which the JSDF could take military action, allowing it, *inter alia*, to assist the Japan Maritime Safety Agency in protecting civilian ships under attack in international waters and to intercept ballistic missiles aimed at US soil. It also enabled JSDF soldiers to approach and fight local armed groups to rescue Japanese nationals as well as military personnel from other countries participating in UNPKO.

Critics claim that the new legislation compromises the 9th Article of the Constitution (i.e., Japan renouncing the belligerency right). According to a May 2017 opinion poll, 41 percent of respondents support the legislation while 47 percent do not. In the same poll, 40 percent believe the legislation violates the 9th Article of the Constitution while 41 percent think it is constitutional.[16] Moreover, the public is still confused about the legal reforms since they were written in such a complicated manner that general readers are not able to fully understand how the regulations have been modified and supplemented. A poll showed that 81 percent of respondents felt that the legislation was not sufficiently explained to the public by the government.[17]

Controversies and confusions also derived from the disputes over whether the JSDF's activities as part of the UN Mission in South Sudan (UNMISS) violate the Five Principles of their participation in UNPKO. The Five Principles of peacekeeping stipulated in Article 6 (7) of the PKO (Peacekeeping Operations) Act specify the conditions under which Japan can participate in UN peacekeeping operations. They include: (1) agreement on a ceasefire reached amongst the parties to the armed conflict; (2) consent from the UN and from the host country allowing Japan to participate in UNPKO; (3) impartiality of the Japanese operations; (4) withdrawal if the above conditions are not met; and (5) the use of weapons within limits judged reasonably necessary. The debate came to the fore when a 300-member strong JSDF engineering unit – stationed in Juba under UNMISS since 2011 – was granted wider permissions for the use of weapons under the auspices of the

---

to the Committee on Audit of the House of Councilors, 14 October 1972. The original Japanese text can be found at <www.kantei.go.jp/jp/singi/anzenhosyou2/dai4/siryou.pdf> (last access: 1 December 2018).

15   On page 166, it reads, "in light of the current security environment, it has been concluded that not only when an armed attack against Japan occurs but also when an armed attack against a foreign country that is in a close relationship with Japan occurs and as a result threatens Japan's survival and poses a clear danger, [...] use of force to the minimum extent necessary should be interpreted to be permitted under the Constitution as measures for self-defense in accordance with the basic logic of the Government's view to date."

16   *The Asahi Shimbun*, 2 May 2017.

17   *Kyodo*, 30–31 May 2017.

2015 Security Legislation. In June 2016, the JSDF encountered serious exchanges of fire between the national armed forces of South Sudan and armed opposition groups. It was the first serious incident in which the JSDF was confronted with dangers that could result in the loss of soldiers' lives (NHK 2017). It touched off a new wave of legal debates weighing the JSDF's right to combat the insurgents (covered by the Security Legislation's permissions for the use of weapons to protect soldiers from local insurgencies) against violating the PKO Five Principles (under which the JSDF must withdraw because the ceasefire of the conflicting parties is compromised).[18] Subsequent polls showed that more than 50 percent of respondents did not support the JSDF's new combat functions as part of PKO activities.[19]

Since the late 2000s, the JSDF has sought to restructure its organization and mission capacity. The aforementioned legal reforms have expanded the JSDF's ability to respond to current changes in the international security environment. They suggest that the JSDF may well be given opportunities to take military action against any substantial threats to the homeland or to JSDF soldiers serving abroad. These unprecedented changes represent a clear and profound departure from the previous situation where only engineering and disaster relief activities were allowed on foreign soil. The JSDF's far-reaching transition has also attracted a great deal of attention from the public, whose questions and concerns have contributed to more alarming discussions amongst critics and journalists in Japan.

A well-circulated essay written in 2016 by Sukeyasu Ito (2016), a former JSDF officer, points out the unrealistic nature of JSDF tactical procedures. He notes that their politicization leaves no room to provision for the possible deaths of Japanese soldiers. Ito warns the Japanese government and the public in general of the dangers of present-day deployments and questions the value of soldiers' personal sacrifices in defense of their country.

More recently, Yujin Fuse and Hideyuki Miura (2018) take up the topic of government concealment. Their book reveals the gap between the realities facing

---

18   "PKO Five Principles to be reviewed after the Security Legislation passes," [original Japanese] *The Sankei Shimbun*, 19 May 2014.

19   *The Asahi Shimbun*, 14 March 2017; and, *The Yomiuri Shimbun*, 19 March 2017. It is noteworthy that once the decision on the JSDF dispatch was made and after the unit had been sent abroad, the National Diet did not conduct periodic reviews to evaluate its decision. The media, likewise, usually put immense attention on decisions about the JSDF's overseas deployments; however, once the forces have arrived on foreign soil, the media is typically not interested in covering the day-to-day events of their PKO activities. A cycle emerges in which the media takes up a controversial topic such as the issue of the Security Legislation package, the public heightens their concerns over the legality as well as the safety of the JSDF in foreign missions, heated opinions are exchanged, and then, as the troops carry on abroad as usual, the matter fades into the background once more.

the Japanese UN peacekeepers in Juba, South Sudan and the limits placed on their actions by current legal restrictions. Fuse and Miura harshly deride the attempt to conceal the JSDF's peacekeeping activity logbooks and accuse the government of euphemizing the vocabulary depicting the realistic – and thus illegal – combat situations the logbooks described. Many of these pieces can be seen to follow a precedent that Shigeru Handa (2009), a liberal journalist, helped to set in 2006 when he raised concerns that Japan's political decisions to dispatch the JSDF's PKO units without carefully evaluating the security situations in deployment zones increased the risks of soldiers being killed in operations. Finally, Yujin Fuse (2015) noted that, given the increasing number of students in debt, many young people will eventually have no choice but to enlist themselves in the JSDF services – despite potential dangers to their lives and well-being – in order to have aspects of their living costs compensated (Amamiya et al. 2017; Fuse 2015).

In sum, these claims fear that either JSDF soldiers will fall victim to a legal system that is unprepared for responding to realities on the ground, resulting in lost morale and public support, or that Japan will be dragged into warfare that forces drastic changes to its peaceful constitution. Typically, they signal perceptible growth of public mistrust in how the government is shaping and implementing its policy toward national defense and contributing to international peace. The general popularity of non-academic works expressing these concerns may reflect the lack of academic studies in critical sociology in Japan.

4   Research Funds for Military Sociology

For similar political and cultural reasons, research funds supporting the study of military sociology in Japan are extremely limited. The shortage of funds does not necessarily mean a lack of budget *per se*, but rather that research opportunities are restricted by insufficient support from academic communities, private enterprises, and, in the case of national and other public research grants, apportionments from Japanese taxpayers.

The sensitivity in sponsoring military studies due to the aforementioned confinement evoked jittery disputes amongst scholars and opinion leaders when the MoD initiated a grant program for research in the field of military sciences.

The situation was poised to improve in 2015 when the MoD launched a new, 540-million-yen (approximately 4.3 million Euro) independent research grant project open to universities, research institutes and private enterprises to foster scientific research for defense technology. This grant program, sponsored by the Acquisition, Technology and Logistics Agency (ATLA), a subbranch of the MoD, accepted a first batch of 109 research proposals studying technologies including those related to laser and micro-bubble coating technology for military vessels. However, it evoked jittery disputes amongst scholars and opinion leaders, coming under fire for feeding on dual-use technologies with applications in both civilian and military domains. The Science Council of Japan, an advisory body to the Cabinet with more than 850,000 Japanese scientists as members, issued a press release condemning the scientists participating in such research and calling for a boycott of their dual-use technology projects and findings (Cyranoski 2017). A number of renowned universities including University of Tokyo, Kyoto University, and Waseda University made charters and guidelines specifically prohibiting researchers from applying for and making use of these ATLA grants, arguing that this field of research could help encourage weapon systems development and threaten international peace (Cyranoski 2017).

Moreover, some of the boycotts initially targeted at the ATLA grants went even further, denouncing all research pertaining to military science. For example, Kyoto University, one of the most renowned national universities in Japan, posted a statement entitled "Kyoto University's principal policy regarding research on military sciences" on its homepage in March 2018. It declared that "the University has since its very foundation long contributed to coexistence and harmony in the international society ... and the University therefore denounces and does not support any military research that could lead to threats to social stability, to happiness of humankind, and to peace."[20] In response to Kyoto University's announcement, some national and private universities followed suit and denounced any research in military science.[21]

The issue presents a difficult problem given the current state of technology, parts that are used in military equipment are likely to be used in electronics (and other components) of civilian technologies. The opposite is also true, particularly in the case of the internet and Global Positioning System (GPS) technology. It is thus unrealistic to distinguish all military technologies from civilian technologies and vice versa. Still, the problem this presents may pale in comparison to the public's more pernicious, if also more abstract biases and fears about the term *military* itself. The post-war decades have taught generations of civilians and academics to reflexively envisage anything associated with the term *military* as dire, contraband, and to be avoided. In this regard, the disputes over dual-use technology in the me-

---

20   Kyoto University, "Basic Principles regarding military research in Kyoto University." (in Japanese) <www.kyoto-u.ac.jp/ja/research/kihonhoshin> (last access: 1 July 2018).

21   E.g., Hosei University, "Regarding the University's policy towards military research and research on civil/military dual-use." (in Japanese) <www.hosei.ac.jp/NEWS/newsrelease/170127.html> (last access: 1 July 2018).

dia and anxious statements by Japanese scholars merely reflect aspects of civilian/ military relations that are characteristic of post-war Japanese society at-large.

5   Obstacles to Military Sociology and Research

Obstacles to research on military sociology and studies in related fields can be characterized by the following closely interrelated factors, *i.e.*, (1) the scarcity of primary sources made available by the MoD and JSDF; (2) the nature of the military culture within the MoD/JSDF; and (3) the de facto taboo on speaking about one's experience pressed upon JSDF soldiers.

The prime obstacle to research in this field is the extreme scarcity of access to primary sources controlled by the MoD and the JSDF. As national defense authorities, the MoD/JSDF's withholding of sensitive information is understandable to a certain degree; however, publicized information concerning the topics in military sociology is unusually limited.

Such behavior starkly contrasts with that of Western militaries like the *Bundeswehr*, which make much more information available to the public (Biehl et al. 2020). This allows for pragmatic discussions amongst citizens, scholars, and other experts that can lead to beneficial long-term changes to military institutions. Conversely, the MoD/JSDF is conspicuously reluctant to release information when it deals with sensitive issues such as soldiers' mental health, deaths in service, suicide, military crimes, and harassment.

This is not to say that no official information on these topics is available; some statistical data regarding these issues can be found on government websites and in the Defense White Paper. On the MoD/JSDF website, for example, basic information including some – albeit minimal – survey results and official guidelines for sexual harassment is available for download (Ministry of Defense 2008, 2016b). The 2017 Defense White Paper also reveals that the number of suicides of servicemen and servicewomen committed in 2015 and 2016 was 101 and 65, respectively (Ministry of Defense 2017). Nevertheless, the MoD/JSDF have been repeatedly criticized for being overly reluctant to disclose internal information that is essential to sustaining long-term national debates and developing radical solutions to current problems. For example, an annual study analyzes statistical data on JSDF cadet morale at the National Defense Academy; however, the study results are not allowed to leave the Academy.[22]

---

22   Authors' interview, 13 April 2017.

The institutions' policing of data is not limited to the disclosure of quantitative information; it is also reflected in their failure to deliver critical qualitative information. A recent example emblematizes the MoD's reluctance in this regard. An official accountability request was placed in 2017 by a journalist hoping for the disclosure of a part of the JSDF's activity logbooks written by an active peacekeeper stationed in Juba, South Sudan. The public's attention had been drawn to one word, *sento*, or *combat*, in an excerpt from one of the logbooks. *Sento* was used to describe the situation when, in June 2016, South Sudanese forces exchanged heavy fire with local armed groups, a moment that threatened to catch the JSDF in the middle (they were forced to prepare to defend themselves against the local insurgents) (NHK 2017). The logbook detailed what and how the JSDF was preparing to respond to this *sento* – combat – situation. Fearing questions of whether this specific wording testifies to a clear violation of the Five Principles, then Defense Minister Tomomi Inada explained to parliament that the use of *sento* was indeed inappropriate and the particular logbook in question had been destroyed and was thus not available to the public.[23]

The fear of public scrutiny and critical reprisal that characterizes the MoD/JSDF's reluctance to disclose information has worked its way to the cultural core of both institutions. For members of the JSDF, speaking about political issues in public is taboo, while other political activities are expressly forbidden. The Self-Defense Forces Act restricts active JSDF personnel from being involved in any political activities except for voting (Article 61). They cannot donate to political parties or run as a candidate in national or local elections. The same clause also forbids them from representing political organizations and associations. While not restricted from sharing political ideas, they seek to avoid the risks of being accused of *civilian control violations* by remaining extraordinarily cautious and hesitant to make themselves heard.

This sensitivity is well-reflected by criticism in the media of a statement by Adm. Katsutoshi Kawano, the then Chief of Staff of the Joint Staff, who expressed his personal support for then Prime Minister Abe's proposed amendments to the constitution. The media, as well as the opposition parties in the National Diet, accused his blunt political address of a stark violation of civilian control.[24] A similar sensitivity is widely shared among JSDF personnel in the lower ranks, too. In general, they remain very hesitant to speak not only about their views on defense

---

23   *The Asahi Shimbun*, 8 February 2017. It was only after a series of criticisms by the media that the MoD disclosed the logbooks in question. Criticisms continued because most of the sentences were sealed in black to make them unreadable for protecting soldiers' privacy. It took further weeks for the MoD to make some logbooks without black-outs public.

24   Sankei Shimbun Editorial Board (2018)

policies and political issues but also about personal reflections on their identity as soldiers and on their service in a variety of settings, including media interviews and academic discussions.[25]

The JSDF officers and soldiers are as such circumspect in their political conversation, to say nothing of more sensitive issues such as service-related deaths and suicide. The death of soldiers is a taboo topic in the JSDF, particularly pertaining to deaths in combat-related situations. Soldiers of all ranks alike are trained not to bring up the topic of death in service – at least openly – unless absolutely necessary, though some exceptions exist.[26] Several unit leaders within the JSDF who were keen on this issue designed a brief, optional workshop as part of their pre-deployment classes and training, allowing their subordinates to discuss deaths in missions and to write their last wills and notes to their families.[27] These are exceptional cases, and their classes were all handled in a personal manner, outside of the official JSDF curriculum. These unit leaders revealed that they often felt pressured by their superiors, who would subtly suggest that they close down such unofficial classes.[28]

A former Joint Chief of Staff made news for violating this taboo subject in another way, revealing to the media that the government had ordered him not to disclose that the JSDF had sent coffins to its Iraq operations (2003–2009). He explained that coffins were sent to Iraq to prepare for the possibility that soldiers would die, which the public construed as a violation of the JSDF's overseas deployment[29] on the condition that the theatre is a non-combat area (NHK 2014).

6   Conclusion

There is a consensus amongst scholars that little study is done in the area of military sociology in Japan. The examinations above make clear that one of the compelling reasons for this deficiency stems from the ways that continuous legal controversies over the legitimacy of the JSDF have divided the Japanese public. They continually generate confusion and concerns about the JSDF and its fundamental defense responsibilities.

The study of military sociology is becoming ever more important and thus necessary in Japan as well as in all Western societies with democratic militaries

---

25   Authors' interview with a major colonel, Ground Self-Defense Force, 23 January 2018.
26   Authors' interview, 3 March 2017.
27   Authors' interview, 3 March 2017.
28   Authors' interview, 3 March 2017.
29   Act on Special Measures concerning Humanitarian Relief and Reconstruction Work and Security Assistance in Iraq, 2003.

and decreasing populations (Ministry of Defense 2018: 391). Studies aimed at improving the wellbeing of soldiers and solving issues regarding recruitment and retention, gender in the military, and care for military families will prove key in developing the militaries and security of democratic countries for the foreseeable future. Nonetheless, in light of the challenges examined above, the development of studies in military sociology in Japan does not appear promising. Changing this situation seems to depend on whether and to what degree the Japanese population can accommodate the nature of the military as a state authority and appreciate that force plays a crucial role in the international political environment of today.

References

Amamiya, K., K. Irie, Y. Kurihara, S. Shirai, W. Takahashi, Y. Fuse, and M. Yang. 2017. *Against Economic Conscription. Wars and Students*. Tokyo: Iwanami Booklets. (Japanese).

Cabinet Office of Japan. 1997. "Public Opinion Survey regarding the Japan Self-Defense Force and Defense Issues." <https://survey.gov-online.go.jp/h08/bouei.html> (last access: 1 December 2018). (Japanese).

Cabinet Office of Japan. 2015. "Public Opinion Survey regarding the Japan Self-Defense Force and Defense Issues." <http://survey.gov-online.go.jp/h26/h26-bouei/index.html> (last access: 1 December 2018). (Japanese).

Cabinet Office of Japan. 2018. "Public Opinion Survey regarding the Japan Self-Defense Force and Defense Issues." <https://survey.gov-online.go.jp/h29/h29-bouei/index.html> (last access: 1 December 2018). (Japanese).

Cabinet Office, Secretariat of the International Peace Cooperation Headquarters. 2019. "Japan's Contribution through International Peace Support Operations as of 8 January 2019." <www.pko.go.jp/pko_j/info/other/pdf/data01.pdf> (last access: 4 February 2019). (Japanese).

Carreiras, H. 2006. *Gender and the Military: Women in the Armed Forces of Western Democracies*. London: Routledge.

Cyranoski, D. 2017. "Japanese Scientists Call for a Boycott of Military Research." *Nature*, 6 April. <www.nature.com/news/japanese-scientists-call-for-boycott-of-military-research-1.21779> (last access: 1 July 2018).

Frühstück, S., and E. Ben-Ari. 2002. "Now We Show It All! Normalization and the Management of Violence in Japan's Armed Forces." *The Journal of Japanese Studies* 28(1): 1–39.

Frühstück, S. 2007. *Uneasy Warriors: Gender, Memory, and Popular Culture in the Japanese Army*. Berkeley: University of California.

Fukuma, Y., G. Nogami, S. Araragi, and S. Ishihara, eds. 2013. *War Sociology: A Conception – The Institutions, the Experiences, and the Media.* Tokyo: Bensei Publishers. (Japanese).

Fukuura, A. 2012. "Getting Involved: Relocation, Overseas Deployment and Spouse Clubs for Japan Self Defense Officers." *Working Paper No. 173*, Shiga University, Faculty of Economics.

Fukuura, A. 2017. "Ambiguous Positioning of Military Wives. Exclusion and Reliance Techniques in Japan." *Working Paper No. 266*, Shiga University, Faculty of Economics.

Fuse, Y. 2015. *Economic Conscription.* Tokyo: Shueisha Shinsho. (Japanese).

Fuse, Y., and H. Miura. 2018. *Concealing the JSDF Activity Logbooks in South Sudan: What Did the Soldiers See in South Sudan?* Tokyo: Shueisha Gakugei Publication. (Japanese).

Handa, S. 2009. *Into War Zones. JSDF in Transition.* Tokyo: Iwanami Shinsho Publication. (Japanese).

Hikotani, T. 2007. "Does a Civil-Military Gap Exist in Japan?" In *The Frontiers of International Security Studies. International Relations and Public Policy in the 21st Century*, edited by T. Murai and A. Mayama, 87–111. Tokyo: Akashi Shoten. (Japanese).

Honda, T. 2018. *In Search of Peace Contribution. Challenges and Aftermaths of the JSDF's Deployments to UNPKO.* Tokyo: Naigai Publishers. (Japanese).

Huntington, S. 1957. *The Soldier and the State.* Oxford: Harvard University Press.

Huntington, S. 1996. "Reforming Civil-Military Relations." In *Civil-Military Relations and Democracy*, edited by L. Diamond and M. Plattner, 3–11. Baltimore & London: Johns Hopkins University Press.

Imanishi, N. 2014. "UN Peacekeeping Operations and Japan's Peacebuilding Policy." *International Public Policy Studies* 19(1): 67–82. (Japanese)

Ito, S. 2016. *Can You Die for the Nation?* Tokyo: Bunshun Shinsho Publication. (Japanese).

Janowitz, M. 1964. *The Military in the Political Development of New Nations. An Essay in Comparative Analysis.* Chicago: University of Chicago Press.

Katayama, Y., ed. 2017. *Managing International Cooperation for Disaster Relief.* Tokyo: Minerva Publishers. (Japanese).

Kawano, H. 2001. "PKO and JSDF: the JSDF Personnel Participated in the UNPKOs. Their Motivations and the Adaptability." *National Defense Academy Repository* 83: 49–91. (Japanese).

Kawano, H. 2004. "Sociology of the JSDF in PKO. The Future of Mission Expansion in International Contribution and the Stress in Mission." In *'War' in post-war Japan*, edited by H. Naka, 214–257. Kyoto: Sekai Shisousha. (Japanese).

Kawano, H. 2007. "Studies of 'the Military and Society' of Today." *Journal of International Security* 35(3): 1–22. (Japanese).

Kawano, H. 2013a. "Studies in Clinical Sociology on the JSDF's Overseas Activities." *National Defense Academy Repository* 107: 1–21. (Japanese).

Kawano, H. 2013b. "How Should We Think about 'New War'?" In *War Sociology: A Conception. The Institutions, the Experiences, and the Media*, edited by Y. Fukuma, G. Nogami, S. Araragi, and S. Ishihara, 389–414. Tokyo: Bensei Publishers. (Japanese).

Kawano, H. 2015. "The JSDF and the Family Support: Building Community Capacity in Japan." In *Military Anthropology*, edited by M. Tanaka, 95–135. Tokyo: Fukyosha. (Japanese).

Kiba, S. 2019. "Parliamentary Debate on Family Support Programs for the Japan Ground Self-Defense Force (JGSDF)." *International Culture* 1: 3–22. (Japanese).

Kiba, S., and A. Yasutomi. 2013. "JSDF-NGO Cooperation. Issues and Challenges in JSDF's 'All-Japan' International Cooperation Policy." *Journal of International Cooperation Studies* 21(1): 119–148. (Japanese).

Lies, E. 2018. "Japan Protests Presence of Chinese Military Ship in Waters near Disputed Islands." *Reuters*, 11 January 2018. <www.reuters.com/article/us-japan-china-submarine/japan-protests-presence-of-chinese-military-ship-in-waters-near-disputed-islands-idUSKBN1F00R8>. (last access: 1 December 2018).

Ministry of Defense. 2008. *Survey on Sexual Harassment.* Tokyo: Ministry of Defense. <www.mod.go.jp/j/press/news/2008/04/21_03.pdf>. (Japanese).

Ministry of Defense. 2009. *Report of JSDF's Act on Special Measures Concerning Humanitarian Relief and Reconstruction Work and Security as of July 2009.* Tokyo: Ministry of Defense. <www.mod.go.jp/j/approach/kokusai_heiwa/iraq/kokaihoudou.pdf>. (Japanese).

Ministry of Defense. 2010. *Report of Refuel Mission under Special Anti-Terrorism Law as of April 2010.* Tokyo: Ministry of Defense. <www.mod.go.jp/j/approach/kokusai_heiwa/hokyushien/pdf/kekka.pdf>. (Japanese).

Ministry of Defense. 2016a. *Defense of Japan 2016* (White Paper). Tokyo: Ministry of Defense.

Ministry of Defense. 2016b. *Studies on Power Harassment.* <www.mod.go.jp/j/approach/agenda/meeting/board/ijime-boushi/pdf/04/jirei.pdf>. (last access: 1 December 2018.)

Ministry of Defense. 2017. *Defense of Japan 2017* (White Paper). Tokyo: Ministry of Defense.

Ministry of Defense 2018. *Defense of Japan 2018* (White Paper). Tokyo: Ministry of Defense.

Ministry of Defense 2020. *Defense of Japan 2020* (White Paper). Tokyo: Ministry of Defense.

Ministry of Defense 2021. *Defense of Japan 2021* (White Paper). Tokyo: Ministry of Defense.

Midford, P. 2011. *Rethinking Japanese Public Opinion and Security*. Palo Alto: Stanford University Press.

Mitani, T., ed. 2008. *War and the Public: Re-examining the War Memories*. Tokyo: Jumposha Publishers. (Japanese).

Moskos, C., ed. 2000. *The Postmodern Military. Armed Forces after the Cold War*. New York: Oxford University Press.

Musashi, K. 2009. *Civilian Control in Post-Cold War Japan*. Tokyo: Seibundo. (Japanese).

Nihon Hoso Kyokai (NHK). 2014. "After 10 years – Reality in Iraq." *Documentary 'Close-up Gendai' No.3485*, 16 April 2014.

Nihon Hoso Kyokai (NHK). 2017. "South Sudan. A PKO Press Officer Talks about the Truth of Crisis." 19 April 2017. <www.nhk.or.jp/kokusaihoudou/archive/2017/04/0419.html>. (Japanese).

Nihon Hoso Kyokai (NHK). 2018. "Opinion Poll. Japanese and Constitution." <www3.nhk.or.jp/news/special/kenpou70/yoron2017.html> (last access: 1 July 2018)

Nuciari, M. 2018. "Women in the Military. Sociological Arguments for Integration." In *Handbook of the Sociology of the Military*, edited by G. Caforio, 279–297. New York: Kluwer Academic/Plenum Publishers.

Osaki, T., and D. Kikuchi. 2018. "Abe Declares 2020 as Goal for New Constitution." *The Japan Times*, 3 May 2018 <www.japantimes.co.jp/news/2017/05/03/national/politics-diplomacy/abe-declares-2020-goal-new-constitution> (last access: 1 December 2018).

Sankei Shimbun Editorial Board. 2018. "Politicians Need to Behave Like Gentlemen, Too!" *The Sankei Shimbun*, 8 May 2018 <https://japan-forward.com/politicians-need-to-behave-like-gentlemen-too/> (last access: 1 July 2018).

Sato, F. 2004. *Military Organization and Gender. Women in the JSDF*. Tokyo: Keio University Press. (Japanese).

Sato, F. 2013. "Sociology of War and the Military from the gender perspectives." In *War Sociology: A Conception. The Institutions, the Experiences, and the Media*, edited by Y. Fukuma, G. Nogami, S. Araragi and S. Ishihara, 233–269. Tokyo: Bensei Publishers. (Japanese).

Sudo, N. 2013. *The Movies Produced in Cooperation with the JSDF.* Tokyo: Otsuki Shoten. (Japanese).

Tanaka, M. ed. 2015. *Military Anthropology*. Tokyo: Fukyosha. (Japanese)

The Asahi Shimbun. 2015. "Security Legislation Bill: Questionnaire to the Scholars." <www.asahi.com/topics/word/%E5%AE%89%E4%BF%9D%E6%B3%95%E6%A1%88%E5%AD%A6%E8%80%85%E3%82%A2%E3%83%B3%E3%82%B1%E3%83%BC%E3%83%88.html> (last access: 28 April 2021). (Japanese).

Uesugi, Y., H. Fujishige, T. Yoshizaki and T. Honda, eds. 2016. *All-Japan Approach towards the World: New Approach to Peacebuilding, Humanitarian Assistance, and Disaster Relief.* Tokyo: Naigai Shuppan. (Japanese).

Whitestone, Y. 2007. "Changing Professional Identity of the JSDF soldiers participating in UNPKO." *Journal of International Security* 35(3): 23–49. (Japanese).

Yasutomi, A. 2018. "Revolution in Information Technology and the Changes in Military Culture." In *War and Peace that Technology Changes*, edited by Michishita Narushige, 55–68. Tokyo: Fuyo Publishers. (Japanese).

Yasutomi, A., and S. Kiba. 2015. "Institutionalizing Interagency Coordination for Disaster Relief. Lessons from the JSDF's Civil-Military Cooperation in the Philippines." *Liaison* 7(Spring): 33–37.

Yoshii, H., and R. Seki. eds. 2016. *War Sociology: Theories, Mass Society, Culture and Representation*. Tokyo: Akashi Publications. (Japanese).

Yoshizaki, T. 2011. "Roles of the Military Organizations during Large-scale Disasters. Roles of the Military Organizations during Large-scale Disasters." *National Institute for Defense Studies International Security Symposium.* Tokyo: National Institute for Defense Studies: 71–88. (Japanese).

Sociological Research of the Military in Slovenia

Marjan Malešič

1   Introduction

The development of Slovenian military sociology started in former Yugoslavia to which Slovenia belonged until 1991. In the West, military sociology as a comprehensive and autonomous sub-discipline started to develop in the 1950s and 1960s with American sociologists playing the leading role. A few years later, the development of military sociology began in Yugoslavia, as well. Before this turning point, some origins of military sociology can be found in works of authors from other disciplinary fields such as history, philosophy, psychology, and law studies (Bebler 1976). As early as 1962, the Yugoslav People's Army introduced a Military Sociology course in the curriculum of its Military Academy[1]. The intention was to enrich future officers with social theory, to stimulate scientific research of the role of the armed forces in society, and to modernize the armed forces (Bebler 1976).

Similarly, as in other socialist countries, publications on the armed forces in Yugoslavia revealed huge imbalances between the quantity of publications and, in average, their extremely low quality (Bebler 1986). Two positive exceptions were Anton Bebler and Jerzy Wiatr who could engage successfully with their Western colleagues in the discussion on the military and related topics from theoretical-conceptual and methodological perspectives.[2] As far as Slovenia was concerned, Anton Bebler's contribution was crucial for the development of military sociology in the 1970s and 1980s.[3] At that time, he critically addressed several topics from sociological and political science perspectives: Marxist views on the war and the military, the Marxist concept of *nation in arms*, the disarmament process and the military, civil-military relations, a classification of political systems based upon the role of the military in the political sphere and society in general, and military rule in Africa.

---

[1]   Mensur Ibrahimpašić was one of key figures in this process. He wrote a reader on military sociology and lectured a Military Sociology course.

[2]   Wiatr's book on Military Sociology (1987) was very influential among military sociologists in former Yugoslavia. It was used as a reader in military academies and civilian defense studies programs alike.

[3]   See more about Anton Bebler's military sociology research in Malešič, 2017.

A key impetus for the development of military sociology in former Yugoslavia was the establishment of civilian educational programs on Defense Studies in five of six republics in mid-1970s. In Slovenia, Defense Studies were established at the then Faculty of Sociology, Political Science and Journalism at the University of Ljubljana. The studies were a product of the official Yugoslav defense and security doctrine (Total People's Defense and Social Self-Protection) that required comprehensive defense and security preparedness of companies and social institutions (extensive defense planning), and teaching of defense topics in high schools and universities (intensive socialization process in the defense field). To professionally support all these activities, civilian defense experts were needed, and Defence Studies programs provided them. Military sociology was, from the very beginning, one segment of that interdisciplinary setting. This is a quite idiosyncratic solution and the development of military sociology in Slovenia has been since inextricably connected to the destiny of Defence Studies as the educational curriculum and research program. The latter had to define its subject of research which was scattered across the social and other sciences. It was also necessary to establish theoretical concepts and to select key methods as a basis for empirical research, to internalize principles of scientific research and norms of academic habitus, to form an autonomous but creative relationship with its context, especially with politics and defense practice, and to search for the reflection of its research work in the international academic arena. It is interesting to note that some of the faculty were not satisfied with the fact that Defence Studies was established within the Faculty of Sociology, Political Science and Journalism (Bebler 1996). They feared that the faculty might be subject to militaristic pressure and they believed the introduction of security, defense and military related topics might reduce the quality of education and research. However, these fears and concerns were exaggerated.

This chapter will describe and analyze the general position of military sociology in the scientific field in Slovenia, military sociology courses that are performed in academic and military educational programs, and the research on and in the military. Periodization will be provided, taking into account prevailing social circumstances that influenced research over the last 35 years. Within each research period the most salient military sociology research projects will be briefly presented. The overview of the entire opus of military sociology research will be presented in a table. I will also introduce the international dimension of research and publishing. Key research approaches and methods will be outlined, as well. That will be followed by explanations on the funding system and on publishing practices. I will offer some concluding remarks at the end of the chapter on the state of education in military sociology, patterns of research in the past and present, on general accomplishments by the *Defence Research Centre* (DRC) and on research-related problems that we need to address in order to assure objectivity of research and the critical assessment of the security context.[4]

2   The Position of Military Sociology in the Scientific Arena

2.1   The Istitutional Setting of Military Sociology in Slovenia

As mentioned above, military sociology in Slovenia has been comprehensively and systematically developed as part of Defence Studies within the Faculty of Sociology, Political Science and Journalism. In the early 1990s, the faculty was renamed as the Faculty of Social Sciences. The Department of Sociology remained an important part of it but Defence Studies has remained within the Department of Political Science since then. Therefore, military sociology as a sub-discipline has been institutionally related to political science. This artificial organizational solution has, in a way, been successfully overcome through multidisciplinary collaboration of Defence Studies not only with sociology, but also with psychology, anthropology, economy, communication sciences, and other disciplines. This collaboration has been taking place at the institutional and individual levels. Some elements of military sociology (not necessarily named as such) research and/or education could be also found at the non-governmental Peace Institute based in Ljubljana and in various analytical bodies of the Ministry of Defence of the Republic of Slovenia and the Slovenian Armed Forces (SAF).

2.2   Teaching Military Sociology Courses[5]

The Defence Studies Program was profoundly reformed in 2005 to be compliant to the Bologna Declaration. Defence Studies, since then, has offered a four-year program, either with a general or a military module,[6] a one-year master program,

---

4   I was personally involved in the development of defense studies and military sociology research in Slovenia from 1985 to the present day: At the beginning as research assistant and teaching assistant, later on as research fellow and professor. I was also Head of Defence Studies (1995–1999) and Head of the Defence Research Centre (since 2000). Therefore, the question of my objectivity is more than appropriate in this context. I will strive to achieve objectivity by focusing on facts, and by avoiding value-weighted evaluation of the research process and its achievements.

5   For detailed information on the different programs and courses see the website of the Faculty of Social Sciences: <www.fdv.uni-lj.si/obvestila-in-informacije/predmeti>.

6   It is important to stress here that SAF do not have a classical military academy but instead recruit candidates for military officers from bachelors of different civilian educational pro-

and a three-year PhD program.[7] There are two relevant courses at the graduate level (Sociology and Political Science of the Military and Peace Operations), one at the master level (Analysis of Contemporary Conflicts) whereas, at the PhD level, the involvement of military sociology themes depends on the PhD dissertation thesis selected by the candidates.[8]

There are also courses of military sociology taught in the educational programs of the SAF, for example, in its Centre of Military Schools which is comprised of Command and Staff School, Officers School and Non-Commissioned Officers School. From 2001, some military educational programs have been related to academic programs in Defence Studies (diploma course program and later Bologna-style master program, respectively), meaning that students from the military organization were taught in military sociology. Nevertheless, frequent changes in military educational programs, in the selection of lecturers and consequently in curricula, and in the manner of cooperation between the Centre of Military Schools and Defence Studies, brought about a lack of continuity and consistency as far as military sociology courses prepared and performed for officers are concerned. There are also other signals (e.g., the announced reform of military education) suggesting that the future of military sociology in the SAF's educational programs is rather unstable.

3   Research on the Military and in the Military – an Overview

Organized and systematic research in the field of security, defense, and the military in Slovenia dates back to the early 1980s when the first projects have been accomplished. The research in the field got its momentum during the process of Slovenia achieving independence from Yugoslavia and in the early years of the newly created state. The Defence Research Centre at the Faculty of Sociology, Political Science and Journalism in Ljubljana had difficulties meeting all the needs of the state in providing an analytical and research basis for the establishment and later modifications of the national security system, and for a gradual approach and integration into Euro-Atlantic security structures.

---

grams, be it social sciences, humanities, science, technical studies etc. The candidates enter a one-year military program in Officers School and, if they are successful, they become military officers. Two to four Defense Studies bachelors annually have joined the Officers School in recent years.

7   Recent reform at the Faculty of Social Sciences introduced a 3+2+4 model of education.

8   In the period of 2008 to 2017, seven PhD candidates successfully defended their theses in the field of military sociology.

From 1982 until 2017, research in the field of military sociology can be divided into several periods. For each period, the prevailing social circumstances have strongly influenced the quantity and content of the research activities. The periods are not clear-cut time frames but rather merge into each other. The scope and content of research is summarized in Table 1; therefore, I will only point out some interesting and important research programs and projects accomplished within each period.

3.1   The Yugoslav Period (1982–1989)

The *Yugoslav* period encompassed the first surveys on general security issues and on the attitudes of the public, especially of the youth towards the military profession. The key framework was a pan-Yugoslav research program on preparedness of the Total People's Defence and Social Self-Protection system. Researchers examined the phenomenon of hyper-institutionalization which caused system entropy and alienated the decision-making process in the narrow military-political structures of the former state, which had contradicted the officially declared policy of socializing [democratizing] defense and security matters. Through the content analysis of defense plans the researchers revealed that some important territorial-political and economic actors were not sufficiently prepared for the defense of the country. Public opinion surveys and interviews revealed that the readiness of people to participate in defense related activities was rather low. That was a striking finding if one takes into account that the system then was based upon the expectation of massive citizens' participation in defense efforts.

A research project on the willingness of citizens of Yugoslavia to choose a career in the defense/military sector was accomplished, as well. It was the first independent research effort in the social sciences on the military profession in the former Yugoslavia. In Slovenia, the project addressed the chronical problem already identified in the past, namely that the population was not interested enough in the military profession which created a huge underrepresentation of Slovenians among NCOs and officers in the Yugoslav People's Army.[9] Nevertheless, there was a considerable interest among Slovenian youngsters in serving in the Air Force and the Navy but not in the Army. The technical factor was an important motivation here, whereas the low standard of living in some Yugoslav republics and autono-

---

9   Bebler (1992) released the data on the ratio of Yugoslav nationalities in the population of the country and the representation of their professional military officers in the Yugoslav People's Army. Slovenians represented 8.2 percent of Yugoslav population whereas only 2.8 percent of military officers were of Slovenian origin. In contrast, Serbs were heavily overrepresented, the ratio was 39.7 percent vs. 60 percent.

mous provinces, the use of the Serbo-Croatian language in the Yugoslav People's Army, relatively low salaries, and rather modest reputation of military profession in Slovenia were among the demotivating factors (Bebler 1992).

3.2   The Independence Period (1990–1991)

During the independence period, Slovenian researchers conducted two surveys. A survey taken before the Ten Day War[10] among the reserve military officers in Slovenia was checking the possibility of the occupational integration of this structure into the emerging Slovenian armed forces. The research focused primarily on the readiness of reserve officers to serve in the armed forces in the future and on the factors that would motivate them to opt for the military profession (Grizold 1990). The first post-war survey in October 1991 focused on the engagement of Territorial Defence members in armed clashes with the Yugoslav People's Army units. Slovenia's Ten Day War offered researchers a unique opportunity to empirically test hypotheses related to the involvement of soldiers in armed clashes and the immediate post-war research was very much focused in this direction (Lubi 1992). Selected questions from the American Soldier research project (1941–1945; Stouffer et al. 1949/50) were applied in the survey. Values and goals of Territorial Defence members were explored, their motivation for fighting, their qualifications and skills acquired to participate in armed conflict, the relationships between soldiers, and between them and commanders within military units, military efficiency, and cohesion. The research revealed that the stereotype of Slovenians being less inclined towards violent solutions in conflicts has been broken. The established characteristics of the armed conflict and the strengths and weaknesses of the functioning of the Territorial Defence were taken into account in the development of the SAF.

3.3   The Post-Independence Period (1992–1997)

The post-independence period brought about the analysis of war in Slovenia (Grizold 1992), the role of the mass media in the Serbian-Croatian conflict (Malešič 1993) but also more sophisticated military sociology themes, particularly civil-military relations in contemporary society, defense restructuring and conversion, and the military profession. Garb (1998) explored the system of relations between the military and civilian authorities in Eastern European countries during the socialist period. The analysis was relevant because it stressed how some patterns of civil-mil-

---

10   The war took place from 27 June to 7 July 1991.

itary relations continued in the post-socialist period. Although the models of civil-military relations differed in socialist countries they had many common character-istics: the double (external and internal) role of the armed forces, extreme political (communist party) control of the military and the social role of the armed forces. Fundamental social changes created conditions in which purges, and a reduction of political control over the armed forces or even armed interventions occurred.

Jelušič (1998) focused on changes in relations between the military and its' civil environment in post-socialist countries. The relationship between the military and civil society and, therefore, the control of the institutional violence was the main topic of the study. It revealed the military's inability to adjust fully to the parliamentary control over the armed forces, the extremely negative public attitude towards the armed forces, and the considerable gap between the democratic rule proclaimed in legal documents and the actual state of affairs.

Grizold (1998) examined the issue of new roles and missions of the armed forces that defined the military profession after the Cold War. He dealt with the transformation of the armed forces which is reflected in new tasks, the formation of supranational military units, a reduction of the numbers of the armed forces, technological modernization, and the improvement of the officer corps. These top-ics were discussed in the light of an international poll conducted among military officers. The survey in Slovenia revealed that the officer corps of the SAF was will-ing to create a contemporary military organization based upon professionalism, responsibility, and cooperation with other social institutions.

3.4 The Integrative Period (1998–2001)

The integrative period was marked with the introduction of the National Research Program *Defence Studies*, which brought stable funding for military sociology re-search. The research focused on defense restructuring and conversion, women in the military, and manning the armed forces. Many European countries, includ-ing Slovenia, were at the time moving toward volunteer and professional armed forces. A related investigation was carried out in two phases. Case studies on eight European countries with either conscription or an all-volunteer system were con-ducted in the first phase. The second phase encompassed the case study of Slovenia, in which national researchers investigated the key factors that had an effect on the recruitment (Malešič 2003).

The research on *sexism* in the military (Jelušič and Pešec 2002) started a socio-logical debate on various ways to involve women in armed formations and their military socialization, from the female members of Partisan units during the na-tional liberation fight on the territory of former Yugoslavia during World War II, the voluntary service of women in the Yugoslav People's Army (1981-1984), to their serving in Slovenian Territorial Defence. Reasons for and against women's participation in the military were examined and critically evaluated from a sociological perspective.

3.5   The Period of Developmental Research (2002–2007)[11]

The period of developmental research encompassed peacekeeping operations and missions in which the participation of the military, the police and civilian functional experts was explored from a social science perspective. The human factor in the military was investigated as well. The research project *Slovenian Armed Forces in Peace Operations* encompassed the review of theoretical paradigms in the field of peace operations, their history and also focused on the international organizations that were involved in carrying them out (Garb et al. 2010; Jelušič 2011; Jelušič et al. 2006; Juvan et al. 2010). Empirical research emphasized the transformation of the *national army soldier* to the *global soldier* and from traditional military tasks to police tasks. Soldiers were away from home, hardly visible in the public, and their return back home was quiet unless they were injured.[12] The research project also focused on other important military sociology topics such as motivational factors for participation of soldiers in peace operations, preparation for and carrying out of operation, reintegration programs for soldiers to their usual working and social surroundings after the operation, and the impact of the SAF's participation in peace operations on future recruitment and retention of soldiers.

The research project *The Human Factor in the Military System* was a synthesis of sub-projects that comprehensively dealt with recruitment, development, management and demobilization of human resources in the Slovenian military system. The project encompassed the analysis of competences and knowledge management in the defense system, women in the SAF, security and defense culture and socialization of youngsters in the security field, social and psychological aspects of the career system in the SAF, and the role of social capital in crisis situations (Garb 2006; Grošelj et al. 2010; Kopač 2006).

---

11   The classification of research in Slovenia refers to fundamental (basic) research, developmental research and problem-solving (applicative) research. Developmental research refers to providing the empirical basis for the development of various processes and activities within institutions and companies.

12   Slovenia started to participate in peace operations in 1997. So far there have been no death casualties registered, however, one female soldier committed suicide during the KFOR (Kosovo Force) mission.

3.6   The Crisis Period (2008–2017)

The final period has been the crisis period, both from the point of view of the economic crisis in Slovenia, which has limited research opportunities, and as a result of the stalemate in relations between the Ministry of Defence and the Defence Research Centre, due to the fact that cooperation among them practically ceased. Officially, the main reason for such a development were austerity measures that heavily hit the Ministry of Defence and especially the SAF. However, it is also important to stress the fact that some civilian and military decision-makers were not keen to support further cooperation with Defence Studies and the Defence Research Centre. This decision was stimulated by the desire to form a classical military academy that would be separated from civilian educational institutions and to establish a military research institute within SAF. Defence Studies and the Defence Research Centre have long been seen as an obstacle of implementing those two initiatives.

A research project on management of human resources in the SAF warned that military reserve forces which were historically based upon a mass army used in great wars had a different role in an all-volunteer force: They were highly-specialized forces that performed military tasks at home and abroad (Kopač et. al. 2010). Compared to other military contract reserve forces, the Slovenian reserve was still at the level of formation of its mission and potential. Members of the reserve forces were confronted with a huge gap between their expectations and the real situation in the units. There were many complications due to the relationship between members of the reserve, their employers and the military organization which made training and deployment of reservists in military operations abroad, and longer absence from regular civilian work extraordinarily complex. Contract reserve service seemed to be a good solution for the soft demobilization of professional soldiers who could, through reserve forces, stay connected to the military organization, and would have an additional source of income.

Military families were also given attention in this period (Vuga 2016). Several counselling programs developed within the SAF to make relations within military families less tense have been explored. Nevertheless, the research revealed that despite social and institutional support, military families in Slovenia rely more on grandparents and on *hired* (paid) support. Military families want more information on the operations and missions their partners participate in, and they also expect a balance between the help of the military organization and its intervention in the privacy of soldiers and their family members. Children often demonstrate the frustration because of absence of their parents through disobedience and rebellion.

3.7   Cross-Cutting Themes over the Entire Period since 1982

To round up this section, it is necessary to emphasize that two constants of the research in the defense studies and military sociology fields from its very origin, through the research periods, have been Slovenian public opinion, and Slovenian youth and the military profession.

Slovenian Public Opinion surveys have been frequent especially during the period following the independence war in 1991 (Bebler 2000; Jelušič 2003; Jelušič and Vegič 2004; Malešič 2013; Malešič and Jelušič 2003, 2004, 2005; Malešič and Kümmel 2011; Vuga 2011).[13] It is important to stress, however, that some general variables were explored from as early as 1982 onwards, while some specific variables are of a more recent date because they have become relevant only recently.[14] The key conceptual fields in the surveys were security threats to Slovenia and its citizens, the national security system, international security structures, the security culture, and the military profession. However, topics such as public support for defense spending, military missions, especially international operations and missions, the issue of public trust in the military, and how the public perceived the military's reputation and performance have been explored as well. We also addressed the public's attitudes towards the manning of the SAF, the issue of women in the military, as well as additional issues referring to the position of the military profession and the socio-economic status of the military. Continuation and consistency of research have given a thorough insight into the legitimacy of official Slovenian security, defense, and military policies. The research findings have suggested that despite usual public criticism towards political decisions, all recent key security projects of the state, namely the participation in peace operations and missions from 1997 on, the introduction of the all-volunteer force in 2002 and the membership in NATO from 2004 on, were accepted and supported by the public. As far as public trust in the SAF is concerned, it is relatively high, but it has never exceeded 60 percent in the last two decades. Although the SAF have been usually placed third or fourth among social institutions in Slovenia, it should be emphasized that the average level of trust in social institutions has been rather low. Additionally, in an international comparative perspective, Slovenia is placed in a group of countries in which the public is less enthusiastic about their military (see details in Garb and Malešič 2016).

---

13   From 1990 on, 10 special surveys on security and the military have been accomplished.
14   Slovenian public opinion surveys have been carried out by the Defence Research Centre in conjunction with the Public Opinion and Mass Communication Research Centre at the Faculty of Social Sciences, University of Ljubljana.

The research project *Slovenian Youth* and the Military Profession arose from the SAF's need to know how prepared Slovenian youth were to engage in the military profession (Malešič et al. 2006). The research on this issue in Slovenia extends back to 1985. Five additional empirical studies have been carried out with similar research tools until 2006. At the general theoretical scientific level, these studies analyzed youth attitudes on security, their homeland, world peace and threats to the modern world. The longitudinal findings of the analyses revealed a gradual change in the value system of youth towards a stronger but not predominant presence of post-modern (post-materialistic) values. Specific variables allowed to explore the attitude of youngsters toward the SAF, the reputation of the military profession, motivational factors that influence the decision to choose the military profession, broader social factors (parents, friends, relatives) that have an impact on the acceptance of the military profession, and the readiness of youngsters to serve in the military reserve forces. Therefore, the practical aim of the research was to investigate the subjective and objective factors that influence youth to choose a military career or reject it. The results suggested that the armed forces were seen as a traditional hierarchical organization among youngsters whereas the military profession was seen as physically and psychologically demanding, with constant exposure to danger and the demand to be fully loyal to the military organization. The soldier was perceived as a traditional warrior and not as a manager, technician, or specialist. The most important characteristics needed to perform in the military profession seemed to be discipline, readiness for action, responsibility, and courage. The expressed interest of youngsters to potentially choose a career in the military was relatively high and so were the expectations of what the employer should offer to those who join the military: predominantly good payment, possibility of further education and smooth demobilization.

4   Some Characteristics of Military Sociology in Slovenia

4.1   International Research Collaboration

Military sociology research in Slovenia has been carried out primarily in an international context, especially with, or stimulated by, associations like the International Sociological Association (ISA), the European Research Group on Military and Society (ERGOMAS), the Inter University Seminar on Armed Forces and Society (IUS) and the International Political Science Association (IPSA). According to Anton Bebler (personal conversation), the first international book project of the Defence Research Centre in the field of military sociology took place in the mid-

1980s when he and Jürgen Kühlmann of the *Sozialwissenschaftliches Institut der Bundeswehr* (SOWI) carried out a project on the motivation of youngsters applying for the military profession. Slovenian military sociologists contributed to several other book projects since then, for example, on cultural challenges in military operations (Coops and Szvircsev Tresch 2007), military cooperation in multinational peace operations (Soeters and Manigart 2008), development of military sociology (Ouellet 2005), soldiers' experiences of asymmetric warfare (Caforio 2013), military unionism (Bartle and Heinecken 2006), and sociological perspectives of conflict resolution (Caforio et al. 2008). Two military sociology methodological book projects should be mentioned as well (Carreiras 2016; Carreiras and Castro 2013). Recently, Slovenian military sociologists have contributed to the handbooks of military sociology (Caforio 2006, Caforio and Nuciari 2018) and to the essays published in honor of Charles C. Moskos (Caforio 2009).

Three research projects (*The Role of Mass Media in the Serbian-Croatian Conflict, Propaganda in War,* and *Peace Support Operations, Mass Media and the Public in former Yugoslavia*) were accomplished for the Swedish partner, National Board of Psychological Defence, in the 1990s (see the country chapter on Sweden in this volume). Also important were the research projects on *Civil-Military Relations in Europe: Learning from Crisis and Institutional Change* sponsored by the Geneva Centre for Democratic control of the Armed Forces, *The Cultural Differences between the Military and Parent Society in Democratic Societies* carried out within the ISA RC 01 framework and *Military leadership, morale and cohesion* and *Security and the military between reality and perception* carried out within ERGOMAS.

The collaboration of the Defence Research Centre as a partner in projects financed by the EU either through COST, FP 7, and Horizon 2020 has been extremely valuable. Out of eight European research projects of the Defence Research Centre, three partly pertain to military sociology: *Defence Restructuring and Conversion, New Challenges of Peace Operations and the Role of the EU in Multilateral Crisis Management,* and *Strengthening European Integration through the Analysis of Conflict Discourses: Revisiting the Past, Anticipating the Future.*

Last but not least, the extensive international collaboration resulted in Defence Research Centre fellows assuming leading positions of international scientific associations, of various expert groups and of editorial boards of scientific journals. Marjan Malešič, for example, was the chairman of ERGOMAS between 2000 and 2002 and the coordinator of its working group on public opinion, mass media, and the military between 1998 and 2019. Ljubica Jelušič (2006–2009) and Uroš Svete (since 2009) were or currently are Executive Secretaries of ISA-RC 01, while Anton Bebler has been a member of the Executive Committee of IPSA between 2006 and 2009.

4.2   Research Approaches and Methods

As we can see from the brief description of the research projects above, Slovenian researchers have applied quantitative and qualitative methodological approaches in their research. Quantitative approaches were applied to accurately measure sociological characteristics of the military and its civilian surroundings. The key methods were surveys (e.g., Slovenian public opinion and the military, Slovenian youth and military profession, thematic surveys in the military), structured interviews (e.g., civilian and military experts, military officers and non-commissioned officers), and the analysis of statistical data (e.g., figures on the military personnel, budget, or participation in peace operations).

Otherwise, qualitative research of the military was more interpretative and critical. The theoretical conceptualization of the military and related phenomena was part of the research itself, based upon *soft* data such as words, impressions, pictures, images, themes, ideas, motives, and gestures. The prevailing methods were observation (e.g., during field research or with direct participation like researchers who were temporarily embedded in defense structures), unstructured interviews (e.g., civilian and military experts, military officers, and non-commissioned officers), scenarios (e.g., on the ways of manning the armed forces), and content analysis (e.g., mass media reporting on military, conflicts, and wars).

In some projects (e.g., *Defence Restructuring and Conversion, The Manning of Armed Forces, Slovenian Armed Forces in Peace Operations*; see Table 1) a triangulation was applied: a combination of qualitative and quantitative research approaches, multi-method approaches, various theoretical paradigms and researchers coming from different walks of science. The project groups have often been international as well.

Vuga and Juvan (2013) explained the methodology of research on and in the SAF in more detail. They mostly focused on qualitative analyses and underlined several practical challenges of field research within the SAF, either when in their barracks or when deployed to peace operations and missions abroad. Issues like entering the military organization as civilian researchers, establishing trust between members of the armed forces and researchers, formation of samples, the sincerity of answers provided by interviewees, adequate selection of methods for various ranks, the question of recording interviews, and the timing of the research were thoroughly addressed in their paper.

As a matter of rule, there are no taboo topics when it comes to various variables in instruments that we apply in empirical research. Therefore, in our surveys and questionnaires participants are asked about their income, religion, political orientation, nationality, and family status. However, the University and the Faculty adopted the rules that stipulate the ethics of research, e.g., how to approach the respondents, how to carry out the research, or how to deal with the data, etc.

4.3 Publishing Practices

Publishing of research results is self-evident in Slovenian military sociology. There are two main reasons for that: The Slovenian Research Agency's policy where the requirement to *publish or perish* is strictly enforced, and the University of Ljubljana's promotion criteria that are rather demanding. The continuation of fundamental research and successful competition at tenders for basic, developmental, problem-solving, and post-doctoral projects have been dependent on publication results and quotations of researchers in recent years[15]. Scientific monographs, articles and various professional publications have been published at home and abroad. Publishing of research results in foreign and international scientific journals has become a standard in Slovenian military sociology. Among recent foreign publications the following stand out: Garb 2015; Malešič 2015; Svete and Juvan 2016; Vuga 2014. Some other important publications are listed in the references to this chapter whereas the entire opus is available in COBISS.[16]

The most prestigious foreign scientific journals that had published recent Defence Research Centre's military sociology research findings have been *Armed Forces & Society, Current Sociology, Res Militaris, Defence and Security Analysis,* and *The Journal of Slavic Military Studies.* The most important domestic scientific journals in which military sociology articles had been published were *Teorija in praksa* (Theory and Practice), *Sodobni vojaški izzivi* (Contemporary Military Challenges) and *Varstvoslovje* (Journal of Criminal Justice and Security). Among books published at home, the six anthologies (Grizold 1992, 1998; Malešič 2002, 2006, 2010, 2016), which epitomized the key research findings of the Defence Research Centre since its establishment in 1985 until 2016, could be considered to be a unique and valuable publishing achievement, as well. Among the monographs published abroad, Bebler (1973), and Malešič and colleagues (2015) should be mentioned.

---

15   For detailed information see the website of the Slovenian Research Agency: <www.arrs.gov.
      si/sl/akti/prav-sof-ocen-sprem-razisk-dej-avg2016.asp>.
16   Cooperative Online Bibliographic System and Services where the data of all publications of
      registered Slovenian researchers are available.

4.4   Research Funding

The Defence Research Centre has been involved in fundamental research funded by the Slovenian Research Agency (since 1999), in developmental and problem-solving research commissioned by various state institutions, primarily the Ministry of Defence whereas the first research project financed by the European Commission was granted in 1996. We have accomplished eight such projects in the role of a partner institution since then.

Financing of fundamental research is provided through the long-term National Research Program *Defence Studies* and through occasional fundamental, developmental, problem-solving, and post-doctoral projects. This kind of funding is very much dependent on the quality of past research and its output. Consequently, the research fellows are under constant pressure to publish in international scientific monographs, and journals with a relatively high impact factor, to be quoted by other colleagues and to raise research funds outside the Slovenian Research Agency. To follow the performance of research groups and individual researchers, a so called SICRIS system (Slovenia Current Research Information System) has been developed by the Slovenian Research Agency. It was introduced in 1998[17] and is a quantitative measurement of scientific items published such as articles, monographs, anthologies, and contributions to conferences[18]. During tenders, there is an additional qualitative grade given by two foreign reviewers who evaluate the quality of the program or project proposals submitted by research institutes.[19] Last but not least, researchers and research groups are expected to raise funds outside the Slovenian Research Agency funding system, either through collaboration with the European Commission and other EU institutions, governmental institutions and local communities, companies, and other organizations.

The Slovenian Research Agency as a main sponsor of research has no direct influence on the selection of topics to be explored, their theoretical background or methodological approach and methods applied however, the foreign reviewers hired by the Agency make decisions on those issues by taking into account the scientific excellence of researchers and the relevance of their achievements, the vitality and functional ability of the research group, the innovation of the research proposal

---

17   The system is based upon COBISS.
18   For detailed information see the website of the SICRIS: <www.sicris.si/public/jqm/cris. aspx?lang=slv&opdescr=home&opt=1>.
19   The quantitative grading system was criticized by the academic community and consequently there is more emphasis on the qualitative grade lately although the quantitative grade is still important as the admission criterion, and as the scientific excellence and relevance criteria.

and the social impact of the anticipated research findings. The Agency's decision on financing the project or not is exclusively dependent on reviewers' grades. It is important to emphasize that program funding granted by the Slovenian Research Agency is stable and long-term, provided that the quantity and quality of research is at the required level whereas all other funds are dependent on occasional tenders or direct commissions.

5   Slovenian Military Sociology and its Political and Societal Context

Defense studies and Military Sociology strive to achieve optimal balance between the autonomy and instrumentalism as far as their relationship with the political and societal context is concerned (Mali 1996). Extreme autonomy might lead to self-sufficiency of the discipline, its social marginalization and irrelevance for practice. The instrumentalist approach which emphasizes the catalyst role of the discipline as far as social development in a certain field is concerned, might lead to uncritical advocacy of official solutions and to servility to parochial political and bureaucratic interests of the elite. An apolitical approach is desired in this context, but it does not mean to neglect the professional needs of practice. On the contrary, such a cooperation is key, given that norms and principles of scientific research and autonomy of scientific institutions are fully respected.

The closest context of defense studies and military sociology are the defense system and the military.[20] Military sociologists have recently not experienced any obstacles, pressures, or manipulations as far as their research about the military and in the military was concerned. On the contrary, the Ministry of Defence and the SAF have been extremely helpful in the entire research process.[21] However, we did experience cases of political pressures and conflicts with politicians and state officials in the past. Nevertheless, it is important to stress that those were anomalies often related to misbehavior of individuals from the defense and military establishment whereas in general the cooperation between the Defence Research Centre and the Ministry of Defence and the General Staff of the SAF before the economic crisis in 2008 was fruitful and rewarding for all actors. Many legal, doctrinal, and

---

20   In the Slovenian case, cooperation in the fields of education, research and publication between the Ministry of Defence and the Faculty of Social Sciences is based upon the Cooperation Agreement signed in 1996.

21   The assertion is made upon the conversations with Ljubica Jelušič, Maja Garb, Jelena Juvan and Janja Vuga who have recently accomplished a bulk of research within the Ministry of Defence and the SAF and on the personal experience of the author.

strategic solutions were formed on the basis of research findings. Security policy was informed and advised to find better solutions. Generally speaking, this role of the Defence Research Centre is not disputed providing that the academic habitus and the autonomy of researchers are fully respected. Additionally, researchers are expected to follow all principles and ethics of scientific research. Based upon occasional conversations, many in academia and in the professional public believe that the educational and research roles of the Defence Studies and the Defence Research Centre contribute to the level of expertise of the national security setting in general and to the quality of civil-military relations. Concurrently, research findings contribute to informed public debate on security topics. Nevertheless, there are also individuals and groups in the society who are critical towards the military and repressive institutions in general. Some colleagues at the Faculty of Social Sciences are among them. Therefore, defense studies involved in educational and research cooperation with national security structures, is a disturbing factor to them.

It is important to emphasize that some colleagues had a chance to change the context discussed so far. Anton Grizold (2000–2004) and Ljubica Jelušič (2008–2011) served as ministers of defence. Erik Kopač (2017–2018) was a state secretary responsible for national security in the Slovenian government. He became a Permanent Representative of Slovenia to NATO in 2019. Anton Bebler (1992–1997) was the Ambassador at the Permanent Mission of the Republic of Slovenia to the United Nations Office in Geneva and to other international organizations that had a seat in Switzerland. All of them returned to the University when their mandates expired. Uroš Svete became an Acting Director-General of the Information Society Directorate at the Ministry of Public Administration in 2018. The entire enterprise was not without questions and dilemmas about politicization of the Faculty, transparency of our work, familiarity, professional standards and autonomy or researchers.[22] Consequently, we ought to be very careful in our contacts with the Ministry of Defence while our colleagues were ministers, especially in the case of new cooperation arrangements. Integrity and transparency were key. Media also accomplished their role by reviewing all contracts, searching for the role of ministers in them and a potential conflict of interests. However, the main burden of those questions and dilemmas was on ministers themselves.

Finally, the research findings have been as a matter of rule embedded into educational programs, and research has become ever more a constituent part of education, not only at the PhD level. Educational cooperation between Defence Studies and the Ministry of Defence and the Armed Forces enabled military sociology and

---

22   Other colleagues from the Faculty of Social Sciences have been elected ministers and members of the Parliament, or were appointed as state secretaries in various fields, as well.

other courses to become part of military education curricula. Some employees of the Ministry of Defence and the SAF were educated in Defence Studies programs of all levels. Highly ranked individuals from the establishment have given lectures to students and faculty of Defence Studies.

Unfortunately, educational and research cooperation between above mentioned actors has been gradually in decline after 2008 when a severe economic and financial crisis hit the country. Slovenian defense and military structures were the greatest victims of the crisis and the austerity measures policy. As a consequence, some contracts between the Ministry of Defence, the Defence Research Centre and Defence Studies were cancelled or were not renewed, and concurrently, the commissioning of research projects ceased. Therefore, formal institutional cooperation was absent however some individuals have been still involved as external experts in some Ministry of Defence activities.

6   Conclusion

The position of military sociology in Slovenia is rather idiosyncratic due to the facts that its origins date back to the former Yugoslavia, and that this sub-discipline of sociology was primarily developed within defense studies. The core of military sociology related education is carried out at the Faculty of Social Sciences, University of Ljubljana. However, a limited scope of activities could be found within the Peace Institute and the SAF, as well. I identified three military sociology courses at the Faculty of Social Sciences, nevertheless, some other courses at the Defence Studies Program are also permeated with (military) sociology themes. Military sociology teaching in the educational programs of the SAF predominantly depended on the ad hoc involvement of military sociology teachers from Defence Studies. After expiration of their agreements, the military sociology topics were almost all deleted from the professional socialization of Slovenian officers. Hence, sociological teaching has been marked with inconsistency and discontinuity. Therefore, at the moment, the prospects for the development of courses related to military sociology in the SAF's Centre of Military Schools are not good.

As far as the research is concerned, the bulk is carried out at the Faculty of Social Sciences, too, mostly but not exclusively within the Defence Research Centre. There is no need to repeat extensive research in the field (see Table 1). However, it is worth mentioning that the most research time, energy and resources have been devoted to Slovenian public opinion on the military: Concepts of trust, reputation, performance, legitimacy, new missions, casualty tolerance and others were investigated. The attitudes of Slovenians, especially the young population towards the military profession have been explored extensively, as well, the main issue being the (de)motivational factors that contribute to the selection or rejection of military profession. Some sociological aspects of wars on the territory of former Yugoslavia, including the role of the mass media, also attracted attention. Several research projects covered the participation of the Slovenian Armed Forces and other actors to peace operations. An incredibly significant part of research encompassed management of human resources within the military organization.

Taking into account the periodization of research activities, it seems that military sociology projects were well represented in all periods of research, especially in post-independence, integrative and developmental research periods. If, in the past, the emphasis was on general topics of military sociology such as the military profession, civil-military relations and the analysis of wars, there has been more focus on specific issues of human resources in the military organization, military families, women in the military, and military reserve forces in recent research.

As far as the methodology of research is concerned, we have seen a combination of quantitative and qualitative approaches. A triangulation of theoretical concepts, sub-disciplines, researchers, and methods was used to achieve comprehensiveness, objectivity, and credibility of findings. The latter have been, as a matter of rule, presented at the international conferences, and published in domestic and foreign scientific and professional journals, anthologies, and monographs. The core of the research funding has been provided by the Slovenian Research Agency, followed by the Ministry of Defence and the European Commission.

The primary accomplishments of the Defence Research Centre since its establishment have been its research-based criticism of the defense system in former Yugoslavia, the creation of a scientific basis for establishing the national security system of Slovenia, its development and solution of practical problems, a critical assessment of Slovenian security policy and structures, including the military, the integration of the Defence Research Centre and researchers in international research, and solid publishing achievements. The participation of individual members of the Defence Research Centre in the management of the Slovenian defense system, including the highest position of Minister of Defence, is a remarkable accomplishment, as well. The members of the Defence Research Centre have also participated in managing international scientific associations in the field. Finally, the research findings have been a constant source of enriching the curricula of programs in civilian and to a certain extent also in military educational institutions.

Despite general success achieved in almost four decades of systematic and consistent research in the field of military sociology in Slovenia, there are certain issues that need to be addressed in the near future. One of them, perhaps not typically Slovenian but universal, is the problem of massive empirical research whereas the findings are not integrated in broader theoretical concepts, meaning we face a danger of empiricism, such as piling-up of empirical facts without adequate generalization and upgrading of existent or creation of new theories. Another issue is the prevailing nature of applicative, problem-solving research and developmental research on the detriment of fundamental research, the phenomenon that is encouraged by the national research policy. It seems that in the past the balance between various types of research in military sociology was more optimal than in the present. Finally, relations between the Ministry of Defence, the SAF and the Defence Research Centre in the research field should be improved in a post-crisis period.

Table 1: Key military sociology research programs/projects of the DRC, 1985–2017[23]

Topic of the project	Duration	Project leader(s)	Key issues	Selected references
Slovenian public opinion on security	1986–1989, 1990, 1994, 1999, 2001, 2003, 2005, 2007, 2009, 2012, 2015/16	France Vreg, Anton Grizold, Ljubica Jelušič, Marjan Malešič	National security system, international security structures, security culture, military profession, trust in the armed forces	Bebler 2000; Garb 2015, Garb and Malešič 2016; Jelušič 2003; Jelušič and Vegič 2004; Malešič and Jelušič 2003, 2005, 2006, 2007; Malešič and Kümmel 2011; Malešič and Vegič 2007; Vuga 2011, 2014
Slovenians and defense/military professions	1985–1986	Anton Bebler	Slovenian youth, military profession, (de)motivational factors, national and social representation in the Yugoslav People's Army (YPA)	Bebler 1992
Macroproject: Preparedness of the socio-political system for total people's defense and social self-protection	1985–1990	France Vreg	Preparedness of citizens, local communities, autonomous provinces, and republics for defense	Vreg 1987, 1995
The attitudes of the Slovenian youth towards the military profession	1989, 1996–1998, 1999–2000, 2003, 2006	Lado Kocjan, Anton Grizold, Marjan Malešič	Values of the young population, expectations related to future profession, attitudes towards professions, interest to choose the military profession, (de)motivational factors	Kopač 2006; Malešič et al. 2006

23   In some comprehensive research programs or projects, such as Slovenian Public Opinion on Security, Macro-Project and National Research Program, the content of research was not limited solely to military sociology but involved general security themes, as well. However, the chapter focuses on military sociology topics.

Topic of the project	Duration	Project leader(s)	Key issues	Selected references
Reserve officers and the military profession	1990	Anton Grizold	Readiness of reserve officers to become active military officers in the future Slovenian Army, motivational factors	Grizold 1990
The Slovenian soldier – members of Territorial Defence during armed conflict with the YPA	1991	Anton Grizold	Fear, courage, cohesion, quality of preparedness, soldier-commander relationship, combat deficiencies, positive experiences	Lubi 1992
The role of mass media in the Serbian-Croatian conflict	1991–1992	Marjan Malešič	The role of media, content analysis of media, psychological warfare	Malešič 1993
Propaganda in war	1996–1997	Marjan Malešič	The case of Bosnia-Herzegovina; propaganda and ideology, routine lies, selective loss of memory, use of language, source criticism, *the other*, iconography, conspiracy theory, context, public	Malešič 1996
Present and future of the military profession in Slovenia	1993–1993	Anton Grizold	Changes in the public attitude towards the military profession in the new state	Grizold 1998
Analysis of war in Slovenia	1994–1997	Anton Grizold	Defense policy, economic warfare, psycho-social role of the human factor in war, prisoners of war	Malešič 1998
Civil-military relations	1995–1998	Ljubica Jelušič	Social acceptability of the armed forces, civilianization of the military, institutional authority of the military, legitimacy	Jelušič 1998

Topic of the project	Duration	Project leader(s)	Key issues	Selected references
COST Action – Defense restructuring and conversion	1996–2001	Ljubica Jelušič	Perception of military threat, conversion of military capacities, social reintegration of former military personnel	Jelušič 2002; Prebilič 2002
National re-search program "Defence Studies"	1999–2017	Anton Grizold, Ljubica Jelušič, Marjan Malešič	Fundamental research of various themes, including military sociology	Garb 2015, 2017; Grizold 2000, 2001; Jelušič 1997, 1998; Jelušič and Pešec 2002; Malešič 2015, Malešič et al. 2015; Svete and Juvan 2016; Vuga 2014
Peace support operations, mass media, and the public in former Yugoslavia	1999–2000	Marjan Malešič	Most influential media in Bosnia and Herzegovina, media habits of the population, points of collision between peace forces and population, image of SFOR, disinformation	Malešič 2000
Armed violence related to the dissolution of the former SFRY (1990–1995, 1998)	1999–2001	Anton Bebler	Cases and forms of violence, space and time dynamics, lethality, pathologi-cal phenomena	Bebler 1991, 2000
The manning of the armed forces	2001–2002	Marjan Malešič	Conscription, all-volunteer force, national service, contract soldiers, factors that influ-ence the way of manning the armed forces-history, threats, alliances, technology, demog-raphy, costs, labor market, psycho-social factors etc.	Malešič 2003; Malešič et al. 2015; Malešič and Garb 2017

Topic of the project	Duration	Project leader(s)	Key issues	Selected references
The SAF in peace operations	2002–2004	Ljubica Jelušič	Theoretical paradigms, history, statistics, characteristics of soldiers' and policemen' participation in peace operations, the SAF in peace operations	Jelušič et al. 2006
Social sciences analysis of factors that influence peace efforts of the SAF	2003–2006	Ljubica Jelušič	Contribution of the SAF to peace operations, motivational factors for soldiers to participate, reintegration programs after operation, the impact of peace operations on recruitment and retention	Garb et al. 2010, Juvan et al. 2010, Vuga 2011
The human factor in the military system	2004–2006	Ljubica Jelušič	Interest for the military profession, analysis of competences in the defense system, women in the military, socialization of youth for security, social and psychological aspects of the career system in SAF, social capital in crisis	Garb 2006; Kopač 2006; Kopač et al. 2010
Social sciences analysis of the functioning of the SAF in missions and headquarters at international duties	2006–2008	Ljubica Jelušič	Preparedness of soldiers for peace operations, motivational factors, recruitment and retention, positive and negative experiences	Jelušič 2007
Civil-military relations after the admission of countries into EU and NATO	2006–2007	Vladimir Prebilič	Legal and political aspects of democratic control of the armed forces, decision-making processes, public support and legitimacy of decisions	Prebilič 2007

Topic of the project	Duration	Project leader(s)	Key issues	Selected references
The role of the state in involving civilian experts into international operations in crisis areas	2007–2009	Vinko Vegič, Marjan Malešič	Integration of military and civilian personnel in peace operations, CIMIC, organization, planning, coordination, comparative analysis of four countries, and Kosovo as a case study	Grošelj et al. 2010
Management of human resources in the SAF: contract reserve forces, families, and the end of conscription	2007–2009	Ljubica Jelušič, Vladimir Prebilič	Military reserve forces, the role, expectations, reality, contract reserve; military families as basic social network, counselling for soldiers and their families	Grošelj 2010; Vuga 2016
COST Action: New challenges of peace operations and the role of the EU in multilateral crisis management	2010–2013	Marjan Malešič	European vision of peace operations, effective multilateralism, EU's security strategy, civilian and military crisis management, Kosovo as a case study	Juvan and Vuga 2015; Malešič 2015
Active citizenship and the homeland	2013–2014	Vladimir Prebilič	The changing role and forms of patriotism, patriotism among primary and secondary school pupils and teachers, comprehension and practicing of patriotism	Juvan and Prebilič 2014; Vuga and Prebilič 2014

Source: Own table based on the DRC's documentation.

References

Bartle, R., and L. Heinecken, eds. 2006. *Military Unionism in Post-Cold War Era: A Future Reality?* London & New York: Routledge.

Bebler, A. 1973. *Military Rule in Africa.* New York: Praeger.

Bebler, A. 1976. "Development of Sociology of Militaria in Yugoslavia." *Armed Forces & Society* 3(1): 59–68.

Bebler, A. 1986. "Social Science Literature in Socialist States. The Contemporary Military." *Armed Forces & Society* 12(3): 453–472.

Bebler, A. 1991. "The Military and the Yugoslav Crisis." *Südosteuropa: Zeitschrift für Gegenwartsforschung* 40(3/4): 127–144.

Bebler, A. 1992. "Jugoslovanska ljudska armada in razpad Jugoslavije." In *Razpotja nacionalne Varnosti*, edited by A. Grizold, 45–57. Ljubljana: Fakulteta za družbene vede.

Bebler, A. 1996. "Dvajset let obramboslovja na Slovenskem." In *Razvoj obramboslovne misli*, edited by Marjan Malešič, 9–12. Ljubljana: Fakulteta za družbene vede.

Bebler, A. 2000. "The Public's Role in the Democratic Control of the Armed Forces in Slovenia." In *International Security, Mass Media and Public Opinion*, edited by M. Malešič, M. (ed.): International Security, Mass Media and Public Opinion. Ljubljana: Fakulteta za družbene vede, 139–148.

Bebler, A. 2000. "Rückkehr des Krieges? Europäische Rundschau." *Vierteljahreszeitschrift für Politik, Wirtschaft und Zeitgeschichte* 28(3): 39–43.

Bebler, A., ed. 2005. Sodobno vojaštvo in družba. Ljubljana: Fakulteta za družbene vede.

Bebler, A. 2017. *Izzivi vojne in miru.* Ljubljana: Fakulteta za družbene vede.

Caforio, G. 2006. *Handbook of the Sociology of the Military.* 1st edition. Cham: Springer.

Caforio, G., ed. 2009. *Advances in Military Sociology: Essays in Honor of Charles C. Moskos.* Bingley: Emerald.

Caforio, G., ed. 2013. *Soldiers without Frontiers: The View from the Ground. Experiences of Asymmetric Warfare.* Rome: Bonano.

Caforio, G., G. Kümmel, and B. Pukayastha, eds. 2008. *Armed Forces and Conflict Resolution: Sociological Perspectives.* Bingley: Emerald.

Caforio, G., and M. Nuciari, eds. 2018. *Handbook of the Sociology of the Military* 2nd edition. Cham: Springer.

Carreiras, H., ed. 2016. *Researching the Military.* Abingdon & New York: Routledge.

Carreiras, H., and C. Castro, eds. 2013. *Qualitative Methods in Military Studies. Research Experiences and Challenges.* London and New York: Routledge.

Coops, C.M., and T. Szvircsev Tresch, eds. 2007. "Cultural Challenges in Military Operations." *NDC Occasional Paper* 23. Rome: NATO Defence College.

Furlan, B. 2013. "Civilian Control and Military Effectiveness. Slovenian Case." *Armed Forces & Society* 39(3): 434–449.

Galantino, M.G., and M.R. Freire, eds. 2015. *Managing Crises, Making Peace. Towards a Strategic EU Vision for Security and Defense.* (Rethinking Peace and Conflict Studies). Basingstoke & New York: Palgrave Macmillan.

Garb, M. 1998. "Razmerje med vojsko in oblastjo v vzhodni Evropi." In *Perspektive sodobne varnosti*, edited by A. Grizold, 60–71. Ljubljana: Fakulteta za družbene vede.

Garb, M. 2002. "Demobilizacija in družbena reintegracija vojaškega osebja V državah vzhodne in Srednje Evrope." In *Nacionalna In mednarodna varnost Slovenije*, edited by M. Malešič, 170–187. Ljubljana: Fakulteta za družbene vede.

Garb, M. 2006. "Demobilizacija in odhodi iz oboroženih sil." In *Varnost v postmoderni družbi*, edited by M. Malešič, 209–226. Ljubljana: Fakulteta za družbene vede.

Garb, M. 2015. "Public Trust and the Military. The Slovenian Armed Forces in a Comparative Analysis." *Current Sociology* 63(3): 450–469.

Garb, M. 2017. "Divergent or Convergent Trends in Professional Military Education in Slovenia?" *Journal of Defense Resources Management* 8(2): 31–41.

Garb, M., and M. Malešič. 2016. "The Causes of Trust and Distrust in the Military." *Defense and Security Analysis* 32(1): 64–78.

Garb, M., K. Grošelj, J. Juvan, and J. Vuga. 2010. "Izbrane teme iz proučevanja mirovnih operacij." In *Mednarodne razsežnosti varnosti Slovenije*, edited by M. Malešič, 161–184. Ljubljana: Fakulteta za družbene vede.

Grizold, A. 1990. *Starešinski kader v oboroženih silah Republike Slovenije* (raziskovalno poročilo). Ljubljana: Obramboslovni raziskovalni center.

Grizold, A., ed. 1992. Razpotja nacionalne varnosti. Ljubljana: Fakulteta za družbene vede.

Grizold, A., ed. 1998. *Perspektive sodobne varnosti*. Ljubljana: Fakulteta za družbene vede.

Grizold, A. 2000. "Contemporary National Security in the Light of Militarization and Militarism." *Politička Misao* 37(5): 128–143.

Grizold, A. 2001. "Civilian Control of the Armed Forces in Slovenia." *Politička misao* 38(5): 123–127.

Grošelj, K., J. Juvan, and R. Zupančič. 2010. "Primerjalna analiza prostovoljnih pogodbenih reezerv Češke, Nemčije, Velike Britanije, Belgije in Nizozemske." In *Mednarodne razsežnosti varnosti Slovenije*, edited by M. Malešič, 303–331. Ljubljana: Fakulteta za družbene vede.

Grošelj, K., P. Fras, S. Arko, and J. Juvan. 2010. "Civilni funkcionalni strokovnjaki v mirovnih operacijah in misijah." In *Mednarodne razsežnosti varnosti Slovenije*, edited by M. Malešič, 207–245. Ljubljana: Fakulteta za družbene vede.

Jelušič, L. 1997. *Legitimnost sodobnega vojaštva*. Ljubljana: Fakulteta za družbene vede.

Jelušič, L. 1998. "Spreminjanje odnosov med vojaštvom in civilnim okoljem v postsocializmu." In *Perspektive sodobne varnosti*, edited by A. Grizold, 76–98. Ljubljana: Fakulteta za družbene vede.

Jelušič, L., and M. Pešec, eds. 2002. *Seksizem v vojaški uniformi*. Ljubljana: Fakulteta za družbene vede.

Jelušič, L. 2002. "Obrambno prestrukturiranje in konverzija." In *Nacionalna in mednarodna varnost Slovenije*, edited by M. Malešič, 146–169. Ljubljana: Fakulteta za družbene vede.

Jelušič, L. 2003. "Slovenian Public Opinion on Security, Defence and Military Issues." In *The Public Image of Defence and the Military in Central and Eastern Europe*, edited by M. Vlachova, 182–200. Geneva & Belgrade: DCAF/CCMR.

Jelušič, L., and V. Vegič. 2004. "Izzivi javnomnenjskega raziskovanja odnosa med državljani in nacionalnovarnostnim sistemom." In *S Slovenkami in Slovenci na štiri oči*, edited by B. Malnarand I. Bernik, 335–350. Ljubljana: Fakulteta za družbene vede.

Jelušič, L., M. Garb, K. Grošelj, J. Juvan, E. Kopač, V. Prebilič, and V. Vegič. 2006. "Mirovne operacije – naložba v mednarodni mir, varnost in stabilnost." In *Varnost v postmoderni družbi*, edited by M. Malešič, 229–257. Ljubljana: Fakulteta za družbene vede.

Jelušič, L. 2007. "Motivation for peace operations." *Revue Internationale de Sociologie* 17(1): 73–85.

Jelušič, L., ed. 2011. *Mirovne operacije in vloga Slovenije*, (Knjižna zbirka Varnostne študije). Ljubljana: Fakulteta za družbene vede.

Juvan, J., J. Vuga, and M. Garb. 2010. "Empirično raziskovanje sodelovanja Slovenske vojske v mirovnih operacijah v obdobju 2002–2008." In *Mednarodne razsežnosti varnosti Slovenije*, edited by M. Malešič, 185–205. Ljubljana: Fakulteta za družbene vede.

Juvan, J., and J. Vuga. 2015. "Civilian Entities in EU Missions: A Comparison of the Slovenian, Italian, Belgian and Danish Approaches." In *Managing Crises, Making Peace. Towards a Strategic EU Vision for Security and Defense (Rethinking Peace and Conflict Studies)*, edited by M.G. Galantino and M.R. Freire, 196–215. Basingstoke & New York: Palgrave Macmillan.

Kopač, E. 2006. "Posameznikovo odločanje za zaposlitev v oboroženih silah." In *Varnost v postmoderni družbi*, edited by M. Malešič, 125–138. Ljubljana: Fakulteta za družbene vede.

Kopač, E., M. Garb, J. Vuga and V. Prebilič. 2010. "Pogodbeni pripadniki rezervne sestave Slovenske vojske." In *Mednarodne razsežnosti varnosti Slovenije*, edited by M. Malešič, 333–352. Ljubljana: Fakulteta za družbene vede.

Kotnik-Dvojmoč, I. 1998. "Nekateri vidiki preoblikovanja Slovenske vojske." In *Perspektive sodobne varnosti*, edited by A. Grizold, 136–155. Ljubljana: Fakulteta za družbene vede.

Lubi, D. 1992. "Slovenski vojak." In *Razpotja nacionalne varnosti*, edited by A. Grizold, 151–169. Ljubljana: Fakulteta za družbene vede.

Malešič, M., ed. 1993. *The Role of Mass Media in Serbian Croatian Conflict.* Stockholm: SPF.

Malešič, M., ed. 1996. *Razvoj obramboslovne misli.* Ljubljana: Fakulteta za družbene vede.

Malešič, M., ed. 1997. *Propaganda in War.* Stockholm: SPF.

Malešič, M., ed. 2000. *International Security, Mass Media and Public Opinion.* Ljubljana: Fakulteta za družbene vede.

Malešič, M., ed. 2002. *Nacionalna in mednarodna varnost Slovenije.* Ljubljana: Fakulteta za družbene vede.

Malešič, M., ed. 2003. *Conscription vs. All-Volunteer Forces in Europe.* Baden-Baden: Nomos.

Malešič, M., and L. Jelušič. 2005. "Popular Perception of Security in Slovenia (selected issues)." In *Sodobno vojaštvo in družba*, edited by A. Bebler, 117–128. Ljubljana: Fakulteta za družbene vede.

Malešič, M., ed. 2006. *Varnost v postmoderni družbi.* Ljubljana: Fakulteta za družbene vede.

Malešič, M., and L. Jelušič. 2003. "Problematika narodnej bezpečnosti v očiach verejnosti: vnimanie NATO a vojska v Slovinsku." *Sociologia* 35(5): 479–494.

Malešič, M., and L. Jelušič. 2006. "Javna percepcija sigurnosti u Sloveniji." *Međunarodne studije* 6(1), 95–112.

Malešič, M., L. Jelušič, V. Vegič, M. Garb, J. Juvan, and K. Grošelj. 2006. "Stališča slovenske mladine do vojaškega poklica." In *Varnost v postmoderni družbi*, edited by M. Malešič, 139−208. Ljubljana: Fakulteta za družbene vede.

Malešič, M., and V. Vegič. 2007. "Javno mnenje o varnostnih temah: splet nakljujčij ali dosleden vzorec?" *Teorija in praksa* 44(1/2): 49−66.

Malešič, M., ed. 2010. *Mednarodne razsežnosti varnosti Slovenije*. Ljubljana: Fakulteta za družbene vede.

Malešič, M., and G. Kümmel, eds. 2011. *Security and the Military between Reality and Perception*. Baden-Baden: Nomos.

Malešič, M. 2013. *Slovenska javnost: spoznavni in zaznavni vidiki varnosti*. Ljubljana: Fakulteta za družbene vede.

Malešič, M. 2015. "EULEX Kosovo: A Test of the EU's Civilian Crisis Management." In *Managing Crises, Making Peace. Towards a Strategic EU Vision for Security and Defense (Rethinking Peace and Conflict Studies)*, edited by M.G. Galantino and M.R. Freire, 157−177. Basingstoke & New York: Palgrave Macmillan.

Malešič, M., L. Jelušič, M. Garb, J. Vuga, E. Kopač, and J. Juvan. 2015. *Small, but Smart: The Structural and Functional Professionalization of the Slovenian Armed Forces*. Baden Baden: Nomos.

Malešič, M. 2015. "The Impact of Military Engagement in Disaster Management on Civil-Military Relations." *Current Sociology* 63(7): 980−998.

Malešič, M., ed. 2016. *Konvencionalna in hibridna varnost: vzorci (dis)kontinuitete*. Ljubljana: Fakulteta za družbene vede.

Malešič, M., and M. Garb. 2017. "A Decade Later: Professionalization of the Slovenian Armed Forces." *Nemzet és biztonság: biztonságpolitikai szemle* 9(Special Issue): 32−41.

Malešič, M. 2017. "O znanstvenem ustvarjanju zaslužnega profesorja dr. Antona Beblerja na obramboslovnem področju." In *Izzivi vojne in miru*, edited by A. Bebler, 5−23. Ljubljana: Fakulteta za družbene vede.

Mali, F. 1996. "Družbena regulacija in avtonomija znanosti." In *Razvoj obramboslovne misli*, edited by M. Malešič, 87−98. Ljubljana: Fakulteta za družbene vede.

Malnar, B., and I. Bernik, eds. 2014. *S Slovenkami in Slovenci na štiri oči*. Ljubljana: Fakulteta za družbene vede.

Ouellet, E., ed. 2005. *New Directions in Military Sociology*. Whitby: de Sitter.

Prebilič, V. 2002. "Upravljanje konverzije vojaških objektov." In *Nacionalna in mednarodna varnost Slovenije*, edited by M. Malešič, 188−209. Ljubljana: Fakulteta za družbene vede.

Prebilič, V. 2007. *Civilno vojaški odnosi po vstopu v Nato in EU: praktični vidik civilnega nadzora nad OS z analizo razmerij med zakonodajno in izvršno oblastjo ter evroatlantskimi povezavami (Severnoatlantsko zavezništvo in EU) (raziskovalni projekt)*. Ljubljana: Fakulteta za družbene vede.

Prebilič, V., and J. Juvan. 2014. "Mladi, domoljubje in nacionalna varnost: vojska kot steber domoljubnih struktur." *Sodobni vojaški izzivi* 16(1): 63–75.

Soeters, J.L., and P. Manigart. 2008. *Military Cooperation in Multinational Peace Operations: Managing Cultural Diversities and Crisis Response*. London & New York: Routledge.

Stouffer, S., E.A. Suchman, L.C. DeVinney, S.A. Star, and R.M. Williams, Jr. 1949/50. *The American Soldier. Studies in Social Psychology in World War II*. Four volumes. Princeton, NJ: Princeton University Press.

Svete, U., and J. Juvan. 2016. "Soldiers' Private Digital Communications as a Factor Disturbing Military Operations Abroad." *Res Militaris* 6(2): 1–13.

Vlachova, M., ed. 2003. *The Public Image of Defence and the Military in Central and Eastern Europe*. Geneva, Belgrade: DCAF/CCMR.

Vreg, F. 1985. *Pripravljenost družbenopolitičnega sistema za SLO in DS*. Ljubljana: RSS.

Vreg, F. 1987. *Družbenopolitični sistem – obramba in varnost*. Ljubljana: Komunist.

Vuga, J. 2011. "Public Perceptions of Casualties in Peace Operations: The Effects of Potential Casualties on Public Support in the Case of Slovenia." In *Security and the Military between Reality and Perception*, edited by M. Malešič and G. Kümmel, 79–93. Baden-Baden: Nomos.

Vuga, J., and J. Juvan. 2013. "Inside the Military Organisation. Experience of Researching Slovenian Armed Forces." In *Qualitative Methods in Military Studies. Research Experiences and Challenges*, edited by H. Carreiras and C. Castro, 116–131. London & New York: Routledge.

Vuga, J. 2014. "Safety Bubble versus Risk Awareness: Casualty Aversion among the Slovenian Public." *Armed Forces & Society* 40(2): 357–381.

Vuga, J., and V. Prebilič. 2014. "Slovenian National Independence in Public Education: In Quest for National Identity among the Slovenian Youth." *European Perspectives/Journal on European Perspectives of the Western Balkans* 6(1): 15–36.

Vuga, J. 2016. "Med družino in delom: očetje, matere in otroci v vojaški organizaciji." In *Konvencionalna in hibridna varnost: vzorci (dis)kontinuitete*, edited by M. Malešič, 239–255. Ljubljana: Fakulteta za družbene vede.

Wiatr, J. 1987. *Sociologija vojske*. Beograd: Vojnoizdavački i novinski centar.

Sociology and its Bearing on Total Defense: Military Sociology in Sweden

Erik Hedlund and Torsten Björkman

1   Introduction: Sweden's Military Sociology in Context

The Kingdom of Sweden has a vast area (more than Germany and the Benelux states combined), long borders at both land and sea, but a relatively small population. That poses many military challenges: How do you defend a coastline of 2,400 kilometers – to mention just one of them? In the 1950s, Sweden had the fourth largest air force in the world, 50 squadrons and 1,000 planes. The conscription system enabled the mobilization of 800,000 soldiers while civil society often exercised its role in total defense. In the major cities nuclear bomb shelters were built for half a million people and the majority of city populations were trained to evacuate to the countryside, *if war were to come.*

Sweden was a neutral country in World War 2. A major lesson learned from the suffering of the neighboring countries was that modern war targets civil populations. Close civil-military cooperation is necessary for successful defense and if the population loses its will to defend itself, the country is doomed. Based on that insight, the new academic subject of sociology was activated in 1947 with its first professor Torgny Segerstedt, in particular to continually study the Swedish population's will to defend itself and the soldiers' adaptation to conscription.

When the Cold War ended with the demise of the Soviet Union and the Warsaw Pact during the dramatic years of 1989–1991, the repercussions on Swedish Defense Policy were far-reaching. Swedish governments first thought that the country had a *strategic timeout,* which should be used for upgrading the military forces according to the ideas of the "Revolution in Military Affairs" (RMA). This turned out to be very expensive combined with the policy of National Self-reliance in Weapons' Procurement (Agrell 2010). Subsequently, at the beginning of the new millennium, policy shifted. According to opinion at that time, the only *real* military need was taking part in international peacekeeping missions. National defense was considered a thing of the past. Within a few years, the Swedish military and civil defense were reduced on average by 90 percent. For example, instead of 36 brigades there remained only two. Most of the regional regiments were closed (called by the media "the death of the regiments"). Local and regional protests from the electorate were mostly ignored by the politicians of those years (Björeman 2011). Sweden, as well as many other Western countries, was slow to realize that Russia had a policy of rearming. The Russian annexation of Crimea was a wake-up call. Now the tide has turned in Swedish defense policy, conscription was reintroduced in 2017, the military budget is increasing each year and civil defense is once again mobilized.[1] However, it is an uphill struggle; many capabilities must be reintroduced starting from close to zero. Military sociology is one of the exceptions. It survived the disarmament years, perhaps by shifting the focus of its research; now being much more international than during the years of the Cold War.

The aim of this chapter is to describe the historical background of military sociology in Sweden and its current position in research, education, and public opinion. The second part of the chapter describes the international birth of military sociology as well as the institutionalization of military sociology in Sweden. Thereafter, we explain current research funding, research methods and main topics of empirical research. Furthermore, we describe some research findings in Swedish doctoral dissertations of interest to military sociology and the role of military sociology in the officer education programs. The conclusion provides a short summary of current military sociology in Sweden and addresses avenues for future research and education at the Swedish Defence University (SEDU).

2   From an International Perspective: Swedish Sociology in General, Swedish Military Sociology in Particular

Sociology is arguably a French invention, at least in the literal sense, since August Comte (the father of sociology) coined the concept in 1838. Sociology was well established in France, the UK, Germany, the US, and a number of other countries, already in the second half of the 19th century. The major theories and findings of classical sociology were well known in Sweden amongst many contemporary scholars, but those scholars were philosophers, economists, statisticians, academics of governmental studies,[2] and not sociologists. Swedish sociology is a newcomer to the discipline, with the first professorship (at Uppsala University) inaugurated as late as 1947. Given the early Cold War period, international relations and military sociology were in focus from the very beginning. The first Swedish professor

---

1   The Swedish Government has recently ordered an investigation of the status of 65,000 (sic!) shelters (many very large and of high standard).

2   The Department of Governmental Studies (and Rhetoric) at Uppsala University is the oldest in that discipline in the World, the department was founded as early as 1622.

of sociology, Torgny Segerstedt, was one of the fathers of the ISA (International Sociological Association) founded in 1948, holding its first World Congress in Zürich in 1950; one of its major themes being *Sociological Research and its Bearing on International Relations*. The World Congresses of Sociology have been very instrumental in the internationalization of sociology. With a European and American bias, only two of the 19 Congresses have taken place in Asia and only one in Africa. Two have been held in Sweden: in Uppsala (1978) and Gothenburg (2010).

In 1949, George Lundberg[3] was a visiting professor of sociology in both Sweden and Norway. His kind of sociology was the one preferred by the first Swedish sociologists; placing substantial emphasis on empirical studies, strict methodology demanding validity, reliability and repeatability of all findings, conscientious theory-building, contempt for "speculation" (Larsson 2001). Very influential studies in military sociology, considered exemplary by most Swedish sociologists, were the ones published by Samuel Stouffer (1949 et al.) under the title: *The American Soldier During WW2, Volume I: Adjustment During Army Life*, and *Volume II: Combat and its Aftermath*. An early Swedish Sociologist, Bo Anderson from Uppsala University who later emigrated to the US and became sociology professor at Michigan State University, became an expert on these studies and inspired the work at two Swedish institutes responsible for research in military sociology, the BN (*The Preparedness Board of Psychological Defense)* and the MPI (*The Institute of Military Psychology)*. We will provide more information on them later on.

The debate between Samuel Huntington (1957) and Morris Janowitz (1960) was followed with considerable interest by the Swedish military. A researcher in military sociology at the MPI, Bengt Abrahamsson, was in favor of Janowitz's interpretation of military professionalism and found it much more applicable to the Swedish officer corps than Huntington's version.[4]

In 1960, the ISA organized its first Research Committee (01)[5] with the name *The Armed Forces and Conflict Resolution*. Morris Janowitz chaired the committee and had Bengt Abrahamsson as its Swedish representative on the board. In 1974, military sociology acquired a journal of its own, *The Journal of Armed Forces & Society*, based on the initiative of Morris Janowitz, sometimes called *the father of military sociology*.

---

3   President of the American Sociological Association for the year 1943 (Presidents of ASA are only presidents for one year). Lundberg, his parents immigrants from Sweden, was one of the leading American sociologists of his time.

4   Bengt Abrahamsson's analysis was published later in 1971, in his dissertation *Military Professionalization and Political Power*.

5   ISA has 57 Research Committees at present, thanks to the early priority of interest given to Armed Forces and Conflict Resolutions.

The ISA's RC 01, *The Armed Forces and Conflict Resolution* has been active at all the World Congresses of Sociology. However, among European scholars there was growing discontent that the problems and challenges of the US military were given too much time and attention in the RC 01. The American military is exceptional, not typical. The problems and challenges of the military in European countries are often drastically different from what is characteristic for the US. In short, European scholars interested in military sociology and related disciplines wanted an organization of their own, focusing on European problems, not American ones. In 1988, the interdisciplinary network of researchers ERGOMAS (European Research Group on Military and Society) was formed. ERGOMAS is the most important international cooperation within military sociology from a Swedish perspective. Swedish researchers have been active in ERGOMAS from the very beginning. In 2007–2009, Alise Weibull was the President of ERGOMAS. Two of the biennial conferences have been held in Stockholm (1998 and 2009). Leading international researchers within ERGOMAS, like Christopher Dandeker and Bernard Boëne, have been invited to Sweden almost on a yearly basis, and they have written extensively on what is specific about the Swedish military and Swedish civil-military relations (Dandeker 1999).

3   Military Sociology in Sweden

3.1   Institutional Organization of Early Swedish Military Sociology

The early sociologists in Sweden defined their discipline as a study of *modern* society, a society in transition from rural to urban, from agriculture to industry, from industry to services and the coming of the post-industrial society. *Modern* also meant a dramatic growth in time spent in an expanding educational system. Rising productivity meant more leisure and more time for activities like sports and media consumption. In military sociology, this focus on sociology and modernity corresponded to an emphasis on *modern warfare*. An overarching aspect of modern warfare was that it was total warfare, and in the case of Sweden, total defense, implying a mobilization of a number of civil sectors of society, such as the media, the infrastructure, all logistics etc. A core concern was how to guarantee a public opinion characterized by the very will to defend the country, a decisiveness never to surrender.

Two governmental agencies are of special interest for early military sociology in Sweden: 1. The Preparedness Board of Psychological Defense (in Swedish: *Beredskaps-*

Nämnden för psykologiskt försvar, BN*)* founded in 1954. Mapping public opinion related to civil-military defense issues was seen as a very *modern* and essential task for this agency, which had the official aim of strengthening civil-military cooperation.« 2. The Institute of Military Psychology *(*in Swedish: *Militärpsykologiska Institutet,* MPI*)* also founded in 1954, which represented a new conception of conscription: Something more than duty. The adjustment and well-being of the conscripts during military service were given priority. Both agencies use the concept *Psychology* (not Sociology) in their names as a result of some conceptual confusion. The Swedish military, during the Cold War decades, grouped academic disciplines into a few broad categories such as social and behavioral sciences. One single discipline amongst these sciences was very well known by the military, namely psychology, but the term was over-applied. Sociology, educational science, governmental studies were all labelled as *psychology.* Psychological warfare was a well-known concept and the same was true of psychological testing, used for selecting conscripts as well as officers. Jan Agrell, the head of the Institute of Military Psychology, was a doctor in educational science, but the military gave him the title of *Supreme Military Psychologist.* Many of the leading researchers at that institute, Bengt Abrahamsson, Walter Korpi, Robert Eriksson, Jan Trost and others, had all defended doctoral dissertations in sociology, but the military called them psychologists[6]. The Swedish military started to use the concept of *sociology* correctly as late as in the 1990s.

3.2 Core Topics of Early Military Sociological Research in Sweden

The institutionalization of military sociology in Sweden is closely linked to how the Cold War became more threatening from a Swedish perspective. This process can be seen as a way of meeting some of those threats by conducting research, in particular sociological research. During the Cold War, the following four themes (fields of study) were dominant and were documented in over two hundred reports and thousands of letters and memoranda from the afore-mentioned institutes. Many of the reports and letters were classified, and still are *top secret,* owing to the conclusion that they are too revealing about Swedish *fighting power* and thereby *interesting* to a potential enemy.

1) *Public opinion.* The main research question was how strong is the general will to defend Sweden militarily, even against an attack by a more resourceful enemy

---

6   A civilian equivalent of conceptual simplification might be the rather common practice of still calling all persons working in the military *soldiers,* regardless of if they are officers, NCOs, or conscripts.

(read: The Soviet Union)? The first questionnaire to measure that will, the attitude to defend, was formulated by Gösta Carlsson, the first professor of Sociology in Lund. His questionnaire is still in use and studies of the Swedish will to defend themselves are still carried out (MSB 2018a, 2018b). In other words, the Swedish will to defend themselves can be compared over a period of more than 60 years (Tubin 2003). A lesson learned from World War 2 was that the enemy tries to manipulate public opinion by spreading fake news in various disinformation campaigns, often skillfully designed. The BN received the additional assignment of spreading the knowledge that all messages proclaiming that Sweden would surrender are false. "We will never surrender!" was the message repeated over and over again (Tubin 2003).

2) *Adaptation during conscription.* The effects of urbanization were of special interest in this domain. A large number of conscripts were city-dwellers like those from Stockholm, but they were supposed to become skillful in warfighting in rural surroundings, such as those at the borders in northern Sweden or out in Sweden's vast archipelagos. During winter, soldiers up in the north had to endure a lot of snow, temperatures 30 degrees below zero and often *stormy weather*. Every Swedish soldier was expected to be proficient on skis. Generally speaking, the adaptation studies by sociologists like Jan Trost (1960) and Robert Eriksson (1964) provided more positive results than expected. Most conscripts from the cities were fast learners of *rural* skills. Another major interest concerning conscription was how well teambuilding functioned and what levels of cohesion were achieved during a year or a year and a half in military service. Another well-known sociologist, Walter Korpi, became an early expert on cohesion, especially in the armored regiments and brigades. Thanks to him and many other scholars and inspired by research in the US, such as *The American Soldier* by Samuel Stouffer et al. (1949) Sweden gained an increasing scientific literature on the Swedish soldiers' adjustment during army life (Korpi 1964).

3) *Military professionalization of the officer corps.* The Swedish labor market in the 1950s was in favor of employees and not employers. Unemployment was down to 2 percent and very capable and highly skilled employees had many alternatives. At the same time, the armed forces had difficulties in keeping officers. Turnover increased, particularly in the Air Force, as civil aviation grew rapidly. The armed forces tried to improve their attractiveness by offering paid education and further experiences, not least in leadership. Leadership education backfired in the sense that officers from all services had such good reputations as leaders that many civil employers wanted to hire them. By paying a lot better than the military, they often succeeded. A lot of sociological research at the two aforementioned agencies dealt with these issues. One Swedish sociologist, Bengt Abrahamsson, made lasting con-

tributions, including internationally, to this field. He wrote a number of reports on the turnover within the officer corps during the 1960s at the MPI before his doctoral dissertation in 1971 (Abrahamsson 1971) *Military Professionalization and Political Power*. Abrahamsson introduced the Huntington-Janowitz debate on the true nature of military professionalization, exclusiveness and uniqueness or integration with the civil society to a Swedish audience. The military was certainly a part of the power elite, as the sociologist C. Wright Mills (1956) claimed in his classic titled, *The Power Elite*. The US President, Dwight *Ike* Eisenhower, 1953–1961 and the French President, Charles de Gaulle, 1959–1969 were former generals and supreme commanders. Abrahamsson argued in favor of the Janowitz perspective of a military profession well integrated into civil society, sharing its norms and values. From his perspective, such an officer corps facilitates civil control of the military, whereas a military according to the Huntington conception poses a constant threat to civil society. In many Latin American countries, military dictatorships were almost the standard and it became common in Africa after decolonization. In Europe at the time of this dissertation, the military dictatorship of Greece (1967–1974) was a closer and much detested example in Sweden.

4) *Leadership studies.* Findings from the impressive study, *The American Soldier*, led by the sociologist Samuel Stouffer had a lasting impact on leadership training in the Swedish Armed Forces. Lundberg, Schrag, and Larsen's (1954) textbook, *Sociology*, became a standard in the early Swedish sociology departments. There was one finding that gained much attention in Sweden: the correlation between morale amongst soldiers and the kind of officers that were their superiors. If the officers were supportive of *their* soldiers and liked by them, the morale, especially in fighting, was much higher than if the officers were simply commanding and controlling, regarding their soldiers as a resource to be spent. This simple finding that there is an important difference between those superiors who are liked and admired by their subordinates and those who are disliked, has had a great impact on most subsequent leadership research. Members of the first category qualify for being called *leaders*, members of the second category fail in most respects as the performance of their subordinates lacks in motivation and flexibility (Hersey and Blanchard 1969).

The Swedish Armed Forces of the 1950s could mobilize 800,000 troops. One consequence was a great demand for active officers and officers in the reserve. Almost all the male population had experienced military leadership during their time as conscripts. Many in the Swedish elite, in business, as well as in the public sector were reserve officers. The armed forces provided a benchmark for *modern* leadership and felt the responsibility to keep up with developments in leadership theory and practice. A favorite was *situational leadership*, or as it was called in the 1970s, "the life cycle theory of leadership" (Hersey and Blanchard 1969). The

Swedish military adapted the theory at the MPI with the help of sociologists and psychologists. Evaluations proved that it was well adapted to *the life cycle of conscription*, designed as four phases denoting the relationship between soldiers and their officers. The first was called *Directive*, when soldiers were supposed to need firmer leadership. *Coaching* was second, with a lot of both direction and support. Next was *Supporting*, with a focus on assistance. Finally, the fourth was *Delegating*, when soldiers had become more independent and had no need for constant leadership. Later, particularly in the 1990s, new fields of documentation and research were added (Tubin 2003).[7]

3.3   The Institutional Development from the 1970s Onwards

The development of the institutions responsible for military sociology in Sweden after 1970 is a story of mergers and relocations, but in retrospect, the 1950s and 1960s were their *golden age*, at least in terms of intensity and the number of studies and reports. In 1974, the MPI merged with the biggest military research establishment in Sweden, the Swedish Defence Institute (FOA, *Försvarsmaktens Forskningsanstalt*). FOA founded in 1945 still exists, but since 2001, under the name of the Swedish Defence Research Agency (FOI, *Totalförsvarets Forskningsinstitut*) and reduced to only some 1,000 employees, 400 of them having completed dissertations in mostly technology and natural sciences.

The political context surrounding FOA/FOI has changed dramatically over the years. Originally, FOA was founded to develop a Swedish nuclear bomb. Swedish industry invested vast resources in nuclear technologies, so the goal was in reach technically, but not politically. FOA became embedded in the Swedish arms industry with an emphasis on research and development into the latest and most advanced military technologies. The focus for FOI was rather on evaluating foreign technologies than developing them in Sweden. A famous case was the evaluation of different tank models. In the final round, the American Abrams, French LeClerc and German Leopard were included. The final decision was to buy the Leopard which proved to be best.

FOA/FOI has a large emphasis on weapon-technology development for the Air Force, the Navy, and the Army, as well as developments in civil defense and logistics. Most of the former MPI became one of the many departments of FOA known as FOA 5. By 1976, it had been already decided amongst the engineers that FOA 5 was a *strange bird*, so a huge part of it was relocated to Karlstad in Western

---

7   These studies were generally published as Swedish reports and not as peer review articles in English. See Tubin (2003) for a comprehensive reference list of such studies.

Sweden. In the 1990s, the lonely years for the FOA 5 section were over, when it was integrated as the Karlstad Campus within the Swedish Defense University with its center of gravity in Stockholm.

The Preparedness Board of Psychological Defense (BN) was reorganized in 1985. The new governmental agency was called the Swedish National Board of Psychological Defense. This new board emphasized research and management to a higher degree, dealing with crises and disasters of varying magnitude during peacetime, for example, repercussions of nuclear fallout after the Chernobyl disaster (1986), rescue efforts during the sinking of the ship Estonia in the Baltic (1994), the tsunami in Thailand (2004) and how Swedish authorities and tourists tried to handle the situation. This Board lasted until 2008, when it became a department within the new *mega* agency, the Civil Contingencies Agency *(MSB, Myndigheten för Samhällsskydd och Beredskap* in Swedish*)*. Some of the research traditions that were characteristic for the earlier Boards of Psychological Defense now have a new home at the Swedish Defence University, currently by far the strongest bastion for research in military sociology in Sweden.

Military sociology research has been placed under the umbrella of the Leadership Department with researchers of different disciplines, such as psychology, sociology, pedagogics, political science, and work science. The processes of identifying research projects are done in close cooperation with the Swedish Armed Forces. They and the SEDU have a channel of communication to discuss and decide each specific research project; some of these projects being under the umbrella of military sociology.

The publication practice is to publish peer reviewed articles, books, and book chapters. In addition, there have been eleven doctoral theses published at the SEDU between 2001 and 2017, which have a military sociology profile. It is difficult to provide an exact number of published articles, books, book chapters and reports in military sociology but there are at least 100 peer reviewed articles, 11 peer reviewed books (doctoral theses), approximately 10−15 peer reviewed book chapters and innumerable non-peer reviewed national reports between 2000 and 2018.

Since the 1990s, lessons learned from peacekeeping and peace-enforcement missions were given priority by several Supreme Commanders, resulting in several reports, (e.g., Ahlquist 1996; Johansson 1996) and later a more monumental work analyzing some 120 Swedish international military missions (Försvarsmakten 2006). Moreover, at the same time, the interest in corporate culture reached the Armed Forces (Magnusson 1998). The differences in corporate culture were shown to be considerable between Army, Navy and Air Force, but also between the various service branches and particularly army regiments, navy squadrons and air force wings. The cultural core values were diverse amongst these units, including bold rangers, aggressive armored brigades, smart reconnaissance, and so on. The 1990s also saw gender studies in the armed forces being introduced (Blomgren and Lind 1997), and later becoming a field of its own.

3.4   Research Funding

Research projects at the SEDU are mostly financed by the Swedish Armed Forces (SAF), which has a research budget per year, meaning that there is a budget closing every year. However, the routine has been an agreement between the SEDU and SAF saying that most research projects will be financed over three years. Another important research sponsor is the Swedish Civil Contingencies Agency (MSB), which is responsible for the Swedish civil emergency management, civil defense, and public defense. The MSB announces research funds for which researchers from the SEDU can apply. There is also some smaller internal research funding available within the SEDU, aimed at promoting research projects between the various SEDU faculties. The amount of money from the SAF for funding research has been decreasing continually, in line with the downsizing of Swedish defense since the beginning of the 2000s. In 2011, the SAF launched a new research policy implying that not only the SEDU will be used for research but also some other universities, such as *Karolinska Institutet, Kristianstad* University and a *network at Chalmers University of Technology,* the Swedish Centre for Studies of Armed Forces and Society. They have collected narratives of the participants in our international military missions and published them in a series of own produced books. They have also installed the Bengt Abrahamsson Award for excellent contributions to the study of the military profession and civil-military relations. It is difficult to say whether this new research policy has been successful, but the new research policy resulted in a decreased research budget for the SEDU of about 50 percent, which is still the case in 2018.

3.5   Preferred Research Methods

The next section will highlight selected findings of Swedish military sociology from doctoral theses completed at SEDU. All these doctoral theses, based on qualitative methods, comprise the main research method in military sociology at the SEDU. Data collection methods such as interviews and participant observations are common, as well as thematic and grounded theory analysis. However, there are also some quantitative studies, especially regarding recruitment and willingness to make a future career in the armed forces (see for example, Österberg 2018; Österberg and Carlstedt 2010; Österberg and Jonsson 2012). Response rates of these surveys are high, even if there is the problem of too many surveys and subsequently widespread fatigue regarding questionnaires. Nonetheless, this indicates there is strong belief in surveys among the Swedish officers.

There are also yearly surveys by the Institute of Society, Opinion and Media (SOM Institute) at the University of Gothenburg as well as the MSB,[8] regarding such questions as public confidence in the Swedish Armed Forces and the Swedish defense policy. It is generally easy to conduct studies within the armed forces and get access to respondents because almost all studies are research on behalf of the armed forces.

4 Selected Topics and Insights of Swedish Military Sociology

This chapter provides an overview of some central examples of research findings which are specific for Swedish military sociology. The examples are based on doctoral dissertations and relevant for broader discussions in the discipline.[9]

4.1 The Great Divide in Military Discipline – from Mechanistic to Organic?

In 1989, Klas Borell defended his doctoral thesis called (Borell 1989) *Disciplinary Strategies – a Historical-Sociological Study of the Professional Military-Disciplinary Way of Thinking 1901–1978*. In it, he gives a sharp characterization of the old paternalistic Swedish military, a total organization in Goffman's (1958, 1991) sense. It was heavily reliant on a *garrison-mechanical* approach to make tough soldiers out of every incoming conscript, in often less than a year (the length of service varied a lot during the 20th century). Former conscripts (now elderly) who have wondered

---

8 See their websites <https://som.gu.se/publicerat/rapporter/rapporter> and <www.msb.se/sv/Insats--beredskap/Psykologiskt-forsvar/Opinioner>.

9 The overview in this section focuses on research, which is specific for Swedish military sociology. However, most of the research is related to issues, which are common in international military sociology. Examples of published peer review articles are the following (ordered by the topics of ERGOMAS working groups): Recruitment and Retention (Österberg 2018; Österberg and Carlstedt 2010; Österberg and Jonsson 2012), Military Profession (Larsson et al. 2016), Civil-military Relations (Hedlund 2013), Leadership and Team Learning (Hedlund 2016; Hedlund et al. 2015; Hedlund and Österberg 2013), Women in the Military (Alvinius and Holmberg 2019; Alvinius et al. 2018; Larsson and Alvinius 2019), Military Organization (Alvinius 2012; Holmberg and Alvinius 2019; Larsson et al. 2015; Ohlsson et al. 2017), Officer and Military Education (Hedlund 2004; Hedlund 2018).

why it was so important to have perfectly polished boots, to be extremely quick in disassembling and reassembling firearms, to leave the barracks in perfect order every morning etc., will understand the theory behind it from Borell's thesis. The hard regime was legitimized by the argument that these are the very demands of war itself. Without strict obedience, an army is already lost at the beginning of a battle.

In 1901, the old Swedish system of allotment (*Indelningsverket*; in practice since 1680) of each soldier living on a croft, supported by neighboring farmers, was abandoned. In many ways, the allotment system functioned well, providing Sweden with an army of some 40,000 experienced and disciplined soldiers but at the end of the 19th century that number was considered too small. In 1901, Sweden introduced a conscription system for both the army and navy. A challenge was to make the young conscripts equally disciplined as the professional soldiers of the allotment system. To achieve that goal, the conscripts were socially isolated in garrisons and barracks encircled by guarded fences and walls. They were the targets of a strict regime of traditional drill; to internalize obedience and docility. In the presence of officers, their first reaction would be to salute them and show readiness to take orders.[10]

In the 1960s and 1970s, this *garrison-mechanical* approach in treating conscripts came into disrepute. Many conscripts simply refused to do what they were told. Old-fashioned officers were openly ridiculed and denied their status as superiors. To punish the *revolting* conscripts turned out to be rather ineffective. If you put too many conscripts in jail, you do not have a functional army any longer. A better strategy was to change the behavior of the officers from disciplinarians to motivating and inspiring role models. They had to be good at persuasion, orders had to be given after some argumentation, not just shouted. In short, these were the years when the Swedish Armed Forces began to change their preferred leadership theory and doctrine from something transactional to transformative leadership (*Utvecklande ledarskap* in Swedish; Larsson et al. 2003).

4.2   Very Skilled when it Counts!

The Swedish Air Force is given the role of being the first line of defense, responsible for uninterrupted Swedish air superiority. The Air Force must always, every second,

---

10   In a recent study (Sundberg 2015) of the French Foreign Legion by a Swedish sociologist, we can read about the same system still in existence. If the *foreign* legionnaires have the courage to suggest anything to their French officers, they are often corrected by these officers with the stereotyped reply: "You have got your head to eat with".

be on alert, ready to detect and intercept an unauthorized intruder in the air or at sea, whenever and wherever along Sweden's borders (or territorial waters), if such an intrusion should occur. The Air Force must, in short, live up to the criteria of a "High Reliability Organization" (Weick et al. 1999). A chain is never stronger than its weakest link and the monitoring of the air space must function without faults and mistakes. The collection of all relevant information to the regional and central command and control centers must work without missing any relevant details. All of this would be in vain if the last link, the fighters, were not to find their targets in time and either deter them (hopefully) or eliminate them (if they refuse orders to turn away).

Alise Weibull (2003a, 2003b) has studied the Air Force for decades, mostly from a vocational skill perspective, but also using organizational and cultural frames of reference. She summed up her major findings in a retrospective thesis from 2003a, *Professional Competence in Readiness (Yrkeskunnande i beredskap)*. Weibull has studied most professional and vocational groups within the Air Force. Pilots, especially fighter pilots, are a select and very skillful group, an elite when it comes to situational awareness, reaction times, the ability to endure 9 Gs etc., which is rather well known. To a lesser extent, the same is true of flight technicians; no one doubts that you must be extremely quality-minded when doing maintenance on a jet engine. However, that the same requirements of quality-mindedness are also true for air observers monitoring airspace is perhaps not as recognized. Weibull has for the first time in Swedish military sociology made a careful study of the inner workings of the command and control (C2) centers of the Air Force and the skill requirements of the interceptor controllers manning these centers. Her C2-study is a dramatic demonstration of the validity of the chain metaphor; every link must be strong. The kind of proficiency that is necessary in this system can only be upheld with a lot of constantly evaluated practice. Learning by doing is a necessity but, given the often-lethal consequences if something goes wrong, operating sophisticated simulators is an important element of learning by doing.[11]

4.3   Changes in Officer Education

The background for this study (Hedlund 2004) was that the Swedish Armed Forces wanted to change the officer education to a more academic one because of the end of the Cold War. The result was that, in 1999, the Swedish Armed Forces introduced a two-year Officer Program with a more academic profile, without on-the-

---

11   In short, a kind of "situated learning", using the concept coined by J. Lave and E. Wenger (1991).

job training at the units and an additional element of joint service. The intention was that the units would arrange local programs so that the new second lieutenants could utilize their specific position knowledge, skills, and capabilities after they finished the Officer Program. Significantly, the on-the-job training, which was the most highly regarded and most central part of all armed forces training, was eliminated from then onwards.

The implementation of a new Officer Program in 1999 was a significant step toward increased subjective civilian control, based on societal imperatives of increased civilian integration into the military establishment. Suddenly, the Swedish Armed Forces had a basic officer education system characterized by almost the opposite of its historical traditions and perceived needs. As a kind of follow up to this study, Hedlund (2013) published an article on civil-military control of the Swedish military profession, which was an analysis from the perspective of officer rank and officer education. Another follow up study by Hedlund (2018) was on a generic pedagogic model for academically based professional officer education. That article presents a proposal for a generic pedagogic model for academic professional officer education, which promotes a process of professionalization within the military profession through officer education, meeting the requirements of higher education systems as well as the demands of the military profession.

4.4   A Complementary View on the Emotional Demands of Serving Abroad

Until the late 1990s, The Swedish Armed Forces kept their focus primarily on national territorial defense, a development that likely delayed the analysis of on-going international engagements. Experiences from soldiers serving under less traumatic conditions were at the time below the radar of both military authorities and the research community. Louise Weibull promoted wider attention to the emotional demands in low-intensity conflict areas in her book, *Emotion matters: Emotion management in Swedish Peace Support Operations* (2012).

The armed forces' view of the need for emotion management in these theatres could roughly be summarized as follows: If there is no direct threat to personal safety, there is no problem. The thesis labels this view on emotions as *hydraulic*, i.e., emotions are seen as something that can be generated on one occasion, locked up and let out somewhere else (e.g., in debriefing sessions or in after-action reviews). Another well-established discourse in the military is to see emotions mainly as friction in high-stake situations, something irrational that may lead to passivity, by which soldiers preferably should avoid being overcome.

Analyzing soldiers' work from an emotion sociological perspective (Weibull 2012) created a broader view, where emotion management is at the core of their work and living experiences abroad. In contrast to stress management theories, this perspective states that the successful soldier is not someone in control, in the sense that he/she 'lacks' feelings towards what he/she is doing. Even when work tasks are more constabulary in kind, being able to manage emotions in a wide range is what it takes to get the job done, i.e., from expressing *the right* emotional display, to changing personal feelings within or those of others, in order to de-escalate a situation. Further, a new concept, Post-Deployment Disorientation (PDD), was introduced to highlight that even a tour of service where nothing happened in military terms, may still influence the soldiers' emotions profoundly. Here, the transformative properties of deployment were expressed in the following three dimensions; A reality check often occurs when leaving the *developed world bubble* and encountering deep civilian poverty. Secondly, personal growth reflects the fact that expeditionary service is generally seen as a greenhouse for personal development. Most often, this is a positive thing, but can also cause social disorientation on return. The third dimension, *A Pocket in Time*, refers to the impact of having lived in an environment where the contrast between intense operations and more tedious work tasks often made way for unusual contemplation and self-reflection.

4.5   Mission Impossible and Discretion

The Swedish Armed Forces have a long history of international military peace-keeping missions. More than one hundred thousand Swedes have volunteered in military peacekeeping missions over the years. One of the biggest in troop size, altogether more than 8,000 soldiers, and the longest, is the one to Afghanistan since 2001, still in operation but now very downsized.[12] In Björkman's evaluation of the reports from the contingents to Afghanistan (Björkman 2012), the short deployment time of the contingents (six months) was proven to be very problem-atic, causing a lot of disruptions and discontinuities. In a study, Johnsson (2017) observes 14 force commanders in Afghanistan between 2006 and 2013, where the mission qualified for being called impossible. A Swedish battalion had the mission of securing four provinces in Afghanistan with a population of 2.4 million and a territory of 60,177 square kilometers.

---

12   During the ISAF-years it used to be a six-month contingent of reinforced battalion size. In the present RSM (Resolute Support Mission) Sweden participates with a small rotating contingent of some 25 military experts.

In his meticulous empirical work, Johnson found support for Huntington's (1957) and Friedson's (2001) theses and assumptions. The civil, political, control of the force commanders is only *objective* (using and verifying Huntington's concept), the colonels as a category have a far-reaching professional autonomy, individual professional "discretion" (using Friedson's terminology). Colonels do not complain that missions are impossible; they do not embarrass the Swedish politicians responsible for promising too much. Instead, they concentrate on smaller parts of the mission and try to make those endeavors, mini-missions, possible, for example, supporting Afghan units both in training and actual warfighting, engaging in various reconstruction efforts like building schools and bridges, supporting and shielding Afghan women who start local cooperatives. The major drawback of these and many similar strategies is the lack of continuity. The contingents are in Afghanistan for only a six-month period, which is rather short; too short for most of these smaller missions to be successful. Another issue with respect to long-term success is that many colonels are more interested in starting new initiatives than continuing those of their predecessor.

As these examples show, research on foreign deployments and missions has been quite common (Andersson 2001; Granberg 2013; Johnsson 2017). There are also several studies in peer-reviewed articles written about different international missions, as well as by individual officers on observation missions in different countries (Liberia: Hedlund et al. 2008; Afghanistan: Larsson et al. 2017; Kosovo: Johansson and Larsson 2001; Larsson et al. 2007).

5   The Relevance of Research: Military Sociology in Officer Education and the Wider Public

There have been elements of military sociology in the Staff and Command Program, as well as in the Advanced Staff and Command Program, from at least 1995 until 2008, but not in the basic Officer Program for the cadets. When the SEDU became a Military University in 2008, it had to adapt to the Bologna and the ERASMUS process. At that point, all Officer Programs from cadets up to the Advanced Staff and Command Programs had to change their curricula to become more academic and, therefore, comparable to civilian universities. This meant that education had to be based on scientific and proven experience and needed to have the same rules and examination requirements as civilian universities. As a result, from 2008 on, the Leadership department developed three programs in leadership and the officer profession for the three different officer programs based on sociology, military sociology, psychology, social psychology, and organizational theory. The military sociology elements were classics such as Samuel Huntington's (1957) *The Soldier and the State* and Morris Janowitz's (1960) *the Professional Soldier*, but also current military sociology research on, for example, civil-military relations, military ethics, leadership, military families, veterans, women in the military, and officer education.

The knowledge of Swedish public opinion relies heavily on polls. As an instrument, they had their break-through in Sweden during World War Two, called Gallups in those days. The results of many of these studies were classified and kept secret from the media and the public. However, after the war, most of them were made public (Håstad 1950), revealing a rather close correlation between the time of the war and common expectations regarding the outcome. In retrospect, Swedish (amongst the majority of Swedes) self-confidence in evaluating the relative strength of their defense seems somewhat exaggerated.

Studying public opinion was top of the agenda for many of the first Swedish sociologists. One of them, Hans Zetterberg, even became the owner of the biggest Gallup institute in Sweden, the Swedish Institute for Opinion Surveys (SIFO; *Svenska institutet för opinionsundersökningar*). However, through the years, the influence of political scientists grew since polls of electoral preferences became very dominant in the media. Political scientists realized that public opinion polls gave them a better understanding of the democratic system as they often showed a wide gap in opinion between the views of politicians and those within the electorate. Studying public opinion became mandatory amongst political scientists. (Petersson 2018). Regardless of who was responsible for the polls, everyone interested in Swedish history has the advantage of an exceptionally long series of studying trends in public opinion. Confidence in the Swedish defense forces, the Swedes' will to defend Sweden (even if the outcome is uncertain) and a number of related issues concerning national security and foreign policy have been studied in a similar way since the 1950s. The MSB still does the same survey annually, started by the BN in 1954. The analysis of the MSB's polls show that public opinion on military defense has changed over the last forty years, from a very high level in 1979 (86 percent) to a lower level during the time when Sweden decided to abolish conscription in 2010 (76 and 77 percent, respectively). Since the security situation radically changed with the Russian invasion of Crimea 2014, public support has increased to an extremely high level again (above 90 percent).

Furthermore, public support for increasing the defense budget has become much stronger as result of the Russian invasion of Crimea 2014. Now there is a solid majority (above 50 percent) in Sweden for enlarged defense spending, as well as a widespread consensus that the present armed forces are inadequate when compared to the new threats to Swedish independence. In 1995, in contrast, (in the years after the fall of the Berlin Wall in 1989 and the demise of the Soviet Union in 1991), the will to increase the defense budget was weak (17 percent) and the support for decreasing it was relatively strong (23 percent).

For the public, *military sociology* is an unknown concept, *psychological defense* is not. The confusion is mirrored within the military. The content and findings of military sociology are rather well known, but they are not associated with the unknown concept of military sociology. The revolution in leadership theory and practice from authoritarianism to participatory and persuasive ideals, in the 1970s and 1980s, was promoted by the findings of military sociology and received a lot of attention from the general public, though it was not associated with military sociology. However, it led to a surge in demand for learning more about the leadership teachings and "tricks of the trade" within the military.

The course in leadership and group dynamics, UGL (*Utveckling av Grupp och Ledare*), in English Development of Groups and Leaders, first used within the military as a vehicle to promote the revolution in leadership approaches, became very popular, for many years the most popular leadership education in Sweden. When the Swedish Armed Forces started downsizing in the 1990s, hundreds of former officers chose to do *UGL-consultancy* as their way of getting an income. Former officers were much in demand in many civilian sectors and organizations such as schools, midsize and big companies as well as municipalities. This was a strong indicator that military leadership, the new military leadership had gained a strong reputation for being *modern*.

6   Conclusion

The system of conscription was introduced in Sweden in 1901 and lasted until 2010, when it was replaced by a system of an all-volunteer force. However, the latter system fell short of expectations, especially numerically. In 2017, conscription was reinstated, although at a low level. The number of conscripts will increase year by year, according to present plans. The study of conscription is a Swedish equivalent to the American study of *The American Soldier*. Adaptation to the life as a soldier, sailor or aviator during conscription has been studied in a hundred ways. The cohesion within platoons, companies, battalions, brigades, and regiments has also been thoroughly documented and evaluated; the same is true of officer leadership experienced from the level of conscripted privates.

At present, public opinion is generally very positive towards the armed forces because of Russian actions in Georgia and the Crimea, and not least the terrorist attacks in Europe in the 2010s and particularly in Stockholm in 2017, when a person named Rakhmat Akilov drove a truck down a pedestrian street. As a result, five people died. Another significant sign of greater consciousness regarding real threats to Sweden is that MSB, for the first time since the 1980s, has published and distributed a brochure to the public with information on how households should prepare themselves for a crisis or a war. This brochure has been very well received among the public.

Moreover, some years ago, Sweden started to rebuild the concept of *total defense*, including all authorities, bigger civilian businesses, and important NGOs to maintain all vital societal functions, thus, contributing to military defense. All staff in the government and public sector as well as specific individuals in companies are now being given wartime postings and told what to do in the event of a crisis or war.

In 2020, there will be a huge civil-military exercise for the armed forces, all authorities and all societal functions and critical companies, such as banks, energy supply companies, companies in sectors for infrastructure, etc. Furthermore, the defense budget is being increased considerably with politicians trying to outwit each other in this matter. These are the same politicians who, some years ago, almost obliterated Swedish military defenses and accused the defense force of not being a special priority.

Consequently, huge steps are now being taken to improve the relationship between civil society and the military. As far as it is possible to foresee, it seems that relations between civil society and the military will continue to develop positively and increase the understanding of each other's activities. Swedish defense will increasingly be characterized by being a defense equivalent to what Janowitz called "the citizen soldier", instead of being a purely professional defense, the aim when conscription was abolished in 2010.

The conclusion is that military sociology has never been a big issue in the Swedish public, albeit it had a stronger position in the 1950s and 1960s. There are some yearly polls by MSB, and the SOM institute related to military sociology such as the willingness to defend Sweden, the defense budget, and whether Sweden should have a defense or not, which gain some attention in the media. At the SEDU, military sociology has been a very strictly defined subject, even though there have been elements of military sociology in the officer programs since the 1980s. When SEDU became a real university with the same academic requirements and regulations as civilian universities, military sociology became a core of the leadership courses together with psychology and social psychology. With the introduction of the new Staff and Command Program in 2019, the leadership courses decreased from about twelve to five weeks, which means that military sociology also decreased considerably. There is no professorship of military sociology. Despite this, several researchers within psychology, sociology and pedagogy research on topics related to military sociology such as officer education, culture in the armed forces, recruitment, and females in the armed forces. The reintroduction of conscription has created a need for research on what makes young people motivated to do military service and make a career in the armed forces. Reconstruction of total defense has highlighted the need for more knowledge concerning difficulties and opportunities in civil-military cooperation. There is no indication that the role of military sociology in research and education will change very much in the future. It will continue to be present, although not as a well-defined topic or one taking a particularly large place.

References

Abrahamsson, B. 1971. "Military Professionalization and Political Power." Doctoral dissertation, Stockholm: Allmänna förlaget.

Agrell, W. 2010. *Fredens illusioner. Det svenska nationella försvarets nedgång och fall 1988–2009.* (The Illusions of Peace. The Decline and Fall of the Swedish National Defense 1988–2009). Stockholm: Atlantis.

Ahlquist, L., ed. 1996. *Co-operation, Command and Control in UN Peacekeeping Operations.* Stockholm: Swedish War College Acta C1.

Alvinius, A. 2012. "The Inadequacy of Bureaucratic Organizations – Organizational Adaption through Boundary Spanning in a Civil-Military Context." *Res Militaris* 3(1): 1–23.

Alvinius, A., and A. Holmberg. 2019. "Silence-Breaking Butterfly Effect: Resistance towards the Military within #metoo." *Gender, Work and Organization* 26(9): 1–16.

Alvinius, A., C. Krekula, and G. Larsson. 2018. "Managing Visibility in Recruitment of Women as Leaders in Armed Forces." *Journal of Gender Studies* 27(5): 534–546.

Andersson, L. 2001. "Militärt ledarskap-när det gäller: svenskt militärt ledarskap med fredsfrämjande insatser i fokus. (Military Leadership – in the Case of Swedish Military Leadership with Peace-Promoting Efforts in Focus)." Doctoral dissertation, Stockholm: HLS Förlag.

Björeman, C. 2011. *Försvarets förfall. Konsten att lägga ner försvaret utan att någon bryr sig. (Defense Decline. The Art of Putting Down the Defense without Anyone Caring).* Stockholm: Santérus.

Björkman, T. 2012. *"Den tioåriga expeditionen" – några lärdomar från Afghanistan.* (*The 10-year Expedition – Some Lessons Learned from Afghanistan*). Stockholm: Försvarshögskolan.

Blomgren, E., and O. Lind. 1997. *Kvinna som man är. (Woman as Man is).* Stockholm: Försvarshögskolan, Ledarskapsinstitutionen, Rapport Serie T:2.

Borell, K. 1989. "Disciplinära strategier. En historiesociologisk studie av det professionella militärdisciplinära tänkesättet 1901–1978. (Disciplinary Strategies. A history Sociological Study of the Professional Military-Disciplinary Way of Thinking 1901–1978)." Doctoral dissertation, Stockholm: Almqvist & Wiksell International.

Dandeker, C. 1999. *Facing Uncertainty. Flexible Forces for the Twenty-first Century* Report no. 1. Stockholm: Försvarshögskolan.

Eriksson, R. 1964. *Yrkesval och officersrekrytering. (Vocational Choices and Officer Recruitment).* Stockholm: MPI.

Försvarsmakten. 2006. *Utlandsstyrkan i fredens tjänst. Försvarsmaktens internationella insatser. (Foreign Force in the Service of Peace. The Armed Forces' International Efforts).* Malmö: Bokförlaget Arena.

Friedson, S. 2001. *Professionalism, the Third Logic.* Cambridge: Polity Press.

Goffman, E. 1958. "Characteristics of Total Institutions" *Symposium on Preventive and Social Psychiatry.* Washington, DC: Walter Reed Army Institute of Research.

Goffman, E. 1991/1961. "On the Characteristics of Total Institutions." In *Asylums: Essays on the Social Situations of Mental Patients and Other Inmates,* edited by E. Goffman, 1–125. London: Penguin.

Granberg, M. 2013. *Kognitivt stöd för lärande i arbetet: En teoretisk modell baserad på en fallstudie av ett svenskt militärt utlandsförband i Kosovo. (Cognitive Support to Learning at Work: A Theoretical Model Based on a Case Study of a Swedish Peace Support Unit in Kosovo).* Uppsala Studies in Education. Place: Uppsala.

Holmberg, A., and A. Alvinius. 2019. "How Pressure for Change Challenge Military Organizational Characteristics." *Defence Studies* 19(2): 130–148.

Håstad, H., ed. 1950. *Gallups och den svenska väljarkåren. (Survey and the Swedish Electorate).* Uppsala: Hugo Gebers förlag.

Hedlund, E. 2004. "Yrkesofficersutbildning, yrkeskunnande och legimitet. (Regular Officer Training, Professional Competence and Legitimacy)." Doctoral dissertation, Stockholm: HLS Förlag.

Hedlund, E. 2013. "Civil-Military Control of the Swedish Military Profession. An Analysis from the Perspective of Officer Rank and Officer Education." *Armed Forces & Society* 39(1): 135–157.

Hedlund, E. 2018. "A Generic Pedagogic Model for Academically based Professional Officer Education." *Armed Forces & Society* 45(2): 333–348.

Hedlund, E. 2016. "Team Learning and Leadership in Multinational Military Staff Exercises." *Armed Forces & Society* 43(3): 459–477.

Hedlund, E., M. Börjesson, and J. Österberg. 2015. "Team Learning in a Multinational Military Staff Exercise." *Small Group Research* 46(2): 179–203.

Hedlund, E., L. Weibull, and J. Soeters. 2008. "Swedish-Irish Cooperation in Liberia." In *Military Cooperation in Multinational Peace Operations*, edited by J. Soeters and P. Manigart, 153–165. Milton Park, Oxfordshire: Routledge.

Hersey, P., and K.H. Blanchard. 1969. "Life Cycle Theory of Leadership." *Training and Development Journal* 23(5): 26–34.

Huntington, S. 1957. *The Soldier and the State. The Theory and Politics of Civil-Military Relations.* Cambridge: Harvard University Press.

Janowitz, M. 1960. *The Professional Soldier.* Glencoe: The Free Press.

Johansson, E. 1996. *I basker blå. (In blue berets).* Stockholm: Försvarshögskolan, Ledarskapsinstitutionen.

Johansson, E., and G. Larsson. 2001. "Swedish Peacekeepers in Bosnia and Herzegovina: A Quantitative Analysis." *International Peacekeeping* 8(1): 64–76.

Johnsson, M. 2017. "Strategic Colonels. The Discretion of Swedish Force Commanders in Afghanistan 2006–2013." Doctoral dissertation, Uppsala: Acta Universitatis Upsaliensis.

Korpi, W. 1964. "Social Pressures and Attitudes in Military Training." Doctoral dissertation, Uppsala: A & W.

Larsson, A. 2001. "Det moderna samhällets vetenskap. Om etableringen av sociologi i Sverige 1930–1955. (The Science of Modern Society. About the Establishment of Sociology in Sweden 1930–1955)." Doctoral dissertation, Umeå: Solfjädern.

Larsson, G., F. Bynander, A. Ohlsson, E. Schyberg, and M. Holmberg. 2015. "Crisis Management at the Governmental Offices: A Swedish Case Study." *Disaster Prevention and Management* 24(5): 542–552.

Larsson, G., C. Brandow, M. Fors Brandebo, A. Ohlsson, and G. Åselius, G. 2016. "Swedish Military Officers through other Nations' Eyes." *International Journal of Organizational Analysis* 24(4): 615–633.

Larsson, G., and A. Alvinius. 2019. "Comparison within Gender and between Female and Male Leaders in Female-Dominated, Male-Dominated and Mixed-Gender Work Environments." *Journal of Gender Studies.* Online First: <https://doi.org/10.1080/09589236.2019.1638233>.

Larsson, G., A. Alvinius, M. Fors Brandebo, P. Hyllengren, S. Nilsson, and A. Ohlsson. 2017. "Leadership Lessons: New Challenges for Smaller Nations in Multinational, Highly Stressed Missions." In *The Swedish presence in Afghanistan: Security and defence transformation,* edited by A. Holmberg and J. Hallenberg, 116–137. London: Ashgate.

Larsson, G., L. Carlstedt, J. Andersson, L. Andersson, E. Danielsson, A. Johansson, and I. Robertson. 2003. "A Comprehensive System for Leader Evaluation and Development." *The Leadership & Organization Development Journal* 24(1): 16–25.

Larsson, G., T. Harem, M. Sjöberg, A. Alvinius, and B. Bakken. 2007. "Indirect Leadership under Severe Stress: A Qualitative Inquiry into the 2004 Kosovo Riots." *International Journal of Organizational Analysis* 15(1): 23–34.

Lave, J., and E. Wenger. 1991. *Situated Learning: Legitimate Peripheral Participation.* Cambridge: Cambridge University Press.

Lundberg, G., C. Schrag, and O. Larsen. 1954. *Sociology.* New York: Harper and Brothers.

Magnusson, P. 1998. *Organisationskulturer i Försvarsmakten. (Organizational Culture in the Armed Forces).* Stockholm: Försvars-högskolan, Ledarskapsinstitutionen; LI. Serie F, 1401–5633; 1.

MSB. 2018a. "Om krisen eller kriget kommer. (If the Crisis or War is Coming)." <www.msb.se/Sok/?query=om+krisen+eller+kriget+kommer> (last access: 22 March 2019).

MSB. 2018b. "Opinioner 2018. Allmänhetens syn på samhällsskydd, beredskap, säkerhetspolitik och försvar. (Opinions 2018. The Public's View of Community Protection, Preparedness, Security policy and defense)." <www.msb.se/sv/Insats--beredskap/Psykologiskt-forsvar/Opinioner> (last access: 5 February 2019).

Ohlsson, A., A. Alvinius, and G. Larsson. 2017. "Shadow Structure within Higher-Level Military Staff: A Qualitative Study." *Res Militaris* 7(2): 1–20.

Österberg, J. 2018. *We Want You as Our New Recruit: Prerequisites for Recruitment to and Retention in the Swedish Armed Forces.* Karlstad: Karlstad University Studies.

Österberg, J., and B. Carlstedt. 2010. "Conscripts Willingness to Sign Up for International Military Service." In *Europe Without Soldiers? Recruitment and Retention across the Armed Forces of Europe,* edited by T. Tresch Szvircsev and C. Leuprecht, 109–126. Montreal and Kingston: Queen's Policy Studies Series, McGill-Queen's University Press.

Österberg, J., and E. Jonsson. 2012. "Recruitment to International Military Service: The Officers' View." In *New wars, new militaries, new soldiers? Conflicts, the Armed Forces and the soldierly subject,* edited by G. Kümmel and J. Soeters, 233–245. Bingley, UK: Emerald.

Petersson, O. 2018. *Medborgarna och det psykologiska försvaret.* (*Citizens and the Psychological Defense*). Stockholm: MSB.

SOM-Institutet. 2017. "Svenska trender. (Swedish Trends)" <https://som.gu.se/publicerat/rapporter/rapporter> (last access: 5 February 2019).

Stouffer, S.A., A.A. Lumsdaine, M.H. Lumsdaine, R.M. Williams Jr., M.B. Smith, I. Janis, and L.S. Cottrell Jr. 1949. *The American Soldier. Combat and Its Aftermath.* Studies in Social Psychology in World War II. Princeton, NJ: Princeton University Press.

Sundberg, M. 2015. *A Sociology of the Total Organization. Atomistic Unity in the French Foreign Legion.* London: Routledge.

Trost, J. 1960. *Undersökningen av anda och trivsel: en arbetsrapport.* (*The Study of Spirit and Well-being: a Work Report*). Stockholm: MPI.

Tubin, E. 2003. *Förfäras ej. 50 år med det psykologiska försvaret – en biografi om en svensk myndighet.* (*Not Horrified. 50 Years of Psychological Defense – A Biography of a Swedish Authority*). Stockholm: Styrelsen för Psykologiskt försvar.

Weibull, A. 2003a. "Yrkeskunnande i beredskap. Om strukturella och kulturella inflytelser på arbete i det svenska flygvapnet. (Professional Knowledge in Readiness. About Structural and Cultural Influences at Work in the Swedish Air Force)." Doctoral dissertation, Stockholm: Försvarshögskolan

Weibull, A. 2003b. *Samlingsvolym 1985–1997. Fyra yrkesgrupper i det svenska flygvapnet.* (*Collection volume 1985–1997. Four Occupational Groups in the Swedish Air Force*). Stockholm: Försvarshögskolan.

Weibull, L. 2012. "Emotion Matters: Emotion Management in Swedish Peace Support Operations." Doctoral dissertation, Karlstad: Karlstad University.

Weick, K.E., K.M. Sutcliffe, and D. Obstfeld. 1999. "Organizing for High Reliability: Processes of Collective Mindfulness." In *Research in Organizational Behavior,* edited by R.S. Sutton and B.M. Staw, 81–123. Stanford: Jai Press, Vol. 1.

Wright Mills, C. 1956. *The Power Elite.* Oxford: Oxford University Press.

Military Sociology in Switzerland

Tibor Szvircsev Tresch

1   Introduction[1]

Swiss military sociology can only be understood against the background of the social structures and the political culture in Switzerland. It is necessary to take a look at the peculiarities of the Swiss militia military system and its integration into society. Compared to other European states, there is a particularly strong interconnection between male citizens and the military in Switzerland. With regard to the Swiss military system, Michael Foot established as early as in the 1960s: "As the whole community is engaged in the task of self-defense, no gulf can open between the armed forces and the nation: The two are virtually one [...] The army is as much an accepted part of everyday life as the weather" (Foot 1961, 69).

Prior to describing military sociology in Switzerland and its inclusion in institutions as well as its access to the research field of the military, it is necessary to provide a brief historical overview outlining the close interconnection between society and the militia-based military. This is an inevitable prerequisite for understanding why militia-based military training for the civilian economy, the motivation to take up a voluntary militia career, or public attitudes in Switzerland on foreign, security and defense policy are key research areas of the Department of Military Sociology at the Military Academy (MILAC) at the Swiss Federal Institute of Technology in Zurich (ETH). Questions regarding foreign operations of the Swiss Armed Forces are of secondary importance, though. Even this brief positioning makes clear that, in contrast to other armed forces where research on operations abroad has become increasingly important since the end of the Cold War, Swiss military sociology represents a special case due to the militia-based military system and the country's unabated adherence to neutrality. Following the historical classification of the relationship between society and the military (section 2), I will outline the current situation of Swiss military sociology (section 3), its links to sociology at universities,

---

1   Large parts of this article are based on four earlier papers which define the place of military sociology in Switzerland (Haltiner 2000, 2003; Szvircsev Tresch 2010, 2011). I venture to quote myself and to name sources in summary. I would like to express my deep gratitude to Karl W. Haltiner. This paper would not have been written without his critical review and his profound knowledge of military sociology in Switzerland.

its integration into institutions and its funding, as well as its access to the military as a field of research. Furthermore, I will take a look at the methods and key topics of research and their public perception.

2   The History of the Swiss Armed Forces and its Relationship to Society

In Switzerland, the military is based on two features. The first one refers to the way in which personnel is recruited, which is done through universal conscription. The second feature is that the constitution prohibits Switzerland from sustaining a standing army. This means that the majority of the members of the army liable to military service do not complete their service en bloc and that militia cadres exercise command and control of the army. As a consequence of this structure, the share of professional personnel as a percentage of the total number of personnel is extremely small. This combination results in the typical Swiss militia system, in which citizens have to serve as soldiers over many years. This system is characterized by its temporary nature and by the part-time employment of citizens at both junior and cadre levels.

Whereas most European states experienced breaks in their military traditions in the course of the past 200 years with consequences for the institution itself as well as for its social and political legitimation, such breaks in tradition did not occur in Switzerland (Jaun 1997, 48−51). To this day, the militia principle is still applied as the constitutive element of the Swiss Armed Forces with regard to organizational and political matters. The idea of the citizen in uniform plays a key role and characterizes the relationship between society and the military (Fuhrer 1999). According to Jaun (1998, 114), 19th century Switzerland, unlike the European great powers, did not have a *military organization* in terms of personnel being strictly isolated from and counterposed to civilian society. Until the turn of the century, only a relatively small number of civil servants and so-called instructor-officers had been employed for the administration and training of the militia army (Jaun 1997, 49). To this day, a unique feature compared to other armed forces remains the fact that there are hardly any professional soldiers as well as no professional officer and NCO corps. With a current effective number of 166,519 troops as of 1 March 2016, the professional component of the armed forces of 3,328 military personnel is less than 2 percent of the overall number (Army Staff 2016). Professional military cadres are primarily engaged in training militia cadres. The command-and-control system of the armed forces eventually resides with the militia officers who for a long time were synonymous with the bourgeois elite (Haltiner 1985; Hollenstein

1979; Jaun 1999, 63; Kriesi 1980). The high civilian reputation of a cadre position in the militia effected a mutual facilitation of military and civilian cadre positions (Haltiner 1987, 138). However, sufficient interest on the part of citizens to accept a cadre position is a prerequisite for the continuation of the Swiss militia system. The Swiss militia system is based on the idea that the civilian society is willing to undertake honorary duties for the benefit of the community. Serving in the military has always been regarded a civil honorary capability which made the army the school of the nation and a symbol of national unity (Haltiner 1986).

The acceptance of a militia officer career was prestigious and offered professional advantages. This was also reflected in numbers: In 1981, the share of officers in the recruitable overall Swiss male population was 7.5 percent (Haltiner 1993, 465). Still in the 1970s, 45 percent of all politicians in the Swiss parliament were officers. Two thirds of all higher civil servants in the Swiss federal administration were also officers. This confirms the high degree of interconnection of political and military leadership positions, which applies to the economy in a similar way. According to a study made in 1987, 53 percent of 485 top managers in the private economy held an officer's rank (Haltiner 1993, 466). John McPhee described this interconnectedness of positions as follows: "More often than not, a high-ranking officer in a Swiss bank will also be a high-ranking officer in the army [...] Chemical companies, insurance companies, construction companies are under the command of majors, colonels, brigadiers." (McPhee 1984, 56–57; translation by the editors).

3   Swiss Military Sociology

This chapter will focus on the development of Swiss military sociology and describe its position in academia and society. Further on, it will take a look at the research methods and funding and outline the current research projects at the Department of Military Sociology at the MILAC.

3.1   The Beginnings of Swiss Military Sociology

In Switzerland, the military was not subject to a sociological scrutiny like in some other European states after World War II, pointing to the established identity between the male population and the militia. With the change in values in society, which has increasingly gotten its grip on Switzerland since the 1970s, it has become apparent that the previously largely homogeneous community had developed into a society of pluralistic lifestyles. The army, previously a model for the citizens (Haltiner 1985) in Swiss society, lost more and more of its special attractive power and positive social standing. As a consequence, active participation in the army has seen a clear downward trend as early as in the late 1970s (Haltiner 1985). The practical benefit and the ideological prestige of the militia officer career have effectively declined since the 1970s (Tanner 1997, 325). In this context, Karl W. Haltiner, paraphrasing Max Weber, speaks of a disenchantment and secularization of the military (Haltiner 1996, 145).

The military was increasingly subject to critical scrutiny and the public's acceptance of the armed forces declined. This was particularly obvious in the 1980s. The peace movement gained momentum also in Switzerland. In 1982, young socialists founded the Group for a Switzerland Without an Army (*Gruppe Schweiz ohne Armee*, GSoA) and launched a popular initiative aiming to abolish the Swiss Armed Forces. The mere idea to abolish the armed forces triggered a major discussion in the Swiss public but astonishingly met with little resonance in the academic sector. The GSoA's main point of criticism regarding the militia system was the concern that its concept of general defense contributed to a militarization of society (Haltiner et al. 2006b, 199). On 26 November 1989, 35.6 percent of the Swiss electorate voted for the initiative to abolish the Swiss Armed Forces, with 68.6 percent of the voters casting their ballot. The fact that the initiative received such strong support was probably also due to the fact that the collapse of the Eastern bloc and the end of the Cold War happened at the same time (Haltiner 1993).

The outlined development made military and political circles increasingly aware of the problem, which resulted in demands for more military sociology research and sociological training of the professional cadre. Since that time, military sociology research has been institutionalized in Switzerland with the establishment of a department of military sociology, then at the former Military Leadership School, which was to become the MILAC at ETH Zurich.

3.2   Position of Military Sociology in the Academic Sector

The lack of military sociology research up into the 1970s is due to the fact that sociology was very late in becoming established as a field of study and research at university level in Switzerland. Up into the early 1970s, sociology as a subject led a shadowy existence at Swiss institutions of higher education; at best it could be studied as a minor subject. Therefore, it was no surprise that there was no significant sociological research in Switzerland. It was only in the course of the movement of 1968, which came late to Switzerland, that sociological problems, such as civil-military relations, were discussed on a broader scale at universities. To be able to better understand the new civil-military relationship, the Institute of Sociology at the University of Bern began to engage in systematic military sociological research for the first time in the mid-1970s. Initial attempts to reflect the changing relationship between society and the armed forces in Switzerland in a sociological context were made in particular by Ruth Meyer Schweizer, who, from 1974 to 1994, worked initially as senior assistant and later as editor and lecturer. In 1994, she was appointed adjunct associate professor. It was basically thanks to her that the Swiss Military and Social Sciences Working Group (*Schweizerischer Arbeitskreis Militär und Sozialwissenschaften*, SAMS), the counterpart of the German Military and Social Sciences Working Group (AMS), was founded in 1976. During this phase, the social position of the military was questioned and analyzed from the viewpoint of changing values (Haltiner and Meyer 1979, 1980; Meyer 1976, 1978).

The SAMS conferences were well attended and its publications found broad interest also among the officer corps and the army leadership. The complex study on internal organizational principles of the military, which was profound in terms of organizational theory and conducted from a functionalist perspective by Zurich sociologist Hans Geser (1981, 1983) was first presented at SAMS and deserves particular mention. In the late 1970s and early 1980s, theoretical and empirical studies on issues of military integration of women (Haltiner and Meyer 1979), on the cadre situation in the militia (Haltiner 1982), on the military socialization of young adults (Steiger 1986) and on the motivation for service (Haltiner and Stadelmann 1990; Leutenegger 1986) were conducted.

In the early 1980s, the Department of Military Sciences at ETH Zurich gave the first teaching assignment in military sociology to Ruth Meyer Schweizer.[2] With the establishment of the Department of Military Sociology under the leadership of Karl W. Haltiner at the newly designed Military Leadership School at ETH Zurich in 1990, military sociology was finally institutionalized in the Swiss educational landscape (Szvircsev Tresch 2010). Since then, military sociology teaching and research in this country have focused basically on the new department and its small research staff. At MILAC, the Department of Military Psychology and Military Pedagogics, also engage in empirical military sociological research to some extent. It strongly focuses on the motivation of soldiers, which is a decisive feature for the selection of prospective militia and career officers. Likewise, the topic of resilience and thus coping with stress is an important field of research. Furthermore, the Department of Leadership and Communication undertakes research in the field of leadership ethics and leadership under extreme conditions; however, it uses classical

---

2 Since Switzerland only has one university at the federal level – the other universities are organized on a cantonal basis – the training of instructors has taken place at ETH Zurich since 1877. The Department of Military Sciences was founded in 1911. Since a broad subject canon ranging from general military history, firing theory, military photography to horse care was offered, the subjects were subsumed under the term military sciences.

quantitative empirical means of research only to a small degree. Instead, it strongly focuses on qualitative research.

With the end of the Cold War, the military sociological view in Switzerland was turned from its initial focus on national issues increasingly to the international environment. Especially questions regarding the forms of military service and the corresponding professionalization of the armed forces were added to the classic topic of the *militia* as focus of research. The new tasks assigned to the armed forces as well as the new multinational peace-keeping missions aroused the interest of sociologists (Szvircsev Tresch 2010). Initially, it was the term *miles protector* by Major General (*Divisionär*) Gustav Däniker which attracted great interest. The focus turned to the changed task area of armed forces. This term often served as food for thought when analyzing the changes in military roles and functions (Däniker 1992, 1995). In this context, the work of Zurich sociologist Hans Geser (1996) needs to be mentioned; he compared the new military tasks, which rather resembled tasks to be assumed by the police, with classic military structures and critically analyzed the consequences for the organizational structures of both types of institutions.

What role did the Swiss Armed Forces play in society after the end of the Cold War? What influence did the GSoA initiative for the abolition of the army have? In order to be able to analyze these questions, the Department of Military Sociology at MILAC in cooperation with the Center for Security Studies (CSS), ETH Zurich, began to conduct representative annual surveys within the framework of the *Security* (*Sicherheit*) study in 1991.[3] It is the objective of these surveys to point out tendencies and long-term trends in the opinion formation of Swiss voters in the fields of foreign, security and defense policy. This institutional cooperation with the CSS, ETH Zurich, is the only long-term cooperation of the Department of Military Sociology among the Swiss university landscape. To this day, Swiss military sociology is hardly integrated into sociology at Swiss universities. In addition to the professorship of Ruth Meyer Schweizer in Bern from 1994 to 2001 and the titular professorship of Karl W. Haltiner at the Department of Humanities, Social and Political Sciences (D-GESS) at ETH Zurich from 2001 to 2011, there were and are no other chairs for military sociology with the authorization to accept doctoral theses. Currently, there is only one appointment to teach at ETH Zurich, offering a bachelor course in Public Policy for future career officers in cooperation with MILAC. To allow assistants at MILAC to submit academic qualification papers, it is necessary to ask external professors to accept doctoral theses. Informal

---

3   In this context, see the website of the Center for Security Studies for details: <www.css.ethz.
      ch/publikationen/studie-sicherheit.html>. Since 1999, the studies have been published in
      the same layout.

cooperation with professors at sociological institutes as Swiss universities developed gradually as a result. In recent years, a number of dissertation projects were successfully completed primarily at Zurich University but also at Basel University (Bennett 2005; Szvircsev Tresch 2005; Würmli 2015).

However, at university level, the teaching of military sociology still leads a marginal existence. The permanent university teaching position at ETH Zurich primarily addresses career officers attending MILAC. Since D-GESS removed military science lectures of MILAC (military history, military psychology/pedagogy, military economy, military sociology, strategic studies, leadership, and communication) from the catalogue of required elective courses in 2015, it has no longer been interesting for ETH students to attend those lectures because they cannot earn ECTS credit points for their course of studies. But since 2020, strategic studies and military sociology are again in the catalogue of required elective courses and therefore students are now again able earning ECTS credit points in military sociology. Although the academic integration and embedding into the Swiss sociology landscape must be considered as low, the Department of Military Sociology at MILAC at ETH has intensively participated in the international academic exchange for decades.

3.3   International Academic Networks

The Department of Military Sociology at MILAC at ETH Zurich has participated, intensively, in the work of the European Research Group on Military and Society (ERGOMAS; see the article by Steinbrecher, Biehl, and Elbe in this volume) since the 1990s. In the 1990s, a number of works were produced within the scope of the Military Profession working group. The focus was on a comparative Europe-wide study on the motivation of career soldiers to work and their satisfaction with work that was conducted between 1991 and 1993 (Caforio 1994). When the topic was resumed in 2007, it resulted in another important publication of this working group (WG) with strong participation of the Department of Military Sociology (Caforio 2007). After the end of the Cold War, the issue of a democratic control of armed forces was paid heightened attention, not only in post-Communist states. The topic was also widely discussed in Europe and the United States (Haltiner 2002). Switzerland played an important role in this context, which was reflected in the establishment of the Centre for the Democratic Control of Armed Forces (DCAF) in Geneva. Since the foundation of the ERGOMAS WG Civilian Control of the Armed Forces in 1998, the Department of Military Sociology has been intensely concerned with aspects of armed forces supervision and has made significant contributions to the publication of a collective volume analyzing civil-military relations from an international comparative perspective (Haltiner and Szvircsev Tresch 2006b; Szvircsev Tresch et al. 2005). This publication was the result of close cooperation with the DCAF.

Since 1999, Swiss contributions within the scope of the *Security* study – series were focused on the "Public Opinion, Mass Media and the Military" Working Group (Ferst et al. 2017; Würmli and Szvircsev Tresch 2011). Since 2016, the research results of the *Social Media and Swiss Armed Forces* project have also been presented in this working group.

As a consequence of the difficulties encountered in the recruitment of career personnel in the Swiss Armed Forces and in Europe, the current representative of the Department, Tibor Szvircsev Tresch, initiated the re-establishment of the Recruitment and Retention Working Group in 2008, of which he is the chairman. A large number of collective volumes and publications are proof of intensive research activities in this working group (Szvircsev Tresch and Leuprecht 2010, Szvircsev Tresch and Moehlecke de Baseggio 2017a, 2017b). In addition, since 2010 the present Head of the Department has been a board member and, since 2014, Vice President of the Research Committee 01 Armed Forces and Conflict Resolution of the International Sociological Association (ISA-RC01). Since April 2013, he has also been a member of the international advisory board for the Center for Military History and Social Sciences of the Bundeswehr (ZMSBw).

In summary, it can be said that the Department of Military Sociology is the only institutionalized research and teaching institute for military sociology in Switzerland. However, it is only rudimentarily integrated into sociological research activities at Swiss universities. Contrarily, the institutional international cooperation is well developed, resulting in extensive publication activities.

3.4   Institutional Integration, Publication Practice and Access to the Research Field of Military Sociology

The Department of Military Sociology is one of six military science departments at MILAC at ETH Zurich. Although the name of the Swiss Federal Institute of Technology (ETH) is used, as far as administrative matters are concerned, MILAC is part of the Federal Department of Defense, Civil Protection and Sports (DDPS), i.e., a federal institution. It is subordinate to the Higher Cadre Training of the Army (HKA) and part of the Training and Education Command of the Swiss Armed Forces. Lecturers also teach as visiting lecturers in the Bachelor program of Public Policy at ETH Zurich.

By being an integral part of the Swiss Armed Forces, MILAC has the advantage of having full access to the research field *army*. As a result, there are hardly any restrictions as far as research is concerned. It was, therefore, possible to conduct interviews with the armed forces leadership, to undertake empirical surveys on various military-related topics among newly drafted recruits or militia soldiers during exercises for reserves, and to conduct polls among the Swiss contingent in Kosovo (SWISSCOY). The insights gained are presented at international conferences and on military-internal occasions and published in national military journals like the *Allgemeine Schweizerische Militärzeitschrift* (ASMZ) or in international journals or edited volumes. There are no actual restrictions for the publications. Freedom of research and teaching is guaranteed and documented in internal directives. Articles to be published in a Swiss journal are submitted to the Commander of MILAC and the relevant entities for information in advance. The topics for the main research project of the Department for Military Sociology, the *Security* series of studies, are determined by the department. Demands of the Department of Defense are taken into account, if possible. One example is a module in the *Security 2018* study on the opinion of the Swiss population on an obligatory information day for women whose results were analyzed and presented in a departmental report (Szvircsev Tresch et al. 2018).

The *Security* series of studies is held in high esteem among members of the armed forces. Prior to the annual publication of the study in a book in late June, the results have been presented to the Head of the DDPS (Minister of Defense) in briefings since 2009. The Chief of the Armed Forces, the army leadership and the generals are informed of the most important findings before the volume is published or they are informed by the Lecturer for Military Sociology in person. Other research projects, such as Social Media and the Swiss Armed Forces, the integration function of the armed forces for members who have a migration background, interviews with personnel managers regarding the significance of a militia-military career, and the like, are often presented in the seminar for senior staff officers, in the army leadership seminar and in military reports.

In recent years, military science at MILAC has become more important in general. The new staff category of project employees was established. In addition to these researchers, who specialize in research on an individual project, the department includes two assistantships. Although the personnel strength of the department depends on the number of current research projects, on a long-term average it has comprised about 5 researcher positions.

3.5 Research Funding

Research funding has to be considered a critical issue. As a federal institution MILAC is not allowed to raise external funds. In the event that MILAC would raise such funds, the funds would have to be administered by the federal cash office and could not be claimed for the approved research projects. For this reason, all research projects are funded by the Department of Defense. The subject matters of the projects are discussed among the team of the Department of Military Sociology. They are closely related to international research and usually fit into current development trends in the field of military sociology. Project outlines need to be presented to the commander of MILAC and afterwards to the commander of HKA. Subsequently, the commander of HKA decides whether the project will be approved or not. As far as their employment situation is concerned, the staff of the department belongs to the Department of Defense. This twofold dependence involves the danger that inconvenient research projects could be rejected or that superior authorities could order projects and thus restrict the freedom of research. Personal preferences of superior authorities, their understanding of science or their wish for practical relevance could be considered intervening variables which may influence the funding of research. But so far, hardly any submitted projects have been rejected.

Nevertheless, this system is obviously based on the goodwill of superior authorities. As long as military sociology research is considered important and the results are discussed in a critical fashion within the armed forces organization, there is no danger that research activities are encroached upon or that research projects can no longer be carried out. The army leadership, the Chief of the Armed Forces and the leadership of the Department continue to be interested in military research. Nevertheless, the funding of research projects at MILAC is dependent on the defense budget. Should the budget be sustainably reduced in the future, it would be doubtful whether all intended research projects could be implemented.

3.6   Preferred Methods of Swiss Military Sociology

To adequately comprehend the above-mentioned research topics in an academic context, military sociology at MILAC considers theoretical perspectives of organizational sociology as well as assumptions from theories examining the change in values.

Analytically, it differentiates between the macro level where questions regarding society as a whole are discussed, the meso level which studies the actual military organization and the micro level which focuses on each individual (Szvircsev Tresch 2010). At the macro level, the department studies the effects of the technological, geostrategic, and social changes for the military (Szvircsev Tresch 2005). At meso level, it is explored whether it is acceptable to regard the military as an institution like any other or if it is a special case as far as organizations are concerned. Special attention is given to the changed civil-military relations and the question is raised whether the bases of common values differ between members of the armed forces and the civilian society to an extent that would endanger the democratic state (Szvircsev Tresch 2010). Furthermore, the department analyses the peculiarities of the Swiss militia model and the significance of a militia-military career in civilian society. This topic is further explored at the micro level.

The Department of Military Sociology first and foremost uses the classical quantitative survey method with paper-and pencil interviews (PAPI). Those are primarily conducted at recruit schools. An example is the project *Integrationsfunktion der Schweizer Armee für AdA mit Migrationshintergrund* (Integration function of the Swiss Armed Forces for members of the Swiss Armed Forces who have a migration background) where 14,503 recruits were interviewed and a total of 32,593 questionnaires were completed (Sokoli et al. 2014; Szvircsev Tresch and Sokoli 2013). This type of quantitative social science research is also used in military exercises for reserves. Recently, on-line surveys have been conducted as well, especially in the Social Media and the Swiss Armed Forces project. The *Security* series of studies is particularly relevant for quantitative research. 1,200 eligible Swiss citizens from the three parts of the country, i.e., German-speaking Switzerland, Romandie, and Ticino, are interviewed through computer assisted telephone interviews (CATI) each January. In addition to these classical quantitative survey methods, all projects since 2008 also use qualitative guideline-based interviews allowing us to generally refer to a mix of methods (Hagmann and Szvircsev Tresch 2013; Szvircsev Tresch and Merkulova 2012).

3.7   Key Topics of Empirical Military Sociological Research

Considering the above-mentioned reasons, it becomes obvious that the issue of Switzerland's social and military militia capability has been a focus of military sociological research of the Department of Military Sociology for years. This topic is closely connected with the recruitment and retention of personnel. In this context, the focus is on the recruiting of militia and professional personnel (Szvircsev Tresch 2008, 2011, 2018; Szvircsev Tresch and Bill 2011; Szvircsev Tresch and Leuprecht 2010). The question of the next generation of militia cadres, in particular, is not only an intra-military issue, but it also has an eminent effect on society and defense policy. It is the pivotal question for the survival of the militia armed forces, as it will be impossible to maintain the Swiss military system without a capable militia cadre (Haltiner and Szvircsev Tresch 2005, 2006a).

Surveys in this respect are conducted in order to assess the motivation of soldiers, officers, and NCOs to pursue a career in the armed forces (Annen et al. 2015;

Geissler 2000; Hedlund and Szvircsev Tresch 2014, 2017; Szvircsev Tresch et al. 2014a; Szvircsev Tresch and Merkulova 2012). Beginning in the early 1990s, periodical surveys have been conducted among a sample of HR managers of civilian enterprises as topic of bachelor or diploma theses in order to assess the value of a militia career in the Swiss economy (Bertossa et al. 1994; Brandalise 2018; Frunz 1991; Haltiner 1997; Kern 2006; Strässle et al. 2002; Szvircsev Tresch et al. 2013). With the help of a large number of studies, it can be established that the civilian prestige of a military career continues to be sound, it has, however, declined over the past three decades.

The *Security* series of studies mentioned above is another important research project, which has been going on since the early 1990s.[4] Since the security political constants that had been valid for Switzerland for centuries had lost their significance with the end of the Cold War, it was the intention of the Department of Military Sociology at MILAC to conduct repeated surveys in cooperation with the Research Unit for Security Policy and Conflict Analysis, today CSS, ETH Zurich, with the objective of understanding how the population assesses the new global political situation. In addition to repetitive core questions, the survey addresses additional topics regarding the current situation (Ferst 2017, 2018; Ferst and Szvircsev Tresch 2017, 2018; Giovanoli et al. 2018; Szvircsev Tresch and Ferst 2016; Szvircsev Tresch et al. 2017). Since 1999, the *Security* series of studies has been supplemented with a *Chronologie potenziell meinungsbildender Ereignisse* (Chronology of potentially opinion-forming events) of the previous year. It is published as an annual volume in a uniform layout.

The analysis of the changes in the force structure of European states is the third important research project. Drawing on a number of time series indicators and a self-developed typology of forms of military service, Karl W. Haltiner was able to show for the first time at the ERGOMAS Conference held at ETH Zurich in 1996 that the change from conscript armies to professional all-volunteer forces was accelerated and encouraged by several aspects: the geopolitical changes since the end of the Cold War, the increasing tendency towards integration of security alliances, and the need for readily available troops for peacekeeping (Haltiner 1998). A dissertation written at MILAC on this topic analyzed these trends in greater detail on the basis of a large survey of security policy experts (Szvircsev Tresch 2005). Further studies on this topic were presented to an international expert audience (Haltiner and Szvircsev Tresch 2009; Szvircsev Tresch and Haltiner 2008).

---

4   In this context, see the website of the Center for Security Studies for details: <www.css.ethz.ch/publikationen/studie-sicherheit.html>.

In addition to the above-mentioned topics, other current research projects of the Department deal with issues concerning traditions in the Swiss Armed Forces (Schwarz and Szvircsev Tresch 2010; Szvircsev Tresch et al. 2012), the integration function of the Swiss Armed Forces for members of the armed forces who have a migration background (Sokoli et al. 2014; Szvircsev Tresch 2015; Szvircsev Tresch et al. 2014b), diversity management (Rinaldo 2018) as well as concerning social media and the Swiss Armed Forces (Schneider et al. 2017).

3.8   Research on Operations Abroad

As mentioned in the introduction, research on foreign operations of the Swiss Armed Forces is of secondary importance for Swiss military sociology. This is due to the fact that Switzerland has only maintained one major contingent abroad (SWISSCOY) within the scope of KFOR since 1999. The few members of the armed forces who serve in other peace-keeping missions are primarily specialists and have not become a topic of research so far. The fact that Switzerland has joined international peace-keeping missions, apart from the traditional Korea mission where five Swiss officers have been supervising the Korean Armistice Agreement together with their Swedish colleagues since 1953, is the result of the country's accession to the Partnership for Peace of the North Atlantic Treaty Organization (NATO) in 1994 and the foundation of three international security policy institutes in Geneva (Geneva Centre for Security Policy [GCSP], DCAF, Geneva International Centre for Humanitarian Demining [GICHD]). The approval of the Swiss electorate for the armament of troops for the United Nations Organization in May 2001 and the accession of Switzerland to the United Nations in March 2002 were other important prerequisites for a stronger international military involvement of Switzerland. In 2001, a survey studied satisfaction of personnel deployed with the fifth SWISSCOY contingent (Bennett et al. 2003, 2005). It turned out that the attractiveness of an individual's official duty was the most important factor for the motivation to serve abroad. Furthermore, the equipment, the infrastructure and the assessment of the training received and provided are most important on operations abroad. This research was supplemented by a study among members of the Swiss Armed Forces regarding their motivation to apply for an operation abroad. The study was based on a survey of 1,644 active service members in a militia, career, and temporary-career status. A total of 13 percent indicated that they would consider taking part in an operation abroad under certain circumstances. It turned out that military personnel who completed their service en bloc and career personnel were more interested than average members of the militia. Furthermore, it was established that the agreement of the partner and the employer are significant determinants for the interest in an operation abroad (CSS 2006).

3.9 The Public's Reception of Findings of Empirical Military Sociology

The work of the Department of Military Sociology is widely perceived in the security policy debate and by the interested public in Switzerland. There are two reasons for this. First, the *Security* series of studies is an empirical work which is presented to the interested public and the media at a press conference in late June each year. The results of *Security* series of studies often make the front page of the press. Moreover, irrespective of the time the annual studies are issued, there are often references to the results of the surveys when a current politico-military topic is discussed in the media. The success of the *Security* series of studies is partly due to the fact that it is conducted in cooperation with the CSS, ETH Zurich. As a result, the series of studies is highly esteemed academically as the Swiss population places great trust in the ETH. Thanks to the close connection with ETH Zurich, the public regards the members of the Department not primarily as employees of the Ministry of Defense but rather as a hybrid of ETH Zurich and the Swiss Armed Forces.

The results of the *Security* series of studies as well as the expertise of the Department of Military Sociology are also taken into account when political decisions are made. An example for this is the *Wehrpflicht*-Initiative (compulsory military service initiative) of GSoA of 23 September 2013. The current head of the Department of Military Sociology spoke at many panel discussions, gave presentations and interviews.

The second reason that the Department of Military Sociology is held in high regard in the general public can be attributed to the fact that it is a unique feature in the Swiss university landscape, as described above. It has a monopoly position which is increased by its direct access to the research field of military. Because of this situation, the public as well as the media as information provider have to rely almost exclusively on the research done by MILAC whenever politicians or Swiss society require explanations in the field of military sociology. Furthermore, there are many military-friendly organizations (officer societies, security, and defense policy associations etc.) in Switzerland, which – often in advance of a referendum – satisfy the public's need for information and provide documents for information or organize events. The Lecturer of Military Sociology is often invited as speaker.

In contrast to the broad reception of military sociology findings in the interested general public, research results receive little attention in the academic debate of Swiss social science. If they obtain any academic attention, it is primarily from Institutes of Sociology at Swiss universities (Kaufmann-Brunner 2012). The reasons for this are a matter of speculation; however, it is safe to assume that social change and a continued aversion to anything military generally plays a role.

4   Conclusion

Military sociological research in Switzerland focuses on the militia capability of the Swiss Armed Forces. The main emphasis is on the recruitment of militia cadres and the related recruitment of professional cadres. In the context of compulsory military service, questions regarding the integration of members of the armed forces and the acceptance of the military system among the population become the focus of studies and security interests. Swiss military sociology first and foremost uses empirical quantitative research methods. Due to the institutional monopoly position of the Department of Military Sociology, military sociology research takes places primarily at MILAC at ETH Zurich. Although, every once in a while, bachelor and master theses on topics of military sociology are also written at other universities, there is no actual military sociological research tradition at other Swiss universities. For this reason, military sociology has few roots in Swiss academic life. Its points of contact are situated at the international level, primarily in the ERGOMAS and ISA-RC01 organizations. As it is part of the Swiss Armed Forces in administrative terms, the Department of Military Sociology at MILAC ETH Zurich has almost unlimited access to the research field of the military. There is a major dependence in terms of research funding, which may put the freedom of research and teaching in jeopardy. Funds are provided almost exclusively by the Swiss Armed Forces. Federal enterprises in Switzerland are not permitted to engage in fundraising campaigns or third-party funding. The findings of military sociological research are often met with great interest among the Swiss general public. Especially the results of the annual *Security* series of studies generate a wide and strong response on a regular basis.

References

Annen, H., P. Goldammer, and T. Szvircsev Tresch. 2015. "Longitudinal Effects of OCB on Cadre Selection and Pursuing a Career as Militia Cadre in the Swiss Armed Forces." *Military Psychology* 27(1): 9–21.

Bennett, J. 2005. *Fitting Security into the Swiss Value Landscape*. Bern: Peter Lang.

Bennett, J., R. Boesch, and K.W. Haltiner. 2003. "Swisscoy – Motivation und Einsatzzufriedenheit." *Allgemeine Schweizerische Militärzeitschrift* 169(3): 20–22.

Bennett, J., R. Boesch, and K.W. Haltiner. 2005. "Motivation and Job Satisfaction in the Swiss Support Company in Kosovo." *International Peacekeeping* 12(4): 562–575.

Bertossa, L., D. Binzegger, and S. Bühler. 1994. "Das Gewicht der militärischen Ausbildung und Karriere." *Schweizerische Arbeitgeberzeitung* 89(3): 65–69.

Brandalise, P. 2018. "Stellenwert der Milizoffiziersausbildung und -karriere sowie zweier Teilaspekte der WEA bei Personalverantwortlichen von Schweizer Grossunternehmen." Bachelorarbeit, ETH Zürich.

Caforio, G. 1994. "The Military Profession in Europe." *Current Sociology* 42(3).

Caforio, G., ed. 2007. "Cultural Differences Between the Military and Parent Society in Democratic Countries." *Contributions to Conflict Management, Peace Economics and Development* Vol. 4. Amsterdam: Elsevier.

CSS (Center for Security Studies). 2006. Rekrutierungspotenzial für friedensunterstützende Operationen. Internationale Trends, Motivationsstruktur in der Schweiz. Ressortforschung zuhanden des Zentrums für internationale Sicherheitspolitik ZISP/EDA und des Bereichs IB V/Stab CdA/VBS Bern. Zürich: ETH Zürich.

Däniker, G. 1992. Wende Golfkrieg: Vom Wesen und Gebrauch künftiger Streitkräfte. Frauenfeld: Huber.

Däniker, G. 1995. "The Guardian Soldier: On the Nature and Use of Future Armed Forces." *United Nations Institute for Disarmament Research (UNIDIR) Research Papers* 36. New York: United Nations.

Ferst, T. 2017. "Sichere Schweiz versus unsichere Welt und angepasstes Reiseverhalten." *Kriminalistik* (8–9): 557–558.

Ferst, T. 2018. Auch in Zeiten terroristischer Bedrohung ist die Schweiz eine offene Gesellschaft, in der man sich sehr sicher fühlt und der Polizei vertraut." *Kriminalistik* (7): 473–477.

Ferst, T., S. De Rosa, and T. Szvircsev Tresch. 2017. "Does Terrorism have an Impact on Travel Behavior?" Paper presented at the ERGOMAS Conference, Athens, 26–30 June 2017.

Ferst, T., and T. Szvircsev Tresch. 2017. "The Swiss Public Opinion Towards the Tasks of the Swiss Armed Forces and the Constitutional Role of the Swiss Armed Forces." *Sociology Study* 7(2): 65–76.

Ferst, T., and T. Szvircsev Tresch. 2018. "Wie die Schweizer Bevölkerung den Terrorismus wahrnimmt." *SKP INFO* 2: 3–7.

Foot, M. 1961. *Men in Uniform: Military Manpower in Modern Industrial Societies.* London: Weidenfeld & Nicolson.

Frunz, U. 1991. "Die Wertschätzung der Offizierskarriere durch zivile Unternehmen." Unpublished Manuscript, Abteilung für Militärwissenschaften, ETH Zürich.

Fuhrer, H.-R. 1999. "Wehrpflicht in der Schweiz – Ein historischer Überblick." In *Wehrpflicht und Miliz – Ende einer Epoche?* edited by K.W. Haltiner and A. Kühner, 67–78. Baden-Baden: Nomos.

Führungsstab der Armee 2016. "Die Armee in Zahlen." <www.vtg.admin.ch/de/aktuell/themen/wirtschaft-und-armee/rueckblick_2016/die-armee-in-zahlen.html> (last access: 13 December 2018).

Geissler, B.M. 2000. "Motiviert, Herr Offizier?" *Allgemeine Schweizerische Militärzeitschrift* 166(7/8): 36–37.

Geser, H. 1981. "Soziologische Aspekte der Organisationsformen in der Armee und in der Wirtschaft." *SAMS-Informationen* 5(2): 88–109.

Geser, H. 1983. "Organisationsprobleme des Militärs." In *Militär, Krieg, Gesellschaft – Texte zur Militärsoziologie* edited by G. Wachtler, 139–164. Frankfurt a.M.: Campus.

Geser, H. 1996. "Internationale Polizeiaktionen: ein neues evolutionäres Entwicklungsstadium militärischer Organisationen?" In *Friedensengel im Kampfanzug? Zur Theorie und Praxis militärischer UN-Einsätze,* edited by G.M. Meyer, 45–74. Opladen: Westdeutscher Verlag.

Giovanoli, M., T. Ferst, and T. Szvircsev Tresch. 2018. "Sicherheit vor Freiheit bei der Terrorbekämpfung." *Allgemeine Schweizerische Militärzeitschrift* 184(6): 30–31.

Hagmann, J., and T. Szvircsev Tresch. 2013. "Der Staat weiss es am besten? Die Schweizer Sicherheitspolitik als verwaltungszentriertes Politikfeld." *Zeitschrift für Außen- und Sicherheitspolitik* 6(2): 199–223.

Haltiner, K.W. 1982. "Voluntary Military Career in a Time of Changing Values. The Case of Switzerland." In: *Public Opinion on Security Policy and Armed Forces – Analyses and Data from Eight Countries,* edited by R. Zoll, 109–128. Forum International, No. 1. München: Sozialwissenschaftliches Institut der Bundeswehr.

Haltiner, K.W. 1985. *Milizarmee – Bürgerleitbild oder angeschlagenes Ideal? Eine soziologische Untersuchung über die Auswirkungen des Wertwandels auf das Verhältnis Gesellschaft – Armee in der Schweiz.* Frauenfeld: Huber.

Haltiner, K.W. 1986. "Struktur, Tradition und Integration der schweizerischen Miliz." *Sicherheit und Frieden* 4(3): 126–133.

Haltiner, K.W. 1987. "Integration der schweizerischen Miliz in die Gesellschaft." In: *Miliz als Vorbild?* edited by D. Bald, 135–146. Baden-Baden: Nomos.

Haltiner, K.W. 1993. "Der Schweizer Offizier." In *Soldat – ein Berufsbild im Wandel,* edited by P. Klein, 455–467. Bd. 2. Bonn: DBW-Verlag.

Haltiner, K.W. 1996. "Das Militär im Wandel der Wertvorstellungen." In *Schweizer Armee – heute und in Zukunft,* edited by L.F. Carrel, 435–447. Thun: Ott.

Haltiner, K.W. 1997. "Privatwirtschaft und Milizkarriere." *Beilage zur Allgemeinen Schweizerischen Militärzeitschrift* Suppl. 10: 1–3.

Haltiner, K.W. 1998. "The Definite End of the Mass Army in Western Europe?" *Armed Forces & Society* 25(1): 7–36.

Haltiner, K.W. 2000. "Military Sociology in Switzerland." In *Military Sociology. The Richness of a Discipline,* edited by G. Kümmel and A.D. Prüfert, 140–148. Baden-Baden: Nomos.

Haltiner, K.W. 2002. "Wer wacht über die Wächter." In *Wer wacht über die Wächter. Demokratische Kontrolle der Armee in der Schweiz. (MFS-Tagung 2002) Beilage zur Allgemeinen Schweizerischen Militärzeitschrift* Suppl. 6.

Haltiner, K.W. 2003. "Die Militärsoziologie als Spiegel gesellschaftlicher und internationaler Umbrüche." Unpublished working paper at Militärakademie an der ETH Zürich.

Haltiner, K.W., and R. Meyer. 1979. "Aspects of the Relationship between the Military and Society in Switzerland." *Armed Forces & Society* 6(1): 49–81.

Haltiner, K.W., and R. Meyer. 1980. "The Woman and the Army in Switzerland. A General Survey." *Arbeitsberichte aus dem Institut für Soziologie der Universität Bern,* No. 4. Bern: Institut für Soziologie der Universität Bern.

Haltiner, K.W., and J. Stadelmann. 1990. *Motivationsrunde RS 90. Militärische Führungsschule ETH Zürich,* Psychologisches Institut, Universität Zürich.

Haltiner, K.W., and T. Szvircsev Tresch. 2005. "Bürgerheer wohin? Alternative Wehrformen in der aktuellen politischen Diskussion." In *Bulletin 2005 zur schweizerischen Sicherheitspolitik,* edited by A. Wenger, 23–44. Zürich: Center for Security Studies, ETH Zürich.

Haltiner, K. W., and T. Szvircsev Tresch. 2006a. "Bürgerheer wohin? Die parteipolitische Wehrformdiskussion in der Schweiz." *Österreichische Militärische Zeitschrift* 44(6): 734–737.

Haltiner, K.W., and T. Szvircsev Tresch. 2006b. "Democratic Control of the Swiss Militia in Times of War and Peace: Ideal and Reality." In *Civil-Military Relations in Europe. Learning from Crisis and Institutional Change,* edited by H. Born, M. Caparini, K.W. Haltiner, and J. Kuhlmann, 191–201. London: Routlegde.

Haltiner, K.W., and T. Szvircsev Tresch. 2009. "From Conscription-Based Defense to Volunteer-Based Constabulary Forces: European Defense Integration and Mission Change as Driving Factors for the End of Conscription in Europe." In *The Transformation of the World of War and Peace Support Operations,* edited by K. Michael, D. Kellen, and E. Ben-Ari, 39–52. Westport, CT: Praeger Security International.

Hedlund, E., and T. Szvircsev Tresch, eds. 2017. *Motivation to be a Soldier. A Comparison of Eight Nations.* Stockholm: Swedish Defence University.

Hollenstein, H. 1979. *Spitzenmanager in Schweizer Unternehmen.* Lizentiatsarbeit, Universität Bern.

Jaun, R. 1998. "Armee, Nation, Staat und Krieg im Widerstreit der Militärdiskurse des 19. Jahrhunderts." In *Etappen des Bundesstaates. Staats- und Nationsbildung in der Schweiz 1848–1998,* edited by B. Studer, 109–125. Zürich: Chronos Verlag.

Jaun, R. 1997. "Vom Bürger-Militär zum Soldaten-Militär: Die Schweiz im 19. Jahrhundert." In *Militär und Gesellschaft im 19. und 20. Jahrhundert,* edited by U. Frevert, 48–77. Stuttgart: Klett-Cotta.

Jaun, R. 1999. *Preußen vor Augen. Das schweizerische Offizierskorps im militärischen und gesellschaftlichen Wandel des Fin de siècle.* Zürich: Chronos.

Kaufmann-Brunner, A. 2012. *"Personen mit Migrationshintergrund in der Rekrutenschule der Schweizer Armee."* Master-Arbeit. Institut für Sozialanthropologie, Universität Bern.

Kern, N. 2006. "Die Bedeutung der militärischen Ausbildung und Karriere bei Stellenbesetzungen für zivile Unternehmen und Verwaltungen. Personalverantwortlichen – Befragung in der Deutschschweiz." Bachelorarbeit am Studiengang Berufsoffizier des Departement Geistes-, Sozial- und Staatswissenschaften der ETH Zürich.

Kriesi, H.P. 1980. *Entscheidungsstrukturen und Entscheidungsprozesse in der Schweizer Politik.* Frankfurt a.M.: Springer.

Leutenegger, E. 1986. "Jugend und Armee. Die Entwicklung der Einstellungen zur Armee während der Rekrutenschule." Dissertation, Bamberg: St. Galler.

McPhee, J. 1984. *La place de la Concorde Suisse.* New York: Farrar, Straus, Giroux.

Meyer, R. 1976. *Befragung über Werte und Wertordnungen in der Schweizer Bevölkerung. Unveröffentlichte Randauszählung.* Bern: Soziologisches Institut der Universität Bern.

Meyer, R. 1978. "Die Einstellung der Bevölkerung zur Milizarmee." *SAMS-Informationen* 2(1).

Rinaldo, A. 2018. "Diversity Management: Herausforderung und Chance." *Allgemeine Schweizerische Militärzeitschrift* 11: 36–37.

Schneider, O., E. Moehlecke de Baseggio and T. Szvircsev Tresch. 2017. "Social Media als Chance für die Kommunikation Verteidigung (Komm V)." *Allgemeine Schweizerische Militärzeitschrift* 11: 32–33.

Schwarz, N., and T. Szvircsev Tresch. 2010. "Militärische Traditionen – Unsinn oder sinnvoll?" *Allgemeine Schweizerische Militärzeitschrift* 176(10): 30–31.

Sokoli, E., C. Nakkas, and T. Szvircsev Tresch. 2014. "Ansehen der Armee und des Militärdienstes." *Allgemeine Schweizerische Militärzeitschrift* 180(11): 44–45.

Steiger, R. 1986. *Werden junge Menschen im Militär überfordert?* Frauenfeld: Huber.

Strässle, T., M. Kessler, and E. Hagen. 2002. *Die Bedeutung der schweizerischen Milizkarriere für zivile Unternehmungen und Verwaltungen. Eine Befragung von Personalverantwortlichen der deutschen Schweiz. Forschungsarbeit am Psychologischen Institut, Universität Zürich.*

Szvircsev Tresch, T. 2005. "Europas Streitkräfte im Wandel: Von der Wehrpflichtarmee zur Freiwilligenstreitkraft. Eine empirische Untersuchung europäischer Streitkräfte 1975 bis 2003." Doctoral dissertation, Zürich.

Szvircsev Tresch, T. 2008. "Personalknappheit beim schweizerischen Berufsmilitär: Rekrutierungsstrategien europäischer Staaten." In *Bulletin 2008 zur schweizerischen Sicherheitspolitik*, edited by A. Wenger, V. Mauer, and D. Trachsler, 59–87. Zürich: Center for Security Studies, ETH Zürich.

Szvircsev Tresch, T. 2010. "Forschung und Lehre an der Dozentur Militärsoziologie der MILAK/ETHZ." *Allgemeine Schweizerische Militärzeitschrift* 176(8): 26–27.

Szvircsev Tresch, T. 2011. "The Transformation of Switzerland's Militia Armed Forces and the Role of the Citizen in Uniform." *Armed Forces & Society* 37(2): 239–260.

Szvircsev Tresch, T. 2015. "The Integration of Cultural Minorities into the Swiss Armed Forces." Presentation at the 13th ERGOMAS conference, Ra'anana, Israel, 8–12 June 2015.

Szvircsev Tresch, T. (Guest Editor) 2018. "Recruitment and Retention as a Challenge of Contemporary Armed Forces and Societies." *Contemporary Military Challenges. Journal of General Staff of the Slovenian Armed Forces*, June.

Szvircsev Tresch, T., D. Allenspach, M. Born, and K.W. Haltiner. 2005. "Is There a Cultural Gap Between the Military and the Parent Society? An Analysis of Switzerland." In *Military Missions and Their Implications Reconsidered: The Aftermath of September 11th. Contributions to Conflict Management, Peace Economics and Development*, Vol. 2, edited by G. Caforio and G. Kümmel, 265–295. Amsterdam: Elsevier.

Szvircsev Tresch, T., and C. Bill. 2011. "Motivating Factors of Swiss Military Cadets to Become Professional Officers." *Journal of US-China Public Administration* 8(5): 519–531.

Szvircsev Tresch, T., J. Craviolini, N. Merkulova, and S. Würmli. 2014a. "Basic Military Training in Switzerland." In *Satisfaction in Basic Military Training. An International Comparison*, edited by E. Hedlund and T. Szvircsev Tresch, 117–132. Stockholm: The Swedish National Defence College.

Szvircsev Tresch, T., and T. Ferst. 2016. "Umfrage massiv pro Armee und noch massiver pro Neutralität." *Schweizer Soldat* 7/8: 8–9.

Szvircsev Tresch, T., T. Ferst, and S. De Rosa. 2017. "Studie *Sicherheit 2017* – Terrorismus und Auswirkung auf das Reiseverhalten." *Allgemeine Schweizerische Militärzeitschrift* 183(6): 36–37.

Szvircsev Tresch, T., T. Gabathuler, and P. Schenk. 2013. *Die Bedeutung der militärischen Ausbildung bei Stellenbesetzungen für privatwirtschaftliche Unternehmen und öffentliche Verwaltungen. Unveröffentlichter Forschungsbericht*. Dozentur Militärsoziologie, Militärakademie an der ETH Zürich: Birmensdorf.

Szvircsev Tresch, T., and K.W. Haltiner. 2008. "New Trends in Civil-Military Relations: The Decline of Conscription in Europe." In *The Heritage and the Present. From Invasion Defence to Mission Oriented Organization*, edited by A. Weibull and B. Abrahamsson, 169–188. Karlstad: Digitaltryck.

Szvircsev Tresch, T., and C. Leuprecht, eds. 2010. *Europe without Soldiers? Recruitment and Retention across the Armed Forces of Europe*. Kingston: McGill-Queen's University Press.

Szvircsev Tresch, T., and N. Merkulova. 2012. *Vorzeitiges Ausscheiden aus dem Berufskader der Schweizer Armee. Eine quantitative Untersuchung. Forschungsbericht, Dezember 2012*. Birmensdorf: Dozentur Militärsoziologie, Militärakademie an der ETH Zürich.

Szvircsev Tresch, T., and E. Moehlecke de Baseggio, eds. 2017a. "Recruitment & Retention, Part 1." *Res Militaris* Ergomas Issue 4.

Szvircsev Tresch, T., and E. Moehlecke de Baseggio, eds. 2017b. "Recruitment & Retention, Part 2." *Res Militaris* Ergomas Issue 5.

Szvircsev Tresch, T., N. Schwarz, and M. Williner. 2012. "Living Traditions in the Swiss Armed Forces." In *New Wars, New Militaries, New Soldiers: Conflicts, the Armed Forces and the Soldierly Subject Contributions to Conflict Management, Peace Economics and Development*, Vol. 19, edited by G. Kümmel and J. Soeters, 143–166. Bingley: Emerald.

Szvircsev Tresch, T., and E. Sokoli. 2013. "Schweizer Rekruten mit Migrationshintergrund: motiviert und leistungsbereit." *Allgemeine Schweizerische Militärzeitschrift* 179(12): 40–41.

Szvircsev Tresch, T., E. Sokoli, and C. Nakkas. 2014b. "Integration of Cultural Minorities into the Swiss Armed Forces. Differences between Soldiers with and without Immigrant Background Regarding Selected Questions." Paper presented at the XVIII ISA World Congress of Sociology, Yokohama, Japan, 14–18 July 2014.

Szvircsev Tresch, T., A. Wenger, S. De Rosa, T. Ferst, M. Giovanoli, E. Moehlecke de Baseggio, O. Schneider, and J.V. Scurrell. 2018. *Sicherheit 2018. Aussen-, Sicherheits- und Verteidigungspolitische Meinungsbildung im Trend.* Zürich: Center for Security Studies, ETH Zürich und Militärakademie an der ETH Zürich.

Tanner, J. 1997. "Militär und Gesellschaft in der Schweiz nach 1945." In *Militär und Gesellschaft im 19. und 20. Jahrhundert*, edited by U. Frevert, 314–341. Stuttgart: Klett-Cotta.

Würmli, S. 2015. "Die Entwicklung der zivil-militärischen Beziehungen in der Schweiz. Eine Analyse anhand von Stimmbevölkerungsrepräsentativen Meinungsumfragen, 1983–2013." Doctoral dissertation, Basel.

Würmli, S., and T. Szvircsev Tresch. 2011. "Neutrality and the Quest for Autonomy as Constraints for the Military: How Does Public Opinion Reflect the Relationship between the Political and the Military System?" In *Security and the Military between Reality and Perception*, edited by M. Malešič and G. Kümmel, 117–133. Baden-Baden: Nomos.

Military Sociology and Critical Military Studies in the United Kingdom

Rachel Woodward and K. Neil Jenkings

1 Introduction

Our point of origin in this review is our observation of the fact that in a recently published *Handbook of Military Sociology* (Caforio and Nuciari 2018), of the 31 chapters and 34 authors across this international collection, only one author (Michael Pugh) is from the UK. This could be taken to indicate an almost-total absence of interest in military phenomena by sociologists in the UK. Yet, such a conclusion would be erroneous as this apparent absence of UK scholarship belies the real state of the study of military phenomena in the UK by sociologists and their affiliates. It perhaps instead indicates a lack of identification with, and consequent minimal visible presence within, the international community of military sociology as a formally recognised sub-discipline. This lack of affiliation should not deflect from the wealth of UK sociological research undertaken on military phenomena. In this chapter, we will explore where in the UK academy this research is undertaken, revealing where in terms of formal military sociology it is hidden (often in plain sight) and why nationally it manifests itself in this fashion. Military research by UK academic sociology has tended to be multi-disciplinary, unaligned to military institutions, and generally adoptive of a critical orientation towards its subject matter. Military sociology as a formal sub-discipline in the UK may initially be difficult to locate, but if we refocus and look for studies of the sociology of military phenomena, particularly over the past decade or so, then a vibrant and engaged field of study is revealed. In this chapter, we proceed by considering the position of military sociology in the UK in broad terms. We discuss the institutional set-up of military sociology and examine publication practices and the ease or difficulty of undertaking research in and on the UK military. We then consider research funding for military research and the research methods that have tended to dominate in the UK. Then we assess some of the key areas of empirical research with which UK military sociology has engaged. Finally, we conclude with a brief assessment of possibly future directions for military sociology research in the UK.

2   The Position of Military Sociology in the Scientific Arena in the UK

We start this exploration of military sociology in the UK by considering its position in relation to the parent discipline of Sociology. Sociology in the UK is characterised by the use of a diverse range of methodologies to generate empirical data through which conceptual questions can be answered about the organisation and expression of social life at a variety of scales. Sociology as an academic discipline is well established in the UK's higher education system and is embedded as a fundamental part of the broader social science base in the UK. This establishment and embeddedness are evident in multiple ways, not least through the presence of degree programmes in Sociology at undergraduate and postgraduate levels across the higher education sector, and the presence of a designated subject panel for Sociology within the UK government's research quality evaluation frameworks. It is a strong and diverse discipline with particular strengths in sub-fields such as medical sociology, industrial, workplace and employment sociology, the sociology of organisations, the sociologies of identities, and conceptual and empirical explorations of social structure, (dis)advantage and inequality. The discipline of Sociology has also been fundamental to the generation of distinctive (and distinctively named) research fields for empirical research and theorising in areas including women's studies, Black studies, Queer studies, criminology, and science and technology studies. It is also a key constituent part of cross-disciplinary analyses, and it is not unusual to find research where social scientific issues are approached via a sociological lens but also drawing on methods and ideas informed by Human Geography, Anthropology, Economics, Political Science or Cultural Studies.

Yet, for all that the discipline of Sociology and its sub-fields have prominence in UK scientific research, military sociology as a sub-field of sociology has a very low profile. It is of course the case that some analysts engaged with the theorising of social structure and social relations in the contemporary period have identified military activities as a component part of contemporary understanding of the nation state. For example, the work of Anthony Giddens (1985) has examined how economic, political, and social transformations within the state are molded and shaped by war and armed violence. The work of Martin Shaw (1984, 1988, 1991) has been influential in shaping sociological thinking about war and the role of armed violence in forming the social and political understanding of the relationship between social structures, society, and conflict.

Yet military sociology itself, as a distinct field, has an extremely low profile in the UK. There are no UK university departments where a self-identified military sociology is presented as being a central and significant component of that department's research and teaching. Instead, we see two patterns in the UK. One of these shows that specific foci or specialisms within military sociological research provide the organising principle for research groups or centres. We can consider, for example, the King's Centre for Military Health Research (King's College London), the Veterans and Families Institute for Military Social Research at Anglia Ruskin University, or the Northern Hub for Veterans and Military Families Research (Northumbria University), each with its specific area of expertise. Beyond this, military sociology is represented in the UK through the activities of single individuals or small teams working within larger departments which have a more varied social sciences remit. Examples include military sociological work undertaken with the Department of War Studies at King's College London, within the School of Geography Politics and Sociology at Newcastle University, or within the Department of Politics, Languages & International Studies at the University of Bath. The position of military sociology within social science in the UK is primarily an outcome of the work of individuals within much larger groupings, rather than of a self-defined military sociology emerging from dedicated research units. As we go on to discuss in this chapter, it is in this work by individuals and small teams that the breadth and depth of military sociology in the UK is evident.

It is useful to contextualise this absence of a critical mass or formalised existence of military sociology in the UK. It is not as if the UK as a nation state has scant interest in military phenomena. The UK is a highly militarised nation state. It has both a long history as well as a recent past of participation in a great array of armed conflicts, in big and small wars, the two World Wars of the 20th century, colonial and imperial wars, and its own civil war if we name *the Troubles* in Northern Ireland as such. Only being protagonists in a war for national independence is missing from the UK's engagements across this typology of armed conflict (although there may be those who would argue that the 1982 Falklands/Malvinas war fits this definition to an extent). One might think, given the UK's persistent involvement in armed conflict and history of military preparedness, and the strength of the discipline of Sociology in the UK, that military sociology might indeed have presence, at least in military institutions, as a means of providing sociological understanding for the armed forces of the social consequences of militarisation in the UK. Yet this is not the case. Instead, it seems that the military training establishments in the UK, no less than the civilian ones, are not keen on the sociology of the military, or at least not interested in the type of research that sociologists in the UK are willing to undertake.

There are two ways of understanding this. From one perspective, there is the history of Sociology itself from the first emergence of the discipline in the early 19th century with its disavowal of the military's future as a form of social organisation. Here, the military is regarded as an archaic form of social organisation that would disappear, like armed conflict itself, from the rational societies ushered into being by the Enlightenment. Consequently, Anglophone sociology has, simply, been reluctant to engage directly with questions concerning war and associated military phenomena (Creighton and Shaw 1987; Giddens and Sutton 2009). Joas and Knöbl (2012) make the point that deep-seated liberal assumptions have avoided being challenged by relegating war and international violence to the subdiscipline of Military Sociology rather than embedding it in sociological theory, where it might have informed a convincing theory of modernity, especially from an analysis of the nation-state. They argue that

> [...] if we fail to take account of war, we can understand neither the consequences of modernity through the *nation-state* – rather than transnational processes – nor many of the social and cultural changes that have occurred in the modern age [...] If sociology continues to argue in this way, if it fails to grasp the significance of wars and continues to suppress them, it will be squandering major opportunities to analyse the contemporary era – with far reaching consequences for the discipline. (Joas and Knöbl 2012, 5)

Although overcome to an extent by historical sociology in the 1970s (Joas and Knöbl 2012, 14), the point remains. Explanations for this state of affairs in Sociology in the UK point to the emergence of Sociology as an early 19th century academic discipline informed by Enlightenment thought, which saw war as an interruption to the regularities of social life and looked at war as a mode of social action which was barbaric, disruptive, and outmoded (Joas 2003; Joas and Knöbl 2012). Joas notes that Durkheim did not take forward Herbert Spencer's "simplistic distinction between 'militant' and industrial societies [...] Furthermore, Durkheim takes the edge off Spencer's prognosis that war would disappear in industrial society by predicting that war would die out gradually, rather than by leaps and bounds" (Joas 2003, 68).

Alas, Durkheim's view of permanent peace through legislation has failed to become manifest, although the legacy of that view, and the consequent seeming aversion of mainstream sociological theory to war and the military (notwithstanding the work of scholars such as Giddens and Shaw, cited above) resulted in the minor position that military sociology has in the sociological canon of substantive topics. Although as West and Matthewman (2016) note, there has been considerable growth in Anglophone sociology's engagement with the sociology of war and of the military over the last 30 years, the need still remains for what they term a "strong program" for the study of the sociology of war and military (see also Barkawi and Brighton 2011). We concur with these arguments, and in the chapter, which follows we contribute to the development of agendas for military sociological research by examining, with reference to the UK, issues such as the institutional set-up of military sociology, publication practices, the ease or difficulty of doing military research, research funding issues, research methodologies, research on deployments, main issues for empirical research, and wider public perceptions of military sociology.

From another perspective, the growth of Sociology in UK universities was spurred by wider social movements with international reach, not least the civil rights movement in the USA and associated struggles for civil rights in Northern Ireland by the minority Catholic population, the emergence of Second Wave feminism with its questioning of the gendered nature of violence, the anti-war movement in the US against the Vietnam conflict and the emergence of the anti-nuclear movement in the UK in the 1960s and 1970s as a result of the Cold War. Of course, these were not the only conditions of relevance to the structuring of UK Sociology in the period following the Second World War, but, without doubt, the Sociology of this period was largely orientated to politically progressive leftist politics, sometimes radically so. Across the second half of the 20th century in the UK, the British military establishment, seen simultaneously as nuclear armed and on the streets of Northern Ireland, were for many working in Sociology seen as *the enemy*. But this was not an *enemy* one needed to understand, but rather an *unspeakable Other* to civil society, the archaic remnants of a mode of societal organisation that sociology saw as its job to *reform*, if not just simply remove. In short, UK Sociology has been profoundly anti-establishment and, given the absolute identification of the UK armed forces with the political and cultural establishment in the UK, Sociology's response to the institution has been muted or absent.

Although we use the term *military sociology* in this chapter to refer to all forms of inquiry into topics of military sociological significance, arguments have been made for a distinction to be drawn between *military sociology* and *the sociology of the military*. The former has been identified as a mechanism for engineering change within military institutions in a manner which leaves questions of power and politics around those institutions unchanged, following the work of the North American school of military sociology represented through the Inter-University Seminar on Armed Forces and Society (IUS). The latter is identified as inquiry in pursuit of enlightenment about the issues of power and politics which structure military institutions, phenomena, and experience (Higate and Cameron 2006). As we go on to discuss, approaches in the UK to sociological questions about military phenomena have more recently taken the latter approach, with its questioning of the power relations that bring these phenomena into being, under the umbrella term *critical military studies*. Within critical military studies, the idea of a distinct disciplinary idea of military sociology is less significant than that of the benefits which derive from conceptual insights from across the social science disciplines. Examples include Enloe's (2015) arguments about the insights to be drawn from feminist studies, or Rech et al.'s (2015) arguments about human geography's contributions. There are also those who would term their analysis as critical war studies and, although focused primarily on armed conflict, as opposed to a wider field of study across military phenomena, this work is important to consider because of the new ways of conceptualising war which this entails (see, e.g., Bakarwi and Brighton 2011).

It is important to note at this point that across the critical military studies and sociology of the military scholarship that we discuss in this chapter, there is an understanding that the study of these phenomena is informed by internationally shared concepts and reference points. So, although publications may be UK-focused, there is a tacit understanding of an internationally shared scholarship informing national contexts.

3   The Institutional Set-up of Military Sociology

Military sociology in the UK is not closely embedded within the UK's military institutions. In this respect, the institutional set up is quite unlike that prevalent in other European and North American contexts, where it is more usual to see academic sociologists, who are civilians, engaged in both teaching and research within military establishments. Where military participation is evident on UK university campuses, this is via the university armed service units (Woodward et al. 2015, 2017) which are not compulsory to students nor a requirement for those who have military funding. In the UK, military sociology as an area for higher education teaching and study is overwhelmingly the preserve of civilian academics working in civilian universities, teaching primarily civilian students. As we have noted, this is mostly through individuals and small groups working in broader Sociology or other social science departments. There are very few individuals undertaking research or teaching that is recognisable as military sociology within UK military institutional contexts, for example the three officer training academies (Royal Military Academy Sandhurst for the British Army, Britannia Royal Naval College for the Royal Navy, and RAF College Cranwell for the Royal Air Force). Under the umbrella of the UK's Defence Academy, which organises in-service education and training usually for military officers, we see some indication that sociological ideas and theories are included in the curriculum for some courses and programs, for example with gender as a focus in research projects on military personnel topics, or the inclusion of anthropological study in military contexts in teaching about military events such as blue-on-blue contacts (Kirk 2014). This seems incidental rather than systematic. If we examine the programmes offered by Cranfield University, which orientates itself almost entirely towards professionals working in science, technology, and business management including in the defence and security sectors, there is no clearly identifiable sociology programme (despite the significance of the discipline for understanding science, technology, and business management issues within the defence and security sectors, of course).

The political and theoretical divide that we identify above dominates. We can take, for example, social studies of technology and the important work of the Edinburgh University- based British sociologist Donald Mackenzie, who had written about militarism and socialist theory (Mackenzie 1983). His highly influential 1990 text (co-edited with Judy Wajcman), *The Social Shaping of Technology*, has a whole section dedicated to military technology, with two chapters by Mary Kaldor (widely read for her international relations-orientated work on new and old wars). Kaldor was a co-founder of the European Disarmament Committee and may not have been a natural ally with the military – at least at that time. Mackenzie himself had written a book entitled *Inventing Accuracy: A Historical Sociology of Nuclear Missile Guidance* (Mackenzie 1990) in which he deconstructs the seeming inevitability of the arms race. The point here is that it was not a case of sociology not being interested in military phenomena, so much as that interest emerging from an ideological opposition to the orientations of the military establishment and being flagged as something other than military sociology.

Neither does military sociology feature visibly within the research commissioned by and delivered to the UK military institutions. The government's Defence Science and Technology Laboratory (Dstl) conducts research and provides its military customers with advice on scientific and technological issues, but although many of its programmes of work engage with issues where social science insights might (from an academic perspective) be assumed to be valuable, such social scientific input appears to be limited to the insights from behavioural psychology. A distinctive sociological approach appears absent. Similarly, whilst a wider range of private sector businesses (Qinetiq and RAND are two examples) contribute academic expertise to the research needs of the UK's military institutions, it is rare that this expertise is informed by the insights a sociological perspective can bring. Where sociological input is evident, it is often not explicitly flagged as such. That being said, we should point out that research commissioned and used by military institutions is often not published or otherwise made publicly available, which in turn raises issues about the possibilities or otherwise for external validation of information used for defence decision-making. Our own experience of undertaking sociological research on personnel issues with the UK's Ministry of Defence and

British Army (Woodward et al. 2014; Woodward and Winter 2001) indicated little understanding within the commissioning institutions of the distinctive requirements of sociological research (e.g., methodologies, conceptual approaches) or of the benefits a nuanced, sociologically informed engagement could bring.

4   Publication Practices

Because most military sociology research undertaken in the UK is done so within academic contexts, the literature is dominated by academic books published by academic publishers, and by academic peer-reviewed journals. Key journals for those working within the dominant military sociology paradigm include *Armed Forces & Society* (published by IUS and representing mainstream military sociology), *Res Militaris* (a European journal of military studies which publishes in both French and English) and *Defence Studies* (which is edited from within the UK and has a broad defence studies remit). Those working with a more critical approach to the sociology of the military are increasingly drawn to *Critical Military Studies*, a journal established precisely to offer a home for more critical cross-disciplinary work. The *Journal of War and Culture Studies* and *War & Society* also carry some sociological work, alongside research informed by the humanities and cultural studies.

However, publication practices for military sociological research include publication in non-specialist journals; individuals or writing teams identifying with particular disciplines will also look to those for publication. For example, the *British Journal of Sociology, Sociology, Sociology Compass,* and *Current Sociology* would be choices for those working in sociology, while feminist international relations scholars might identify *International Feminist Journal of Politics*, or *Millennium*, or *Security Dialogue* as publication destinations for work that is, essentially, sociological.

It is hard to make general, definitive observations about the publication of military sociology books in the UK. A number of publishers, including Palgrave Macmillan and Peter Lang, will publish books on military sociological topics, including within a series that may be interdisciplinary; Routledge's *War, Politics and Experience* series is a case in point. Yet some publishers are primarily interested in books that can be adopted for student courses, especially as core textbooks or books that can be positioned in reading lists as recommended texts. With few courses on military sociology in the UK, there is no clearly identifiable market for publishers to address through the commissioning and publication of nationally-orientated military sociology books. We should point out that the recent growth of critical military sociology is gradually starting to have an impact on publishing practices, with for example Edinburgh University Press's new series on *Advances in Critical Military Studies*. Ironically, the increasing profile for critical sociological assessments of military phenomena is at least in part due to the military's own determination to raise its own public profile, especially in the cultural life of the UK. The public response to the repatriation of dead military personnel from the wars in Iraq and Afghanistan and the increased visibility of overt support for British military personnel, although not necessarily the wars themselves, had led to a transformation in the representation of military service and those that serve, at least at an abstract level. Thus, the military has become a much more documented and publicly recognised phenomenon, and this is feeding through into sociology albeit in its critical contemporary variant rather than as more traditional military sociology.

We should note also that military sociology publication does also take place outside academic life. For example, we would argue based on our experience of researching contemporary military memoirs (Woodward and Jenkings 2018) that many of these constitute sociological accounts of UK military personnel on deployment and contain sociological insights (see, e.g., Bury (2010) or Parker (2016)). We could also consider things like governmental reports which contain sociological analysis of information about military phenomena; examples here include the British Army's *Speak Out: Sexual Harassment 2018 Report* or the British Parliament's House of Commons Defence Committee's recent reports and evidence published as part of its inquiry into mental health and the UK armed forces.

5   The Ease and Difficulty of doing Research in and on the Military

The experiences of those undertaking research in and on the UK military are hugely diverse and providing a meaningful analysis of these experiences is difficult. We could start by noting the distinctions that could be drawn between, for example, military sociological research that is commissioned by the UK military and that which is not, or research which is conducted by those with prior military experience and those without, or research which has a policy objective and that which does not. However, for all the binaries that we can invoke around a spectrum of research practices, there are examples that confound these. Furthermore, in our considerable experience of doing military sociological research in the UK, and of discussing military research practice with our peers over the years, we conclude that chance and circumstance play as significant a role in doing research as careful planning and appropriate contacts. Officially, according to the UK Ministry of Defence, research in and on the UK military has to have both official permission

at senior levels and has to be approved via the Ministry of Defence's own Research
Ethics process. Both these requirements can present barriers to researchers who do
not have the necessary institutional support for research access to military personnel or facilities. That said, we know of individuals who have been given full approval to proceed but have still found difficulties with access to military personnel
at the local level. In addition, some researchers have gained very high levels of close
access to personnel through the support of individual commanding officers who
have determined that, for whatever reason, access to personnel should be granted.
Vron Ware's (2012) analysis of military multi-culture and the role of recruitment
from the Commonwealth in maintaining the British Army's recruitment levels is a
case in point, as is Alex Hyde's (2015, 2017) close ethnographic study of military
wives on a British overseas military base.

A good example of the difficulties encountered when setting out to do sociological research on the military is recounted in Mark de Rond's (2017) *Doctors at
War: Life and Death in a Field Hospital.* Mark de Rond is a professor of organizational ethnography at Cambridge University, and in the epilogue to his book he
begins "You weren't meant to read this" (p. 132). He highlights the origins of the
study in an approach by "a high ranking medical officer" who initially facilitated
the research, recounting that same officer's later loss of nerve (indeed betrayal),
and the attempts of the UK Ministry of Defence to censor the final draft version
of the book. These included contacting Cambridge University's Vice-Chancellor
personally about the matter and calling the author and his Head of Department
to a meeting at Whitehall, the centre of Ministry of Defence (MoD) activities in
London. The MoD had numerous objections of which he notes that "Perhaps unsurprisingly, of these objections, 90 percent related to concerns with the Ministry
of Defence's reputation" (p. 136). When de Rond commissioned a legal opinion by
a specialist legal firm on this matter, they "made it clear that the Ministry had no
legal basis on which to file [a threatened] injunction against, or otherwise prohibit
publication of the book, and reassured me that the MoD's bravado and bullying
were entirely true to type" (p. 137). This treatment of a Professor at an internationally prestigious university is significant as MoD treatment of lesser establishment
figures is reportedly even more robust. Experience of MoD attempts at policing
research and publication on military phenomena, especially studies of military personnel and their activities, is frequently reported as unpleasant. Similarly, former
military personnel – of all ranks – can also be the recipients of MoD prohibitions
and restrictions on publications (or threats thereof) when they write their accounts
of life in the military (Woodward and Jenkings 2018). Unsurprisingly, within UK
military sociology, and particularly within critical military studies, there is considerable discussion about the politics and practices of doing military research (Baker

et al. 2016; Bulmer and Basham 2017; Cree 2019; Gray 2016a; Rech et al. 2015; Williams et al. 2016).

6 Research in Practice: Funding, Methods, Public Perceptions, and Key Research Topics

6.1 Research Funding

There are a number of different sources of research funding for military socio-logical research in the UK. The UK's Economic and Social Research Council is the key source of public funds for academic research, and grants are awarded on a competitive basis in response to applications through schemes which may be thematic or may be open to any topic. Success rates are low (around 20 percent). The Ministry of Defence provides some funding for research which is sociological in nature, although it should be pointed out that there is very little public trans-parency as to exactly what research the MoD has funded, and this is not research where the expectation is of publication for scrutiny of research findings by aca-demic peers. The MoD has from time to time engaged in match-funding with research councils, and we ourselves have been recipients (Woodward and Winter 2001; Woodward et al. 2014). European Union funding is potentially available for research through the various framework programs and through the European Research Council (see, e.g., Alex Edmonds and his team's work on combat veter-ans and mental health from an anthropological perspective (Edmonds undated)). Although the UK Government has publicly stated that it will continue to support UK participation in EU funding schemes, many within the UK academic sector are skeptical of the Conservative Government's ability or willingness to do so fol-lowing the UK's departure from the European Union. Internally within universities funding may be available on a modest basis for small projects (often on a seed-corn basis). There is also an important role played by charitable organisations such as the British Academy, Leverhulme Trust and Joseph Rowntree Foundation for funding for military sociological research (see, e.g., Vron Ware and colleagues' work on "the military in our midst" at the University of Kingston, funded by the Leverhulme Trust (Ware et al. 2018)).

6.2 Preferred Research Methods

Military sociology uses a range of research methods, although, historically, quan-titative methods have dominated and are still associated with mainstream military sociology (Jenkings et al. 2010). Whether that range is fully accepted across the military studies community in the UK is a different matter; there are those who are critical of qualitative methods, preferring the (in their view) reliability of quantitative methods and the use of numeric data and statistical testing to confirm or disprove hypotheses. Equally, there are those who are critical of the reduction of the richness of lived experience to numeric indicators, who argue that some issues, questions, or problems can only be adequately examined through qualitative methods where the objective is the generation of data on experience to facilitate analytic insight. We ourselves endorse a pluralism around methodologies, advocating the use of the most appropriate methodology to address the question at hand, but would also note that consideration of the politics of different methodological approaches requires continued consideration (Williams et al. 2016). In a recent paper, Jenkings (2018) has suggested that ethnomethodology, and other sociological disciplines too, reappraise what it considers to be military phenomena and to consider which methodological approaches can be adopted to collect data and analyze them. He notes especially that the use of new technologies can be used creatively to overcome some of the difficulties ethnomethodology has, and others need to consider these in selecting research phenomena whilst avoiding ironicising members' practices and understandings of the military. He gives as an example of this creative methodology the studies of UK sociologists (and German collaborators) into the phenomenon of friendly fire (Elsey et al. 2016, 2018). Key is Jenkings' call for a broader conception of what constitutes military phenomena for military sociology and how they are "accounted for" methodologically.

What becomes clear, even from a very quick perusal of some of the recent edited collections on research methods in military social science research, is that qualitative methods are proving increasingly useful in addressing many contemporary military sociological research questions (within the UK, across Europe, and including in North America). Further, the diversity within that broad group, as applied to military sociological questions, is indicative of the strength in the UK of military sociology research (Williams et al. 2016).

6.3   Public Perceptions of Military Sociological Research

There is a question, which has not been specifically addressed in UK contexts as far as we are aware, concerning the extent to which military sociological understandings of military phenomena may or may not have purchase on non-academic understanding of military issues in the UK. It is certainly the case that the work of military sociologists has impact in some quarters, in terms of understanding within military institutions of the nature and consequences of military transformations for example (Edmunds 2014; King 2014). We can also see how research on issues affecting military veterans feeds directly into wider public and policy debate about the costs and consequences of military activity. It is also the case, however, that having a clear understanding of *exactly* how academic research on issues such as identity impacts on public understanding or military institutions is difficult to determine with precision. For many working within critical military studies, the objective of research is not to support specific policy interventions but rather to widen a more conceptual understanding of what is at stake when we talk in social terms of military phenomena.

6.4   Main Topics of Empirical Research

There are certain areas of research where military sociological inquiry in the UK has concentrated its efforts. Of primary interest has been the experiences of military personnel. There has been some engagement from sociological approaches with organizational sociology within the armed forces, as the pages of the journal *Defence Studies* make clear. Anthony King's research on military change and transformation (King 2011, 2014) and Tim Edmunds and Anthony Forster's research on civil-military relationships (2007), and Edmunds et al.'s (2016) studies of the transformation of military reserves, are all examples (on the Reserves, see also Bury 2017a, 2017b, 2018; Basham and Catignani 2018; Higate et al. 2019; Jenkings et al. 2018). However, institutional and organisational issues have not been the primary focus of those working from an academic perspective on military sociology, and in this respect military sociology in the UK is quite distinct from the US where the inheritance of traditional military sociology has dominated.

The question of military identities – what it means to be a military operative – has generated a rich literature. The first significant sociological text on this – and one which still, over three decades after its first publication, is used, cited, and held up as an archetype of rigorous, critical military sociology, is John Hockey's *Squaddies: Portrait of a Subculture* (1986). Framed by a symbolic interactionist theoretical approach, this is an account drawing on intensive ethnographic fieldwork with an infantry unit, during both training and deployment. It is a highly influential book, indicating the possibilities of ethnographic analysis in military sociology, and of viewing military practice as embodied. Hockey is one of the leading practitioners of the phenomenology of sport, the embodied practices of running, in particular, and is an ex-military member who did a PhD on the practices of a small military unit which came to be published as *Squaddies*. This study still stands as one of the few ethnographies by a sociologist of the UK military. Hockey, who kept his field-notes from that study, has revised them with the latterly acquired skills of phenomenology and embodied practice (Hockey 2002, 2016, 2017). Interest in the embodied aspects of military participation continues, with Kevin McSorley, a sociologist at Portsmouth University, producing a number of significant sociological texts on the impact of war and militarism on the body (2014, 2016, 2018, 2019), and his edited collection on *War and the Body* brings together accounts of embodiment in practice and experience (McSorley 2013, see also the special issue of *Journal of War and Culture Studies* 2013 and Dyvik and Greenwood 2016). Significantly, these topics are not the sole preserve of military scholars or even sociology itself, and research is informed by cognate subject areas such as gender studies, human geography, politics and international relations, and anthropology. Duncanson, Winter and Woodward's work on gender and the military is a case in point (Duncanson and Woodward 2016, Woodward and Duncanson 2016, 2017; Woodward and Winter 2007).

Research on military identities has provided insightful accounts of the military experience and has examined both soldiers' own perceptions of themselves and their work (Woodward and Jenkings 2011) and as reported by others, embracing close studies of military cultural practices including cohesion (Bury 2017c; Bury and King 2015; King 2013). Paul Higate's work on military masculinities (Higate 2003, 2012, 2017) has been influential in opening up the field for closer scrutiny (see, e.g., Atherton 2009; Basham 2013; Bulmer and Eichler 2017; Duncanson 2009, 2013, 2015, 2016; Dyvik 2016a, 2016b; Woodward 2000). Studies of sexuality (Bulmer 2013) have informed our understanding of cultural change within the armed forces. Studies of ethnicity and of experiences of soldiers as racialized within the military are notable by their absence, although Vron Ware's examination of the recruitment and experience of Commonwealth soldiers to the British Army sheds light on this experience (Ware 2012). Sociological analysis of military activities as gendered is evident in Woodward and Duncanson's *Handbook of Gender and the Military*. Work by Alex Hyde (2015, 2017) and Harriet Gray (2016b, 2016c, 2017) takes a gendered analysis to examine military families and the ways that familial relationships with the military are constructed through gender relations.

Research on military veterans is growing in prominence in UK military sociology, especially that focusing on the problems of transitioning from military service to civilian life (Walker 2013; Williams et al. 2018), including attendant mental health issues (Caddick et al. 2015a, 2015b, 2015c). The importance of veteran-led analysis of veteran sociologies has also been noted (Bulmer and Jackson 2016). Research on remembrance, memory and memorial practices around military phenomena has also seen increased focus in recent years, coinciding with both the centenary of the First World War, but also with significant UK government efforts to reframe the meanings of military participation around noble sacrifice, in the face of public disquiet about the effects of that participation on military personnel through death and life-changing injury in wars that were broadly unpopular with the wider public (see Jenkings 2017 for an overview).

The sociology of security is an increasingly significant aspect of military sociology. This is because of the close connections between military and security practices, and the interconnections amongst personnel between the military and security forces. The sociology of private security firms has emerged following their prominence in the coalition forces during first the Iraq and then the Afghanistan wars. Much of this work has come from within International Relations studies, but has included some key work by sociologists, most notably in terms of the UK, Paul Higate. Through work supported by the ESRC he has undertaken ethnography of the training and deployment of private security contractors to Afghanistan (Higate 2014, 2016). What is particularly notable to military sociology is the fact that private security operatives are almost invariably former state military personnel, and there are significant issues around the social organisation and identity politics of private security contractors which follow from this.

Studies of the representation of military phenomena from a sociological perspective are also significant to military sociology in the UK (e.g., Woodward et al. 2009). The role of military communications management is an important component of research (Maltby 2012; Maltby and Keeble 2007), in particular the interactions of government, media, military and public reception (see, e.g., Sarah Maltby's (2016) research on media operations and memory in the Falklands War). Social media activity by military personnel and their families is also of interest (Adey et al. 2016; Maltby and Thornham 2016, Maltby et al. 2018).

There is some evidence for research on or with UK military forces when on deployment. As we have noted above, access to military forces for these purposes can be impossible or problematic (as in de Rond's case, which looked at medical practices during UK military deployment to Afghanistan). John Hockey's *Squaddies*, which we discuss above, is one of the few sociological accounts of deployment in Northern Ireland. As we also note above, there may be texts that draw on experiential activities which are sociological, which speak to deployments (as with the memoirs of military personnel; a good example would be the memoirs of Afghanistan deployments by UK military personnel, and individuals' reflections on the sociology of this feature of their service, see Woodward and Jenkings 2012a, 2012b). Military memoirs are not of course sociological research as commonly understood, but nonetheless texts such as memoirs generate sociological data. In contrast to the US, the incorporation of anthropological understanding in UK deployment contexts has not been significant. Although there are accounts (e.g., Charles Kirke's engagements with British military forces over the last two decades (2011)), there has not been a significant amount of engagement by UK academic researchers for the purposes of military learning about social phenomena in deployment or occupation situations, again a reflection of the vast distance between military imperatives and the imperatives of UK academic scholars. We noted above the international dimensions of UK military sociology, and this of course extends to the international dimensions of personnel deployments as part of multinational forces. For this reason, we can consider the work of Paul Higate and Marsha Henry (2009) on United Nations and NATO personnel deployments in peace-keeping operations. This work illustrates for military sociology the complexity of the work of political, military, and civilian (i.e., non-governmental) organizations in peace keeping and peace support in conflict zones, and particularly the gendered dimensions of this.

7   Conclusion

As may be clear from our overview, although military sociology as a formally recognised sub-discipline of sociology has limited organised presence in the UK, there is in fact a wealth of research on the sociology of the military to be found in UK academic life. In particular, we would point to the energising of the field through the broad critical military studies project. This is a real strength in the UK at the present time. The weakness in UK military sociology, we contend, stems not from the research activities that take place, but rather from the disconnect that is sometimes apparent between academic research findings, and consideration of these within the defence community. The reasons for this are complex and beyond our scope here, but we would argue for continued efforts on the part of academic researchers to engage with military institutions in terms of communicating research findings, and in turn a curiosity about externally driven research on military matters from within military institutions. The potential advantages for military institutions of engagement with researchers as critical friends seem to us to be obvious.

In terms of future research directions, there are two broad areas where we see specific sociological issues at play, which suggest the need for closer analysis. The first is the broad issue of recruitment, and the on-going issue (difficulty, even) faced by the UK armed forces in recruiting sufficient numbers of suitably qualified and capable men and women. Research on recruitment exists, of course (Bury 2017a; Dandeker 2010; Kearns 2019; Rech 2014) but we would advocate further involvement of military sociology in this area, not least in order to situate the on-going recruitment problems faced by the UK military within more informed sociological explanations around the changing social structures, expectations in social life, and civil-military relationships. This should also include a serious consideration of the functions of institutional and social racism and discrimination in shaping the recruitment of British citizens identifying as Black, Asian, or from other minority ethnic backgrounds, and continued attention to gender and class in shaping recruitment and military experience. The second broad area where we see great potential for sociological investigation is around the privatization of the military. This is a large and complex issue, which to date has primarily been the preserve of those focusing on the private security industry and individual contractors. However, we suggest that broader sociological issues around military outsourcing of basic functions related with the maintenance of personnel (e.g., training facilities, housing, catering and so on) merit a greater degree of scrutiny.

We conclude by returning to an observation made at the outset to this chapter, that although our focus has been on UK military sociology, in fact when engaging with this body of work it is clear that military sociologists consider their field to be an international one. The concepts, methodologies and approaches guiding military sociology in the UK are not necessarily specifically national; there is not, as far as we are aware, a *British* or *UK School* of military sociology in existence. Rather, military sociology in the UK is enriched through its engagements with ideas, practices and approaches originating in a wider range of different national and international contexts. To return to the point made at the start of this chapter, about the absence of sustained engagement with military phenomena by the discipline of Sociology, we note that this is not a national issue. Lindy Heinecken's (2015) argument on the value of critical sociological analysis for understanding military phenomena makes clear, through her engagement with literatures emanating from European, North American, and African scholarship, that the strengths of military sociology rest on its international nature. We concur.

References

Adey, P., D. Denney, R. Jensen, and A. Pinkerton. 2016. "Blurred Lines: Intimacy, Mobility, and the Social Military." *Critical Military Studies* 2(1–2): 7–24.

Atherton, S. 2009. "Domesticating Military Masculinities: Home, Performance and the Negotiation of Identity." *Social and Cultural Geography* 10(8): 821–836.

Baker, C., V. Basham, S. Bulmer, H. Gray and A. Hyde, A. 2016, "Encounters with the British Armed Forces: Reflections on Research, Ethics, and Access." *International Feminist Journal of Politics* 18(1): 140–154.

Barkawi, T., and S. Brighton. 2011. "Powers of War: Fighting, Knowledge, and Critique." *International Political Sociology* 5(2): 126–143.

Basham, V. 2013. *War, Identity and the Liberal State*. London: Routledge.

Basham, V., and S. Catignani. 2018. "War is Where the Hearth is: Gendered Labor and the Everyday Reproduction of the Geopolitical in the Army Reserves." *International Feminist Journal of Politics* 20(2): 153–171.

Bulmer, S. 2013. "Patriarchal Confusion? Making Sense of Gay and Lesbian Military Identity." *International Feminist Journal of Politics* 15(2): 137–156.

Bulmer, S., and V. Basham. (2017): "Critical Military Studies as Method: An Approach to Studying Gender and the Military." In *The Palgrave International Handbook of Gender and the Military*, edited by R. Woodward and C. Duncanson, 59–71. London: Springer.

Bulmer, S., and M. Eichler. 2017. "Unmaking Militarized Masculinity: Veterans and the Project of Military-to-Civilian Transition." *Critical Military Studies* 3(2): 161–181.

Bulmer, S., and D. Jackson. 2016. "'You do not Live in My Skin': Embodiment, Voice, and the Veteran." *Critical Military Studies* 2(1–2): 25–40.

Bury, P. 2010. *Callsign Hades*. London: Simon and Schuster.

Bury, P. 2017a. "Recruitment and Retention in British Army Reserve Logistics Units." *Armed Forces & Society* 43(4): 608–631.

Bury, P. 2017b. "The Changing Nature of Reserve Cohesion: A Study of Future Reserves 2020 and British Army Reserve Logistic Units." *Armed Forces & Society* 45(2): 310–332.

Bury, P. 2017c. "Barossa Night: Cohesion in the British Army Officer Corps." *The British Journal of Sociology* 68(2): 314–335.

Bury, P. 2018. "Future Reserves 2020: Perceptions of Cohesion, Readiness and Transformation in the British Army Reserve." *Defence Studies* 18(4): 411–432.

Bury, P., and A. King. 2015. "A Profession of Love: Cohesion in a British Platoon in Afghanistan." In *Frontline: Combat and Cohesion in the 21st Century*, edited by A. King, 200–215. Oxford: Oxford University Press.

Caddick, N., B. Smith and C. Phoenix. 2015a. "Male Combat Veterans' Narratives of PTSD, Masculinity, and Health." *Sociology of Health and Illness* 37(1): 97–111.

Caddick, N., B. Smith and C. Phoenix. 2015b. "The Effects of Surfing and the Natural Environment on the Well-being of Combat Veterans." *Qualitative Health Research* 25(1): 76–86.

Caddick, N., C. Phoenix and B. Smith. 2015c. "Collective Stories and Well-being: Using a Dialogical Narrative Approach to Understand Peer relationships among combat veterans experiencing PTSD." *Journal of Health Psychology* 20(3): 286–299.

Caforio, G. and M. Nuciari, eds. 2018. *Handbook of the Sociology of the Military*. 2nd edition. New York: Springer.

Cree, A. 2019. "Encountering the 'lively' in Military Theatre." In *A Research Agenda for Military Geography*, edited by R. Woodward, 162–173. London: Edward Elgar.

Creighton, C., and M. Shaw, eds. 1987. *Sociology of War and Peace*. London: Palgrave.

Dandeker, C. 2010. "Recruiting the all-volunteer force: continuing and change in the British Army, 1963-2008." In *The New Citizen Armies: Israel's Armed Forces in Comparative Perspective*, edited by S. Cohen, 32–47. London: Routledge.

De Rond, M. 2017. *Doctors at War: Life and Death in a Field Hospital*. Ithaca: Cornell University Press.

Duncanson, C. 2009. "Forces for Good? Narratives of Military Masculinity in Peacekeeping Operations." *International Feminist Journal of Politics* 11(1): 63–80.

Duncanson, C. 2013. *Forces for Good? Military Masculinities and Peacebuilding in Afghanistan and Iraq*. New York: Palgrave Macmillan.

Duncanson, C. 2015. "Hegemonic Masculinity and the Possibility of Change in Gender Relations." *Men and Masculinities* 18(2): 231–248.

Duncanson, C. 2016. *Gender and Peacebuilding*. Cambridge: Polity Press.

Duncanson, C., and R. Woodward. 2016. "Regendering the Military: Theorizing Women's Military Participation." *Security Dialogue* 47(1): 3–21.

Dyvik, S.L. 2016a. "Of Bats and Bodies: Methods for Reading and Writing Embodiment." *Critical Military Studies* 2(1-2): 56–69.

Dyvik, S.L. 2016b. "'Valhalla rising:' gender, embodiment and experience in military memoirs." *Security Dialogue* 47(2): 133–150.

Dyvik, S.L., and L. Greenwood. 2016. "Embodying militarism: exploring the spaces and bodies in-between." *Critical Military Studies* 2(1–2): 1–6.

Edmonds, A. Undated. *The Afterlives of War: Combat Veterans' Reintegration and Mental Health, an Anthropological Approach*. European Research Council Grant, University of Edinburgh, <www.san.ed.ac.uk/research/grants_and_projects/current_projects/the_afterlives_of_war> (last access: 7 February 2020).

Edmunds, T. 2014. *Strengthening Democracy, Security and Civil-Military Relations Through Security Sector Reform*. Research Excellence Framework Impact Case Study, <https://impact.ref.ac.uk/casestudies/CaseStudy.aspx?Id=40298> (last access: 7 February 2020).

Edmunds, T., A. Dawes, P. Higate, K.N. Jenkings and R. Woodward. 2016. "Reserve Forces and the Transformation of British Military Organisation: Soldiers, Citizens and Society." *Defence Studies* 16(2): 118–136.

Edmunds T., and A. Forster. 2007. *Out of Step: The Case for Change in the British Armed Forces*. London: Demos.

Elsey, C., M. Mair and M. Kolanoski. 2018. "Violence as Work: Ethnomethodological Insights into Military Combat Operations." *Psychology of Violence* 8(3): 316–328.

Elsey, C., M.D. Mair, P.V. Smith, and P.G. Watson. 2016. "Ethnomethodology, Conversation Analysis and the Study of Action-in-Interaction in Military Settings." In *The Routledge Companion to Military Research Methods*, edited by A.J. Williams, K.N. Jenkings, R. Woodward and M.F. Rech, 180–195. Abingdon: Routledge.

Enloe, C. 2015. "The Recruiter and the Sceptic: A Critical Feminist Approach to Military Studies." *Critical Military Studies* 1(1): 3–10.

Giddens, A. 1985. *The Nation State and Violence*. Cambridge: Polity Press.

Giddens, A., and P. Sutton. 2009. *Sociology*. 6th edition. Cambridge: Polity Press.

Gray, H. 2016a. "Researching from the Spaces In-Between? The Politics of Accountability in Studying the British Military." *Critical Military Studies* 2(1–2): 70–83.

Gray, H. 2016b. "The Geopolitics of Intimacy and the Intimacies of Geopolitics: Combat Deployment, Post-Traumatic Stress Disorder and Domestic Abuse in the British Military." *Feminist Studies* 42(1): 138–165.

Gray, H. 2016c. "Domestic Abuse and the Public/Private Divide in the British Military." *Gender, Place and Culture* 23(6): 912–925.

Gray, H. 2017. "Domestic Abuse and the Reproduction of the Idealised 'Military Wife'." In *Palgrave International Handbook of Gender and the Military*, edited by R. Woodward and C. Duncanson, 227–240. London: Palgrave.

Heinecken, L. 2015. "The Military, War and Society: The Need for Critical Sociological Engagement." *Scientia Militaria, South African Journal of Military Studies* 43(1): 1–16.

Higate, P., ed. 2003. *Military Masculinities: Identity and the State.* Westport, CT: Praeger.

Higate, P. 2012. "Drinking Vodka from the 'Butt-Crack': Men, Masculinities and Fratriarchy in the Private Militarized Security Company." *International Feminist Journal of Politics* 14(4): 450–469.

Higate, P. 2014 "From Squaddie to Bodyguard: Towards a Remilitarized Agency?" In *Studying the Agency of Being Governed,* edited by S. Hansson, S. Hellberg, and M. Stern, 150–166. Abingdon: Routledge.

Higate, P. 2016. "Catfood and Clients: Gendering the Politics of Protection in the Private Militarized Security Company." In *Handbook on Gender and War*, edited by S. Sharoni, J. Welland, L. Steiner, and J. Pedersen, 86–104. London: Edward Elgar.

Higate, P. 2017. "Men, Masculinity and Global Insecurity: Fighting for and against Islamic State." In *Handbook of Gender and Security*, edited by L. Sjoberg, C. Gentry and L. Shepherd, 70–82. London: Routledge.

Higate, P., and A. Cameron. 2006. "Reflexivity and Researching the Military." *Armed Forces & Society* 32(2): 219–233.

Higate, P., A. Dawes, T. Edmunds, K.N. Jenkings and R. Woodward. 2019. "Militarization, Stigma and Resistance: Negotiating Military Reservist Identity in the Civilian Workplace." *Critical Military Studies*. Online First: <https://doi.org/10.1080/23337486.2018.1554941>.

Higate, P., and M. Henry. 2009. *Insecure Spaces: Peacekeeping, Power and Performance in Haiti, Kosovo and Liberia.* London: ZED Books.

Hockey, J. 1986. *Squaddies: Portrait of a Subculture.* Exeter: University of Exeter Press.

Hockey, J. 2002. "'Head down, Bergen on, Mind in Neutral:' The Infantry Body." *Journal of Political and Military Sociology* 30(1): 148–171.

Hockey, J. 2016. "The Aesthetic of Being in the Field: Participant Observation with Infantry." In *The Routledge Companion to Military Research Methods*, edited by A.J. Williams, K.N. Jenkings, M.F. Rech, and R. Woodward, 207–218. London: Routledge.

Hockey, J. 2017. "The Experience of Zulu (Military) Time: An Examination of the Temporal Practices and Perceptions of UK Infantry." *Sociological Research Online* 22(3): 78–94.

Hyde, A. 2015. "The Present Tense of Afghanistan: Accounting for Space, Time and Gender in Processes of Militarization." *Gender, Place and Culture* 23(6): 857–868.

Hyde, A. 2017. "The Civilian Wives of Military Personnel: Mobile Subjects or Agents of Militarisation?" In *Handbook of Gender and the Military*, edited by R. Woodward, and C. Duncanson, 195–210. London: Palgrave.

Jenkings, K.N. 2017. "War and Conflict Commemoration: Identities, Memories and Place." *Symbolic Interaction* 41(2): 285–288.

Jenkings, K.N. 2018. "Unique Adequacy in Studies of the Military, Militarism and Militarisation." *Ethnographic Studies* 15: 38–57.

Jenkings, K.N., A. Dawes, T. Edmunds, R. Higate, and R. Woodward. 2018. "Reserve Forces as the 'Privatization' of the Military by the Nation State." In *The Sociology of Privatized Security*, edited by O. Swed and T. Crosbie, 107–136. New York: Palgrave Macmillan.

Jenkings, K.N., R. Woodward, A. Williams, M. Rech, A. Murphy and D. Bos. 2010. "Military Occupations: Methodological Approaches and the Military-Academy Research Nexus." *Sociology Compass* 5(1): 37–51.

Joas, H. 2003. *War and Modernity: Studies in the History of Violence in the 20th Century*. Cambridge: Polity Press.

Joas, H., and W. Knöbl. 2012. *War in Social Thought: Hobbes to the Present*. Princeton, NJ: Princeton University Press.

Kearns, M. 2019. "Military Masculinities and Contemporary Recruitment Practices to the British Armed Forces." Doctoral dissertation, Newcastle University.

King, A. 2011. *The Transformation of Europe's Armed Forces: From the Rhine to Afghanistan*. Cambridge: Cambridge University Press.

King, A. 2013. *The Combat Soldier: Combat and Cohesion in the Twenty and Twenty-first Centuries*. Oxford: Oxford University Press.

King, A. 2014. *Understanding and Influencing Military Transformation and Operations*. Research Excellence Framework Impact Case Study, <https://impact.ref.ac.uk/casestudies/CaseStudy.aspx?Id=36246> (last access: 7 February 2020).

Kirk, C., ed. 2014. *Fratricide in Battle: Unfriendly Fire*. London: Bloomsbury.

Kirke, C. 2011. *Red Coat, Green Machine: Continuity in Change in the British Army 1700 to 2000*. London: Bloomsbury.

Mackenzie, D. 1983. "Militarism and Socialist Theory." *Capital and Class* 7(1): 33–73.

Mackenzie, D. 1990. *Inventing Accuracy: A Historical Sociology of Nuclear Missile Guidance*. Cambridge, MA: MIT Press.

Mackenzie, D., and J. Wajcman, eds. 1990. *The Social Shaping of Technology*. Buckingham: Open University Press.

Maltby, S. 2012. *Military Media Management: Negotiating the 'Front' Line in Mediatized War*. Abingdon: Routledge.

Maltby, S. 2016. *Remembering the Falklands War: Media, Memory and Identity*. London: Palgrave.

Maltby, S., and R. Keeble. 2007. *Communicating War: Memory, Media & Military*. Bury St Edmunds: Arima Publishing.

Maltby, S., and H. Thornham. 2016. "The Digital Mundane, Social Media and the Military." *Media, Culture and Society* 38(8): 1153–1168.

Maltby, S., H. Thornham and D. Bennett. 2018. "'Beyond' Pseudonymity: The Socio-Technical Structure of Online Military Forums." *New Media and Society* 20(5): 1735–1754.

McSorley, K., ed. 2013. *War and the Body: Militarisation, Practice and Experience.* London: Routledge.

McSorley, K. 2014. "Towards an Embodied Sociology of War." *The Sociological Review* 62(2): 107–128.

McSorley, K. 2016. "Doing Military Fitness: Physical Culture, Civilian Leisure and Militarism." *Critical Military Studies* 2(1–2): 103–119.

McSorley, K. 2018. "Doing Military Fitness: Physical Culture, Civilian Leisure, and Militarism." In *Embodying Militarism: Exploring the Spaces and Bodies In-between*, edited by S. Dyvik and L. Greenwood. London: Routledge.

McSorley, K. 2019. "Predatory War, Drones and Torture: Remapping the Body in Pain." *Body and Society* 25(3): 73–99.

Parker, H. 2016. *Anatomy of a Soldier.* London: Faber and Faber.

Rech, M. 2014. "Recruitment, Counter-Recruitment and Critical Military Studies." *Global Discourse* 4(2–3): 244–262.

Rech, M., D. Bos, K.N. Jenkings, A. Williams, and R. Woodward. 2015. "Geography, Military Geography, and Critical Military Studies." *Critical Military Studies* 1(1): 47–60.

Shaw, M., ed. 1984. *War, State and Society.* Basingstoke: Palgrave Macmillan.

Shaw, M. 1988. *Dialectics of War: An Essay on the Social Theory of Total War and Peace.* London: Pluto.

Shaw, M. 1991. *Post-Military Society: Militarism, Demilitarization, and War at the End of the Twentieth Century.* Cambridge: Polity Press.

Walker, D. 2013. "Anticipating Army Exit: Identity Constructions of Final Year UK Career Soldiers." *Armed Forces & Society* 39(2): 284–304.

Ware, V. 2012. *Military Migrants: Fighting for YOUR Country.* London: Palgrave.

Ware, V., P. Dixon, and A. Dawes. 2018. *The Military in Our Midst.* Leverhulme Trust Project Grant. London: University of Kingston.

West, B., and S. Matthewman. 2016. "Towards a Strong Program in the Sociology of War, the Military and Civil Society." *Journal of Sociology* 52(3): 482–499.

Williams, A., K.N. Jenkings, M. Rech, and R. Woodward, eds. 2016. *The Routledge Companion to Military Research Methods.* London: Routledge.

Williams, R., J. Allen-Collinson, J. Hockey, and A. Evans. 2018. "You're Just Chopped Off at the End: Retired Servicemen's Identity Work Struggles in the Military to Civilian Transition." *Sociological Research Online* 23(4): 812–829.

Woodward R. 2000. "Warrior Heroes and Little Green Men: Military Training and the Construction of Rural Masculinities." *Rural Sociology* 65(4): 640–657.

Woodward, R., and C. Duncanson. 2016. "Gendered Divisions of Military Labour in the British Armed Forces." *Defence Studies* 16(3): 205–228.

Woodward, R., and C. Duncanson, eds. 2017. *The Palgrave International Handbook of Gender and the Military*. London: Palgrave.

Woodward, R., T. Edmunds, P. Higate, and K.N. Jenkings. 2014. Keeping Enough in Reserve: The Employment of Hybrid Citizen-Soldiers and the Future Reserves 2020 Programme. Economic and Social Research Council with Ministry of Defence and British Army, grant reference ES/L012944/1. Newcastle University, <https://gtr.ukri.org/projects?ref=ES%2FL012944%2F1> (last access: 7 February 2020).

Woodward, R., and K.N. Jenkings. 2011. "Military Identities in the Situated Accounts of British Military Personnel." *Sociology* 45(2): 252–268.

Woodward, R., and K.N. Jenkings. 2012a. "Military Memoirs, their Covers, and the Reproduction of Public Narratives of War." *Journal of War and Culture Studies* 5(3): 349–369.

Woodward, R., and K.N. Jenkings. 2012b. "'This Place isn't Worth the Left Boot of One of Our Boys': Geopolitics, Militarism and Memoirs of the War in Afghanistan." *Political Geography* 31(8): 495–508.

Woodward, R., and K.N. Jenkings. 2018. *Bringing War to Book: Writing and Producing the Military Memoir*. London: Palgrave.

Woodward, R., K.N. Jenkings, and A.J. Williams. 2015. *The Value of the University Armed Service Units*. London: Ubiquity Press.

Woodward, R., K.N. Jenkings, and A.J. Williams. 2017. "Militarisation, Universities and the University Armed Service Units." *Political Geography* 60(1): 203–221.

Woodward, R., and T. Winter. 2001. *Gendered Bodies, Personnel Policies and the Culture of the British Army*. Economic and Social Research Council award, with Ministry of Defence, under joint funding scheme. Newcastle University and Sunderland University, <https://core.ac.uk/download/pdf/19743755.pdf> (last access: 7 February 2020).

Woodward, R., and T. Winter. 2007. *Sexing the Soldier: The Politics of Gender and the British Army*. London: Routledge.

Woodward, R., T. Winter, and K.N. Jenkings. 2009. "Heroic Anxieties: The Figure of the British solider in Contemporary Print Media." *Journal of War and Culture Studies* 2(2): 211–223.

The Armed Forces and Society in the United States. Current Trends and Issues

Michael John Williams

1 Introduction

The United States is a fertile subject for the field of military sociology. The military services play a central role in the public discourse and the American military is glorified by the public and soldiers are often referred to as *heroes*. The United States routinely deploys military forces around the world and actively uses violence to achieve policy objectives. As a result, the United States is a fascinating country of study for military sociologists. The academic community in the United States has produced some of the most influential scholarship in the field, but the field itself is a fractured and variable landscape. Like in most other countries, the focus of military sociology in the United States is predominately devoted to evidence-based knowledge of the military, using both quantitative and qualitative methods, rather than development of purely sociological theory. For example, much of the work done on the fundamental issue of civil-military leadership is conducted by political scientists, rather than sociologists. Thus, military *sociology*, in the United States, is to a large extent a dialogue between disciplines rather than an accumulation of theoretical knowledge within one field. Although military sociology could be considered a subfield of sociology, the writing on the military in the United States is usually undertaken by scholars from across a range of fields including sociology, law, political science, and history.

Military sociology in the United States began to blossom at the end of the Second World War when Samuel Stouffer, a sociologist from Sac City, Iowa, conducted a survey of 500,000 GIs. Stouffer was the head of Army's Information and Education Division's Research Branch. He wanted to apply empirical methods to create a sociological understanding of the draftee soldier (Ryan 2013). The research found major discrepancies between what military leadership believed soldiers thought, and their actual views. Stouffer's research was praised by the likes of General George C. Marshall as he set new parameters in survey research and provided the most comprehensive understanding of the American citizen soldier at that point in time. as the US found itself headed into the Cold War.

The impetus for scholarly interest into the military was a fundamental concern about the survivability of democracy in an era defined by a large standing military. The roots of this American concern can be traced back to the British colonial origin of the United States. English political theorists were concerned that a large standing military would be a potential threat to the established political order in England. Having a monopoly on the use of force meant that if it so desired, a large, standing military could intervene in the governance of a country, via a coup, and oust a civilian government from power. The aim of this English policy was to reduce the size of the military, specifically the Army, in times of peace.[1] The United States, once independent from Great Britain, pursued a similar policy through to 1945. When necessary an army was raised, and when no longer needed, the army were drastically shrunk. The operational requirements of the Cold War, however, necessitated a permanently large, standing military which raised concerns in the United States about the potential for a coup, about too much military influence on political decision-makers, and about tendencies towards a militarization of civil society. Thus, the cornerstone of American military sociology became at this time the theoretical debate about military professionalism and the relationship between civilian masters and the military (Finer 1962; Huntington 1957; Janowitz 1960, 1964). It remains a subject of inquiry and concern (Desch 1999; Feaver 2003). However, a large standing military also opened up a wealth of other avenues of study and interest and, thus, the field began to expand, looking at the effects of military service on individuals, the wider relationship of soldiers and society, as well as the social composition of the armed forces. The interest in this topic became embodied in the Inter-University Seminar on the Armed Forces and Society founded in 1961 under the leadership of Morris Janowitz. The advent of the *Journal of Political and Military Sociology* (1973) and *Armed Forces & Society* (1974) heralded the development of the field, as an interdisciplinary one. In the US, these four areas of interdisciplinary study are essentially: military organization, civil-military relations, the experience of war and the use and control of force (Segal and Burk 2011). Whilst it is difficult to engage the most *impactful* research the initial discussions about civilian control of the military and more recent scholarship on the integration of different identity groups has been seemingly quite influential.

The study of the military in the United States is not specifically driven by the military itself. Naturally, the military does conduct organizational and personnel studies, and the military does contract outside scholarship. However, much

---

1   This standard applied only to the Army, not the Royal Navy, as the Royal Navy was directed outward towards threats and the development of the Empire, not barracked at home and idle.

American military sociology is done by civilian scholars at civilian institutions. The internal research sponsored by DOD is conducted by individuals trained by outsiders and there is an engaged, consultative relationship between the top scholars in the academy and those running studies within the military. The benefit of outsides scholars is that they are not beholden to institutional interests, which may exert pressure on studies conducted inside the military. Likewise, scholars on the inside of the military establishment have access to empirical data that is not available to outsiders.

Before going further, it is necessary to define, for the purposes of this chapter, the military. In this study the military is an organized entity (composed of both full-time and reserve forces), under the control of a state government, with the function of using arms and directed violence to defend the state from attack or to advance the policy of the state in relationship to other states (and sometimes non-state actors, such as terrorist networks) in the international system. This definition does not include police forces, private military companies, local militias, special agencies, or mercenary groups. Definitions are important when defining the parameters of any study, but they are particularly important here given one of the fundamental challenges to military sociology today is the relationship between the military and private military companies.

Although the field of military sociology is characterized by a diversity of methodological and disciplinary contributions, it is still possible to discern several key areas of investigation. Given space constraints this chapter focuses on the three most prolific areas of inquiry at the moment, including the Military as a Profession (section 2); the Post-Modern Military (section 3) and the Military as Social Structure (section 4). The Military as a Profession section explores the discussion of the military as an institution or occupation, before going on to describe how the rise of Private Military Companies (PMCs) is challenging role concepts. The section on the Post-Modern Military focuses on the challenges confronting the contemporary US military. In addition, it addresses how theorists view these challenges in light of the ideal role concept of the military in the 20th century. Finally, the Military as Social Structure section concentrates on the most pressing social changes in the US Armed Forces.

2   The Military as a Profession

2.1   The Profession of Arms

The literature of the military as a profession is one of the foundational elements of American scholarship on the relationships between the armed forces and society. A profession can be broadly categorized as a community having a monopoly on the body of knowledge related to a subject vital to humankind. A profession involves lengthy, formal training and is a full-time, career-oriented form of occupation. Society regards a profession as praiseworthy and special and the relationship between the profession and the society is based on altruistic service between the professional practitioner and the client. The skills developed within the profession are not easily available to the layman. Samuel Huntington's *The Soldier and the State* argued that the military profession distinguishes itself from other occupations on the basis of the distinctive knowledge and set of skills related to the *management of violence*, he argues that the duties of the military officer – organizing, equipping, and training the force; planning activities; and the direction of operations in and out of combat – make up the essential elements of the profession (Huntington 1957). One failing of Huntington's argument is that the *management of violence* fails to take into account a large number of other tasks that the military professional involves – particular as the technology used by the military expands. Constant technological change requires soldiers that are adept in programing and data management to deploy force, rather than to wield it themselves. This is a particular challenge in the 21ˢᵗ century where the increasing use of technology has resulted in great participation of civilians into the military realm.

Charles Moskos (1977) built on Huntington's work, but preferred to analyze the military with respect to the concepts of calling, profession, and occupation. Moskos' thinking on professionalism follows the argument above with the key factor being the legitimation of the profession according to specialized expertise. Related is the idea of a military career as a calling, where institutional values transcend narrow self-interest for the greater good. Those *called* to service regard themselves as apart from the wider society and their calling is associated with self-sacrifice and is based not on high remuneration, but rather a moderate level of remuneration bolstered by an array of social benefits. Meanwhile, the occupation is legitimized in terms of the marketplace. The occupation model, as it is known, is based on self-interest rather than the task or the position in the employing organization. Employees are compensated with appropriate salary and work conditions. Historically, militaries, including the US military, resisted the occupational model approach. However, trends over the last fifty years have pushed the US military, and other global militaries, in this direction. Indeed, the Gates Commission, formally known as The President's Commission on an All-Volunteer Force (1970), recommended monetary inducements guided by marketplace standards be the main vehicle for recruitment and retention. The termination of the active selective service (the draft) in the United States was one step in this direction. More recently, the use of high financial incentives to retain military personnel indicates that the military, although retaining both features of the calling and professional model, is increasingly one occupation among many in the workplace.

2.2 Private Military Companies and the Professional Soldier

The blurring between profession and occupation in the early 21st century is facilitated through the expansive use of private military companies (PMC) by the United States Government (USG). Much scholarly energy has been devoted in recent years to the rising use of PMC's and how this reinforces a contemporary concept of the military as an occupation legitimized by the market rather than professional norms or public esteem. At the height of the Iraq campaign, there were 140,000 US service personnel in theater. The next largest group of armed personnel was not any American ally, but private military contractors. As the US military drew down, the number of contractors grew in number, so much so that four years later, one-fifth of all armed combatants in Iraq was not a soldier, but an employee of a private company (O'Hanlon and Campbell 2009). Contractors are not an entirely new phenomenon. In the Second World War, contractors made up about 15 percent of the personnel (Glanz 2009). Over the course of a decade from 1997–2007 contracts with private military companies went from 20 percent of the total armed forces budget to 40 percent, this change is due in part to a downsizing of the US military. In 1989, US military forces, including Guard and Reserve Forces was 3.2 million, but in 1995 there were only 1.5 million active duty soldiers under arms, with the total force structure (including Guard and Reserves) at 2.4 million. Exacerbating the trend is the use of more commercial technology that requires skilled contractors with a professional capacity not built-in to the military for operation and maintenance (Stockman 2007). Traditionally contractors have filled support roles, but increasingly contractors provide *security services* meaning that they are doing the shooting and engaging in combat. This raises legal and ethical issues, but it also stresses ideas about the military as a profession.

Contractors for the USG in both Iraq and Afghanistan conducted not just support operations, but also combat operations (Carter 2004). On one occasion in September 2007, Blackwater employees detailed to protect State Department civilians in Iraq opened fire at a busy civilian intersection killing fourteen unarmed civilians and wounding twenty others. A US investigation led by the Department of Justice concluded that one civilian had been shot in the chest whilst his hands were raised in the air in surrender (Robinson 2008). Such incidents raise a number of issues of concern to both policymakers and scholars interested in the military. First of all, there is the accountability issue. Contractors are not formally part of the military and were not, at the outset of the War on Terror (2001–2007), accountable to the Uniformed Code of Military Justice (UCMJ; Wilber 2008). The 2007 US Law stated that contractors operating in contingency operations could be held to account under UCMJ. However, this does not resolve the problem as there is no procedure as to how to apply to rules to non-uniformed combatants (Stockman 2007). The current system only managed uniformed combatants. Accountability, however, is only the first part of the problem, perhaps more important are the challenges they raise to the military profession.

Private military contractors are paid significantly more than those serving in the military. This creates a perverse incentive for soldiers, trained by the USG, to leave the military at the end of their service contract and to take up work as a contractor. This problem is not specific to the US. In 2007, Tom Ricks reported that there were more former British Special Forces working in the private sector for PMCs than there were in the actual British Special Forces (Ricks 2007). The central challenge here is that the military profession is choosing to outsource core duties outside of the profession. There has been little attention paid within the military, and not enough attention among scholars, as to what it means to the military profession if the core competencies of the military are undertaken by those outside. It is highly detrimental to morale within an organization to see any tasks outsourced, not to mention core tasks. Especially if contractors operate in the same combat environments but do not hold the same ethical standards. This not only erodes morale in the military but will also contribute to possible ethical lapses within the military, not to mention a blurring of the line between contractor and military in the operational environment, which may have adverse effects on mission objectives (Abrahamsen and Williams 2009; Avant 2005; Bruneau 2012; Crosbie 2018; McCoy 2010).

All of this ties back into research, debate, and discussion of the military as a professional force or a calling, as opposed to an occupation. The use of PMCs reinforces Moskos' argument that the military is increasingly based on a market-oriented occupation (Avant 2005; McCoy 2010). There are also legal concerns for the military profession. The contemporary law of armed conflict rests on a distinction between jus ad bellum and jus in bello. Professional soldiers that fight for their country are not considered guilty for a country's decision to go to war – the moral culpability of the soldiers fighting an unjust war is mitigated (Walzer 1977). The legal line may be blurred, if the profession of arms is diluted by the extensive use of military forces in combat operations (McCoy 2010). Contractors have the ability to pick and choose what conflicts they fight in. Thus, the military contractor who chooses to provide security in an unjust war, may be held responsible not just for her just conduct in security operations, but also, theoretically, the justness of the war in which she has chosen to work (Shah 2014). As Hedahl writes, "The only way for a citizen to nobly serve her country and fight for the rights of innocents is to fight in the military and forfeit her ability to choose the wars in which she fights" (2009, 30). The challenge here is that the presence of the mercenary, aka, the private contractor, makes it possible for the citizens to choose their form of *service*, thereby undermining the normative distinction the soldier enjoys as just combatant in an unjust war.

3 The Post-Modern Military

3.1 Post-Modern Warriors

The US military excelled at war within the western paradigm and, in particular, at total war, where the result is the annihilation of the enemy and eradication of the enemy government as was the case in the Second World War. However, US politicians have been less adept at war as a conversation, the use of force to achieve limited aims, with an acceptance that the opponent may remain in power after the conclusion of a military campaign. In short, the end of the Cold War and the rise of the ensuing *War on Terror* has led to significant changes in the mission parameters of the US military. During the Cold War, the US military was charged with fighting a large-scale conventional war against a symmetric enemy. This clearly defined mission allowed for a modernist culture oriented at the destruction of a clearly defined enemy using traditional military tools, tactics, and strategies. The decade of the 1990s started off with a brief confirmation of the US military mission during the 1990–91 Gulf War where a US-led coalition ousted Saddam Hussein's military forces from Kuwait. But, aside from this war, the challenges of the 1990s began to muddy the waters of hitherto clearly defined military missions. Soon, US military forces found themselves guarding UN aid shipments in Somalia and protecting civilians in the Balkans. The early 2000s again saw two largely conventional military campaigns in Afghanistan (2001) and Iraq (2003), but after the conventional phase of the war, the US military, and their allies, found themselves in an extremely blurred operational environment that required a set of skills such as policing, development, political reconciliation – not fostered in US military training.

In short, the US military has found itself moving into post-modernity, along with the rest of the country. Modernity has been defined

> as positivistic, techno centric, and rationalistic. Universal modernism has in general been identified with the belief in linear progress, absolute truths, the rational planning of ideal social orders, and the standardization of knowledge and production. Postmodernism, by way of contrast, privileges heterogeneity and difference as liberating forces in the redefinition of cultural discourse. Fragmentation, indeterminacy, and intense distrust of all universalizing or totalizing discourses are the hallmark of postmodernist thought (Moskos et al. 2000, 4−5).

It is not difficult to see how this shift could cause serious disturbances within national military forces, but the problem is also a political one, as politicians seek to navigate a world that is all too often far less defined than it was in the past. As Gerrard Toal states:

> One can find evidence of this counter modern tendency in certain geopolitical crises where global threats are territorialized as threats from 'rogue states'. The problem of weapons of mass destruction, for example, becomes the problem of Saddam Hussein and what to do about Iraq. The problem of ballistic missiles becomes the problem of Iran, Iraq, North Korea and China. Territorialism becomes the problems of 'rogue states' like Sudan and Afghanistan (Toal 1998, 24).

This is not a challenge unique to only one party in the US political system. The United States-led 2011 intervention in Libya by the Obama Administration was predicated on the same logic of risk that the Bush Administration used to justify the invasion of Iraq in 2003 and state-building in Afghanistan. NATO justified the ISAF mission arguing that Afghanistan "poses a threat to international and regional security", but Afghanistan posed no military threat as traditionally understood. Rather than a preponderance of power, it was the absence of power in Afghanistan – the inability of the government to hold a monopoly on the use of force, to curb narcotics production, to root out warlordism and to defeat an insurgency – that causes problems for NATO allies. When policymakers spoke about Afghanistan, they were not referring to the threat posed by Afghanistan, rather they used it as shorthand for a host of issues. Afghanistan became synonymous with security risks from narco-trafficking to terrorism. For the major powers within NATO, however, dealing with these problems in Afghanistan was better than dealing with any consequences that might manifest themselves domestically.[2] Assigning the military to deal with these challenges necessitates a range of challenges for the military as an institution and the people serving in the armed forces.

3.2 Peacekeeping, Policing and the Provincial Reconstruction Team (PRT)

In the most recent wars fought by the United States – Iraq and Afghanistan – the country's soldiers have had to work across multiple issue areas from soldier to peacekeeper, development agent to service provider. Trained in the application of lethal force, soldiers from senior leadership on down were placed into positions where the roles were blurred and the very idea of a profession of arms was called into question. This trend is all part of the increasing global ambiguity of threats, risks, and challenges whereby it is difficult to define strategic objectives and enact plans. This challenge was embodied in both the US led war in Iraq (2003–on) and the mission in Afghanistan (2001–on) where the US was not just called on to wage counter-insurgency military operations, but increasingly took on significant portions of development work to advance military permissibility. This process was native to the United States but spread to allies involved in the NATO ISAF mission (2003–2014). By 2006, the Pentagon realized that development was a critical part of winning the peace, and the White House, the Office of the Secretary of Defense and the State Department had all sent out a number of missives on the issue (Department of Defense 2006; Department of State 2005a, 2005b; The White House 2005). It was then that the idea was labeled the 'comprehensive approach' (CA; Petersen and Binnendijk 2007).

The US military dominated the comprehensive approach in Afghanistan in particular for a number of reasons. The overriding objectives of the CA are military in nature. This was the case despite the objection from those specialized in development aid that humanitarian relief is not a military objective in and of itself. The reality is that the CA in Afghanistan was implemented by NATO forces with two central goals in mind: (1) force protection, and (2) advancement of the military goals. The problem of military dominance is compounded by the fact that the military often has a larger chunk of funds to develop and support capacity. In the US, Donald Rumsfeld essentially created his own state within a state, and the funding for both the Iraq and Afghan wars came year after year from emergency

---

2   For small allies, there was a different logic at work, one that was predicated on being involved with NATO to accumulate good will toward their European-based security concerns, i.e. Russia.

supplemental appropriations rather than the regular annual budget. The military dominance of the operations in Afghanistan is illustrated well in NATO's earliest attempt to instrumentalize the nascent comprehensive approach in Afghanistan – the PRTs (Provincial Reconstruction Team). The PRT, which I will explore below, represents what Rosén labels Third Generation civil-military relations:

> Third-generation civil-military relations are the product of military organisations embarking on civil governance roles and the creation of deep partnerships between military and civil agencies. They appear to be less dramatic than 'traditional' civil-military relations (Blue Helmets, PRTs) in that they do not create the same visible alignment on the ground between military and non-military identities. Yet they do represent a momentous development for the US military's engagement in Afghanistan in particular, as well as challenging our understanding of the role of the military in global security, thus adding a new complexity to international security cooperation (Rosén 2009, 3).

The advent of the PRT recalls Charles Moskos' 1976 work *Peace Soldiers*. The PRT is one of the more recent manifestations of the post-modern military. The PRTs were a way to provide security and reconstruction, whilst avoiding committing too many troops on the ground. The PRTs followed on from ad-hoc civil-military enterprises such as the Combined Joint Civil Military Operations Task Force created during the invasion of Afghanistan in 2001 (Oliker et al. 2001). There was, however, divergence among NATO members as to the best model for the PRT. Perhaps reflecting the relatively militarized nature of American society, the US-led PRTs were generally heavy on troops and lighter on civilian experts (Bacevich 2005). Three relatively distinct models of PRTs developed in Afghanistan, with the most militarized model being the American one. The American model is comprised of around 80 personnel, three to five of whom are civilians. The team is led by a military commander who focuses on delivering 'quick impact projects' in hostile areas. The British model has a higher percentage of civilians, roughly 30 out of 100 personnel, and the group is led by a civilian. The emphasis is not on doing but teaching: local capacity building in short. The British PRTs also operate in hostile environments. The third model is German. The German PRTs tend to be very large, around 400 personnel with about 20 of them civilians. The German PRTs are run by joint command (one civilian and one military) with a focus on long-term development strategies. They operated in permissive environments but could arguably be considered a more balanced approach to the problem than the more militarized models, considering the long-term challenge was political and economic.

The PRT challenges Huntington's idea that the military's autonomous nature is directly related to its ability to act effectively in war, and in particular the idea of professional officer corps free from civilian interference. The PRT model raises serious issues about the future of the military as specialists – should the military engage in policing? Development? What impact might the overall militarization of US policy have on American domestic society? To what extent is the military supporting or substituting civilian efforts? (Zaalberg 2006).

Over time, the American model began to have a slightly larger civilian component, however, US-led PRTs tended to be overly militarized and this perhaps, reflects a broader trend within the United States whereby politicians view the Department of Defense and the military as the *can do everything* department. This view provides a number of challenges, e.g., the atrophying of other parts of the government – such as the State Department, responsible for foreign affairs, and the US Agency for International Development (the development agency that is housed in the State Department). The Trump Administration seems to be openly warring against the State Department but previous administrations, in particular Republican ones, have tended to view all foreign policy challenges through the lens of America's robust military, more so than anything else. This naturally raises the question and concern, how much peace a military can actually instigate (Tomforde 2018).

4   Military as Social Structure

As the US military further enters a period of post-modernity, there is an expansion of multiculturalism within the ranks of the service. Membership in the US military continues to diversify, albeit in fits and starts. Service personnel increasingly are more representative of the diversity in American society and the diversity in the military is increasingly found across the ranks. The increasing diversity of the military helps to reinforce the diversity of citizen identities in American society and to legitimize formerly ostracized minority groups in a cyclical policy of expansion of growth and acceptance within American society (Bristol and Stur 2017). Progress, however, is slow although the US military today is more diverse than it used to be, ethnic and sexual minorities, as well as women in the military, report a multitude of difficulties.

The United States military is a highly diverse organization and one that looks more and more like the society it serves. The military is racially integrated, women serve in a number of capacities and lesbian and gay service members are allowed, although the issue of transgender service members remains confused due to changes by the Trump Administration.

4.1   Race and Ethnicity

The United States military is often viewed as an institution that is emblematic of good race relations. In a country where race remains a hotly contested topic, this is no minor achievement especially keeping in mind that in 1925, just less than 100 years ago, the US Army War College in a study of black soldiers opined

> In the process of evolution the American Negro has not progressed as far as the other sub-species of the human family [...] As a race he has not developed leadership qualities. His mental inferiority and the inherent weaknesses of his character are factors that must be considered with great care in the preparation of any plan for his employment in war. (Wolfe 2019)

Among its conclusions was that the, "Negro officers should not be placed over white officers, noncommissioned officers or soldiers." In just 60 years, however, the US military moved away from institutional segregation to integration. The process began with Executive Order 9981 (1948) that mandated the desegregation of the military. Military compliance was not immediately forthcoming, but the large-scale mobilization required for the Korean War led to the recruitment of African American soldiers and desegregation in 1954 (Armor and Gilroy 2010). This did not mean, however, that race relations in the military had improved overnight. Only through a process of reforms were racial disparities gradually reduced within the institution.

The military was able to move beyond the segregated past by casting aside the old moral contract between the institution and service members based on racism, but challenges to race relations still exist (Burk 2007). Burk defines a moral contract as the practices an institution undertakes regarding the treatment of those under its control (Burk 2007). Instead of a racist moral contract, the military embraced the meritocratic principle, based on equality of the members (Walzer 1983). The basis of equality was necessary in the new all-volunteer professional military that emerged out of the Vietnam War. Minorities, in particular African Americans, volunteered to serve in large numbers helping to make the all-volunteer force a success during a period of American history when the military was extremely unpopular (Janowitz and Moskos 1979; Rostker 2006). The wars fought by the United States over the last twenty years have not been characterized by negative race relations, which is a marked difference from conflicts in the early and mid-twentieth century. This is not to say that the military is a paragon of perfection when it comes to issues of race. Moskos and Butler (1996) concluded already in 1996 that the new moral contract worked, but an array of literature can be found illustrating racial disparities across a number of issue areas. In particular Burk and Espinoza identify five key goods: admission into enlisted ranks, promotion rates, administration of military justice, combat deaths and care of wounded where there was significant and active research on the issue of race.

Minority representation in the US military changed markedly after the desegregation and the launch of the all-professional military force. The military releases demographic data via two annual Department of Defense reports, the *Population Representation in the Military Service* and the *Annual Demographic Profile*. The population of African Americans serving in the US military doubled in nearly a decade from 1972 to 1981. Whereas in 1972 the number of African Americans serving in the military equaled their share of the civilian population (11 percent) by 1982 there was a 2:1 ratio (22 percent). The Army saw the highest rates of African American participation hitting a high of 33 percent in 1981. Throughout the 1990s enlistment rates of the African American population hovered around 20 percent. The Hispanic population participation rates totaled around 4 percent for the better part of the period from the mid-1970s to 1991. The enlistment rates increased to around 11 percent in 2007. It is important to note that in 1973 Hispanics represented just 1 percent of enlisted force numbers. Racial disparities in military enlistment are based on three factors according to the research: merit-based criteria, propensity to enlist, and the socio-economic context (Burk and Espinoza 2012).

The Armed Forces Qualification Test (AFQT) is a merit-based approach to determining suitability for the armed forces. The test can be a barrier to entry to those that fail to satisfy the requirements, which goes some way to explaining lower service rates among African American populations in the 1980s and Hispanic populations in the 1990s (Segal et al. 2007). However, as both groups became better educated, their performance on the AFQT improved. This improvement also led to shifts in where populations served. Historically, a larger number of the African American population served under combat arms, but over the years this has shifted. As African Americans scored better on the AFQT they moved away from combat arms into combat support and administrative jobs. These positions tend to provide one with more transferrable skills, which make the individual more marketable in the civilian labor force (Segal and Verdugo 1994).Willingness to serve is a key metric that the US DOD follows using its own Youth Poll as well as a study conducted by the University of Michigan called Monitoring the Future Survey. When high school seniors indicate they are willing to enter the military within two years of graduation they are marked with a *propensity to serve*. Woodruff concluded that more than two thirds of high school seniors indicating a propensity to serve actually joined the armed forces within six years of completing high school. African

American and Hispanic youth have a higher propensity to serve than whites, with the highest propensity to serve amongst Hispanic males (Dempsey and Shapiro 2008; Segal et al. 2007). Finally, the socio-economic state of the individual can impact who serves, although not uniformly. For example, African Americans from poor families have higher rates of service than similarly poor white families. Interest in the military from these individuals proved a good investment, within one decade they escaped poverty. Studies also indicate that minorities that serve in the military accrue significant social capital both within their own cultural group as well as across society (Burk 2007; Krebs 2006; Salyer 2004). Despite accruing economic and social capital, minority group enlistment has dropped off in recent years. The US-led post-Cold War military interventions have been decidedly less popular with minority communities which has made it difficult to attract and retain minority talent. Crisis was averted in the ranks only though enlistment bonus and a lowering of entry standards.

4.2   Women in the Military

Women have been critical to war efforts, including on the front lines, for centuries. They have not always, however, been critical as uniformed components of the military, but they have served in a variety of roles (D'Amico and Weinstein 1999). The advent of nursing, for example, was one of the more beneficial developments in military medicine and the services provided largely by women. In the US, the 1948 Women's Armed Services Integration Act established the formalized presence of women in all departments of the military, albeit restricting them to two percent of the total force and keeping them away from combat roles. Although the percentage of women in the military grew above two percent, the restriction remained in effect until recently. In 2011, the Military Leadership Diversity Commission recommended that the Department of Defense remove all combat restrictions. This issue has been hotly debated. The core issues of concern to military sociologists over the past 20 years in the US have been focused on questions such as *should women serve in combat* and *do women increase or decrease military effectiveness*, much of the writing on these topics has focused on the concept of gender roles in society and the relationship between social change in the wider society against the relief of developments in the military. The military is fascinating in that it is a highly masculinist culture and thus, at the core, hostile to women in the forces, especially women serving in what would be seen as traditionally male roles – such as frontline combat (Browne 2007; DeGroot 2001; Gutman 2002; Segal 1995; Stiehm 1996; van Creveld 2002; Ziegler and Gunderson 2005). Scholars have deconstructed these positions demonstrating how the ban reinforces a patriarchal society, whilst limiting the legitimization of women's equality (MacKenzie 2013).

Whilst theorists have focused on gender roles in the military, empiricists have fastened onto studying the integration and roles of women in the military. Women serve extensively, although the women that serve differ in many ways from their male counterparts. A higher percentage of female soldiers are black – 31 percent compared to only 16 percent of men. Fewer women are married than male counterparts (46 percent vs 58 percent). Women generally have seen fewer combat tours of duty, although record numbers of women have been deployed in combat over the last 20 years. Approximately 24 percent of post-1990 female veterans saw combat, as opposed to 7 percent of pre-1990 female veterans. Women tend to be more critical of the US military missions in places like Iraq and Afghanistan, as opposed to their male counterparts – this is similar to the trend amongst minority communities that serve in the military. Historically the number of women in the military is at a historic high. The number of women in the enlisted ranks rose from 42,000 (2 percent) in 1973 to 167,000 in 2010 (14 percent). The percentage of women in the officer corps rose from 4 percent to 16 percent – during this time one must keep in mind that the overall size of the US military also decreased. As of 2015 women were allowed to enter frontline combat roles, as well as to train to become Navy SEALS. There has been little public upset at the issue. More recently the public has been focused on the attention on the issue of female registration for the Selective Service. In March 2019, a US District Court Judge ruled that requiring Selective Service for males only violated the equal protection clause of the Constitution (Page 2019). At the time of writing, this had no impact on the registration process. But it highlights the continuing opening up of the US military along the lines of America's diverse society.

One issue area that appears to be gaining more traction is the abuse of women serving in the military (Mengeling et al. 2014, 17–25). Senator Martha McSally's recent revelation at a Capitol Hill hearing on sexual assault was yet another opening up of the discussion on this critical issue that remains pervasive in the US military (Cochrane and Steinbauer 2019). This important issue finds some theorization in the discussion of the equivalency debate within a military model based on patriarchy and the call for scholars to shift more to a discussion of kinship as the basis for female success in the military (Brownson 2017). Known as Military Sexual Assault (MSA) in the literature, the opening up of public discussion in this area has been further driven by the start of the 'Me Too' movement which emerged out of Hollywood when several female actresses began to push back against sexual harassment and assault by male colleagues in positions of power (Bennet 2017). MSA has been an issue for some time, but it has not been a front burner issue for years. Military sociologists, however, have been following the issue closely. The literature finds that sexual assaults against women are higher in the army than in the other branches of the service (Department of Defense 2018). The report for fiscal 2017 says the department received 6,769 reports of sexual assault involving service members as either victims or subjects of criminal investigation, a 9.7 percent increase over the 6,172 reports made in fiscal 2016. Nathan W. Galbreath, deputy director of the Sexual Assault Prevention and Response Office, believes that this reflects more confidence in reporting such assaults, as opposed to an actual increase in assaults, however, it is impossible to determine the accuracy of the statement. Galbreath noted that about 1 in every 3 military members now choose to report their sexual assault, up from about 1 in 14 in 2006. "We're seeing a bigger slice of the problem – in other words, more people coming forward to participate in the justice system, to get the help that they need, and to give us a chance to hold offenders appropriately accountable" (Ferdinando 2017). One of the more disturbing aspects of the research indicates that the US military as a professional, volunteer force and, thus, a self-selecting group, is composed of individuals with a higher predisposition to sexual violence. One study, for example, reported that in three large samples of Navy recruits approximately 9.9 to 11.6 percent across samples reported perpetrating a completed rape of a woman prior to entering the Navy. This is significantly higher than the 4.4 percent rate reported by large samples of college-aged men (Koss et al. 1987, 9; see Merrill et al. 2001 for a wider discussion). Interestingly, Hunter (2007) found that several elements of military culture may promote sexual violence. These elements included sexualized and violent language, an acceptance of violence, objectification of people as well as the in-out dichotomy of a masculinist military. Undoubtedly, this links back to the discussion of gender and gender roles at the beginning of this section.

4.3   Sexual Minorities

Sexual minorities have most likely been present in the US military since the inception of the force, but they have only been a subject of open discussion and debate over the last several decades (Berube 1990; Shilts 1993). Like much of the literature cited elsewhere in this chapter, much of the research conducted in this area is done by sociologists focused on gender and queer theory, rather than the military. Naturally, it has implications for the broader field of military sociology. This literature is generally empirical, rather than theoretical in nature. Scholarship in this area has argued that much of the decisions around the *Don't Ask, Don't Tell* (DADT) policy that banned homosexual service members until 2011 was built around a specific conception of masculinity and in particular military masculinity (Britton and Williams 1995). DADT was contested since its inception in 1993, the policy reflected the confusion, doubt, and discord within American society as to the rights of homosexual citizens. The removal of the law in the military would help to set a standard of wider acceptance and indeed, it has not resulted in the ensuing chaos that proponents of the ban predicted should it be revoked. However, openly LGBTQ (Lesbian, Gay, Bisexual, Transgender, Queer) individuals in the service report difficulties with being out in the military (Fanning 2019). Predictions that openly LGBTQ individuals in the ranks, however, would lead to a less effective US military have not come to pass (Halley 1999). Although some cases were made that argued that heterosexuals did not like homosexuals, and this would hinder group cohesion (Miller and Williams 2001). The necessity of *liking* a fellow soldier, however, has been found to have no impact on unit effectiveness (Kier 1998; Segal and Kestnbaum 2002; Wong et al. 2003). Evidence does show, however, that LGBTQ veterans posit unique challenges to the Veterans Healthcare network and require that the Veterans Administration which provides healthcare to all veterans, adjusts to become a more LGBTQ affirmative health system (Ramirez et al. 2013).

Although homosexuals and bisexuals can now openly serve in the military, the situation regarding transgender individuals has greatly deteriorated since the end of the Obama Administration. Contrary to the Obama White House which allowed transgender to serve in the military, the Trump Administration has been outright hostile to the idea of transsexuals in military service. This is cause for concern amongst those transgenders within the military who feel they may be forced out, and it also helps to delegitimize transgender people in wider American society, much like the ban on homosexuals did so earlier (Cruikshank 1994). Research indicates, however, that there would be no major drawback of transgender individuals in the service, the current ban is more a projection of social norms than a reflection of the individuals' capacity to benefit the services through their professional expertise (Yerke and Mitchell 2013).

5   Conclusion

The field of military sociology is alive and well in the United States, however, it is far from a cogent discipline. Rather, the military is a unit of study that is approached from a variety of disciplinary and methodological perspectives as we have seen above. Political scientists, for example, as we have seen above, have done most of the research related to coup and coup theory, whereas queer theorists have looked at the role of the LGBT community in the military, whilst feminist scholars have tended to focus on the role of gender. This makes for a rich and diverse array of scholarship; however, it also means that it is difficult to silo it all into a single category of military sociology. Much of the sociological scholarship remains empirically oriented and descriptive in nature. There is, however, a surprising amount of more theoretical critical literature, in particular when it comes to issues such as homosexuals, women and race in the military. The theoretical advancement, however, is more in the realm of critical theory, rather than military sociology per se. Despite the overly empirical and descriptive nature of much of the work, the contribution it makes to our understanding of the armed forces should not be undervalued.

References

Abrahamsen, R., and M.C. Williams. 2009. "Security Beyond the State: Global Security Assemblages in International Politics." *International Political Sociology* 3(1): 1–17.

Armor, D.J., and C.L. Gilroy. 2010. "Changing Minority Representation in the US Military." *Armed Forces & Society* 36(2): 223–246.

Avant, D.D. 2005. *The Market for Force: The Consequences of Privatizing Security.* Cambridge: Cambridge University Press.

Bacevich, A.J. 2005. *The New American Militarism: How Americans are Seduced by War.* Oxford: Oxford University Press.

Bennet, J. 2017. "The #MeToo Moment: When the Blinders Come Off." *The New York Times*, 30 November.

Berube, A. 1990. *Coming out under Fire: The History of Gay Men and Women in World War Two.* New York: The Free Press.

Bristol, D., and H.M. Stu, eds. 2017. *Integrating the US Military: Race, Gender and Sexual Orientation Since World War II.* Baltimore: Johns Hopkins University Press.

Britton, D., and C. Williams. 1995. "Don't Ask, Don't Tell, Don't Pursue: Military Policy and the Construction of Heterosexual Masculinity." *Journal of Homosexuality* 30(1): 1–21.

Browne, K. 2007. *Co-ed Combat: The New Evidence that Women Shouldn't Fight the Nation's Wars.* New York: Sentinal Books.

Brownson, C. 2017. "Rejecting Patriarchy for Equivalence in the US Military: A Response to Anthony King's 'Women Warriors: Female Accession to Ground Combat'." *Armed Forces & Society* 42(1): 235–242.

Bruneau, T.C. 2012. *Patriots for Profit. Contractors and the Military in U.S. National Security.* Stanford: Stanford University Press.

Burk, J. 2007. "The Changing Moral Contract for Military Service." In *The Long War: A New History of U.S. National Security Policy Since World War II*, edited by A. Bacevich, 405–455. New York: Columbia University Press.

Burk, J., and E. Espinoza. 2012. "Race Relations within the US Military." *Annual Review of Sociology* 38: 401–422.

Carter, P. 2004. "Hired Guns: What to Do about Military Contractors Run Amok." *Slate*, 9 April.

Cochrane, E., and J. Steinhauer. 2019. "Senator Martha McSally Says Senior Officer in the Air Force Raped Her." *The New York Times*, 6 March.

Crosbie, T., and O. Swed. 2019. "Introduction: Sociology and the Privatization of Security." In *The Sociology of Privatized Security*, edited by O. Swed and T. Crosbie, 1–19. London: Palgrave Macmillan.

Cruikshank, M. 1994. "Gay and Lesbian Liberation: An Overview." In *Gays and Lesbians in the Military: Issues, Concerns, and Contrasts*, edited by W. Scott and S. Stanley, 3–16. New York: Aldine De Gruyter.

D'Amico, F., and L. Weinstein, eds. 1999. *Gender Camouflage: Women in the US Military*. New York: New York University Press.

DeGroot, G. 2001. "A Few Good Women: Gender Stereotypes, the Military and Peacekeeping." *International Politics* 8(2): 23–38.

Dempsey, J.K., and R.Y. Shapiro. 2008. "The Army's Hispanic Future." *Armed Forces & Society* 35(3): 526–561.

Department of Defense. 2005. *Directive 3000.5 Military Support for Stability, Security, Transition and Reconstruction (SSRT) Operations*, 28 November.

Department of Defense. 2018. *Department of Defense Annual Report on Sexual Assault in the Military: Fiscal Year 2017*, 4 May.

Department of State. 2005a. *Post-Conflict Reconstruction: Essential Tasks*. Office of the Coordinator for Reconstruction and Development, 1 April.

Department of State. 2005b. *National Security Presidential Directive 44/NSPD-44: Management of Interagency Efforts Concerning Reconstruction and Stabilization Operations*, 7 December.

Desch, M.C. 1999. *Civilian Control of the Military: The Changing Security Environment*. Baltimore: Johns Hopkins University Press.

Dunigan, M. 2011. *Victory for Hire: Private Security Companies' Impact on Military Effectiveness*. Stanford: Stanford University Press.

Fanning, N.L. 2019. "I Thought I Could Serve as an Openly Gay Man in the Army. Then Came the Death Threats." *The New York Times*, 10 April.

Feaver, P.D. 2003. *Armed Servants: Agency, Oversight, and Civil-Military Relations*. Cambridge: Harvard University Press.

Ferdinando, L. 2018. "DOD Releases Annual Report on Sexual Assault in the Military." *The Department of Defense*, 1 May. <www.defense.gov/Explore/News/Article/Article/1508127/dod-releases-annual-report-on-sexual-assault-in-military> (last access: 11 June 2021).

Finer, S.E. 1962. *The Man on Horseback: The Role of the Military in Politics*. New Brunswick: Transaction Publishers.

Glanz, J. 2009. "Contractors Outnumber US Troops in Afghanistan." *The New York Times*, 1 September.

Gutman, S. 2000. *The Kinder, Gentler Military: Can America's Gender Neutral Fighting Force Still Win Wars?* New York: Lisa Drew Books.

Halley, J. 1999. *Don't: A Reader's Guide to the Military's Anti-Gay Policy*. London: Duke University Press.

Hedahl, M. 2009. "Blood and Blackwater: A Call to Arms for the Profession of Arms." *Journal of Military Ethics* 8(1): 19–33.

Huntington, S. 1957. *The Soldier and the State: The Theory and Politics of Civil-Military Relations*. Cambridge: Belknap Press.

Janowitz, M. 1960. *The Professional Solider: A Social and Political Portrait*. New York: Free Press.

Janowitz, M. 1964. *The New Military: Changing Patterns of Organization*. New York: Russel Sage Foundation.

Janowitz, M., and C. Moskos. 1979. "Five Years of the All-Volunteer Force: 1973–1978." *Armed Forces & Society* 5(2): 171–218.

Kier, E. 1998. "Homosexuals in the U.S. Military: Open Integration and Combat Effectiveness." *International Security* 23(2): 5–39.

Koss, M.P., C.A. Gidycz, and N. Wisniewski. 1987. "The Scope of Rape: Incidence and Prevalence of Sexual Aggression and Victimization in a National Sample of Higher Education Students." *Journal of Consulting and Clinical Psychology* 55(2): 162–170.

Krebs, R. 2006. *Fighting for Rights: Military Service and the Politics of Citizenship*. Ithaca: Cornell University Press.

MacKenzie, M. 2013. "Introduction: Women in Combat: Beyond 'Can They' and 'Should They'." *Critical Studies on Security* 1(2): 239–242.

McCoy, K. 2010. "Beyond Civil-Military Relations: Reflections on Civilian Control of a Private, Multinational Workforce." *Armed Forces & Society* 36(1): 671–694.

Mengeling, M.A., B.M. Booth, J.C. Torner, and A.G. Sadler. 2014. "Reporting Sexual Assault in the Military: Who Reports and Why Most Servicewomen Don't." *American Journal of Preventive Medicine* 47(1): 17–25.

Merrill, L.L., C.J. Thomsen, S.R. Gold, and J.S. Milner. 2001. "Childhood Abuse and Premilitary Sexual Assault in Male Navy Recruits." *Journal of Consulting and Clinical Psychology* 69(2): 252–261.

Miller, L., and J. Williams. 2001. "Do Military Policies on Gender and Sexuality Undermine Combat Effectiveness?" In *Soldiers and Civilians: The Civil-Military Gap and American National Security*, edited by P.D. Feaver and R. H. Kohn, 361–402. Cambridge: MIT Press.

Moskos, C. 1976. *Peace Soldiers: The Sociology of a United Nations Military Force.* Chicago: University of Chicago.

Moskos, C. 1977. "The All-Volunteer Military: Calling, Profession, or Occupation?" *Parameters* 7(1): 2–9.

Moskos, C., and J. Butler. 1996. *All That We Can Be: Black Leadership and Racial Integration the Army Way.* New York: Basic Books.

Moskos, C., J. Williams, and D.R. Segal. 2000. *The Postmodern Military: Armed Forces after the Cold War.* New York: Oxford University Press, 4–5.

O'Hanlon, M., and J. Campbell. 2009. "Iraq Index: Tracking Variables of Reconstruction and Security in Post-Saddam Iraq." *Brookings*, 26 February.

Oliker, O., R. Kauzlarich, J. Dobbins, K. Basseuner, D. Sampler, J. McGinn, M. Dziedzic, A. Grissom, B. Pirnie, N. Bensahel, and I. Guven. 2001. *Aid During Conflict: Interaction between Military and Civilian Assistance Providers in Afghanistan, September 2001–June 2002.* Santa Monica: RAND.

Page, T. 2019. "Drafting Only Men for the Military is Unconstitutional, Judge Rules." *The New York Times*, 24 February.

Petersen, F.A., and H. Binnendijk. 2007. "The Comprehensive Approach Initiative: Future Options for NATO." *Defence Horizons* 58.

Ramirez, M.H., S. Rogers, H. Johnson, W. Seay, B. Tinsley, and A. Grant. 2013. "If We Ask, What They Might Tell: Clinical Assessment Lessons from LGBT Military Personnel Post-DADT." *Journal of Homosexuality* 60(2–3): 401–418.

Ricks, T. 2007. "US Policy in Iraq." *Georgetown Public Policy Institute Lecture*, 4 December.

Robinson, E. 2008. "A Whitewash for Blackwater?" *The Washington Post*, 9 December.

Rosén, F. 2009. "Third Generation Civil-Military Relations and the 'New Revolution in Military Affairs'." *DIIS Working Paper 03*. Copenhagen: Danish Institute for International Studies.

Rostker, B. 2006. *I Want You! The Evolution of the All-Volunteer Force.* Santa Monica: RAND.

Ryan, J.W. 2013. *Samuel Stouffer and the GI Survey: Sociologists and Soldiers during the Second World War.* Knoxville: University of Tennessee Press.

Salyer, L.E. 2004. "Baptism by Fire: Race, Military Service, and US Citizenship Policy, 1918–1935." *The Journal of American History* 91(3): 847–876.

Segal, D.R., and J. Burk. 2011. *Military Sociology*. London: Sage.

Segal, D.R., and M. Kestnbaum. 2002. "Professional Closure in the Military Labor Market: A Critique of Pure Cohesion." In *The Future of the Army Profession*, edited by D.M. Snider and G.L. Watkins, 441–458. Boston: McGraw-Hill.

Segal, D.R., and N. Verdugo 1994. "Demographic Trends and Personnel Policies as Determinants of the Racial Composition of the Volunteer Army." *Armed Forces & Society* 20(4): 619–632.

Segal, M.W. 1995. "Women's Military Roles Cross-Nationally: Past, Present and Future." *Gender and Society* 9(6): 757–775.

Segal, M.W., M.H. Thanner, and D.R. Segal. 2007. "Hispanic and African American Men and Women in the US Military: Trends in Representation." *Race, Gender & Class* 14(3–4): 48–64.

Shilts, R. 1993. *Conduct Unbecoming: Lesbians and Gays in the Military, Vietnam to the Persian Gulf.* New York: St. Martin's Press.

Stiehm, J.H. 1996. *It's Our Military Too! Women and the US Military*. Philadelphia: Temple University Press.

Stockman, F. 2007. "Contractors in War Zones Lose Immunity: Bill Provision Allows Military Prosecutions." *The Boston Globe*, 7 January.

The President's Commission on an All-Volunteer Armed Force. 1970. *The Report of The President's Commission on an All-Volunteer Armed Force*. Washington, DC: Library of Congress.

Toal, G. 1998. "Deterritorialized threats and Global Dangers: Geopolitics, Risk Society and Reflexive modernization." *Geopolitics* 3(1): 24.

Tomforde, M. 2018. "How Much Peace Can the Military Instigate? Anthropological Perspectives on the Role of the Military in Peace Intervention." In *Ethnographic Peace Research. Rethinking Peace and Conflict Studies*, edited by G. Millar, 207–229. Cham: Palgrave Macmillan.

Van Creveld, M. 2002. *Men, Women and War: Do Women Belong on the Front Line.* London: Cassell & Co.

Walzer, M. 1977. *Just and Unjust Wars: A Moral Argument with Historical Illustrations*. New York: Basic Books.

Walzer, M. 1984. *Spheres of Justice: A Defense Of Pluralism And Equality*. New York: Basic Books.

Wilber, D.Q. 2008. "Blackwater Guards Indicted in Deadly Baghdad Shooting." *The Washington Post*, 6 December.

Wolfe, C.P. 2019. "Sir, I Never Thought I'd See the Day When I'd be Working for a Colored Officer." *The New York Times*, 7 February.

Wong, L., T. Kolditz, R. Millen, and T. Potter. 2003. *Why they Fight: Combat Motivation in the Iraq War.* Carlisle: Strategic Studies Institute.

Yerke, A., and V. Mitchell. 2013. "Transgender People in the Military: Don't Ask? Don't Tell? Don't Enlist!" *Journal of Homosexuality* 60(2−3): 436−457.

Zaalberg, T.B. 2006. *Soldiers and Civil Power: Supporting or Substituting Civil Authorities in Modern Peace Operations.* Amsterdam: Amsterdam University Press.

Ziegler, S.L., and G.C. Gunderson. 2005. *Moving Beyond GI Jane: Women and the US Military.* Lanham: University Press of America.

List of Contributors

Eyal Ben-Ari (Prof. Dr.) is an anthropologist and sociologist at the Kinneret Center for Society, Security and Peace in Israel.

Heiko Biehl (Dr.) is the head of the military sociology research unit at the Center for Military History and Social Sciences of the Bundeswehr.

Torsten Björkman (Dr.) is a professor emeritus in Leadership at the Swedish National Defence University and in Work Sciences at the Royal Institute of Technology. He now works as a senior consultant.

Martin Elbe (Prof. Dr.) is a military sociologist and social psychologist at the Center for Military History and Social Sciences of the Bundeswehr.

Erik Hedlund (Dr.) is an associate professor in Leadership and military sociologist at the Swedish National Defence University in Stockholm.

Barbara Jankowski (Dr.) is a Senior Research Fellow at the Institute for Strategic Studies in Paris since 2009 and works on civil-military relations, the influence of the generals in defense policy-making, and war and public opinion.

K. Neil Jenkings (Dr.) is an ethnomethodologist and sociologist working as a Senior Research Associate in the School of Geography, Politics & Sociology, Newcastle University, UK.

Saya Kiba (Dr.) is a political scientist and Associate Professor at Komatsu University, Japan.

Ina Kraft (PhD) is a political scientist at the Center for Military History and Social Sciences of the Bundeswehr.

Marjan Malešič (Dr.) is a professor and Head of the Defence Research Centre at the Faculty of Social Sciences, University of Ljubljana.

Joseph Soeters (Dr.) is a retired professor of sociology and organization studies at the Netherlands Defense Academy and Tilburg University.

Markus Steinbrecher (Dr.) is a political scientist and military sociologist at the Center for Military History and Social Sciences of the Bundeswehr.

Tibor Szvircsev Tresch (Dr.) is a military sociologist at the Military Academy (MILAC) at the Swiss Federal Institute of Technology (ETH) Zurich.

Michael John Williams (PhD) is Associate Professor of International Affairs at the Maxwell School for Citizenship and Public Affairs at Syracuse University, USA.

Rachel Woodward (PhD) is Professor of Human Geography in the School of Geography, Politics & Sociology at Newcastle University, UK.

Atsushi Yasutomi (Dr.) is Associate Professor at Eikei University of Hiroshima, Japan.

Julius Hess

Leviathan Staggering

A Quantitative Analysis of the State's
Coercive Capacity and Intrastate Violence

From Afghanistan to Africa's Sahel region, from the Congo to Central America, deadly violence within state borders is a major threat to peace and security in the contemporary world. Today, internal violence involving rebels, terrorist groups, or organized crime has a higher death toll than wars between nations. Meanwhile, rates of violent deaths have reached historical lows in other parts of the world. Why are some countries ravaged by internal strife while others enjoy lasting stability?

Building on a wide variety of data, this study provides fresh perspectives on the question of how peace within nations may be achieved. It explores Thomas Hobbes' argument that it takes a militarily powerful state to overcome the scourge of violence and asks whether this helps us understand conflict in the contemporary world. The findings show that recent efforts at stabilizing violence-ridden nations, such as the multinational missions in Mali or Afghanistan, are likely to run into serious dilemmas.

2020, 395 S., 36 s/w Abb.,
47 s/w Tab., kart, engl.,
47,– €, 978-3-8305-5063-1
[eBook PDF] 978-3-8305-4228-5
(Sozialwissenschaftliche Studien des Zentrums für Militärgeschichte und Sozialwissenschaften der Bundeswehr, Bd. 21)

DER AUTOR

Dr. Julius Hess, born 1980, obtained a Master's degree in Sociology at the University of Hamburg. 2010 Deputy Head of Department of Scientific Analysis at the State Criminal Police of Hamburg. 2012 Research Associate at the Bundeswehr Centre for Military History and Social Sciences. 2019 Doctorate at the University of Erfurt. He currently works as a data analyst at the German Federal Foreign Office. His research interests include conflict research, international security and military sociology.

AUS DEM INHALT

Theoretical and Empirical Approaches | The Hobbesian Approach to Intrastate Violence | The Great Decline: Violence in History | The Great Surge: Coercive Capacity in History | Quantitative Research on Coercive Capacity and Intrastate Violence | The Research Gap | Theoretical Framework | Research Design | Results

Berliner Wissenschafts-Verlag | Behaimstr. 25 | 10585 Berlin
Tel. 030 84 17 70-0 | Fax 030 84 17 70-21
www.bwv-verlag.de | bwv@bwv-verlag.de

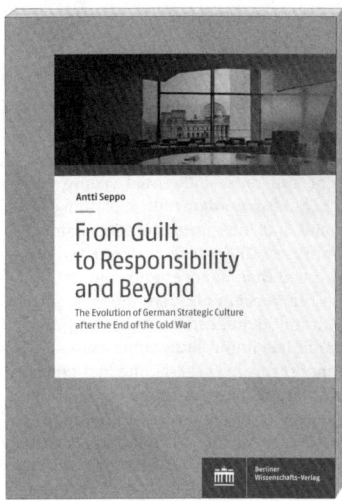

Antti Seppo

From Guilt to Responsibility and Beyond

The Evolution of German Strategic Culture after the End of the Cold War

From Guilt to Responsibility and Beyond tackles the ever-controversial topic of German security and defence policy from the perspective of strategic culture. In particular, it describes the way in which German strategic culture – the ways of thinking and acting in terms of peace and war – has gradually changed after the end of the Cold War.

The book delivers a comprehensive picture of the evolution of German strategic culture from the end of the Second World War to present times with a focus on Post-Cold War events. It also discusses hitherto unexplored ways and methods of how to study continuity and change in strategic culture e.g. through counterfactual thought experiments. The book offers a novel scientific-philosophical take on strategic culture based on Critical Realism and concludes that a combination of present and past experiences of warfare is one of the key generative mechanisms in facilitating strategic cultural change.

2020, 378 S., 4 s/w Tab., kart., engl., 46,– €, 978-3-8305-5067-9
eBook PDF 978-3-8305-4231-5
(Sozialwissenschaftliche Studien des Zentrums für Militärgeschichte und Sozialwissenschaften der Bundeswehr, Bd. 22)

DER AUTOR

Antti Seppo studied political science and holds a PhD. in International Relations from the University of Helsinki. Between 2018 and 2020, he was a visiting scholar at the Center of Military History and Social Sciences, Potsdam. His research focuses on German and European security and defence policy, and strategic culture.

AUS DEM INHALT

Germany and Strategic Culture: The Prophecy of Continuity | Understanding Strategic Cultural Change | The Evolution of German Foreign and Security Policy and Strategic Culture from 1945 to the War in Kosovo | Im Einsatz – German Strategic Culture from Afghanistan to Libya and beyond | Re-Interpretation of the Past and German Strategic Culture | Future Challenges for German Strategic Culture

Berliner Wissenschafts-Verlag | Behaimstr. 25 | 10585 Berlin
Tel. 030 84 17 70-0 | Fax 030 84 17 70-21
www.bwv-verlag.de | bwv@bwv-verlag.de

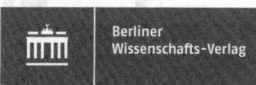

Berliner Wissenschafts-Verlag

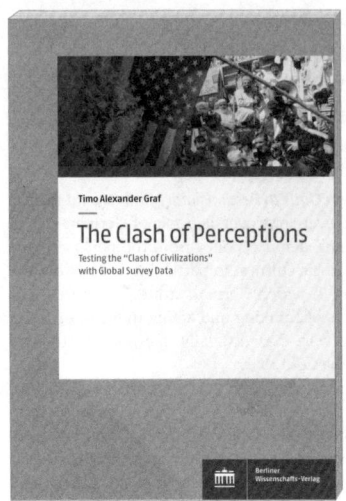

Timo Alexander Graf

The Clash of Perceptions

Testing the "Clash of Civilizations"
with Global Survey Data

The Clash of Perceptions offers a novel perspective on and a unique empirical test of one of the most influential, controversial and popular paradigms for explaining international and intergroup conflict: Samuel P. Huntington's Clash of Civilizations. Huntington argued that alliances and conflicts in the post-Cold War era are determined primarily by cultural identification. Although previous research has found little empirical evidence to support this hypothesis, the fear persisted that due to its popularity the Clash of Civilizations could become a self-fulfilling prophecy. Building on the assumption that (mis) perceptions of intergroup relations can cause real conflicts, Huntington's core hypotheses are tested for the very first time as a Clash of Perceptions by analyzing empirically the pattern and the determinants of conflict in intercivilizational intergroup perceptions with global survey data. The findings suggest that the Clash of Civilizations may exist after all, if only in our heads.

2020, 295 S., 5 s/w Abb., 5 farb. Abb.,
34 s/w Tab., kart., engl.,
37,– €, 978-3-8305-3985-8
eBook PDF 978-3-8305-4146-2
(Sozialwissenschaftliche Studien des
Zentrums für Militärgeschichte und Sozialwissenschaften der Bundeswehr, Bd. 20)

DER AUTOR

Timo Graf holds a Bachelor's degree in Integrated Social Sciences from Jacobs University Bremen, a Master's degree in Political Science from the University of Cambridge, and a PhD in Political Science from the Bremen International Graduate School of Social Sciences. He is employed as a research associate at the Bundeswehr Center of Military History and Social Sciences. His research focuses on international relations, security and defence policy, civil-military relations, and public opinion.

AUS DEM INHALT

The "Clash of Civilizations": A Review of Theory and Evidence | Theoretical Framework: From "Clash of Civilizations" to "Clash of Perceptions" | Macro-Level Analysis: "Clash of Perceptions" at the Macro Level? | Micro-Level Analysis: Individual-Level Determinants of Civilizational Out-Group Images | General Discussion and Conclusion.

Berliner Wissenschafts-Verlag | Behaimstr. 25 | 10585 Berlin
Tel. 030 84 17 70-0 | Fax 030 84 17 70-21
www.bwv-verlag.de | bwv@bwv-verlag.de

Berliner
Wissenschafts-Verlag